Benedictus de Spinoza, Robert Willis

Tractatus Theologico-Politicus

A critical Inquiry into the History, Purpose, and Authenticity of the Hebrew

Scriptures

Benedictus de Spinoza, Robert Willis

Tractatus Theologico-Politicus
A critical Inquiry into the History, Purpose, and Authenticity of the Hebrew Scriptures

ISBN/EAN: 9783337132545

Printed in Europe, USA, Canada, Australia, Japan

Cover: Foto ©ninafisch / pixelio.de

More available books at **www.hansebooks.com**

TRACTATUS THEOLOGICO-POLITICUS:

A CRITICAL INQUIRY INTO THE HISTORY, PURPOSE, AND
AUTHENTICITY OF THE HEBREW SCRIPTURES;

WITH

THE RIGHT TO
FREE THOUGHT AND FREE DISCUSSION
ASSERTED,

AND SHOWN TO BE NOT ONLY CONSISTENT BUT NECESSARILY
BOUND UP WITH TRUE PIETY AND GOOD GOVERNMENT.

BY

BENEDICT DE SPINOZA.

FROM THE LATIN,
WITH AN INTRODUCTION AND NOTES BY THE EDITOR.

"Hereby know we that we dwell in God, and God in us, because he hath given us of his spirit."—1 JOHN iv. 13.

LONDON:
TRÜBNER & CO., 60, PATERNOSTER ROW.
1862.

"It is not true that speculations upon these things have ever done harm or become injurious to the body politic. You must reproach, not the speculations, but the folly and tyranny of checking them."—*Lessing. Education of the Human Race, Translation.* 12mo, London, 1858.

TABLE OF CONTENTS.

	PAGE
INTRODUCTION—The Editor to the Reader	1
Scope and Purpose of this Work—Author's Preface	19

CHAP.
- I. Of Prophecy 31
- II. Of the Prophet 51
- III. Of the Election of the Hebrew nation. Was the gift of Prophecy peculiar to the Jews? 71
- IV. Of the Divine Law 89
- V. Of Religious Rites and Ceremonies, and Belief in Historical Narratives. Why Rites and Ceremonies are required .. 104
- VI. Of Miracles 120
- VII. Of the Interpretation of Scripture 142
- VIII. Of the Pentateuch, and the Books of Joshua, Judges, Ruth, Samuel, and Kings, and their Author or Authors. Of Ezra as their Compiler 169
- IX. Of the same Books of the Old Testament. Did Ezra put the finishing hand to his work? Are the Marginal Additions to the Hebrew Codices variorum readings of the text? 186
- X. Of the remaining Books of the Old Testament 204
- XI. Did the Apostles write in the character of Prophets, or merely as Teachers? Of the office of the Apostles 218
- XII. Of the True Covenant of the Divine Law. Of the reason why the Scriptures are called Sacred, and are spoken of as the Word of God. The Hebrew Scriptures in so far as the Word of God is concerned have come down to us uncorrupted 228

CHAP.		PAGE
XIII.	Scripture teaches nothing that is not extremely simple, requires nothing but obedience from man, and imparts nothing of the Divine Nature, that men, by following a certain rule of life, may not imitate	240
XIV.	Of Faith, and the Distinction of Faith from Philosophy	249
XV.	Theology does not assist Reason, nor does Reason aid Theology. The grounds of our belief in the authority of the Sacred Scriptures	259
XVI.	The Foundations of a Commonwealth, or Policied State. Of the Natural and Civil Rights of Individuals, and of the Rights of Rulers	270
XVII.	No one can cede the whole of his rights to the ruling power of a State. Of the Jewish Republic, as it was during the Life of Moses and after his Death, before the election of Kings. Of the excellence of this Republic and the causes of its decline	287
XVIII.	Certain political Axioms derived from the Constitution of the Hebrew Republic and the History of the Jewish People	316
XIX.	All Authority in religious matters rests with the Civil Power. Religious Worship must be in harmony with the Institutions of the State, if Peace is to be preserved and God to be truly obeyed	327
XX.	In a Free State every one is at liberty to think as he pleases and to say what he thinks	342

INTRODUCTION.

THE EDITOR TO THE READER.

THE theological and political Treatise (Tractatus Theologico-politicus) of Benedict de Spinoza, now presented to the English reader, is the most generally interesting of the works of this celebrated writer,—*celebrated*, we say, for there is no one of any culture who has not heard of Spinoza, though it must be owned that few know more of the man than his name. Spinoza, nevertheless, set his mark upon the chart of human progress, and no history of Philosophy would be complete that did not devote a chapter to the consideration of his metaphysical views and conclusions. The vulgar, however, and their ministers the theologians, have hitherto been the grand arbiters in matters touching the mysteries of God, the Soul, and the religious and moral nature of man, and Spinoza, opposed to theologians and filled with contempt for the vulgar, having no reverence for mere antiquity and no respect for prescription, daring moreover to think independently, and, above all, daring to give utterance to his thoughts, has still been denounced as a dangerous person, called atheist as matter of course, his writings proscribed, and his really spotless name and fame vilified and put to the ban. In the exegetical and critical Treatise which follows we are at no loss to discover the grounds of all the theological hate that has so long clung to the name of Spinoza. Purely philosophical and speculative writings scarcely attract the notice of the many, and only afford matter of discussion to philosophers and learned persons, whose interests never differ from those of the body politic at large; but critical inquiries, in whatever spirit conceived, almost necessarily jar with the opinions and prejudices of individuals, and perchance are found in opposition to the interests of large and influential classes of society, who forthwith band themselves together and declare war to the death against the inquirer. So has it fared with Spinoza. Brought into intimate contact, as a mere youth, with the Hebrew Scriptures, the Talmud, and the exegetical writings of the Jewish Rabbins,—particularly, as it would seem, with the Moré Nebouchim, or Perplexed one's Guide of the celebrated Rabbi Moses Maimonides of Cordova, and little satisfied with the accredited and orthodox mode of getting over the many difficulties encountered in the Old Testament, Spinoza was led by natural taste to examine the ancient records of the faith of his forefathers for himself, and bringing to the task great abilities, abundant learning, entire freedom from prejudice, and a fearless spirit, he gradually arrived at conclusions little in accordance with those generally entertained. The results of his inquiries he embodied in the work now given in an English dress, the purpose of which, besides the critical and exegetical element, is to show that the freest discussion, both of religious and political principles, is not only consistent with true piety and the safety of the State, but cannot be forbidden without detriment and danger to both.*

It is not surprising that the appearance of this remarkable work should immediately have produced a great sensation in the theological world, nor that it should have been regarded as a most serious assault against the accredited systems of religious prescription and belief of Christendom.

* For the original title in extenso vide p. 16.

Yet was this, or such another book, almost a necessity of the advancing European enlightenment. It is, in fact, but the first-fruits in religious criticism of that spirit of discussion which had been evoked by the Reformation—or rather of that spirit of free inquiry of which the Reformation itself was the expression. When the shackles of tradition had been cast off, when the prison of unreasoning submission to irresponsible authority had been broken, and the Bible, as the sole record of the religious system of Christendom, had been made accessible to all in the vulgar tongue, the first grand step in the wonderful history of European progress may be said to have been taken. But it was the first step only, for the same spirit of inquiry, the offspring of doubt, which in questioning the *Old* had led on to the *New*, assailed the new in its turn, and by and by began to ask if what had been been won were indeed the *End* and the *All?* The Tractatus Theologico-politicus of Benedict de Spinoza was the philosophical answer to this question, though the work is to be regarded as the result of the writer's own meditations and inquiries, rather than the embodiment of any peculiar sceptical or critical temper rife in his time. With the Reformation, indeed, the world had but transferred its allegiance from one system of dogmatic theology to another; and though it was no longer necessary to swear fealty to the Church of Rome, and the individual had come to be reckoned for something in the scheme of Christian polity, it was still almost as dangerous to indulge in what each succeeding age never fails to designate as heterodox opinions, and to take nobler views of God's providence, as it had been in the time of Socrates, of One much greater than Socrates, of the long array of Christian martyrs, and of all the persecuted for religious opinion's sake to the present hour. Belonging essentially to the epoch of its publication, then, the remarkable work of Spinoza, nevertheless, did not see the light without heralds of its coming; nor were the minds of scholars and philosophers altogether unprepared for its appearance, though the newness of the views it proclaimed, and of the information it imparted, seems to have taken somewhat aback even the most advanced of these. Copernicus and Galileo, however, had already come into open collision with the literal text of Scripture and the dicta of dogmatic theology in the field of physical science, and Bacon and Descartes had successfully asserted man's right to freedom of opinion in the domain of philosophy. Spinoza's work, consequently, however ill received by professed theologians, appears to have met with countenance enough in the world of science and letters. Copernicus, Luther, Galileo, Bacon, Descartes, Leibnitz, and, though last not least, Spinoza,—these are the mighty names to whom we owe the intellectual freedom we now enjoy; Spinoza not least in the illustrious roll, we say, for—though in arrear as regards political principles of our own great writers and actors of the time of the first Charles,—as true original of the school of biblical criticism, he continues to influence the religious opinions of Europe in a greater degree, perhaps, than any other man of modern times.

In these our own days of freer individual thought and of greater general enlightenment, when authority and prescription in matters of faith no less than in subjects of science are ignored by the truly educated in all classes of society, an English version of the Tractatus of Spinoza appears to be a want that ought to be supplied. In this favoured land we have long attained to a salutary conviction of the unmixed advantages that accrue from the open discussion of political and social questions; but in regard to subjects of Faith and Religion, it must be confessed that public opinion is less advanced; the many still fear to meddle here, and from the pulpit we are anxiously cautioned against too curious inquiry and bidden to believe. Nevertheless, and in spite of all dissuasion to the contrary, mankind will inquire; and of late there are unmistakeable signs of greater freedom, and of some progress in the consideration of the subject of subjects— the Relations of man to his Creator. A ray of the light that has long illumined the scholars of Germany and the North has at length broken in upon the stagnant theological atmosphere of England, and though it has so dazzled our accredited spiritual chiefs that they now appear disposed to turn their backs upon the brightness, at the risk even of being left behind by the science and common intelligence of the country, they will learn to bear it by and by. For England cannot remain in arrear of the rest of the world in her speculative theology, any more than she dare lag in science and the mechanical arts. With the happy constitution of her people she ought rather to lead here, as she has already led in all that ministers to the material well-being of man, and that characterizes true civilization—respect for law, regard for the rights of others, and the assertion of civil and religious liberty. Religion is indeed an eternal entity in human nature, and outcries against the freest discussion of its elements, and against inquiry into the worth and authenticity of the ancient records of the systems that have obtained among the earliest of the policied races of men, have no meaning in fact but this,—that present professors incline to be left alone in their faith, whatever it may chance to be. But as surely as there has been an *Old* Covenant and a *New* so surely will there be another and another newer still, each more than the last in harmony with the knowledge and the aspirations of ever-advancing humanity. The terrible Jehovah of the Pentateuch, who exacted as a burnt-offering for himself every male that opened the womb, whether of man or beast, and whose altar reeked duly morning and evening with the blood of victims, gave place to the milder conception of subsequent ages, who "delighted not in the blood of bullocks or of rams," who "required not from his people their first-born for their transgression, the fruit of their body for their sin," but only asked of his worshippers that "they should do justly, love mercy, and walk humbly with their God." The whole of the exclusive sensuous and blood-stained ritual of the ancient Hebrew people had therefore yielded to the more humane and spiritual views of the later prophets; and they in their turn, all in preparing the way for his coming, veiled their heads and sank into the shade when the culminating point in the religious history of humanity was attained, and Jesus the son of Joseph appeared upon earth. Our grand Exemplar and Teacher, however, left not his doctrine to the world in a comprehensive and absolutely authentic form, dictated by himself, and with the stamp of his authority upon it; or if he did, the record has perished in the lapse of ages. His views, his precepts, have to be gathered from imperfect narratives put together long after the events which they recite had occurred, by men who often plainly give their own colouring to the matters recorded, and who seem at times not well to have understood their Teacher. Christ, in fact, scattered his sayings among curious or careless multitudes. His precepts often fell upon ears that did not know their meaning. Hence the early dissidence in the world's estimate of the entire scope of the Christian doctrine, and the differences in the specific ideas that began to obtain, soon after the death of Christ. This gives us the assurance that his simple moral doctrine speedily waned from its pristine brightness, and became mixed and contaminated with the rites and notions of the Pagan systems with which it necessarily came into such intimate contact. Many of these ideas and rites indeed belonged to the Jews, in common with the whole of the policied nations of antiquity, and were therefore familiar to the earlier Christians as children of Hebrew parents. One of the most widely spread of all the religious ideas of antiquity was that of propitiation by sacrifice. An animal—well if it were not a human being!—was slaughtered upon the altar of the divinity addressed, and in its death was held to propitiate the Deity and to expiate the sins of the people. Christianity ought to have escaped this barbarous idea, and doubtless was at first entirely free from it, though this certainly did not continue for any length of time. The deliverer whom the Jews had anticipated in their misfortunes was beyond all question a temporal leader or ruler. Jerusalem was to become the centre of the empire of the world, and all the nations of the earth were there to bow down before Jehovah, and to serve the chosen people led by his anointed. But this new law-giver and victorious leader failing to appear about the time anticipated, the Christian sect of the Jews by and by came to the conclusion that it could not have been a deliverer with an arm of flesh who had been promised by the prophets. They conceived the nobler idea that it was a spiritual deliverer, one who should set them wholly free from the bondage of the ceremonial law, now become well-nigh intolerable; and this grand deliverer a certain number of his countrymen satisfied themselves anon that they recognized in Jesus, who had emphatically declared his kingdom not to be of this world. Like all religious reformers, Christ was necessarily obnoxious to the priesthood of his day, and was, as the New Testament writers tell us, put to death as a blasphemer and subverter of the law of Moses. Long afterwards—when several generations had passed away, and this sad, though natural, conclusion of the religious Reformer's career was growing dim in the distance, the old Hebrew and Pagan elements began to bear fruit. The pure heart which Christ had proclaimed, the holy life he had inculcated, were not held sufficient to make man acceptable to God. The Deity must be propitiated in some more sensible and striking way; and as the victim in the olden time was chosen without spot or blemish, and Christ, the pure, the holy, had died in the assertion of his ennobling principles, what sacrifice so fit as the noblest form which humanity had yet assumed upon earth, even Christ himself? Christ therefore was held the sacrifice: he died, and in his death was an offering to offended Deity for the sins of the people. Hence the doctrine of the *Atonement;* and, as a corollary to this, in conformity with uniform and invariable custom, the *Communion.* Waxing in their reverence and admiration as time went on and their numbers increased, and virtually without other guide than blind feeling and a wonderful tale handed down from sire to son, the followers of Christ next assumed him to have been not a man, but God. The old heathen gods had often appeared on earth in human shape — Bacchus, Hercules, &c., — as instructors and benefactors of mankind; why should not Christ have been an incarnation of Deity also? He must have been more than man; he was man and he was God; he was not spiritually or figuratively, but actually, υιος Θεου, Son of God, whence the further corruptions derived from Paganism of the miraculous conception and the virgin mother, with a birth at the winter solstice and a triumph over death and decay at the vernal equinox. In short, as the life and doctrines of the Last and Greatest of the Prophets in the course of successive generations became more and more misunderstood, and more and more mixed up with Pagan and superstitious ideas, he came at length to differ little in the popular apprehension from the Nature-god of the heathen world. Well and truly has it been said by the great writer whose loss we had reason so lately to deplore, that "Christianity conquered Paganism, but Paganism infected Christianity; the rites of the Pantheon passed into her worship, and the subtleties of the Academy into her creed," —a sentence full of meaning to him whose eyes are unsealed, but without significance to the untutored sight. In what precedes will be found the key to Macaulay's pregnant words.

It is time that superstitious notions and Pagan contaminations were discarded from the grand ideal of religion, as it was undoubtedly conceived by the Author of Christianity, and that mankind escaped from the labyrinth of unreason in which they are still seen wandering led by the untutored religious sentiments. The religious sentiments, it should never be forgotten, are in themselves *blind;* they require enlightenment by the intellectual faculties, direction by the moral powers, before their promptings can conduce to good. They were doubtless intended by a beneficent Creator for the happiness and ennoblement of mankind; but what misery has been endured, what crimes have been committed, under their influence and sanctioned by their award! Intelligence and its offspring, Science, must intervene at length, and appealing to the ever-extant Revelation which God makes of himself in the mind he has furnished us withal, and in the universe around us which we are privileged to scan, reassert the ABSOLUTE RELIGION that was taught by Christ, and that does not differ from the Religion which reason and nature at one, declare alone to be true. Another of those great religious waves that roll over the world from time to time would seem to have been long gathering in Europe, and is certainly compact on this occasion of no new superstition, but rises under the influence of science, of general enlightenment, and of that refinement in manners wherein true civilization so essentially consists. Religious philosophers of what are called heterodox opinions—and of such men the educated world is full—are no enemies to Religion in itself, and to establishments for the instruction of mankind in their religious and moral duties. On the contrary, they regard these as means to an end designed by God, and as essential elements in the social fabric; they are only hostile to what to them seems unreasonable and objectionable in the matters taught; they would amend, improve, not pull down or destroy. In the system of the Church of England rightly used, in especial, they see perhaps the most admirable instrument ever imagined for the general improvement of mankind. With their pastors at their head, the various parochial communities of worshippers in England constitute the Church. In the parish all have a voice in the administration of their local affairs, as in the estates of the realm in Parliament assembled the best men among them have a voice through their representatives in the settlement of the articles of their creed and the ritual of their worship. The parochial system in which the Church is so principal a part is the true cradle of our English liberties. The pastor himself, as we now meet him, at once the gentleman and the scholar--the man of good breeding and liberal acquirement, the equal of the highest in the social scale, the friend, the adviser, and the comforter of the lowest, and more than all perhaps in its humanizing influences, as Head of the Family—as husband and father—he is at once the centre and the ensample of the civic and domestic virtues, duties, and affections—the very core of all that most endears man to the world, and the world in its greenness and loveliness to mankind. England had need beware how in suffering a narrow theology to be forced upon her she indisposes her best intellects and highest moral natures from seeking admission into her ministry; men who cannot get the better of doubts and difficulties by "taking a curacy;"* nor, by higher preferments, i.e. by richer bribes, be kept from apostatizing to the effete and supersensuous Church of Rome.† Credulity and mystery have lost their hold upon the educated mind of the 19th century, and he who has made any progress in reasonable, as distinguished from dogmatic, religion finds no satisfaction for the aspirations of his spirit towards the Infinite in ritual observance, in parrot-like iteration of set formulæ, and in a mendacious prostration of his moral sense and understanding in terms that make God a tyrant and man a slave. If matters are unhappily pushed to extremity by the narrow-minded among her overseers ($\epsilon\pi\iota\sigma\kappa o\pi o\iota$) there must needs occur a rent in the fair fabric of the English Church; but the secession here, should it come to pass, will not have the effect of that which took place so lately in a neighbouring country,—to rivet the fetters of superstition more firmly than ever on the soul. In our Father's house are many mansions; in the constitution of the human mind there is endless variety; but all, with the most diverse speculative views, may meet on the common ground of reason, justice, and charity. GOD the creator, ordering, ruling, from *eternity*, by laws harmonious and unchanging; CHRIST coming into the world in *time*, the example and the teacher of mankind; LOVE OF GOD, which means obedience to his eternal decrees on the one hand, and NEIGHBOURLY LOVE, which means doing as we would be done by on the other; to which let us add a *Sense of Accountability* for deeds done here, and the *Hope of Immortality* hereafter—and we have the

* Vide Life of Dr Arnold.

† Vide Report of a parley between a certain Bishop and the late Prince Albert, in the *Examiner* Newspaper of Dec. 21st, 1861.

essential elements of a truly Catholic faith.* Speculative opinions have little influence on action, beliefs have still less. Some of the best and most gifted men the world has ever seen have had a very small measure of believingness in their nature, yet have they lived beloved by their friends, and have often made mankind their debtors to the end of time by the noble works they have left behind them. And, again, it is notorious that the zealous and perfectly sincere professor—to say nothing of crimes of far deeper dye perpetrated by the fanatic—the perfectly sincere professor, we say, has occasionally been proved the spoiler of the widow and the orphan confided to his care, the forger of deeds that made innocent children beggars, the selfish sybarite who consumed in sensual indulgence the hard-won earnings of the labouring poor. It is time that another test of human worth were appealed to, besides religious profession; and especially that men of letters and good breeding should cease bespattering those who differ from them in their speculative theology with such epithets as infidel and atheist.

The path entered upon at the glorious Reformation, in short, cannot now be quitted, neither may we loiter on the way. Forward, ever forward, without hurry, but without pause,† is the motto inscribed in letters of light on the modern banner. Infallibility and dogmatism are no more; scientific truth associated with reason, justice, and charity must henceforth point the way, and it were wilful mistrust of the Almighty to question the wholesomeness of the conclusions to which they will lead, however these may clash with preconceived opinion and particular interest. Our science is not that of the Jews of the days of Moses and Joshua, it is not the science of our fathers, nor even of yesterday, but ever progressive, ever extending, ever becoming

---

* The grounds of a universal religion are admirably given, and at greater length, by our author in chapter xiv.—*Ed.*

† Ohne Hast, aber ohne Rast; Goethe's motto, with a sun in the centre as cognizance.

more precise, each and all of its parts are seen arranging themselves in their several places, as elements of one vast and harmonious whole, overruled by eternal and unchanging laws, the ordinances of the Almighty and all-comprehending God who is their Author. Shall not the religious elements in our nature dovetail with the rest of our wonderful economy; our sensational be worthy of our scientific conceptions of God and the universe? The day has long gone by for assuming that man can only be religious according to the Hebrew Scriptures. Religion is a thing apart from parchment, ink, and paper, and the Hebrew Scriptures, themselves but evidences of the existence of a certain order of primitive faculties in the mind of man, are neither the only nor yet the oldest records of a religious system extant. The Hindoos preceded the Hebrews in civilization by hundreds, perchance by thousands, of years, and in their Vedas, which existed in writing centuries before the Jews became serfs to Egyptian task-masters, they have not only given us a clear insight into their religious world, but have actually transmitted the record of this in the tongue which is the root of all the dialects spoken in Europe to the present day. It might have been that the Sanscrit Vedas had descended to us as our especial religious inheritance, when we should have had Brahm, Vichnou, and Siva, as our triune divinity. The Zends, again, the religious books of the ancient Persians, are of great antiquity; and as the Persians were nearer neighbours of the Jews than the Hindoos, so do we find that they have influenced Jewish ideas in a much greater measure. We now see very clearly the Zoroastrian idea that is the foundation of the Book of Job.—But we must not be tempted to pursue this line of reflection any further; the field that opens up before us is all but limitless.*

---

* The existence of the ancient sacred books referred to above could not have been known to Spinoza, though the learned Thomas Hyde must have been engaged upon his great work, the "Veterum Persarum et Medorum Religionis Historia," in his day. The religious literature of India is the discovery of the latter half of the last century only, a field in which Sir Wm. Jones, H. T. Colebrooke,

Spinoza, whose work it is our present business to introduce to the reader, like all the great thinkers of the world, was much in advance of his age; and, almost as matter of course, was persecuted by that section of his contemporaries who only felt an interest in having things remain as they were. He made himself especially obnoxious to the narrow-minded among the religious community to which by birth he belonged, but which on attaining to manhood he forsook—the Jews; and, intolerance and fanaticism having still the upperhand in human affairs, there is perhaps no name to which the odium theologicum has so pertinaciously clung as to that of Spinoza. He by whom the conception of Deity is declared to be the foundation of all knowledge, of all mental capacity to know, who sees God in everything, and maintains that without God there were nothing, is nevertheless charged with the folly of atheism. He who held the love of God and rapt contemplation of the Infinite to be the chief joy and privilege of existence, is familiarly spoken of as a man without piety! And he who led a life of saint-like purity, despising the wealth and honours that were within his easy reach, is denounced as a heartless and avaricious impostor! Time has already, however, in a great measure righted the memory of Benedict de Spinoza. To many of the great in intellect, of Germany especially, Spinoza has now for some time been better known, and is at length

---

M.A., Anquetil de Perron, and others, have made the world their debtors for ever. Spinoza expresses his wish for some authentic proof that the Book of Job was written by a Gentile, as we should then be certain, he says, that Gentile nations had their religious books as well as the Jews.

The reader who is anxious for information on the History and Progress of the Religious Idea among mankind is referred with confidence to the noble work of Creuzer and Guigniaut, "Histoire des Religions d'Antiquité," (4 vols. 8vo, Paris). Save in a single direction which is not entered on, this work exhausts the subject. It is a grand monument both of learning and industry. The omission noticed—the Hebrew system—has lately been most ably supplied by an English scholar of the highest attainments, Mr R. W. Mackay, whose masterly work on the Progress of the Intellect, in connection with the religious idea among the Greeks and Hebrews, will be read with pleasure by every lover of learning and good taste, and with an eye and an ear for sterling English.

regarded with feelings of entire respect, even where his peculiar views do not command assent. God, as conceived by Spinoza, has indeed been the Divinity of many of the most distinguished in letters and science of the middle and north of Europe since his day. Lessing, the great scholar, critic, and poet of his age, holding up the works of Spinoza in his hands, exclaimed to his distinguished contemporary Jacobi on a certain occasion, Εν και παν!—behold the sum and substance of philosophy. Goethe, to the end of his long life, was in the habit of seeking refuge and refreshment from other studies in "The Ethics." Herder used to wish he could for once find Goethe engaged with another book than the Ethics, and Goethe himself, in one of the pleasantest of his works—"The Fact and Fiction of my Life (Aus meinem Leben Dichtung und Wahrheit)"—expands with delight over the remembrance of the new world that was awakened in his mind by the study of this work. Novalis, another of Germany's great writers, is in raptures with the "Divine Nature," as portrayed by the traduced Spinoza; and Schleiermacher, the eloquent preacher, in his enthusiasm, upon a certain occasion exclaimed from the pulpit to his astonished auditory,—"Sacrifice with me a lock of hair to the manes of the pure and misunderstood Spinoza. The sublime spirit of the Universe filled his soul; the Infinite was his beginning and his end; the Universal his sole and eternal love. Living in saintly innocence and in deep humility, he viewed his being in the glass of everlasting nature, and knew that he too reflected something that was not unworthy to be loved. Full of religion, full of the Holy Spirit, he appears to us as dwelling apart from the world, raised above the vulgar and master in his art, but without disciples or a school."

Spinoza has therefore had his fervid admirers among the learned and eloquent men of Europe; but he has not been fortunate in finding apologetic or admiring biographers; and the greatest critic and dialectician of the 17th century, Bayle, has not only shown himself unmitigatedly hostile to the philosophy of Spinoza, but cold and hardly just to the philosopher himself. To Bayle, indeed, may be traced the frequent, though by no means universal, disfavour among the learned in which the name of Spinoza was so long held.* The Pastor Colerus, whose Life of our author is best known, was personally acquainted with him; and though there are doubtless some points which a thorough admirer would have seen through a different medium, the blameless life, the gentle and really attractive character of the man are made sufficiently to appear. It is not difficult for us to excuse in the Lutheran minister a spice of splenetic feeling against so bold a thinker as Spinoza—the theologian could not away with the uncompromising critic of the Hebrew Scriptures—but he has evidently no dislike of the man. It is with much regret that we discover a different spirit in a quarter where we should not have looked for such a manifestation, in the last and certainly one of the most able of the translators and editors of Spinoza, M. E. Saisset. In a learned and instructive article on the Philosophy of the Jews and Arabians, lately published (vide Revue des deux Mondes, Janv. 15me, 1862), M. Saisset has been strangely led away by his dislike of Pantheism and other points in the philosophy of Spinoza, to attempt to degrade him from the place he assuredly holds in the world both of intellect and of morals. For our own part, we have no more affection for Pantheism than M. Saisset; neither do we care to ship in the brain-built bark that carries Spinoza's metaphysical freight; but looking simply to truth, and careless of consequence, we are bound to aver that in all we can make out of the man Spinoza in his works, in his letters, in the character he bore when alive, and the social position of those who were his friends, we discover nothing that is not great intellectually, good, gentle, and loveable morally. And yet, strangely as it seems to us, this is the man of whom M. Saisset speaks disparagingly, as a heartless recluse and a merely selfish dreamer. Spinoza very certainly was neither one nor other. He was much rather one of nature's own nobility, great intellectually, and as self-reliant and independent, as he was courteous, considerate, and generous.

* Dictionary, sub voc. Spinoza.

Spinoza's writings are extremely rare in England. His name does not even occur in the catalogue of some of our greatest libraries. His works have nevertheless been several times reprinted in the original Latin in Germany, and there are translations by competent hands into both French and German. That by Herr Berthold Auerbach* into German is extremely faithful, and is preceded by a good Life of the author; and M. Emilius Saisset's French version, which has now reached a second edition,† has the great merit of being both accurate and readable. It further contains Colerus' Life of the Philosopher, and an able exposition of his doctrines from the pen of M. Saisset himself.

Spinoza in his life-time published the following works:— 1. Renati Descartes principia philosophiæ; cujus accesserunt cogitata metaphysica. Amstelodami, 1663. 2. Tractatus Theologico-politicus continens dissertationes aliquot, quibus ostenditur libertatem philosophandi non tantum salva pietate et republicæ pace posse concedi, sed eandem nisi cum pace republicæ ipsaque pietate tolli non posse, 4to. Hamburgi 1670. 3. After his death were published under the superintendence of his friends Louis Meyer and Jarig Jellis, under the general title of B. de Spinoza Opera Posthuma, the *Ethica*, Spinoza's great philosophical work; a short political treatise entitled *Tractatus Politicus*; another short essay, *De Emendatione Intellectus*; a *Compendium Grammatices Linguæ Hebraicæ*; and a selection of *Letters* to and from friends and correspondents, fol. Amst. 1677.

Besides these works it is known that Spinoza at one time occupied himself with a translation of the Hebrew Scriptures into Latin; and if the versions which follow the Hebrew texts quoted in the Tr. Theol.-polit. are from his pen, it is much to be regretted that he himself, shortly before his death, committed this work to the flames.

For the translation of the Tractatus Theologico-politicus

---

* B. von Spinoza's sämmtliche Werke, 5 Bde., 12mo, Stuttgart, 1841.

† Œuvres de Spinoza, 2 Tom. 12mo, Paris, 1842.   2me Ed. 3 Tom. 12mo, Paris, 1862.

now given to the English reader, the writer makes beforehand every apology that can be admitted. Many years had elapsed since he first read the work in the original Latin, but his attention was recalled to it lately, first by Bunsen's Biblical Criticisms, and then by Essays and Reviews, in which he seemed to meet with many things that were already familiar to him in the Tractatus. For occupation in an enforced solitude, and to bring the subject nearer to his mind, he began a translation of the chapter on Miracles, the subject there treated being one that seemed particularly to engage the public attention, and the work once entered on was found so attractive that it proceeded pretty regularly until completed. For his own part, the writer is ready to avow that his task has been both interesting and edifying; and as all the better spirits of the world are now of opinion that a moral bed of Procrustes is even as sorry an idea as the original contrivance was cruel, he trusts that generally they will bear him out in his estimate of the worth of Spinoza's short but masterly work.

Spinoza himself informs us in his preface that he wrote only for the liberal-minded and the lettered. He had indeed a great contempt for the vulgar, and did not care that any one unacquainted with the learned languages should be able to peruse his work. But in the course of two centuries the world has advanced in its notions of what constitutes real vulgarity and true learning, and has decided that neither one nor other necessarily inheres in the possession or in the want of Greek and Latin. The despot and the bigot, the advocate of popular ignorance and superstition, alone begrudge their freedom whether of thought or action to mankind. But freedom of thought and the vernacular are inseparable, and are even as necessary to human progress as is the light of the sun to the life of the world. In the present day we have no misgivings of the inestimable advantages of free discussion in terms accessible to all. The light only puts out the dark; it is dreaded by none but those who have selfish ends to serve, or who are possessed by unworthy fears of their fellow men.

SCOPE AND PURPOSE OF THIS WORK.

DID men always act with understanding and discretion, or were fortune always propitious, they would never be the slaves of superstition. But as they frequently fall into straits and difficulties, and find no counsel in themselves, as they mostly strive without measure for the questionable favours of fortune, and in their vain aspirations after these are often tossed miserably betwixt hope and fear, so is their spirit commonly disposed to credulity. The mind involved in doubt, indeed, is easily swayed by every impulse, more especially when wavering between hope and fear, as in other moods it is but too apt to be self-sufficient and presumptuous.

No one, I imagine, can be ignorant of these things, though I believe that few know themselves; for whoever has lived in the world must assuredly have seen that in prosperity the mass of mankind, however ill informed, seem to themselves so full of wisdom that they deem it an insult does any one presume to offer them advice; whilst in adversity they appear not to know whither to turn, but seek counsel and countenance from every one, and nothing can be suggested so vain, so unreasonable, so absurd, but they incline to follow it. The most inadequate causes, further, mostly suffice to make men now hope for better things, now fear for worse; for if aught occurs when they are depressed by fear which brings to mind some former good or ill that has befallen them, they forthwith imagine that it betokens a happy or a disastrous issue to their plight; and though the same thing may have occurred a hundred times before without a consequence, they still persist in calling it a lucky or an unlucky omen. If aught unusual happens, again, and their wonder is aroused, they believe it to be a prodigy, a portent, implying the displeasure or the anger of God, whom the superstitious then think it impious and irreligious not to seek to propitiate by vows and supplications. In this way do thousands of strange fancies take their rise, and as if all nature were delirious like themselves men interpret its processes in the most unreasonable manner.

Such being the state of things, we see that they who are most under the influence of superstitious feelings, and who covet uncertainties without stint or measure, more especially when they fall into difficulty or danger and cannot help themselves, are the persons who, with vows and prayers and womanly tears, implore the Divine assistance, who call reason blind, and human wisdom vain, and all forsooth because they cannot find an assured way to the vanities they desire! These are the men who credit the whisperings of fancy and their own puerile conceits, and call them divine promptings and responses, yea, who think that God turns his face from the wise, has written his decrees, not in the mind of man, but in the entrails of beasts, and has given the idiotic and insane among themselves, or the birds of the air, the power of foretelling events by instinct or divine inspiration! Such power has fear in making men irrational!

The mainspring of superstition, then, is fear; by fear, too, is superstition sustained and nourished. Were proof of this beyond what has just been said required, were particular illustrations of our position demanded, we have but to turn to history—to Quintus Curtius' Life of Alexander, for instance—to observe that the great commander first began to consult soothsayers when he had learned to mistrust fortune by reverses in the Cilician passes. After his triumph over Darius, however, he no longer troubled himself about seers and oracles; but when again alarmed by the defection of the Bactrians and the threatened hostility of the Scythians, whilst he himself lay sick on his bed disabled by a wound, he once more, as Q. Curtius says, "returned to the superstitious absurdities of soothsaying, and ordered Aristander, to whom he had confided his own scepticism on the subject, to inquire into the course of events by sacrifice" (Q. Curt., lib. v. § 4, and lib. vii. § 7). Many other instances of a parallel kind could be easily adduced to prove that men are chiefly assailed by superstition when suffering from fear, and that all they then do in the name of a vain religion is in fact but the vaporous product of a sorrowful spirit, the delirium of a mind overborne by terror. These instances would further show that seers and soothsayers have always had the greatest influence with the multitude in times of affliction, and of disaster to the State, and have then also been found most formidable to sovereign or ruling powers.

From the cause of superstition assigned it follows that all men are by nature disposed to be superstitious (whatever others may say who maintain that superstition arises from the confused idea men in general entertain of Deity); that superstition assumes a vast variety of shapes, that it is inconstant also, like all the other uneasy feelings and impulses of the mind, and that it can only be held in countenance by desire, deceit, hatred, and anger, since it has nothing in common with reason, but is the product of mere affection of the most obnoxious kind. How readily soever, therefore, men fall into any sort of superstition, with even as great difficulty are they to be kept true to the form it first assumes; yea, inasmuch as the mass of mankind are always equally miserable, therefore are they never long in the same mind; that generally pleases them best which is newest, and which supplies a sort of excitement they have not yet experienced, and this inconstancy is well known to have been the cause of innumerable commotions in States, and of many sanguinary wars; for, as Q. Curtius admirably observes (lib. iv. ch. 10), "Nothing more constantly sways the multitude than superstition." And superstition is in fact the cause why at one time nations have been led to worship their kings as gods, and at another to execrate them as prime pests of humanity, and why vast pains have always been taken to surround the true or false religions that have prevailed in the world, with such pomp and circumstance as should cause religious observance to be esteemed of greater moment than aught besides, and a matter to be regarded by all with the highest reverence. This purpose, though it have had success enough nearer home, seems to have been most thoroughly accomplished among the Turks, who even hold it unlawful to question or discuss anything, and whose minds are filled with so many prejudices that there is no room left for reason to find an entrance or curiosity to raise a doubt.

If, however, it be the grand object in despotisms to have mankind deceived, and means of terror always at hand by which they may be coerced; if religion be there made the pretext for inducing citizens to fight for slavery as though it were salvation, and it is not held base but highly becoming to venture limb and life for the vain-glory of one man, I can think of nothing more disastrous for a free State than the imposition of such a system upon it. I hold that it is in every way repugnant to the general weal to fill the minds of the community with prejudices, or to seek to coerce them save by the laws. And as to those seditious movements that take place under pretext of religion, they only become possible because laws are passed upon speculative matters, and because opinions are made subjects of punishment like crimes. The propounders and defenders of such laws indeed are moved by no regard for the public safety, but only by the desire of reaching their opponents and sacrificing them to their vengeance. Were it otherwise, were the law of the land to declare nothing criminal but overt act, seditious movements could not be undertaken under the cloak of religion; were words free and where they involved no threat to be spoken with impunity, controversy could never be turned into rebellion. As we however have the rare felicity of living in a State where entire freedom of opinion prevails, where all may worship God in their own way, and where nothing is held sweeter, nothing more precious, than such liberty, I have thought that I should undertake no ungrateful nor useless task did I show that such noble privileges might always be conceded, not only with safety to the State and to true religion, but further that they could not be denied without compromising the interests of true piety and good government. And this is indeed the main purpose of my Treatise, in the arrangement of which I have deemed it especially necessary in the first instance to discuss the principal prejudices that surround the subject of Religion; in other words, to point out and wipe away the traces of the ancient slavery that surround this momentous subject. After this I have considered the erroneous conceptions entertained in regard to the rights and privileges of sovereign powers, which certain parties, with the most barefaced licence, and under pretext of religion, have arrogated to themselves, striving to turn the minds of the multitude, still held in the bondage of a heathen superstition, from their natural rulers, and to sink the world again into a state of abject slavery. Before indicating the order in which I have set the several parts of my work, however, I shall beg to be allowed to say a few words on the causes which have induced me to write at all.

I have often wondered within myself that men who boast of the great advantages they enjoy under the Christian dispensation — the peace, the joy they experience, the brotherly love they feel towards all in its exercise—should nevertheless contend with so much acrimony, and show such intolerance and unappeasable hatred towards one another. If faith had to be inferred from action rather than profession, it would indeed be impossible to say to what sect or creed the majority of mankind belonged. Christian, Turk, Jew, and Heathen, in fact, are not to be recognized save by complexion and habiliment, or by their frequenting this or that place of public worship, and the profession of this or of that system of opinion, each being wont to swear by the dictates of one master or another. As regards life and conversation it is the same with all. Inquiring into such a state of things, I have been led to conclude that it is due to this: The majority of mankind regard the ministry of their Church as a dignity, its offices as benefices, and its priests or pastors as objects of the highest reverence. With the vulgar, such is the sum and substance of religion. As soon, indeed, as abuses had crept into the Christian Church, every worthless person seemed seized with a desire to administer its offices, and the propagation of a Divine Religion was made to subserve the ends of sordid avarice and base ambition; its temples were degraded into show-houses; orators, not teachers, appeared in the pulpits, for no one really thought of instructing the people in their duties, but only of carrying off applause for rhetorical power, and of attacking opponents; and as the subjects of discussion were mostly novelties and paradoxical propositions (these taking greatest hold on the vulgar, and being most admired of them), endless disputes arose, and such hatred and envy and uncharitableness were engendered as no length of time has yet been able to abate. I do not wonder, therefore, that nothing by and by was found to remain of the primitive religion but its trappings and outward forms, in which the vulgar seem rather to flatter God than to adore him, and their faith degenerates into mere credulity and prejudice—and what prejudice! such as makes brutes of rational men, opposes obstacles of all kinds to the entertainment of freedom of opinion, and the use of those faculties by which alone truth is to be distinguished from error; obstacles, of which the purpose is, as it seems, entirely to extinguish the light of the understanding in the soul. Piety, great God! and religion are thus turned into foolish mysteries, and men who contemn reason and reject understanding as corrupt in nature are strangely believed to be possessed of heavenly light! Had they, in truth, but one spark of that divine fire, they would not babble as they do, but would cease from their arrogant ravings, learn to worship God with reverence and understanding, and as they now excel in hate would be seen distinguished among all for humility and loving kindness; they would no longer persecute those who conscientiously differ from them in opinion; and were it the eternal salvation of these, and not their own fame and worldly estate, that was in question, they would rather be found to pity and compassionate them. Did a single ray of the divine light reach these men, it would moreover show itself in their doctrine; but I confess that whilst with them I have never been able sufficiently to admire the unfathomable mysteries of Scripture, I have still found them giving utterance to nothing but Aristotelian and Platonic speculations, artfully dressed up and cunningly accommodated to Holy Writ, lest the speakers should show themselves too plainly to belong to the sect of the Grecian heathens. Nor was it enough for these men to discourse with the Greeks; they have further taken to raving with the Hebrew prophets, which sufficiently proclaims that they have known nothing of the divineness of Scripture even in their dreams. The more they have abandoned themselves to their mystical reveries, indeed, the more plainly have they shown that they do not so much *believe* in as *assent* to the Scriptures; a conclusion that further appears in this, that they mostly assume as the basis of all inquiry into the true meaning of the Bible, that it is everywhere inspired and literally true. But this is the very matter in debate, and should first appear from a careful examination and close criticism of the text; whereby, indeed, a right understanding of Scripture is much more certainly attained than by any amount of human ingenuity and gratuitous speculation.

Weighing these things in my mind, and seeing that our natural understanding was not only despised as a guide, but even condemned as the well-spring of impiety by many, and further, that human commentaries were frequently substituted for divine decrees, that credulity was accounted faith, that philosophical controversies were waged with the utmost heat, both in the pulpit and before the judge, and that out of these sprang the most cruel hatreds and dissensions, seditious movements, and other acts which it were tedious to enumerate here, I resolved with myself forthwith to examine the Scriptures anew, in a spirit of entire freedom and without prejudice, to affirm nothing as to their meaning and to acknowledge nothing in the shape of doctrine, which I did not find most plainly set down in their pages. Fortified with these resolutions, I drew up " A method of studying and interpreting the sacred volume " for myself, and guided by this I set out by inquiring in the way of preliminary, What is Prophecy? and In what manner may God have revealed himself to the prophets? Why were these men accepted of God? was it because they had sublime ideas of God and Nature? or was it because of their signal piety? Having satisfied myself on these points, I found it easy to determine that the authority of the prophets was only of weight in those things that regard the usages of life and virtuous conduct, and that in other directions their opinions do not much concern us. These conclusions formed, I next inquired why the Jews were called the chosen people of God? and when I had discovered that it was only because God had selected a certain district or country wherein they might dwell securely and commodiously, this led on to the further inference that the laws revealed to Moses by God were nothing more than a code appropriate to the peculiar state or empire of the Hebrews; consequently, that no nation but themselves need be held bound to receive this code, nor even the Jews themselves to observe its precepts, save whilst their empire endured. Moreover, in order that I might know from Scripture whether the human heart and understanding were naturally corrupt, I proceeded to inquire whether the Roman Catholic system of religion, or the Divine law propounded by the prophets and apostles to the whole human race, was different from the religion which the light of nature teaches? Next I asked whether miracles happened in contravention of the order of nature or not? and whether the Being and the Providence of God were more certainly declared by miracles than by the things which we clearly and distinctly understand by their first causes? But when I had found nothing that Scripture taught which expressly contradicted, nay, nothing which did not entirely accord with reason and understanding, and saw, moreover, that the prophets taught none but plain and simple things which could readily be apprehended by all, and that their communications were made in a style and manner, and enforced by references and reasons, that are most apt to move the popular mind to devotion to God, I fully persuaded myself that Scripture left reason absolutely free, and had nothing in common with, no dependence on, Philosophy, but that this as well as that must support itself on its own footing.

Now that I may demonstrate these conclusions systematically, and set the whole matter at rest, I first show in what way Scripture is to be interpreted, insisting that the whole of our knowledge of the spiritual matters contained therein is to be derived from Scripture itself, and not from what is known to us by the light of our natural understanding. I then speak of the prejudices that have arisen from the vulgar having worshipped the Book of Scripture rather than the Word of God—the vulgar, abandoned to superstition and loving the relics of time more than eternity itself! After this I show that the Word of God was revealed in no set or certain number of books, but is the simple conception of the Divine mind imparted to the prophets, and that it is proclaimed to consist mainly in love and obedience to God with the whole heart and mind, and in the practice of justice and charity to our neighbour. I then exhibit the teachings of Scripture as in accordance with the capacity and opinions of those to whom the prophets and apostles were wont to preach this, the true Word of God. They spoke in a way that should excite no repugnance in the minds of their hearers, in a style that should lead to a ready acceptance of their doctrines. The foundations of faith next made known, I conclude that the end and object of revealed knowledge is nothing but *obedience*, and is so distinct from natural knowledge as well in its objects as in its grounds and means as to have nothing in common with it, but that each may possess its own province without clashing, and neither need be subordinate to the other. Further, as one man differs notably from another in capacity and disposition, as one agrees and another disagrees with this or that opinion, as one is moved to devotion by that which disposes another to laughter, I conclude that freedom of opinion belongs of right to all, and that the privilege of interpreting articles of faith is to be left to every man according to his capacity, no one being adjudged pious or impious save by his works. On this footing will all be able to obey God with unconstrained mind, and justice and charity be held in universal estimation.

After thus proclaiming that which the Divine Law, as revealed, allows to all, I proceed to another part of my subject, and argue that this liberty may be conceded with safety to the peace of the State and the rights of the sovereign or ruling powers; that it ought always to be enjoyed, and that it cannot be denied without great peril to the peace and much damage to the well-being of the whole commonwealth. In the demonstration of this principle, I begin with a summary of the natural rights of man, which I show extend as far as the desires and power of the individual extend, and that no one is bound by natural law to live according to the pleasure of another, but that every one is by natural title the rightful asserter of his own independence. I show, besides, that no one can truly cede this right unless he transfer the power of defending himself to another; and that he necessarily acquires this right absolutely to whom is transferred the right of each individual to live in his own way and to defend himself; hence I prove that whoever holds the sovereign or supreme authority in the State has a title to all he can command, and is the sole arbiter of right and liberty, the other members of the body politic being bound to act exclusively on his decrees. But as no one can so divest himself of the right of self-defence as to cease to be a man, I conclude that no individual can be absolutely deprived of the whole of his natural rights; but that he still retains something by the law of nature, as it were, of which he cannot be deprived without danger to the State, and which is therefore either tacitly conceded to him, or is expressly bargained for with the sovereign authority. Having advanced so far, I go on to consider the Hebrew Republic particularly, in order to show in what way and by whose command religion acquired the force of a right, and take occasion by the way of discussing other matters that seem to me worthy of special attention. In conclusion, I show that whoever holds the reins of the sovereign or supreme power in the State is not only the arbiter of civil right, but is also the judge and interpreter in religious matters, and alone has the title to decree what shall be held just or unjust, what shall be reputed pious or profane; and I wind up by avowing my conviction that he or they govern best who concede to every one the privilege of thinking as he pleases and of saying what he thinks.

This is a summary, philosophical reader, of what I now present for your examination; and I trust it will prove not ungrateful to you, by reason of the excellence and importance of the argument as a whole, as well as of its several parts, to the number of which I could readily have added. But I must not have this Preface grow to the size of a volume, especially as I know that the matters I handle are sufficiently interesting to persons of philosophic and inquiring minds. To others indeed I do not commend this Treatise, there being nothing in it which I could hope would by any possibility give them pleasure; for I know full well how pertinaciously those prejudices stick to the mind which have been embraced by it as a kind of religion; I know, too, that it is impossible to divest the vulgar mind of superstition and puerile fear; I know, in fine, that by the vulgar constancy is accounted contumacy, and that they are never governed by reason, but always moved to praise or blame by impulse or affection. I invite not the vulgar, therefore, nor those whose minds like theirs are full of prejudices, to the perusal of this book. I would much rather they neglected it entirely than, by misconstruing its purpose and contents after the fashion usual with them, that they proved troublesome, and, whilst advantaging themselves in nothing, became obnoxious to those who would show a freer spirit in their philosophy, stood not this one obstacle in the way: The idea that Reason should be subordinate to Theology. To these I would fain believe that my work may indeed be serviceable.

In conclusion, since many may have neither the time nor the inclination to read all I have written, I take occasion to say here, as I do at the end of my Treatise, that I have written nothing which I have not carefully considered, and which I have not submitted to the chief authorities of my native country. Should aught however that I have said be held to contravene the laws of the State, or to be opposed to the common good, I would have it impugned and rectified; for I know that I am man and liable to err; but I have taken great pains not to err, and I have been especially solicitous so to express myself, as that all I have written should be found in harmony with the laws of my country and with piety and good manners.

CHAPTER I.

OF PROPHECY.

Prophecy or revelation is certain knowledge communicated by God to man. A *Prophet* is one who interprets things revealed by God to those who of themselves cannot have certain knowledge of them, and who consequently can only receive the revelations imparted as articles of faith. The Hebrew word *Nabi*, commonly translated Prophet, signifies orator or interpreter, but is always used to signify an interpreter of the Divine will, as appears from Exodus (vii. 1), where God says to Moses,—"See, I have made thee a god to Pharaoh: and Aaron thy brother shall be thy prophet;" which is as much as if he had said,—"Since Aaron in interpreting what thou sayest to Pharaoh plays the part of a prophet, thou shalt therefore be as a god, or stand in the stead of a god to Pharaoh."

It will be our business to treat of the Prophet in the next chapter; here we shall speak of Prophecy only. From the definition given above, it follows that all natural knowledge may be entitled Prophecy; for what we know by the light of nature depends entirely on a knowledge of God and his eternal decrees. But as this natural knowledge is accessible to all men, resting as it is does on foundations that are common to mankind at large, therefore is it not so highly esteemed of the vulgar, whose disposition it is still to be attracted by rare and strange incidents, to the contempt of natural events. This is the reason why the vulgar, when there is question of Prophecy, always presume natural knowledge to be set aside, although it has a like title with any other kind of knowledge to be called divine, seeing that it is imparted to us by the nature of God and his decrees, and is not different from the knowledge which by all is called divine, save that divine knowledge surpasses the limits of natural knowledge, and that the laws of human nature considered in themselves cannot be its cause. As regards certainty, however, which natural knowledge always involves, and the source whence it proceeds, namely, God, it yields in nowise to prophetic knowledge,—unless, forsooth, it were thought or rather dreamed that the prophets possessed human bodies, indeed, but had minds other than human, whereby their sensations, consciousness, &c., would be entirely different from ours. Although natural knowledge be truly divine, then, still its teachers cannot be called prophets;* for the things taught may be perceived and understood by mankind at large with the same certainty as by those who teach, in virtue of common natural powers, and without the aid of faith.

Since our mind, therefore, in containing the nature of God objectively within itself, and thereby participating in his nature, has the power of forming clear and certain ideas which explain the nature of things and teach the purposes of life, it may be assumed on the ground of its excellence to be the prime cause of Divine revelation. For all that we clearly and adequately understand is dictated to us by the idea of God and

* Prophets, i. e. God's interpreters. He alone is God's interpreter, in fact, who makes known Divine commandments revealed to him by God to those who have not been so favoured, and whose belief consequently rests on no ground but the authority of the prophet and the confidence he inspires. Were it otherwise, did they who hearkened to the prophet become prophets in their turn, as they become philosophers who listen to philosophical discourses, the prophet would no longer be the sole interpreter of the Divine will to man, for then would they who heard him know the truth, not on the faith of the prophet, but by a kind of Divine communication like his own, and by internal testimony. It is thus that the sovereign in a despotic monarchy is the sole interpreter of the law, because his authority alone enacts and enforces it. [N.B.—The notes without the signature *Ed.* are the author's.—*Ed.*]

nature, as has been already said, not in words, indeed, but in a much more excellent way, a way which agrees entirely with the nature of mind, and which has been experienced by every one undoubtedly who has tasted the delights of intellectual certainty. But as my object is to speak of those things especially which bear upon the Scriptures, I must be content in this place to say nothing more of the light of nature, and therefore proceed to discuss at length the other causes and means by which.God has revealed to man those things that are beyond the sphere of natural knowledge, as well as those that do not surpass its compass; for there is no assignable reason wherefore God should not also in other ways impart to man those things of which he is cognizant by the light of nature.

Now whatever is said on this subject must be deduced from Scripture alone. For what can we possibly say of things that surpass our understanding but that which we have from the mouths of the prophets and the pages of Holy Writ? And since, in so far as I am aware, we have now no prophets among us, there is nothing for it but to draw from the sacred writings what has been left to us by the prophets of old, taking care always to ascribe nothing to them, to set down nothing as theirs, which they have not plainly and distinctly declared. But here it is to be especially observed that the Jews never make mention of mediate or particular causes; neither do they seem ever to regard or consider these; but from religion, from piety, or, as is commonly said, from devotion, they always refer everything immediately to God. If, for example, they have made a profit of their traffic, they say the advantage has been given to them by God; if they desire anything whatsoever, they say that God inclines their hearts thereto; and if any thought comes into their minds, they say that God has put it there. Wherefore we see that we are not to assume everything as prophecy and supernatural communication which Scripture says God imparted to any one, but so much only as Scripture declares expressly to have been revealed, or as from the context plainly appears to be revelation.

If we turn to the sacred volume, therefore, we shall find all that God reveals to the prophets to be imparted to them either by words or by visions, or in both ways at once—both by words and visions. The words, and the visions likewise, were, however, either real, actual, and independent of the imagination of the prophet who heard or saw them, or they were imaginary, the imagination of the prophet, even though watching, being so disposed as to lead him to believe that he clearly heard certain words, or distinctly saw certain visions.

Now, that God by a real voice revealed to Moses the laws which he desired should be given to the Jews appears from Exodus (xxv. 22), where we find these words, "And there I will meet with thee, and I will commune with thee from above the mercy-seat, from between the two cherubims," words which show that God made use of an actual voice in giving them utterance; for there, in the place pointed out, Moses, when he so desired, found God ready to hold communication with him; and I shall by and by show that it was by a true voice that the law was made known. The voice with which God called Samuel I also suspect to have been a real voice, for we find the incident stated thus (1 Sam. iii. 21), "And the Lord appeared again in Shiloh: for the Lord revealed himself to Samuel in Shiloh by the word of the Lord;" as though it had been said that God manifested himself to Samuel by vocal sounds, or that Samuel heard God speaking. Nevertheless, as we have to distinguish between Moses and the rest of the prophets, we are compelled to hold that the voice heard by Samuel was imaginary; a conclusion which is also forced upon us from what has gone before in the narrative, where we find Samuel referring the voice to Eli, with whose voice he was of course familiar; for, called on three several occasions by God, he still imagined that he was summoned by Eli. The voice which Abimelech heard was imaginary, for we find it stated in Genesis (xx. 6.), "And God said unto him in a dream," the communication of God's will to him being therefore made not when he was wide awake, but when asleep and dreaming, a state in which the imagination is most apt to bring up things before the mind that have no existence in fact.

That the words of the Decalogue were not actually pronounced by God is the opinion of some among the Jews. They conceive that the Israelites only heard a noise, and no distinct words, during the continuance of which they became mentally aware of the Laws of the Decalogue. And to this view I have myself sometimes inclined; for I see that the words of the Decalogue as delivered in Exodus differ considerably from those of the Decalogue as it occurs in Deuteronomy, a circumstance from which it seems to follow (inasmuch as God spoke but once) that the Decalogue does not give the very words of God, but is intended to convey his precepts only. Nevertheless, unless violence be done to the plain sense of Scripture, we must admit that the Israelites heard a real voice on the occasion when the Decalogue was communicated, for in Deuteronomy (v. 4) it is said expressly, "The Lord talked with you face to face," &c., i. e. spoke as two persons hold verbal communication with one another by means of their corporeal organs. Wherefore it seems more in accordance with Scripture to conclude that God created a certain real voice by which he revealed the Decalogue; and in our eighth chapter we shall take occasion to explain how it happens that the words and precepts of one of these Decalogues differ from those of the other. Even then, however, every difficulty will not have been removed; for it does not seem slightly in contradiction with reason to imagine that any created thing, depending like all else on God, should have power given it to express the essence or existence of God in word or deed, and to assume his personality, as is done when we find such language as this in the first person, "I, Jehovah, am thy God," &c. And although when any one says with his mouth "I understand," no one imagines that it is the mouth but the mind of the speaker which understands, because the mouth speaking is referred to the nature of the man who speaks, and he to whom the words are addressed appreciates by the nature of his own mind the mind of the speaker; still I do not see how they who previously knew nothing of God but his name, and who desired speech with him that they might be assured of his existence, —I do not see, I say, how their desire would be satisfied by a creature having no more intimate dependence on God than any other created thing saying to them, "I am God." I ask, Had God disposed the lips of Moses—but why of Moses? —of any created thing to articulate such words as these, "I am God," would the existence of God have therefore been understood? And then Scripture seems invariably to imply that God himself spoke when the Decalogue was delivered. He came down from heaven upon Mount Sinai for the special purpose of divulging the law, and the Jews not only heard his voice, but their chiefs and elders saw him (Exodus xx. 10, 11). Nor does the law revealed to Moses, from which it was not permitted to take, and to which it was not lawful to add, anything, and which was the binding code of the country, ever teach that God is incorporeal, that he is without form and features, but only that he is God; that he alone is to be believed in and worshipped, and that no image of him is to be made lest his true worship should be compromised. Image or likeness of God never having been seen, none could be fashioned in semblance of him, but must needs be formed after some created thing which had been seen; and thus, having homage paid it, the thing represented, and not Jehovah, would be thought of, and have the honour and worship due to him alone bestowed upon it. Nevertheless Scripture in several places clearly declares that God has a form; and to Moses' petition, whilst conversing with God, to be shown his glory, he is informed that no man shall see God and live. Putting him in a cleft of the rock, however, God covers him with his hand as he passes, but withdrawing it for a moment, shows Moses "his back parts." And here, in this account, I make no doubt but that some mystery or allegory lurks, of which I shall speak more at length by and by. At present I proceed to point out those passages in Scripture that indicate the means by which God has revealed his decrees to man.*

That revelation has been made by visions only appears from the First Book of Chronicles (xxii.), where God declares his anger to David by an angel having a sword in his hand. The same means are also employed in the case of Balaam. And although Maimonides and others have maintained that these and other histories in which apparitions of angels are mentioned (that of Manoah, that of Abraham, when he thought of immolating his son, &c.), are based upon dreams, inasmuch as no one with his waking sense can see an angel; this seems to me but idle talk, in which Scripture is tortured into Aristotelian vanities and poetic figments, than which I find nothing more reprehensible. God certainly revealed to Joseph his future greatness, not by an apparition or vision, but by his imagination. To Joshua, on the contrary, God revealed himself by a vision, and words addressed to the ear, showing him an angel armed with a sword like the leader of a host, and in speech by the angel's mouth bidding him do battle for the people. To Isaiah also it was shown in a vision how Jehovah had withdrawn his favour from the Israelites, the thrice holy God being imagined as seated on a

---

* The following note, from a paper by a distinguished writer, will probably satisfy the unprejudiced reader on the subject of direct *verbal* communication from the Almighty.—*Ed.*

"Shall we, dare we, conceive God as speaking? Did God speak, we must then presume him to be possessed of human parts, with the several corporeal organs in especial upon which articulate speech depends. To me, however, it appears as absurd to imagine a human body without each and all of its members—without teeth, for example—as to think of Deity with a set of teeth, and, as a sort of necessary sequence to this, engaged in mastication, for the teeth, with the wise economy of means so conspicuous in our wonderfully compacted frames, whilst subservient to articulate speech, are nevertheless especially provided for the comminution of the food."—Jacob Grimm, *Ueber den Ursprung der Sprache*, S. 27. 4te Aufl., 8vo. Berlin, 1858.

lofty throne surrounded by the heavenly host, and the Israelites beneath plunged in their wickedness and sin, and so removed to the uttermost from his presence and protection. The abject state of the Hebrew nation in his day was understood and keenly felt by Isaiah, and the calamities in store for it were revealed to him in words as it were from the lips of God. It were easy for me to cite many similar instances from the Scriptures, did I not believe that they were generally well known.

All that has been said above, however, is particularly confirmed by the text of the Book of Numbers (xii. 6, 7), where we find these words: "If there be a prophet among you, I the Lord will make myself known unto him in a vision, and will speak to him in a dream," i. e. by figures and hieroglyphics, not by actual words and a real voice. The text proceeds: "To my servant Moses not so; with him will I speak mouth to mouth, even apparently, and not in dark speeches, and the similitude of God shall he behold," that is, Moses in the presence of God should speak to him as a friend without fear, as may be seen more at large in Exodus (xxxiii. 17). The passage just quoted makes it evident that the prophets generally did not hear real voices or words, a conclusion still further confirmed by Deuteronomy (xxxiv. 10), where it is written: "And there arose not a prophet since in Israel like unto Moses whom the Lord knew face to face," words which must still be understood as referring to knowledge by voice only, for not even did Moses ever behold the very face of Jehovah (Exod. xxxiii.).

Other than these means I find none in Scripture whereby God ever held communication with man; so that, as has been shown above, none others are to be imagined or admitted. And although we clearly understand that God can communicate his will to man in various ways,—for without having recourse to corporeal media, he does communicate his essence to our souls,—yet that a man should by his mind alone be able to perceive aught which is not included within the fundamentals of his understanding, and which cannot be deduced therefrom, would imply that he possessed a mind much more excellent, much nobler, than that which belongs to humanity at large. Wherefore, I do not believe that any one save Christ alone ever attained to such superiority over others as to have had the precepts of God which lead to everlasting life, revealed to him immediately, and without the intervention of words or a vision. God, I opine, manifested himself by the mind of Christ Jesus immediately to the apostles, as He formerly revealed himself to Moses by the medium of the voice. The voice of Christ, consequently, even as the voice which Moses heard, may be called the voice of God, and in this sense also may we say that the wisdom of God, that is, the wisdom which is more than human, put on humanity in Christ, and that Christ, consequently, is the way of salvation.

But it is necessary for me here to admonish my reader that I do not speak either in affirmation or negation of those things which some churches declare concerning Christ, for I freely confess that I do not understand them. What I affirm I derive from the Scriptures alone; and there I nowhere read of God having ever appeared to or spoken with Christ, but of God revealed through Christ to the apostles as the way of life, and finally of the old law having been delivered through an angel or a voice, but not immediately revealed by God to man. Wherefore, if Moses spoke face to face with God, as one man speaks with another, i. e. by means of their corporeal organs severally, Christ, it must be maintained, communicated with God in the way of mind with mind.*

Our position therefore is, that with the exception of Christ no one has received the revelations of God save by the aid or medium of imagination, viz. by means of words, signs, or visions; so that in order to excel in prophesying there was no need of a more perfect mind, but only of a more vivid im-

---

* Is not all communication with the Supreme effected in the way of mind with mind? God incarnate in Christ, in the Man Christ, in man furnished with mental aptitudes to receive and understand the decrees of his Maker, whether issued in words or visions, mentally apprehended, or read on the everlasting page of nature—in no case is it ear or eye or any *sense*, but *mind*, that is in communion with the Supreme Intelligence.—*Ed.*

agination, as I shall clearly show in the next chapter. Here, meantime, it seems proper to ask what is to be understood by the expression, "The spirit of God infused into the prophets," or, "The prophets spoke from or inspired by the spirit of God," an inquiry in which it is important, in the first place, to learn the true significance of the Hebrew word רוח *ruagh*,* commonly translated spirit.

Now in its most simple sense the word *ruagh* signifies wind or vapour, but it is also used in a great variety of other senses: 1st, in Psalm cxxv. (17), for example, we find the word employed to signify the breath of the mouth: "Neither is there any breath in their mouths." 2nd, In 1 Samuel (xxx. 12) *ruagh* imports strength in the sense of bodily power: "And when he had eaten, his *spirit* came again to him." 3rd, The word means courage or moral strength, as in Joshua (ii. 11), "Neither did there remain any more courage (*ruagh*) in any man." In Ezekiel the word occurs with the same meaning (ii. 2), "And the spirit entered into me and set me on my feet." 4th, The word is further used to signify virtue or aptitude, as in Job, where we find these words (xxxii. 8), "There is a spirit in man, and the inspiration of the Almighty giveth them understanding," words in reply to Elihu who has just expressed himself diffidently, "on account of his youth," in the presence of Job and his friends, "because they were very old:" "great men," continues Job, "are not [necessarily] wise, neither do the aged understand judgment," which is as much as if he had said that knowledge and understanding depend on the capacity of each individual man. In the same sense, nearly, do we find the word employed in Numbers (xxvii. 18), "Take thee Joshua, a man in whom is the spirit." 5th, The word *ruagh* is still further used to signify conduct or disposition, as in Numbers (xiv. 24), "But Caleb, my servant, because he had another spirit with him, him will I bring into the land," &c. In Proverbs (i. 23) we find these words, "I will pour out my spirit (i. e. make known my purpose) unto you." In this sense the

---

* Ruagh, Heb., Rauch, Germ., Reek, Scotch: smoke, vapour.—*Ed.*

word signifies will, desire, mental impulse, as in Ezekiel (i. 12), where it is written, "Whither the spirit was to go they went," and in Isaiah (xxx. 1), "Woe to the rebellious children that cover with a covering, but not of my spirit;" and again (xxix. 10), "The Lord hath poured out on you the spirit (i. e. the desire) of deep sleep." In Judges (viii. 3*) we have this phrase, "Then was their spirit softened," and here the word implies temper; and in Proverbs (xvi. 32) we are told that "He that is slow to anger is better than the mighty, and he that ruleth his spirit (i. e. his passions) than he that taketh a city," and yet again in the same book (xxv. 28), "He that hath no rule over his own spirit (i. e. temper) is like a city without walls." In Isaiah again (xxxiii. 11) the word breath (*ruagh*) evidently signifies evil disposition, in these words, "Your breath as fire shall devour you."

The word *ruagh*, moreover, as it signifies disposition of mind, is used to express all the passions and even modes of the soul. We have therefore the phrase lofty spirit for proud spirit or pride, lowly spirit for humility, good spirit for benevolence, spirit of jealousy for jealousy, spirit of lust for fornication, spirit of wisdom, of counsel, of fortitude, &c., for these qualities severally, though, in the Hebrew, words are more frequently used substantively than adjectively. 6th, *Ruagh* signifies the mind or soul itself, as in Ecclesiastes (iii. 19), "All have one breath, and all go into one place." 7th, Finally, the word *ruagh* is applied to the quarters of the world, because of the winds which blow from these, and also to the sides of anything that look towards these quarters. (Ezekiel xxxvii. 9 and xlii. 16 *et seq.*)

And here it is proper to observe that in the Hebrew Scriptures everything referred to God is very commonly said to be of God. 1st, Because nature belongs to God, and is as it were a part of himself, as when the "Power of God," the "Eye of God," is mentioned. 2nd, Because everything is in the power of God, and is obedient to his will. Thus the

* The citation here appears to be wrong.—*Ed.*

heavens are the heavens of God, because they are his chariot and his dwelling-place. Assyria is entitled the "Scourge of God," and Nebuchodonosor the "Servant of God," &c. 3rd, Because the thing spoken of is dedicate to God, as the temple of God, the bread of God, a Nazarene of God, &c. 4th, Because things are made known by the prophets, not revealed by the natural understanding, whence the law imparted by Moses is entitled the Law of God. 5th, When things have to be spoken of in the superlative degree, they are said to be of God; thus, very high mountains are called mountains of God, very deep sleep is a sleep of God, and it is in this sense that Amos (iv. 11) is to be understood, when he makes Jehovah himself speak thus: "I have destroyed you as the destruction of God destroyed Sodom and Gomorrah," that is to say, completely, like the memorable instance of destruction quoted; for, as God himself speaks, it is impossible to explain the passage appropriately in any other way. The natural wisdom of Solomon is entitled wisdom of God; in other words, Solomon was very wise, he possessed wisdom much above the common. In the Psalms great cedar-trees are designated cedars of God, to indicate their unusual size. In 1 Samuel (xiv. 7) we find the expression, "And the fear of God fell upon the people," used to signify that it was a great fear which seized them. In the same way indeed was everything habitually spoken of that surpassed the comprehension of the Jews, and of which the natural causes were to them unknown: "The thunder is the muttering or angry voice of God, the lightnings are his arrows, &c." The Jews indeed believed that God kept the winds confined in certain caverns, which they called treasures of God, differing in their views from the Pagan in this only, that they thought Jehovah, not Æolus, was the ruler of the storm. On the same grounds miraculous works are called works of God, or mighty works. And, indeed, all natural events are the work of God, and happen by the Divine will and authority alone. It is in this view that the Psalmist calls the miracles of Egypt powers of God, because they opened up a way of safety to the Jews, expecting nothing of the kind, whereby their wonder and admiration were the more excited.

When in the Scriptures, then, we observe that unusual events in nature are called works of God, and trees of mighty dimensions are spoken of as trees of God, it is not to be wondered at that we find men of great stature and strength, though spoilers and ravishers, designated sons of God, as we do in the Book of Genesis. The ancients generally indeed, heathen as well as Jew, were accustomed to refer everything of peculiar excellence to God. Pharaoh, when he had heard Joseph's interpretation of his dream, declared that the understanding of the gods dwelt in him, and Nebuchodonosor told Daniel that he possessed the understanding of the sacred gods. Among the Latins, again, nothing is more common than to find works of art of great excellence ascribed to the Divine hand, or, as the Jews would have said, to the hand of God.

Those passages in Scripture, consequently, in which there is mention made of the spirit of God are easily interpreted and understood. The words *ruagh* Elohim, and *ruagh* Jehovah —spirit of God and spirit of Jehovah—signify nothing more in many places than a violent and excessively dry or blighting wind. Thus, in Isaiah (xl. 7) we have, "The grass withereth, the flower fadeth: because the spirit of the Lord bloweth upon it," that is to say, because blown upon by a very parching and strong wind. In Genesis (i. 2) it is said that the spirit of God, i. e. a strong wind, moved on the face of the waters. In other places the word *ruagh* is used to designate a mighty soul. Gideon and Samson, for instance, are spoken of as spirits of God; otherwise they were daring men prepared for every emergency. So also all virtue, all power, beyond the common, is virtue or power of God, as appears in Exodus (xxxi. 3), where we find these words, "And I will fill him with the spirit of God," which means, as the text itself immediately proceeds to explain, with genius and art, beyond the common run of men. In Isaiah

(xi. 2) it is written, "And there rested upon him the spirit of God," which signifies, as the prophet by and by informs us, in a way that is very common in Scripture, such virtues as wisdom, counsel, fortitude, &c. The melancholy of Saul, moreover, is designated an evil spirit of God, which means no more in fact than a very great or deep melancholy; for the servants of Saul who called the melancholy with which he was possessed a melancholy of God, were those who suggested to him that he should summon a musician to his presence, who by playing on the harp might calm his mind and soothe his distemper, a course which plainly shows that by the phrase melancholy of God the persons about Saul understood a common but very great melancholy. The expression spirit of God, again, is used to signify the soul, life, and mind of man, as in Job (xxvii. 3), "And the spirit of God is in my nostrils," allusion being evidently made to what is said in Genesis of God's breathing the breath of life into the nostrils of man. In the same way Ezekiel, prophesying to the dead (xxxvii. 14), says, "And I shall give my spirit to you and ye shall live," i. e. breathing on them he would restore them to life. It is in the same sense that we are to understand these words in Job (xxxiv. 13), "If he (God) set his heart upon man, if he gather unto himself his spirit (i. e. the mind he has given) and his breath, &c." So also must we read the passage in Genesis (vi. 3), where it is said, "My spirit shall not always strive with man, for that he also is flesh," the interpretation being, that henceforward man would act according to the dictates of the flesh, and not of the understanding, which he had at first for his guidance. In Psalm li. (10, 11) we find this imprecation, "Create in me a clean heart, O God, and renew a right spirit within me; cast me not away from thy presence, and take not thy holy spirit from me;" the meaning of which becomes obvious when we know that all sins were believed to proceed from the flesh, and that the spirit, mind, or understanding, prompted only to good, wherefore the Psalmist invokes the help of God against the lusts of the flesh, whilst he prays that the spirit of understanding, which the blessed Lord himself bestows, may be preserved to him. Scripture frequently representing God in the likeness of man, and ascribing to him mind, understanding, passions, a body, breath, &c., in order to accommodate itself to the weakness of the vulgar, we therefore frequently find in Holy Writ the words spirit of God used in the sense of mind, understanding, the passions, strength, and breath of the mouth of God. Thus Isaiah (xl. 13) asks, "Who hath directed the spirit (or mind) of the Lord, or being his counsellor hath taught him?" i. e. Who but God himself has ever determined the Almighty mind to will or decree aught? In lxiii. 10 of the same prophet we read, "But they rebelled, and vexed his holy spirit."* Here the phrase, holy spirit, or spirit of God, is used synonymously with the law as delivered by Moses, because this law explains and makes known the mind of God, as Isaiah himself proceeds to show in the verse immediately following the one just quoted: "Where is he who put his holy spirit within him?" in other words, who dictated the law to Moses; an interpretation which plainly appears from the whole of the context. Nehemiah, when he says (ix. 20), "Thou gavest also thy good spirit to instruct them," is speaking of the time when the law was delivered; and the same thing is alluded to in Deuteronomy (iv. 6), where Moses says, "For this (the law) is your wisdom and your understanding, &c." The Psalmist also says (cxliii. 11), "Thy good spirit leads me into level lands," i. e. Thy revealed will guides me on the way of life. The word *ruagh* also signifies, as has been said, spirit in the

---

* The Scripture texts in the original are presumed to be Spinoza's own version from the Hebrew, which is always given along with the Latin. The translation of the above text is as follows: "Et ipsi amaritudine et tristitia affecerunt spiritum suæ sanctitatis,"—"and they afflicted with sorrow and bitterness the spirit of his holiness;" words that are certainly much more striking and forcible than those in the common English Bible. Spinoza is known to have made a translation of the Hebrew Scriptures, which he himself, it is much to be regretted, destroyed shortly before his death. The English texts in this translation are usually from the accredited version.—*Ed.*

sense of breath, as in the phrase "breath of God," which, like mind or soul and body, is often inappropriately ascribed to God in the Scriptures. The word occurs with this signification in Psalm xxxiii. 6, "By the word of the Lord were the heavens made, and all the host of them by the breath of his mouth." The word again, in connection with God, sometimes implies power, force, virtue, as in Job (xxxiii. 4), "The spirit of God hath made me, and the breath of the Almighty hath given me life;" that is to say, the power, or, if you will, the decree of God hath given me life. The Psalmist speaking poetically says: "By God's command were the heavens fashioned, and by his spirit or the breath of his mouth (i. e. his decree uttered as it were in a breath) the whole of the heavenly host." So also in Psalm cxxxix. 7 we have these words, "Whither shall I go from thy spirit, or whither shall I flee from thy presence?" expressions which the Psalmist proceeds to amplify, and to show that by them he means he cannot go where he should be beyond the reach of the Almighty's power and protecting care. Finally, the word *ruagh*, translated spirit of God, is used in Scripture to express modes of affection of the Supreme mind, such as mercy, lovingkindness, &c. This is seen in Micah (ii. 7), where the prophet asks, "Is the spirit (i. e. the mercy) of God straitened?" and in Zechariah (iv. 6), where we have this, "Not by might, not by power, but by my spirit (in other words, by my mercy), saith the Lord." In the same sense, I believe, are we to understand ver. 12 of ch. vii. of the same prophet: "And they made their hearts as an adamant stone, lest they should hear the law, and the words which the Lord of hosts hath sent in his spirit (i. e. his mercy), by former prophets." Haggai also has the following (ii. 5), "So my spirit (i. e. my grace) remaineth among you, fear not;" and further, Isaiah (xlviii. 16), "And now the Lord God and his spirit hath sent me;" a verse in which the word spirit may be variously interpreted indeed, and taken to signify either the mind or the mercy of God, or his will revealed in the law; for the prophet continues: "From the beginning I have not spoken in secret, from the time that it was, there am I, and now the Lord God in his spirit hath sent me." This is as much as to say the prophet made no secret at first of God's anger and of the sentence that had gone out against the nation, but now was he a messenger of good tidings, come to preach the mercy of God, and to announce their restoration to his favour. That the verse may also be understood as referring to the will of God revealed in the law of Moses, or as saying that the prophet had come in obedience to that law to admonish the Jews, might be assumed from what is said in Leviticus (xix. 17). Isaiah certainly admonishes the children of Israel in the same way as Moses was wont to do, and also winds up as the great first prophet did, by foretelling their restoration. The first interpretation, however, is that which I myself prefer.

Returning to our subject, from this long array, illustrative of particular and diverse applications of the same word, I think we may safely conclude that Scripture phrases such as these, "To the prophets was given the spirit of God," "God shed his spirit upon man," "Men filled with the spirit of God, or with the Holy Ghost," &c., have no other meaning than that the prophets possessed certain special and extraordinary powers,* that they were men more than commonly devout, and that they apprehended or knew the mind and purposes of God; for we have shown that the word spirit, *ruagh* in Hebrew, signifies as well the mind or soul itself as the modes or affections of the mind or soul; whence

---

* Although there are men endowed with certain advantages which nature has denied to others, it is not said that these men are raised above human nature; because for this it were necessary that they possessed qualities in peculiar, which are not comprised in the essence or definition of humanity. The stature of a giant, for example, is something rare, but entirely human. In the same way, the talent of making verses impromptu is far from common, but there is nothing in it which surpasses the power of ordinary humanity. I say the same of that faculty which some men have of representing certain things to themselves very vividly by means of their imagination, and this not in sleep, but wide awake, precisely as though the objects were present to them. Were we to encounter one who possessed other means of perception than those that belong to mankind at large, we should then have to admit that he was more than mortal.

it comes that the law as it makes known the mind of God, so is it often spoken of as the spirit or understanding of God, and by an extension of the same principle, the imagination of the prophets (inasmuch as by this are the decrees of God revealed) may be styled the mind of God, and the prophets themselves be said to be possessed of the mind of God. And although the mind of the Almighty and his eternal decrees are written upon our minds also, and we therefore and thereby perceive and know the mind of God*—and here I speak by the letter of Scripture—still, inasmuch as the knowledge of natural things is common to all, it is not held in such high esteem by the vulgar, as has been already said, and was even wont to be despised by the Jews, who boasted themselves superior to all other peoples, and cared nothing for knowledge and understanding of a kind that was shared with the world at large. Finally, the prophets were said to have the spirit of God within them, because men, being generally ignorant of the cause of prophetic knowledge, marvelled at its exhibition, and referring it as they do other wonderful or portentous things immediately to God, they called it divine knowledge.

We may therefore affirm, without hesitation or reserve, that the prophets perceived not the revelations of God save by the aid of imagination; that is to say, by the medium of words, visions, or signs, and these either actual or imaginary. For, as we find no other means of communication besides these referred to in Scripture, we are not to hold ourselves at liberty to conceive any other, as I have already shown. Wherefore, or by what law of nature, this is so, I am free to confess my ignorance. I might say indeed, as others have done, that it is by the power or will of God; but then I should seem to myself to talk idly; for it would be as if I pretended to explain the form of any particular thing by the use of some transcendental term. All things are made by the power of God : yea, because there is no power in nature but the power of God alone ; and it is certain that in our ignor-

* Vide Editor's note, page 39.—*Ed.*

ance of the causes of natural things, we can have no knowledge of the power of God. The power of God is therefore very foolishly invoked when the natural cause of anything, in other words, the very power of God, is unknown. But neither is it necessary to our purpose that we should understand the cause of prophetic knowledge; for, as I have already declared, I here pretend to do no more than to discuss the documents of Scripture, that from these, as in natural science from the data supplied by nature, I may draw my conclusions:—we have nothing to do with the causes of the documents themselves.

Admitting, then, that the prophets by imagination were made cognizant of the things God willed to reveal, there is no doubt but that they perceived many things beyond the limits of the understanding; for from words and visions a much longer array of ideas may be composed than from those principles and ideas on which the whole of our natural knowledge reposes.

And this consideration explains to us why the prophets almost always make their communications allegorically or enigmatically, and give bodily shape and form to spiritual things in general. The procedure is in entire conformity with the nature of the imaginative faculty. On the same ground also we no longer feel surprise when in Scripture we find the Supreme so inappropriately spoken of as we do in the Books of Numbers, xi .17, and 1 Kings, xxii. 2; when we meet Micah describing God as seated on a throne; Daniel portraying the Almighty as an old man clothed in white raiment; Ezekiel figuring him as fire; those about Christ fancying that they saw the Holy Ghost in the likeness of a dove descending, whilst the apostles conceived that they saw it in the shape of fiery tongues, and Paul, on his conversion, believed that he beheld a great light. All such notions and images are obviously in consonance with vulgar ideas of God and spirits. Again, and to conclude, since the imagination has something of a flighty and inconstant nature, we should expect, as we find the case to be in fact, that the power of prophecy is not common, that it does not remain long at a time with those who possess it, and that neither does it come upon them frequently. On the contrary, prophetic power is rare—very few men possess it, and in these it is only manifested at distant and uncertain intervals. Now this being the case, we are led to inquire whence might accrue to the prophets the certainty of the things which they perceived by force of their imagination, and not from the assured principles of the understanding? But all that can be said in answer to this query must be derived from Scripture: inasmuch as we have no true or actual science of such matters, we cannot explain them upon first principles or causes. The teaching of Scripture, however, in regard to the certainty of prophetic teaching can be elicited, and this we shall proceed to ascertain in the following chapter.

Imaginary, Imagination. These words are evidently used by Spinoza to signify internal, sensual conceptions, occurring independently of external agency. The cerebral parts, to which impressions made on the organs of sense are conveyed, and where these become mental conceptions, being spontaneously active, cause impressions or conceptions that are referred to the outer world. It is in this way that men see spectres, hear ghostly sounds when awake, or ravishing music in their sleep, sit at wonderful banquets, are visited by well-remembered forms and faces in their dreams, &c. In the same manner we account for the idea of spirit, and of the spiritual world in general, which is wholly a creation of our own—without ourselves it has no existence, it is within us, not without; and though metaphysicians tell us that it is the mental act which evokes the material world, still this dictum is to be differently understood. Till we were, to us very certainly the world was not; but we have the intuitive assurance that before we were, the world was, and that when we are gone, it will continue to be.—*Ed.*

CHAPTER II.

OF THE PROPHET.

From what has been said in the preceding chapter it appears that prophets were not gifted with any peculiar superiority of understanding, but only with a certain more lively faculty of imagination, than the rest of mankind. This indeed appears plainly from the Scripture narratives themselves. Solomon, for instance, excelled all his contemporaries in wisdom, but he was not therefore possessed of the gift of prophecy. Those most sagacious persons, Heman, Darda, and Kalchol, were not prophets; whilst others, mere rustics without culture, and even ignorant women, such as Hagar, the servant of Abraham, were possessed of prophetic powers. And this is consonant with reason and experience; for those who greatly excel in strength of imagination are often less able to see things truly by the pure light of intellect; and those, on the contrary, who are distinguished for the vigour of their understanding, are apt to have the power of imagination more tempered, more under command, as it were, and distinct from pure intelligence. They therefore who go in search of wisdom and a knowledge of natural and spiritual things from the writings of the prophets completely mistake their way, as I shall now proceed to show at length; little caring what the superstitious may say, since the time, philosophy, and the subject itself, demand plain speaking;

and superstition has no greater hatred of aught than of those who advocate simple truth and strive to find out and follow the true way of life. And with grief I am compelled to say that many who openly admit that they have no idea of God, and know nothing of him save by created things, of the causes of which they are utterly ignorant, yet do not hesitate to accuse religious philosophers of Atheism.

That I may proceed regularly, however, I shall now go on to show that prophecies have varied in their purport, not only by reason of the imagination and bodily temperament of each prophet, but also by reason of the opinions with which they were severally imbued; from whence it is to be inferred that the gift of prophecy never made prophet wiser or more learned than it found him, as I shall show more in detail immediately. Here, at the outset, we have to inquire as to the *certainty of the prophets;* first, because this bears upon the entire argument of the present chapter, and next, because it serves us somewhat in the demonstration at which we aim.

Imagination of itself not involving certainty from its own nature, as does every clear and distinct idea, in order that we may be sure of the things we conceive by imagination, it is necessary to supplement it by reasoning; whence it follows that of itself prophecy, as the effect of imagination, can never involve certainty; and this is the reason why the prophets were never certain of the revelation of God by the revelation itself, but always by some supplementary sign or condition. This is obvious from Genesis xv. 8, where Abraham, after having heard the promise made him by God, asks for a sign, not because he did not believe God, or had not faith in him, but that he might know it was God indeed who had made him the promise. The same view appears still more clearly from Gideon, where he says to God, "Show me a sign that [I may know] thou talkest with me" (Judges vi. 17). God also says to Moses, "And this [shall be] a sign to thee, that I sent thee." Hezekiah, who had long been aware that Isaiah was a prophet, nevertheless asks for a sign by way of assurance of the prophecy of restored health which was made him. These instances suffice to show that the prophets always looked for a sign as an assurance of the things they prophesied from imagination; and this is the reason why Moses admonishes the people always to demand of the prophet a sign, such as the predication of some event about to happen, as a security that he did not speak falsely. Prophecy, therefore, in this case yields the palm to natural knowledge, which requires no sign, but by its own nature involves certainty. Prophetic certainty, however, was not mathematical, but only moral, certainty, as appears by Scripture; for Moses (Deut. xiv.) instructs the Jews to put the prophet to death who should propose new gods, even though he supported his doctrine by signs and miracles; "for," Moses proceeds to say, "God sometimes sends signs and miracles to tempt and try the people." Christ, even, spoke in very similar terms to his disciples, as appears from Matthew (xxiv. 24), "For there shall arise false Christs and false prophets, and shall show great signs and wonders, insomuch that, if it were possible, they shall deceive the very elect." Then Ezekiel clearly teaches (xiv. 9) that God sometimes deceives men through prophets by false revelations,—"And if the prophet be deceived when he hath spoken a thing, I, the Lord, have deceived that prophet," &c.; and Micah (1 Kings xxii. 22) speaks in the same way of the prophets of Ahab (who by their false predictions led him to do battle at Ramoth-Gilead, where he was slain).

Now though all this seems to imply that prophecy and revelation were very doubtful matters, still there was much of certainty in them, as has been said; for God never deceives the truly pious and elect; but, according to that old proverb quoted by Samuel (1 xxiv. 13), and as we gather from the history of Abigail and the words employed, we are to conclude that God makes use of the pious as instruments of his mercy, and of the impious as means and functionaries of his wrath. This clearly appears from the instance of Micah cited above; in which, though God had resolved to deceive

Ahab by means of prophets, he only made use of false prophets for this end, revealing matters as they were to be in fact to the true prophet, who was not prohibited from uttering the truth. Still, as I have said, the certainty of prophecy was moral only; for no man can justify himself before God, nor boast that he is the instrument of God's clemency, as Scripture and the thing itself declare, for the displeasure of God seduced David into taking a census of the people, although Scripture bears abundant testimony to his piety.

The whole of prophetic certainty was founded upon these three considerations: 1. That revealed things were imagined by the prophets in a most vivid manner, and as men are wont to be affected or impressed by objects whilst awake. 2. That they were conceived by signs. 3. Lastly and especially, that they were conceptions of prophets having minds disposed to justice and goodness alone. And although Scripture does not regularly make mention of a sign, it is still to be believed that the prophets always received one; for Scripture does not constantly enumerate all the conditions and circumstances of an event, but often proceeds on the supposition that these are known. Besides, we may concede that the prophets who foretold or spoke of nothing new, and that was not contained in the law of Moses, did not require a sign; inasmuch as what they said was confirmed by the law. The prophet Jeremiah, for example, speaking of the desolation of Jerusalem, was confirmed by all the other prophets and by the denunciations of the law, and therefore he did not require a sign; but Hananiah, who, in opposition to Jeremiah and the rest of the prophets, foretold the speedy restoration of the city, necessarily required a sign: his prediction must be doubted, until the event had declared its truth or falsehood (vide Jer. xxviii. 9), and the prediction not being borne out by the event in this case, Hananiah was put to death as the reward of his false prophesying.

Since the assurance which the prophets had from their signs, then, was not mathematical, or such as arises from the necessity of the thing perceived or seen, but was only moral, and signs were merely accorded to the prophets as additional testimonies, it follows that the signs exhibited must be in accordance with the opinions and capacity of the prophets; so that the sign which would have sufficed to render one prophet certain of his prediction, would have been altogether inadequate to convince another, professing different views and opinions. The consequence of this was that the signs exhibited varied with each individual prophet; even as we have shown that the revelation varied with every prophet, in harmony with his natural temperament, his imagination, and the kind of opinions he had already espoused. In regard to temperament, for example, if the prophet were of a hopeful and lively spirit, his prophecies spoke of victory, peace, abundance, and all that moves mankind to gladness; if, on the contrary, he were of a sad and gloomy disposition, then disaster, defeat, and every evil became the burthen of his revelation. Hence as the prophet was mild and merciful, or irascible and cruel, &c., was he apt or disposed to make revelations of an agreeable or harrowing nature. Again, as the prophet was a man of taste and culture, so did he receive and make known God's communications in an elegant and ornate style; but as he was rude and uncultivated, so were his revelations confused and inelegant. The same thing holds good as regards the revelations made by the imagination: were the prophet a rustic, then oxen, cows, &c., were the figures that presented themselves to him; were he a soldier, then armies with their leaders; were he a courtier, then the royal throne and attendant ministers were the images that served the purposes of communication. Finally, the prophecy varied according to the variety of opinion entertained by the prophet. The magi, for instance (vide Matthew ii.), who believed in the vanities of astrology, had the nativity of Christ revealed to them by the imagination of a star appearing in the east. To the augurs of Nebuchadnezzar (Ezek. xxi. 26) the destruction of Jerusalem was revealed in the entrails of the sacrificial victims, and the king himself had information of the same event from the oracles he consulted, and from the direction of the arrows which he shot into the air over his head. And to conclude, God was revealed as indifferent to and unwitting the actions of men to those prophets who believed that men acted of their own free will and proper power. These several positions I proceed to demonstrate seriatim from the text of Scripture.

The first position is proved by the case of Elisha (2 Kings iii. 15), who, that he might prophesy to Jehoram, desired a minstrel, or a musical instrument, to be brought to him; and it was only after he had been composed by sweet sounds that he was enabled to speak joyful tidings to Jehoram and his associates, which he had not been in a condition to do before, on account of the wrath of the king; for they that are angry with any one, though they be apt enough to imagine evil, are little inclined to imagine good of him. Some indeed have said in connection with this matter, that God does not reveal himself to the angry and the sorrowful; but these persons plainly dream; for Moses in anger against Pharaoh, and without having recourse to music, foretold that wretched slaughter of the firstborn of Egypt (Exodus xi. 5, 8). God was also revealed to Cain in a paroxysm of rage. To Ezekiel, impatient from anger, were revealed the misery and the contumacy of the Jews (Ezek. iii. 14); and Jeremiah, plunged in sorrow and weary of his life, prophesied the calamities that were to befall his countrymen in such dark colours that Josias would not consent to consult him, but preferred a female contemporary prophetess, the task of declaring God's mercy and loving-kindness, of which he wished to hear, seeming more especially adapted to the female genius (vide Paralipomena or Chronicles, Book ii. ch. xxxv.). Micah, also, never prophesied any good to Ahab, which other true prophets did nevertheless, as appears from 1 Kings xx., but all his life long prophesied evil (1 Kings xxii. 7 and still more clearly 2 Chron. xviii. 7). Prophets therefore, according to their various temperaments, were more apt for revelations of one kind than of another.

The style, again, of the several prophets varies greatly as regards elegance of diction. The prophecies of Ezekiel and Amos are not like those of Isaiah and Nahum, but are written in a much ruder style. Any one somewhat familiar with the Hebrew tongue who would look into this matter more curiously, by comparing the different prophets chapter by chapter where the argument happens to be the same, would discover a vast difference in their several styles. To cite one or two examples: Let the courtier Isaiah (i. 11—20) be contrasted with the rustic Amos (v. 21—24) in the passages now referred to. Let the arrangement and reasoning of Jeremiah (xlix.) writing to Edom be compared with the order and ratiocination of Obadiah, and the 40th (19, 20) and 44th (8) chapters of Isaiah be compared with the 8th (8) and 13th (2) chapters of Hosea. And so of other instances, all of which along with those particularly quoted, when rightly considered, seem clearly to show that God used no particular style in making his communications; but, in the same measure as the prophet possessed learning and ability, his communications were either concise and clear, or, on the contrary, they were rude, prolix, and obscure.

Prophetic representations and hieroglyphics, although meaning to express the same thing, varied nevertheless. The glory of God leaving the temple was represented differently to Isaiah and to Ezekiel. The Rabbins indeed will have it that the two representations are nearly identical, only that Ezekiel, a rustic person, having been beyond measure surprised, gave a more particular and circumstantial account of what he saw. But unless the Rabbins have a traditional and certain account of the matter, which I by no means believe, they plainly invent what they say; for Isaiah saw seraphim with six wings, whilst Ezekiel saw beasts with four wings; Isaiah saw God in white raiment and sitting on a royal throne, Ezekiel saw him as fire:—each undoubtedly presumed he saw God in the way or likeness in which he was wont to conceive him.

Nor do prophetic accounts vary only in particulars; they

differ much in perspicuity. The representations of Zechariah, as we learn from the accounts themselves, were so obscure, that without an explanation they could not be understood by himself; and those of Daniel were so dark, that even when explained they were still unintelligible, not to others only, but also to the prophet himself. And the obscurity here was not because of any difficulty in the matter to be revealed, (for the subjects were purely human, and in no wise surpassed human capacity, save in so far as they were prospective,) but only because the imagination of Daniel was not so active or did not possess equal prophetic power when he was awake as when he slept; a fact which appeared in this, that in the beginning of his prophesyings he was so much alarmed as almost to despair of his strength to bear their burthen. It was probably by reason of this weakness of his imagination and bodily powers that his visions came before him so obscurely, that even with the help of an explanation he could not rightly comprehend them. And here it is to be observed that the words heard by Daniel were imaginary only (as has been shown before); wherefore it is not wonderful that he, in the perturbation of the moment, should have heard things so indistinctly and imperfectly that he found it impossible afterwards to understand them. They who maintain that God did not design to reveal himself clearly to Daniel appear not to have read the words of the angel, who says expressly (x. 14) that he had come to make Daniel understand what should befall his people in the latter days. What was intended has therefore remained an enigma, for there was no one then living with such strength of imagination as would have made a clearer revelation possible. Finally, when we observe the prophets to whom it was revealed that God was about to take away Elias endeavouring to persuade Elisha that Elias was only removed to another place where he might still be found by them, it was plain that they did not rightly understand the revelation made to them. It seems unnecessary to carry this discussion further: nothing appears more manifestly from Scripture than that God endowed one prophet much more largely with the gift of prophecy than another. I shall therefore proceed to show that prophecies, or things foretold or imparted, varied in conformity with the opinions of the several prophets, and that different prophets entertained various and even contrary opinions and prejudices (I speak of merely speculative matters thus; for of those which bear on morals and conduct a totally different view is to be taken). And here I shall proceed inquiringly and at some length; for I esteem this subject one of great moment, and I think I shall be able to show from it that prophecy never rendered prophet more learned than he was before, but still left him in possession of his preconceived opinions; whereby we shall escape the bondage of feeling ourselves tied down in matters purely speculative by anything that the prophets have said.

It is indeed wonderful with what eagerness men have still tried to persuade themselves that the prophets knew all that the human understanding could embrace. Although several parts of Scripture clearly inform us that the prophets were ignorant of certain things, the world have preferred to maintain that they did not understand these passages of Scripture rather than admit that the prophets were ignorant of anything; or they have striven so to twist the words of Scripture, as to make it say what there plainly was no intention of saying. But, if either of these courses be permitted, it is all over with Scripture as an authority; for we should then seek in vain to prove aught from Scripture, if those things that are most clearly set forth are put among the obscure or impenetrable matters, or the plainest text is to be arbitrarily interpreted. Nothing in Scripture, for example, is clearer than that Joshua and the writer of his history also were of opinion that the sun moved round the earth—that the earth was at rest, the sun in motion—and that the sun stood still in the heavens for a certain time upon a certain occasion. Many, however, who will not allow that any change takes place in the heavenly bodies, explain the passage detailing this extraordinary event in such a way as to make it declare nothing of the kind; others, again, farther advanced in philosophy, and aware that the sun is at rest whilst the earth revolves around him, have striven with all their might to extort this doctrine from words which say the very contrary,—at which I confess my amazement! But I would ask, whether we were bound to accept Joshua the warrior as a competent astronomer, or to believe that by a miracle it was revealed to him that the light of the sun might remain longer above the horizon than wont, from causes of which he was ignorant? To me either conclusion appears equally absurd. I prefer saying openly that Joshua was ignorant of the true cause of that longer continuance of the light which he witnessed, and that he and those about him believed that the sun, revolving round the earth in its daily course, had stood still on the day in question, and so been the cause of the phenomenon they witnessed. They never thought of referring it to any less obvious cause, such as to the ice and hail which then filled the air (vide Joshua x. 11), and which might have given rise to a higher refractive power in the atmosphere than usual, or, in fine, to any other condition, into the nature of which it is not our business to inquire. In the same way and according to his light was the vision of the backward shadow revealed to Isaiah, viz. by a retrograde movement of the sun; for he too thought that the sun was in motion whilst the earth was at rest; and probably not even in his dreams had he ever thought of parahelia. Let us, then, without hesitation admit so much, and say that a sign might appear, and Isaiah prophesy before the king, although the prophet knew nothing of the true cause of the wonders he witnessed.

Of the temple of Solomon, although its construction was revealed by God, the same thing is to be said, viz. that all its proportions and parts were in conformity with the capacity and opinions of Solomon; for as we are not held to the belief that Solomon was a great mathematician, we may be permitted to affirm that he was ignorant of the true relation between the circumference of a circle and its diameter, but that with common workmen he believed it to be as three to one. If, on the contrary, it is said that we do not understand the meaning of the text in 1 Kings (vii. 23)* I know not, I vow, what can ever be made out of any other part of Scripture; for the construction of the molten sea is detailed simply and as matter of history; and if we are told that Scripture meant otherwise, but for some reason unknown to us, chose to write in such a way, this were equivalent to a subversion of all its authority; for then might the same thing be said with equal right of every individual passage, and thus whatever human folly and perversity could imagine might come to be paraded and defended on the teaching of Scripture. But what we have ourselves advanced has nothing of impiety about it, for Solomon, Isaiah, Joshua, &c., although prophets, were still men, and men who thought that nothing interesting to mankind at large was indifferent to them.

To Noah, too, according to his knowledge, was revealed God's purpose of destroying the human kind, because he thought that beyond the confines of Palestine the world was uninhabited. Nor indeed does true piety run any risk when the prophets are maintained to have been ill informed on such matters;† they show their ignorance of things of much greater moment, teaching nothing grand or comprehensive of the Divine nature, but uttering merely vulgar opinions, with which the revelations they imparted were in conformity, as I shall immediately show by numerous references to their writings in the sacred volume. The prophets therefore, as it appears, are less to be commended for sublimity of genius and extent of knowledge than for piety and constancy. Adam, to whom God was first revealed, did not

* Referring to the molten sea 10 cubits across and 30 cubits round about.—*Ed.*

† No one in much later days, when the news arrived in Paris, took the French drummer's account of the state of matters in Switzerland, *au pied de la lettre*, when he informed his friends at home that the army had now reached the end of the world: "Nous sommes ici au bout du monde! Ici on touche le soleil de la main!"—*Ed.*

know that God was omnipresent and omniscient; for he tried to hide himself, and strove to excuse his sin before God, precisely as he would have done in the presence of another man. Hereby we see that the revelation of God made to Adam was according to his capacity, as of a person who was not ubiquitous, who was not cognizant of all things, and of Adam's guilt in particular; for Adam heard or seemed to hear the voice of God when walking in the garden, calling him by name, and demanding where he was; and finally, when, in the conversation which ensues, Adam speaks of his nakedness, God asks him whether he had not eaten of the fruit of the forbidden tree? Adam plainly knew nothing more of the attributes of God than that he was the creator of all things. To Cain, in like manner, God was revealed according to his condition, viz. as ignorant of human affairs; nor was any higher idea of God necessary to Cain to lead him to repent of his crime. To Laban, again, God revealed himself as the God of Abraham, because Laban believed that every people had its own peculiar god (vide Genesis xxxi. 29). Abraham himself did not know that God was ubiquitous, and had foreknowledge of all things; for when he heard the sentence against the Sodomites, he entreated God not to carry it into execution, until he should discover whether all in the city were alike deserving of punishment (Genesis xviii. 24):—peradventure, he says, there be fifty righteous within the city.* Nor on other occasions was God revealed otherwise to Abraham, for thus in his imagination does God speak to him (ver. 21), "I will go down now and see whether they have done altogether according to the cry of it which is come unto me; and if not, I will know." The divine testimony concerning Abraham indeed contains nothing but in reference to his

---

* And then the thing of clay proceeds to reason with, and fix, as it were, on the horns of a dilemma, the Almighty maker of the Universe! Far be it from thee to slay the righteous with the wicked; shall not the judge of all the earth do right? Peradventure there be 40, 30, 20, 10, &c.—And what shall be said of the next succeeding chapter, containing the terrible story of Lot and his daughters?—*Ed.*

obedience, and the strictness with which he commanded his children and household that they should do justice and judgment; there is not a word of the sublime ideas which it were fit should be entertained of God. Moses himself does not sufficiently perceive that God is omniscient, and governs all human actions by his decrees alone. Although God himself has said to him (Exodus iv. 1) that the Israelites would confide in him, Moses nevertheless calls the matter in question, "But behold they will not believe me, nor hearken to my voice." God was consequently revealed to him as indifferent to, and ignorant of, the future actions of mankind; for he gave him two signs, and said (Exodus iv. 8), "And it shall come to pass, if they will not believe thee, neither hearken to the voice of the first sign, that they will believe the voice of the latter sign, * * and if they will not believe these two signs, * * then thou shalt take of the water of the river, and pour it upon the dry land, and it shall become blood," &c. And indeed whoever weighs the words and views of Moses without prejudice will readily perceive that his opinion of God amounted to this: that he was a Being who had always existed, who existed now, and who would exist for ever; and for this reason it was that he called God by the name of Jehovah, the letters composing the Hebrew word expressing the three times of existence, past, present, and future. Of his nature, however, God taught Moses nothing, but that he was merciful, long-suffering, &c., and especially that he was jealous [of his position as God above all other gods], as appears from very many passages of Scripture. Moses, moreover, believed and taught that this Being differed so much from all other beings that he could not be expressed by the image of any visible thing, nor could be even looked upon, and this not because of anything terrible or repugnant in God, but because of human weakness. Further, Moses taught that God by reason of his power was one and alone; though he acknowledged that there were other entities or beings which (doubtless by the order and command of Jehovah) ruled in his stead; in other words, that there were beings to whom God gave power and authority to govern nations, and to provide for and protect them; but the Being whom the children of Israel were to worship was the High and Supreme God, or, to use the Hebrew phrase, the God of all gods. Thus in the Song of Moses (Exodus xv. 11), he says, "Who among the gods is like unto thee, O Jehovah?" and further (xviii. 11) Jethro exclaims, "Now I know that the Lord [Heb. Jehovah] is greater than all gods;" as if he had said, "Now am I compelled by Moses to allow that Jehovah is greatest among the gods and of singular power." Whether Moses believed that those beings who administered in the place of God were created by Jehovah may be doubted; inasmuch as he has said nothing, in so far as I know, of their creation or beginning; though he taught that God [Heb. Elohim] reduced this visible world from chaos into order, scattered over it the seeds of natural things, and so had highest power and highest authority over all; further (vide Deut. x. 14, 15), in virtue of this supreme right and authority, that he had chosen the Hebrew people for himself, and given them a certain territory or land to dwell in, leaving other nations and regions of the earth to the care of other gods his substitutes (Deut. iv. 19, xxxii. 8, 9), whence he was called the GOD of the Israelites, or the God of Jerusalem in the singular, whilst the rest of the gods—those appropriate to other nations—were called GODS, in the plural. For this reason the Jews believed that the country which Jehovah had chosen for himself required a peculiar form of worship, different from that adapted to other lands, and that the worship of the gods of other lands was on no account to be tolerated within their own boundaries. The Jews even thought that some of the people whom the King of Assyria had brought into the land of Judea were torn in pieces by lions "because they knew not the manner of the gods of that land" (vide 2 Kings xvi. 25, *et seq.*). According to the opinion of Eben Ezra,* it was for this reason that Jacob, about to journey to his native

---

* A Jewish writer of liberal views much esteemed by Spinoza.—*Ed.*

country, admonished his sons and servants that they should prepare themselves for the new worship, and give up the worship of strange gods, i. e. of the gods of the land wherein they were then dwelling. (vide Genesis xxxv. 2, 4): "Put away the strange gods that are among you," says he; "and they gave unto Jacob all the strange gods which were in their hand," &c. David also complained to Saul, when forced by his father's wrath to flee his country, that he "had been driven from the heritage of Jehovah, and thrown upon the service of other gods" (1 Sam. xxvii. 19). Finally, the Jews believed that this Supreme Being—God—had his dwelling-place in heaven,* an opinion very prevalent among heathen nations (vide Deut. xxxiii. 27).

When we carefully consider the revelations of Moses, therefore, we find that they are all accommodated to such opinions as he himself entertained: inasmuch as he believed God to be endowed with such attributes as mercy, graciousness, jealousy, &c.; therefore was Jehovah revealed to him alternately as a merciful, as a gracious, as a jealous God, &c. This plainly appears in the account which we have (Exodus xxxiii. xxxiv.) of the way and manner in which God appeared to Moses, when he besought God to show him his glory, and was informed that the goodness of the Lord should be made to pass before him, but that he could not see the face of the Lord. Now Moses not having formed any idea of the similitude of God in his brain, and as God was only revealed to the prophets in conformity with the character of their opinions and imaginations, God could not present himself to Moses in any definite similitude. And this occurred, I say, because it was repugnant to the imagination of Moses to conceive God in the likeness of any created thing; for other prophets—Isaiah, Ezekiel, Daniel, &c.—testify to having seen God. It was for this reason too that we find these words added, "For there shall no man see me and live," an opinion in harmony with the views of Moses;

---

* A firmament; a solid crystalline sphere surrounding the earth; not infinite space as conceived by us.—*Ed.*

for God does not say that to show himself were in contradiction with the Divine nature, as the thing is in truth, but that it cannot be, because of human infirmity. Further, when God informed Moses that the Israelites in worshipping a calf had made themselves like other nations, he says (xxxiii. 2, 3) that he would send an angel, that is, a being who should have charge of the Israelites, in place of himself, the Supreme Being, for that he would not remain among them; whereby nothing was left to Moses by which it might appear that the Israelites were more cherished of the Lord God himself than foreign nations, which had been put under the charge of other gods (ver. 16). Finally, because God was presumed to dwell in heaven, therefore was he revealed as descending from heaven upon the mountain, and Moses also ascended the mountain that he might hold intercourse with God; nothing of which would have been necessary had he conceived God as alike present in all places.

The Israelites, in fact, knew almost nothing of God, although he was peculiarly revealed to them, a truth which appears but too plainly when a very few days afterwards they abandoned the honour and worship of Jehovah, bowed themselves before a golden calf, and declared that the gods they had brought with them out of Egypt should be their deities. Nor indeed was it to be expected that men accustomed to the superstitions of Egypt, rude in manners, degraded by most miserable slavery, should have had any right understanding of God, or that Moses should even have taught them anything beyond the way of living justly, which he did, not indeed as a philosopher, that they might enjoy freedom of spirit, but as a legislator, compelling them to a good life, by commandments issued under pain of the penalties of law. Whence it came to pass that the rule of living aright, or the true life—the love and adoration of God—was to them a slavery rather than a real liberty and gift by the grace of God, for Moses ordered them to love God and to keep his commandments that they might show themselves grateful for past favours, viz. their escape from Egyptian bondage, &c., and whilst he threatened them with the heaviest penalties if they transgressed, he promised them ample recompense if they were found obedient to his precepts. Moses therefore treated the Jews as parents are wont to treat children before they have arrived at years of discretion. It is certain therefore that as a people the Hebrews were ignorant of the excellence of virtue, and of all that constitutes true happiness. When Jonah thought to flee from the presence of God by shipping for Tarshish, we can only conclude that he believed God gave charge over the countries beyond Judea to other powers as his substitutes. There is no one named in the Old Testament who has spoken of God more reasonably than Solomon, who surpassed all his contemporaries in natural capacity; but for this very reason he held himself above the law (this being only delivered for the guidance of those who are without reason and great natural abilities), and paid little attention to, nay he openly violated, those clauses which refer especially to the king (Deut. xvii. 16, 17). And herein it may be observed, in passing, that he showed little wisdom; neither did he act in a way becoming a philosopher, for he sought his chief delight in merely sensual pleasures. Still he taught that all the good things of fortune were vanities to man; that there was nothing more excellent than understanding, and that the greatest punishment a man could suffer was to be afflicted with foolishness (Eccles., and Prov. x. 23).

But let us return to the prophets, of the discrepancy of whose opinions we had already begun to take notice. Now the views of Ezekiel have been found by the Rabbins so discordant with those of Moses that they had almost come to the determination of not admitting his books into the Old Testament as canonical (vide Tractatus de Sabbato, ch. i. fol. 13); nay, these writings would certainly have been excluded, had not a certain Chananias undertaken to explain them, a task which, we are informed, he only accomplished with great labour, and after all it is not certain what the nature of this explanation was, for his work is lost; whether it was in the nature of a commentary, or whether he ventured daringly to alter the words and statements of Ezekiel. However this may have been, it is certain, referring to Ezekiel as we have him, that his 18th chapter does not appear to agree with Exodus (xxxiv. 7), nor with Jeremiah (xxxii. 18), &c. Samuel believed that God having once passed a decree never repented him of having done so; for Saul, contrite for the sin he had committed, and desiring to worship God and obtain his forgiveness, still says that God's decree against him will not be changed. Jeremiah, on the other hand, had it revealed to him that God was subject to repentance, when having made a decree, whether for good or evil, to a people, they were found subsequently to alter their ways for better or worse (vide 1 Samuel xviii. 8—10). Joel again taught that God only repented him of the evil he had inflicted (Joel ii. 13). Finally, it appears most clearly from Genesis (iv. 7) that man may overcome temptations to sin, and do well: "If thou doest well shalt thou not be accepted? and if thou doest not well, sin lieth at the door;" words which are addressed to Cain, who, however, did not get the better of his evil passions, as appears from Scripture itself and the history of Josephus. The same thing is gathered very plainly from the passage in Jeremiah just referred to, where God is made to say, "If a nation do evil in my sight, and obey not my voice, then I will repent of the good wherewith I said I would benefit them; but if that nation against whom I have pronounced, turn from their evil, I will repent of the evil that I thought to do unto them." Paul, however (Epist. to Romans ix. 10 *et seq.*), declares quite positively that men have no power over the temptations of the flesh save in the special election and grace of God; though, speaking of the justice of God (iii. 5, and vi. 19), he corrects himself, and says that he has been speaking as a man, after the manner of men, and because of the infirmities of the flesh.

From all that precedes it seems sufficiently, and more than sufficiently, proved, that the revelations of God were accommodated to the natural capacities and adopted opinions of the prophets, and that the prophets may have been ignorant of things having reference to speculation merely, and not bearing upon the charities and usages of life; nay, it plainly appears that they were ignorant in this wise, and entertained most opposite and mutually contradictory speculative opinions. Wherefore we infer that we are never to look to the prophets for information either on natural or spiritual subjects, and come to the conlusion that they are to be believed only in so far as the matter and purpose of their revelations are concerned, every one in all other particulars being at liberty to believe what he pleases. Take the instance of the revelation of Cain by way of illustration; Cain informs us that God only admonished him to lead a good life, "If thou doest well," &c., but taught him nothing about the freedom of the will or other subjects of philosophy; wherefore, although in the words made use of freedom of will is clearly implied, we still feel ourselves at liberty to take an opposite view, when we find the words and reasoning entirely accommodated to the capacity of Cain. So also we see that the revelation of Micah was merely meant to inform Ahab of the real issue of the battle against Aram; and so much only are we bound to believe; all the other particulars set forth in that revelation, as of the true and false spirit of God, of the armies of heaven standing on either hand of God, &c., do not really concern us, so that every one may believe what to him seems good or accords with his mental constitution. In the same way are we to view the reasons given for the revelation made by God to Job of his power over all things, if indeed it be true that any such revelation was ever made to Job, and that the purpose of the writer was to compose a proper narrative, and not, as some have thought, to give an embroidered version of his own conceits. However this may be, the allegations are still entirely in consonance with the views of Job, and made to satisfy him alone, not as of universal application and calculated to convince mankind at large. Nor are the reasonings of Christ to be otherwise regarded, by which he convicted the Pharisees of ignorance and contempt, and exhorted his disciples to newness of life; his reasonings were accommodated to the opinions and principles of those about him. When he says to the Pharisees, for example (Matt. xii. 26), "And if Satan cast out Satan, he is divided against himself, how then shall his kingdom stand?" he desired nothing more than to convince the Pharisees on their own principles, not to teach that there were devils or any kingdom of Satan. So, again, when to his disciples he says (Matt. xviii. 10), "Take heed that ye despise not one of these little ones; for I say unto you that in heaven their angels do always behold the face of my Father which is in heaven," he intended only to admonish them against pride in themselves, and contempt of others, not teaching anything positive about angels or heaven, but using the language he does the better to persuade his disciples. The same view, in fine, is to be taken of the reasonings and signs of the apostles; but of these I need not speak more at length; for were I to quote all the passages of Scripture which were certainly written with a special view to the persons to whom they were addressed, and which cannot be referred to as embracing divine doctrine without great detriment to true philosophy, I should have to wander far from the path of brevity which I have marked out for myself. Let it suffice, therefore, that I have touched upon a few topics of universal application; particulars and further information I leave to the industry and research of the curious reader himself. The subjects now discussed, namely, Prophets and Prophecy, falling in an especial manner within the scope of my purpose, which is to sever Philosophy from Theology, as I have only dealt with them in a general way, it will be necessary further to inquire whether the gift of Prophecy was peculiar to the Hebrews alone, or was common to them and other nations, and then to come to a conclusion in regard to the election of the Hebrew people. These matters will form the subject of the following chapter.

CHAPTER III.

OF THE ELECTION OF THE HEBREW NATION. WAS THE GIFT OF PROPHECY PECULIAR TO THE JEWS?

TRUE happiness consists in Fruition of The Good, not in any glory or advantage which one alone enjoys to the exclusion of others. He who esteems himself blessed because he alone enjoys, or enjoys more than others, for he is more prosperous in any or in every way than his neighbour,—that man, I say, knows nothing of real happiness, of the soul's true joy; such happiness as he tastes, if it be not childish or merely sensual, has its source in envy and evil disposition alone. Man's true happiness consists in wisdom and understanding, in the study of truth, and no wise in this, that he is wiser than others, or that the rest of the world are without true understanding; for such a conclusion would not add to his wisdom or his real happiness. Whoever should rejoice on such grounds would, in fact, rejoice in the misfortunes of others, and so show himself envious and evil-disposed, and as knowing nothing of true wisdom and peace of mind. When Scripture, therefore, in order to keep the Jews obedient to the laws, declares that God had elected them to himself in preference to other nations (Deut. x. 15), that he was nigh to them and not to others in the same degree (Ib. iv. 4—7), that to them alone he had prescribed just laws (Ib. ver. 8); and, lastly, setting others aside, that he had made himself known to them alone (Ib. ver. 32, &c.), we can only conclude that such language was used as adapted to the mental state and capacity of the Jews, who, as has been shown in the preceding chapter, and, as Moses himself bears witness (Deut. ix. 6, 7), knew nothing of happiness; for it is obvious that they as a people would have been no less happy and prosperous had God called all other nations to salvation as well as them. God would have been no less propitious to the Jews had he chosen to be equally near to other nations; neither would the laws he gave them have been less just, nor they themselves less understanding, had he given like laws to all; neither would the signs and wonders he showed them have less proclaimed his power had they been manifested over a wider range, nor would the Jews themselves have been held less bound to worship him had he elected to pour out his bounties upon all mankind alike. If God, therefore, says to Solomon (1 Kings iii. 12) that he had given him more wisdom than any man who had ever lived, or who should ever come after him, this is probably to be understood as meaning no more than that God had given him a very large measure of understanding,—at all events, it seems impossible to believe that God, for the greater delectation of Solomon, had engaged henceforward to bestow no such ample measure of understanding on any man as he had shed on him; for such a promise could have added nothing to Solomon's wisdom, nor would a wise king have been less thankful for the Divine beneficence, had he been informed that God intended to be no less bountiful to all.

But yet, and admitting that Moses spoke to the Jews, in the passages just quoted, according to their powers of apprehension, we would not be held as denying that God had delivered those laws of the Pentateuch to them alone, or that he had spoken with them only, or, in fine, as saying that the Jews had not seen such wonders as no other people had ever witnessed. What we meant to say amounts only to this, that Moses, for the reasons especially assigned, proceeded as he did in order that he might the more easily lead the Jews to the worship of the true God; and then we desired to show that the Jews excelled other nations neither in natural knowledge, nor in piety, but in very different things. In other words—and here with Scripture I use language on a level with their capacities—I say that the Jews were plainly chosen by God before all other nations for reasons other than because of the good lives they led, or the sublime speculations in which they indulged. It will now be my business to show, seriatim, on what grounds the preference was founded.

Before I begin, however, I would explain in a few words what I understand by the government of God; by the outward and inward aid of God; by the election of God; and finally, by what is called fate, fortune, or destiny. By government or guidance of God I understand the fixed and immutable order of nature, or concatenation of natural things; for I have already said, and shall have further occasion to show, that the universal laws of nature, according to which all things come to pass, are nothing else than the eternal decrees of God, which always involve eternal truth and eternal necessity. Whether we say, therefore, that all things happen according to the laws of nature, or are ordered by the decree and direction of God, we say the same thing. Again, since the power of all things natural is nothing but the power of God himself, by whom alone all things are determined and come to pass, it follows that whatever man, who is himself a part of nature, does for his help and the upholding of his being, or whatever nature presents to him for this end, without his co-operation, is all in virtue of the divine power, whether it acts through human nature or by means that are external to the nature of man. Whatever, therefore, human nature can accomplish of itself towards the preservation of existence may with right be called the inner help of God, and whatever happens for our good through the force of things external to us may be entitled the outer help of God. On this ground we easily gather what is to be understood by the election of God; for, inasmuch as no one does anything save by the predetermined order of nature, in other words, by the eternal decree and direction of God, it follows that no one chooses for himself a certain course of life, or does aught save by the special vocation of God, who elects him in preference to others for this course of life, or for this peculiar work. Lastly, by fortune, or destiny, I understand nothing more than the direction of God, in so far as he governs human affairs by outward and unexpected causes. These things premised, we return to our subject, which is to discover on what grounds the Hebrew nation was said to have been chosen by God for his people in preference to all other nations.

All that we rightly desire may be referred to these three heads, viz. to know things by their first causes; to subdue our passions, or acquire virtuous habits; to pass our lives in safety and in health. The means which subserve the first and second heads directly, and which in so far may be regarded as proximate and efficient causes, inhere in the nature of man himself; so that the attainment of knowledge and of virtuous habits lies entirely within our own power, or depends on the laws of human nature alone. For this reason it may be confidently maintained that these gifts belong to no nation in particular, but are common, and always were common, to the whole of the human race; unless, indeed, we incline to dream, and fancy that nature formerly created different kinds of men. The means, again, which insure security of life and good health, are principally comprised in externals, and are therefore spoken of as gifts of fortune; because they mostly depend on the current of external things, of the reason of which we are often ignorant, so that here the foolish may be as happy or unhappy as the wise. Still, human forethought and watchfulness are of vast avail in attaining security of life, and in escaping injury from other men, from savage beasts and from adverse influences. To this end reason and experience alike declare that there is no better or more certain way than the establishment of a society or state, governed by definite laws, with a certain district or country for a dwelling-place, the strength of all the members being concentrated in one body, as it were, that, namely, of the Society, Commonwealth, or State. To the formation and preservation of such a society, however, no small amount of genius and watchfulness is required; wherefore, that society will be the most secure and lasting, and least liable to the assaults of accident, which is founded and administered by wise, prudent, and watchful men; as, on the other hand, the state established and ruled over by men of a ruder mould will be more dependent on fortuitous events, and less enduring. Should a state so founded and governed endure for any considerable length of time, this will be due to the guidance of another, not of itself; and should it have survived great dangers, and affairs have even prospered with it, then will it be impossible for the people not to admire and to adore the guiding hand of God (i. e. in so far as God acts by hidden external causes, and not by means inherent in the mind and nature of man), for then nothing will have happened otherwise than unexpectedly and against likelihood, in ways and by means, indeed, which would be apt to be regarded as miraculous.

Now, nations are particularly distinguished from one another by the institutions and laws under which they live, and by which they are governed, and it was on such grounds, and not by reason of superior intelligence or nobler qualities of soul, that the Jews were chosen by God in preference to other nations, their polity being calculated to secure prosperity, to extend their empire, and to endure for a great length of time. All this appears very plainly from Scripture itself; for whoever peruses the Hebrew Scriptures, even in a cursory manner, will perceive that the Jews excelled other nations in this only, that they conducted the business that bears upon security of life successfully, and that they overcame many great dangers, and this especially by the outward aid of God; in other respects the Jews appear to have been upon a par with other nations, to which God herein was as propitious as to them. In respect of understanding, indeed (as has been shown in the preceding chapter), the Jews were not distinguished: they entertained very poor notions of nature and of God, and were not therefore elected of God on the score of superior understanding; neither could it have been by reason of the virtuous and true lives they led; for in this particular other neighbouring nations were their equals, and very few elect could have been found among them. The election or calling of the Jews, therefore, was grounded on their temporal prosperity and the fitness of their system of polity for its end; and we never find that God promised anything but this to the patriarchs and their successors.* Even for obedience to the law nothing whatever is promised beyond continuing supremacy to their power, and the sensual enjoyments of life; as, on the other hand, for contempt of the law they are threatened with a cancelling of the bond that bound them to Jehovah, with an end to their power, and disasters of different kinds. Nor is this wonderful, for the end of all society, the purpose of all authority, is security of life and estate; but no authority can exist without laws to be observed by all; for were the several members of any society to bid adieu to law, they would by this alone dissolve their society, and bring the authority it had ever possessed to an end. Nothing therefore could be promised to the Jewish people for steady observance of their law but security of life, and the comforts and conveniences that thence ensue;† and for disobedience no more certain penalty could be predicted than dissolution of their empire and the evils that usually follow such an event, to say nothing of certain special evils which, from the peculiar constitution of their society, would have befallen them alone. But on this matter it is not necessary to speak here at greater length. I only add that the laws of the Old Testament were revealed and

---

* In the 15th chapter of Genesis God promised Abraham to be his defender, and to reward him amply; and Abraham replies that he can now look for nothing that should be precious in his eyes, as he is childless, and far advanced in years.

† "All that could have been promised the Jews was therefore security of life." On this point, viz. that to the attainment of eternal life it was not enough to have kept the precepts of the Old Testament, see Mark x. 19, 21.

prescribed to the Jews alone, for when God chose them to form a peculiar people, and to found a new state, they necessarily required peculiar laws. Whether God also prescribed especial laws to other nations, and revealed himself to them in a prophetic manner, or with those attributes with which they were accustomed to believe God to be endowed, does not appear to me quite certain. This much, however, is manifest, and to be gathered from Scripture, that other nations possessed authority and particular laws by the outward providence or direction of God; in illustration of which position I quote no more than two passages from Scripture. 1st, In Genesis (xiv. 18, 19, 20) it is said the Melchisedek was king of Jerusalem, and priest of the most high God, and that he blessed Abram, as it was the privilege of the priest to do (vide Numbers vi. 23), and, lastly, that Abram for the glory of God gave a tithe of all spoil to this priest of God; particulars which plainly show that God, before he had founded the Hebrew nation, had already established kings and priests in Jerusalem, and prescribed rites and laws for their observance; but whether this were done prophetically is not, as I have said, sufficiently determined. Of this, however, I feel assured, that whilst Abraham abode there he lived religiously, and in conformity with the laws of the country; for Abraham never received any special law or ritual from God, and it is said, nevertheless (Genesis xxvi. 5), that Abraham obeyed the voice and kept the statutes and laws of God, words which without doubt are to be understood as referring to the voice, charges, statutes, and laws of the God of king Melchisedek. 2nd, The Jews are addressed in the name of God in these words, by the prophet Malachi (i. 10, 11): "Who is there among you that would shut the doors [of my temple] for nought? neither do ye kindle fire on my altar for nought. I have no pleasure in you, &c.—for from the rising of the sun even unto the going down of the same, my name shall be great among the Gentiles, and in every place incense shall be offered unto my name, and a pure offering, for my name shall be great among the heathen, saith the Lord of hosts." Now these words, inasmuch as without violence they can be held to refer to no time but that in which they were spoken, more than sufficiently show that the Jews in those days were not more cherished of God than other nations; nay, that God at that time was manifested even more to other nations by miracles than to the Jews, who had again partially and without miraculous interposition regained their empire. At a later period the Jews adopted the rites and ceremonies of the nations accepted of God.

But I pass on; for, with the end I have in view, it is enough for me to have shown that the election of the Jews was based on nothing but their temporal prosperity and liberty; to have made known the manner and means by which their position as a state was obtained, and the nature of the laws under which they lived, *in so far* as they bear upon the establishment of their peculiar polity; and, finally, the manner in which these laws were revealed. In other respects, in those conditions especially in which the true happiness of man consists, the Jews were no more than the equals of other nations. When we find it stated in Scripture, therefore (Deut. iv. 7), that the gods of no other nation were so nigh to them as God was nigh to the Jews, we are to understand this as referring to temporal superiority alone, and to the time when the Jews were the subjects of so many miraculous interpositions; for in respect of understanding and virtue, that is, of true happiness, God, as has been already said, and as reason proclaims, is equally propitious to all; a truth, indeed, which is abundantly attested by Scripture also, for see what the Psalmist says (Ps. cxlv. 18), "God is nigh unto all them who call upon him, to all that call upon him in truth;" and further (Ib. ver. 9), "The Lord is good to all, and his tender mercies are over all his works." In the 33rd Psalm (ver. 15) it is distinctly said that God gave the same understanding to all. Here are the words, "He fashioneth their hearts alike," heart being here synonymous with understanding, the Jews regarding the heart as the seat of the soul and of intelligence, a fact which I presume to be sufficiently well known. From Job (xxviii. 28) we learn that God said to man, "Behold, the fear of the Lord, that is wisdom, and to depart from evil is understanding." Job, therefore, although a Gentile, was most accepted of all men by God, inasmuch as he surpassed all others in piety. Still more to the point is Jonah (iv. 2), who, speaking generally, declares God to be gracious, merciful, slow to anger, of great kindness, and ready to repent of the evil he had intended to do. "Should not I spare Nineveh, that great city, wherein are more than sixscore thousand persons that cannot discern between their right hand and their left hand?" Let us conclude, therefore, since God is equally propitious to all, that every one beyond the pale of the Jewish society, save in the particular respects already indicated, was just as much favoured as any of its members; in short, that the Jew and the Gentile were alike. Now as the business of the prophet was not so much to teach the laws peculiar to his nation as the rules of a virtuous life, there is no doubt but that other nations had their prophets, and that the gift of prophecy was by no means peculiar to the Jews. This is a matter borne witness to by profane as well as sacred history; and although it does not appear from the books of the Old Testament that other nations had so many prophets as the Jews, or, indeed, that any Gentile prophet was ever expressly commissioned by God, this is of no moment, for the Jews have been little careful to write the history of any other people but themselves. It is enough if in the Old Testament we find mention made of more than one Gentile and uncircumcised man—Noah, Enoch, Abimelech, Balaam, &c.—who appeared as prophets; and then the later Hebrew prophets were sent not only to their own people, but to all other nations by God. Ezekiel prophesied to all the nations then known; Obadiah, so far as we know, to the Idumeans alone, and Jonah to the Ninevites especially. Isaiah not only bewails and predicts the misfortunes that were to befall the Jews, and the joyful restoration of that people, but he does the same in regard to other nations, as, for instance, where he says (xvi. 9),

"I will bewail with the weeping of Jazer the vine of Sibmah: I will water thee with my tears, O Heshbon and Elealeh," &c. In chapter xix. (19—25) he first foretells calamities to the Egyptians, and then their restoration to favour,—that God "should first smite and then heal them;" that he should "send them a Saviour, a great one, who should deliver them;" that, entreated of them, he should be known to Egypt and the Egyptians; and that, finally, they doing sacrifice and oblation, the Lord of hosts should bless them, saying, "Blessed be Egypt my people, and Assyria the work of my hands, and Israel mine inheritance,"—words which are indeed every way worthy of especial remark. Jeremiah, lastly, is called the prophet, not of the Hebrew people alone, but of the nations (vide Jer. i. 5). He also laments over the evils which he prophesies, and rejoices over the good which is to follow, "Therefore will I howl for Moab, therefore mine heart shall sound for Moab like a drum "* (xlviii. 31, 36); and then he foretells the re-establishment of the Moabites, as well as of the Egyptians, Ammonites, and Elamites. Wherefore it is not matter of question that other nations had their prophets like the Jews, who prophesied to them and to the Jews likewise, and although Scripture makes mention of one only— Balaam, to whom the future, as affecting the Jewish and other nations, was revealed, it is not to be presumed that Balaam prophesied but once upon the particular occasion indicated; indeed, from his history it appears clearly enough that he had shown himself endowed with prophetic and divine gifts at other times. When Balak orders Balaam to be summoned before him, for example (Numb. xxii. 6), he says, "For I wot that he whom thou blessest is blessed, and he whom thou cursest is cursed;" words which show that Balaam was endowed with the same virtue as that conferred by God on Abraham (Gen. xii. 3). Balaam, then, as accustomed to prophetic visitations, replies to the messengers that he must be lodged for the night, and in the morning that he would bring them what the Lord should speak to him,

* Like *pipes*, Eng. version.—*Ed.*

informing Balak himself (Numb. xxiv. 4), that " he (Balaam) hath said, which heard the words of God, which saw the vision of the Almighty, fallen into a trance, but having his eyes open." Then when he had blessed the Jews by command of God, he began, as he was wont, to prophesy of other nations, and to predict future events. All these things sufficiently indicated that Balaam had always been a prophet, or had frequently used his gift of prophecy, and that he possessed the quality of soul which of all things made prophets sure of their predictions, viz. a mind only disposed to justice and truth; for he could neither bless nor curse any one of himself, as Balak supposed, but only those whom God desired that he should bless or curse; wherefore, he replied to Balak that though he should give him his house full of gold and silver, he would not go beyond the commandment of God, to do either good or evil of his own mind, "But what the Lord sayeth that will I speak." God, however, was angry with Balaam for setting out on his journey towards Balak, as he was also with Moses when about to return into Egypt, though it was by command of the Lord (Exod. iv. 24), and likewise with Samuel, because he had taken money for the exercise of his prophetic powers (1 Sam. ix. 2, 8); " For there is not a just man upon earth that doeth good and sinneth not " (Eccles. vii. 20). The sayings of Balaam indeed appear to have been held of great weight by God; and his power of cursing must have been extraordinary, for we find it mentioned oftener than once in Scripture that God, to show his great mercy and loving-kindness towards the Israelites, refused to hear Balaam, and even changed his cursing into blessing; whereby we may conclude that he was much regarded of God, for the sayings and maledictions of the impious are unheeded by the Supreme. Balaam is to be esteemed a true [prophet, then, though by Joshua he is called a " soothsayer" (xiii. 22); we must conclude, therefore, that this epithet was used in no bad sense, and that they whom the Gentiles called soothsayers and augurs were true prophets, whilst they whom Scripture frequently denounces and condemns were false soothsayers, who as false prophets deceived the Jews, as clearly appears from many passages in Holy Writ.

Let us conclude, therefore, that the gift of prophecy was not peculiar to the Jews, but was common to them and the nations around them. The Pharisees, however, eagerly contend for the contrary view, maintaining that the divine gift of prophecy was given to the Jewish nation alone, whilst in other nations future events were foretold by virtue of some—I know not what—demoniacal power, which superstition has not yet defined. The part of Scripture on which they particularly rely, as authority for their opinion, is that verse of Exodus (xxxiii. 16) where Moses says to God, "For wherein shall it be known here that I and thy people, have found grace in thy sight? Is it not in that thou goest with us? So shall we be separated, I and thy people, from all the people that are upon the face of the earth;" a verse from which they pretend to infer that Moses besought God to be nigh to the Israelites alone, reveal himself exclusively to them by prophecy, and withhold this grace from all other nations. Now to me it appears absurd to suppose that Moses should have grudged the presence of God to other nations, or that he would have dared to ask anything of the kind imagined from the Supreme. The truth is that Moses, after he came to know the genius and contumacious temper of his nation, saw clearly that he would never succeed in the course on which he had entered without many and great miracles, and the singular external aid of God; nay, that without such aid the Jews would even perish utterly as a people. It was, therefore, that he might have testimony to God's will and wish towards them that he sought the singular outward and manifest assistance of God. Thus he says (Exod. xxxiv. 9), "If now I have found grace in thy sight, O Lord, let my Lord, I pray thee, go among us; for it is a stiff-necked people," &c., where the reason plainly appears for the unusual aid he required, viz. that they were a stiff-necked people whom he had to guide; though, indeed, the motive is still more clearly exposed in the answer he immediately receives, which is to this effect (Ib. ver. 10): "Behold,

I will make a covenant: before all thy people I will do marvels, such as have not been done in all the earth, nor in any nation," &c. Here Moses, according to my interpretation, treats of the election of the Israelites only, and asks for nothing else from God. In the Epistle of Paul to the Romans, however, I find a passage (iii. 1, 2) which moves me greatly, wherein Paul appears to teach otherwise than we do here; he says, "What advantage then hath the Jews? or what profit is there of circumcision? Much every way, chiefly because that unto them were committed the oracles of God." But if we consider the doctrine which Paul is here enforcing, I think we shall not only find nothing repugnant to the view we have taken, but even derive countenance and support for it; for Paul shortly after adds (Ib. ver. 29), that " God is not the God of the Jews, but of the Gentiles also;" as he had said previously (ii. 25, 26): "For circumcision verily profiteth, if thou keep the law: but if thou be a breaker of the law, thy circumcision is made uncircumcision. Therefore if the uncircumcision keep the righteousness of the law, shall not his uncircumcision be counted for circumcision?" Then he says (iv. 9) that God's blessing comes upon uncircumcision as well as upon circumcision, and that (ver. 15) where no law is, *there* is no transgression. Whence it appears most manifestly (as indeed has already been shown from the Book of Job) that the law, under which all alike should live, was revealed absolutely to all,—that general law, to wit, which alone points the way to true virtue, not that particular law which was adapted to especial ends of empire, and accommodated to the genius of an individual nation. Finally, Paul concludes that as God is the God of all nations, alike propitious to all, and that as all were equally under sin and the law, therefore had God sent his Christ to all mankind, to free them alike from the bondage of the law, and that they should no longer do justice because of the commands of the law, but from inherent rectitude of soul. Paul, therefore, teaches the very doctrine in favour of which we have above been arguing. So that when he says, "To the Jews alone were intrusted the decrees of God," he must be understood as meaning either that the Jews alone had a written law delivered to them, whilst other nations received their laws mentally by revelation or imagination; or Paul may be speaking on the level of the Jewish capacity and commonly received opinions (and here, indeed, he is combating objections which the Jews alone would be apt to raise), in conformity with his principle when teaching things which he had partly seen and partly heard, of being Greek with the Greeks and Jew with the Jews.

We have only further to reply to the views of those who would persuade themselves that the election of the Jews was not temporary and for political reasons only, but eternal and from special favour; for they say the Jews are still seen, so many years after the dissolution of their empire, scattered over every country and rejected by every nation, yet subsisting as a distinct people, in a way that has happened to no other nation. And then the Scriptures certainly seem in many places to teach that God had elected the Jews to himself for ever; so that, though their empire is gone, they nevertheless remain the chosen people of God. The passages particularly pointed to as teaching this eternal election of the Jews most clearly are the following: 1st, The 32nd and 33rd chapters of Jeremiah, where the prophet declares "that the seed of Israel should remain a nation to the Lord for ever, that God would make an everlasting covenant with them, nor turn away from them to do them good, and that they should be as the host of heaven that cannot be numbered." 2nd, The 20th chapter of Ezekiel, where the Jews are promised, though they have forsaken the worship of the true God, that they shall be gathered together again from all the countries over which they have been scattered, and led into the wilderness, even as their fathers had been brought out of Egypt into the desert; and at length, the rebellious and erring having been purged from among them, that they should be led to the holy mountain, where the whole of the house of Israel should serve Jehovah together.

There are other passages besides these, which are often referred to, especially by the Pharisees; but when I have replied to the two particularly quoted I shall think that I have answered all. And my task will be neither long nor difficult, when I have shown from Scripture itself that God did not elect the Jews for all eternity, but only on the same conditions as he had already elected the Canaanites, who also, as we have seen above, had their priests religiously to conduct the worship of their divinity, and whom God nevertheless subsequently rejected on account of their luxury, and indifference, and evil courses. And Moses admonishes the Israelites (Levit. xviii. 27, 28) that they should not defile themselves by incests as the Canaanites had done, lest the earth should cast them forth, as it had cast out the nations that dwelt in those lands before them. In Deuteronomy again (viii. 19, 20) we see the Jews threatened, in so many words, with total ruin and rejection in case of disobedience: "And it shall be if thou do at all forget the Lord thy God, and walk after other gods, and serve them, and worship them, I testify against you this day that ye shall surely perish; as the nations which the Lord destroyeth before your face, so shall ye perish, because ye would not be obedient to the voice of the Lord your God." There are indeed many passages of similar import in the Old Testament, in which we read plainly that God had not absolutely, unconditionally, and for ever, elected the Hebrew nation to himself. If, therefore, the prophets be found preaching to the Jews a new and eternal covenant of grace and love, this must be understood as having reference to the good and pious only among them; for in the very same chapter of Ezekiel which is quoted above, we find it distinctly stated that God had separated the rebels and shortcomers from them; and in Zephaniah (iii. 11, 12) God says, "Then I will take away out of the midst of thee them that rejoice in thy pride, and I will leave in the midst of thee an afflicted and poor people, and they shall trust in the name of the Lord." Now as the election here plainly points to true goodness, it is not to be thought that it had reference to the pious among the Jews only, but that it extended to Gentile nations also, and we have shown that other nations besides the Jews had their faithful prophets, who made promises to the pious among their peoples, who found themselves consoled and edified thereby. Hence the eternal covenant of grace and mercy, under consideration, is to be esteemed as of universal application; a view the correctness of which appears from another passage of Zephaniah (iii. 9, 10). Here therefore no difference need be admitted between the Jews and Gentile nations; neither is any election to be imagined other than that which we have described. And if the prophets are found mixing with their account of this election, which refers to true virtue alone, many things about sacrifice and other ceremonies, the Temple and its rebuilding, &c., this is only from custom and wont, and because it was usual with the prophets to explain spiritual matters of prophecy by such means, and that they might speak with effect to the Jews, whose oracles they were, of the restoration of their power, and the rebuilding of the Temple, events which were commonly looked for in the time of Cyrus. In the present age of the world the Jews certainly have nothing which can be ascribed to them as greater or more excellent than other nations. And that they have remained for so long a time dispersed over the globe, and without political power, is not to be wondered at, seeing that they so kept themselves apart from other nations as to have drawn down the hatred of all upon their heads, not only by their general rites and ceremonies, always opposed to those of other peoples, but by their special rite of circumcision which they most religiously observe. But that this dislike or hatred of other nations has proved a cause of the preservation of the Jews as a distinct people, is matter of experience; for when a king of Spain in former times obliged the Jews either to receive and profess the religion of the kingdom, or to go into exile, very many of them made profession of the Roman Catholic faith; and as all who did so were at once admitted to the privileges and immunities of Spaniards generally, and were held eligible to all the distinctions of the country, they almost immediately became so intermingled with the Spaniards that very shortly afterwards no trace and no memorial of their descent remained. A totally different effect was produced in Portugal, where the Jews, compelled to profess and professing the religion of the State, but declared incompetent in respect of all honours and dignities, have continued to live among themselves, apart from the rest of the community, and have consequently preserved all their national characteristics unimpaired.* The rite of circumcision, too, I am fain to persuade myself, is of such moment in this matter that it alone, methinks, were enough to preserve this people distinct for ever; indeed, unless the fundamentals of their religion bring upon them effeminacy of mind and character, I am inclined to believe that, with the opportunity afforded, since human affairs are notoriously changeable, they may again recover their empire, and God elect them to himself anew.† We have a remarkable example of the influence of a particular observance, in the Chinese, who most religiously preserve a lock of hair on the crown of their heads, whereby they are distinguished from all other people; and thus distinguished they have kept themselves apart for thousands of years, so that in point of antiquity they far surpass all other nations; nor have they always preserved the supreme authority to them-

---

* Spinoza's explanation of the continued separate existence of the Jewish people is unquestionably the right one. With the more charitable and tolerant views of these later times the prejudice against the Jews is fast dying out. With no mark of civic distinction denied them, they will soon become absorbed into the larger Christian communities, surrounded by whom they now dwell in all the countries of Europe.—*Ed.*

† The preceding note and the Spanish absorption make against the probability of any restoration of a Jewish sovereignty. No longer persecuted by Pope and Kaiser, or Christian communities, the Jews will finally disappear, and leave only historical records of their existence. The immediate cause of the above curious persuasion in Spinoza's mind may have been this, that under a certain Sabbathai Zewi, who appeared in Greece about the year   , and pretended to be the Messiah, such a commotion took place among the Jews, as at one time made their regeneration and reconstitution into a sovereignty appear not impossible. B. Auerbach, Leben Spinoza's.—*Ed.*

selves, though they have still recovered it when it had been lost; and without doubt they will recover it again, when the minds and bodies of their Tartar conquerors have declined from their old vigour under the deteriorating influences of wealth and luxury and irresponsible dominion.* To conclude, were any one disposed to maintain that the Jews, for the cause assigned, or for any other cause whatsoever, had been especially chosen by God to all eternity, I should not gainsay him, provided he allowed that this choice was made in respect of nothing but empire and personal advantages (in which only can one nation be distinguished from another), for as regards understanding and true virtue, no nation is more remarkable than another, and so cannot on such grounds be looked on as elected by God.

* Spinoza must be ranked among the number of the prophets here. The above was published in 1670; in 1861 the Tai-Ping, or national Chinese party, called rebels of course by the Tartar or ruling sept, are making head against their conquerors and oppressors; and may possibly recover the sovereignty. Nations that keep possession of the land appear in these later days at all events very difficult of extirpation. In 1862 we have seen Italy all but restored to the Italians, in spite of centuries of suffering and foreign domination. We now also see the Poles insisting on their nationality, in spite of half a century of oppression, and Hungary resolutely asserting her status among the nations, against attempts, as wicked as they are foolish, to blot her out of the map of Europe.—*Ed.*

CHAPTER IV.

OF THE DIVINE LAW.

THE word Law, taken in an absolute sense, signifies that in virtue of which things of the same species act in a certain determinate manner. Now this comes either of natural necessity, or it depends on the will and pleasure of an agent. The law which depends on natural necessity is that which follows from the nature of things; that which depends on the will and pleasure of an agent—say man—again, and which were well entitled Jurisprudence (Jus), is prescribed by men for themselves and others, with a view to the safety and commodity of life, or for any other reason. For example,— It is a universal law of ponderable matter, and a natural necessity, that bodies in motion impinging on other bodies lose as much of their proper motion as they communicate to these. So, again, it is a law which follows necessarily from the constitution of human nature, that in recollecting some particular thing we bring to mind another similar thing, or something of which we were cognizant at the same time with the former. But when men cede or are forced to cede any of the rights which they have by nature, and restrict themselves to a certain manner of living, this depends on the human will and pleasure. And although I admit without reserve that all things are determined in their being and doing in certain definite ways by virtue of universal laws of nature, still I say that the kind of law in question depends on the will and consent of man. 1. Because man, in so far as he is a part of nature, in so far is he also a part of the power of nature. Consequently, what happens from nature, in so far as we conceive this determined by human nature, still follows and necessarily follows from human agency. Therefore do we say, with perfect propriety, that laws for the regulation of society depend on the will, pleasure, and consent of man. They are plainly so immediately connected with the faculties of the human mind, that though mind itself, in its power of perceiving things in their relations to the true and the false, can be perfectly well conceived without these laws, it cannot be conceived without the idea of divine or necessary law, as we have but just defined it. 2. I have also said that jurisprudence or human social law depends on the will of man, because we ought ever to define and explain things by their immediate causes; inasmuch as general considerations of the order of nature, and the concatenation of causes, cannot in the least assist us in our considerations of particular things; and further, as we are plainly ignorant of the co-ordination and concatenation of things, in other words, of the way and manner in which things are co-ordinated and enchained, we see that in regard to the usages of life it is better to consider things in their immediate connections, as contingencies or possibilities, and not as necessities. So much of law, considered absolutely.*

As the word Law, however, by an extension of its meaning, has been applied to common things; and as by the term nothing more is very usually understood than a precept or command which men may observe or neglect—something which human capacity may overpass, nothing which is beyond the power of man—it seems requisite to define law in a more particular manner, as a rule of conduct, which man imposes on himself and others for a definite end. As the

* The above paragraph in the original is exceedingly obscure, made so, plainly, by the recondite metaphysical ideas of the author, which it would require large references to his Philosophy or Ethics to explain.—*Ed.*

true ends and objects of law are understood by very few, however, the great majority of mankind being incapable of apprehending these, the course which legislators have taken to enforce obedience upon all alike is this: They have proposed an object entirely different from that which necessarily follows from the nature of laws, promising occasionally rewards the most prized by the vulgar for their observance, much] more constantly attaching pains and penalties the most dreaded for their neglect or violation. Legislators may be said to have undertaken to dominate mankind in the same way as a horse is controlled by his provender, the bit, and the spur. From this it has come to pass that it has been usual to designate as law rules of conduct imposed by a certain man or by certain men on all the rest of their tribe or nation, and to speak of those who obey these laws as living under them, and in a sort of slavery. And the truth is, that he who only renders their own to others through fear of the prison or the gibbet obeys an alien authority, and acts under constraint of an evil which he fears: the title of *just* does not belong to him. He, on the contrary, who renders to every one his due because he knows the true reason of laws and their necessity, acts with a resolved soul, not from any foreign authority, but of his own proper will, and truly deserves the title of *just*. This without doubt is what the Apostle Paul intended to say when he tells us that they who lived under the law could not be justified by the law (Rom. iii. 20). Justice, indeed, according to the definition usually given of it, consists in a strong and settled will to render to every one his due. This is why Solomon says that it is joy to the just to do judgment, but destruction to the wicked (Prov. xxi. 15).

Since, then, law, as commonly understood, is nothing more than the rule of life which for certain ends men prescribe to themselves and others, therefore is it to be distinguished into Human and Divine. By human law I understand that which applies to the security of life and estate, and the advantage of the commonwealth. By divine law I mean that which solely regards the highest good or true happiness, viz. the knowledge and love of God. The reason why I call this law divine is because of the nature of the supreme good, which I shall here explain as briefly and as clearly as I can.

Seeing that our better part consists in our understanding, it seems certain that if we would seek for what were truly good for us, we should strive above all things to have our understanding as perfect as possible; for in the perfection of this ought our chief good to consist. But since all our knowledge and certainty, all that removes doubt from the mind, depends entirely on the knowledge of God, then, as without God nothing is nor can be conceived, and, inasmuch as we doubt of everything so long as we are without a clear and distinct idea of God, it follows that our supreme good and highest perfection depend on the knowledge of God alone. Again: since, as we have said, nothing is nor can be conceived without God, it is certain that all that is in nature involves the conception of God; and since we, the more intimately we know natural things, acquire a larger and more adequate conception of God, or, inasmuch as the knowledge of an effect from a cause is nothing more than the knowlege of a certain property of a cause, the more we know of natural things the more do we enter into the essence of God, who is the cause of all things, so, and by so much the more, does the whole of knowledge resolve itself into a knowledge of God, in which indeed it may be said entirely to consist. The same conclusion follows from this, that man is the more perfect according to the nature and perfection of that which he loves and strives to know above all things; and he therefore is necessarily the most perfect, and participates most fully in the supreme good, who most delights in the intellectual cognition of God, the most perfect of beings. Our supreme happiness, therefore, our highest joy, again resolves itself into a knowledge and love of God. The means calculated to attain to this, the end of all human thought and striving, viz. the knowledge and love of God, in so far as we have an idea of him, may well be called his commandments; for they are prescribed to us by God himself, inasmuch as God dwells in our souls; and so the rule of life which regards this end is most properly entitled the Divine Law. But what these means are, and what constitutes the rule of life which this end requires, as well as how the true foundations of the commonwealth rest on them, are all particulars which properly belong to ethics, and here I have no intention to treat of the divine law otherwise than generally.

Assuming, then, that the love of God is the supreme good, the chief end of man, the purpose of all human action, it follows that he only observes the divine law who is sedulous to love God not from affection for any other thing, such as sensual pleasure, fame, riches, &c., not from fear of punishment or any other motive, but from this only, that he knows God, or rather that he knows the knowledge and love of God to be the highest bliss. The first precept of the divine law, therefore, indeed its sum and substance, is to love God unconditionally as the supreme good—unconditionally, I say, and not from any love or fear of aught besides; for the idea of God informs us that he is the supreme good, and that the knowledge and love of HIM are the final issue to which all our thoughts and actions are to be directed. The carnal or animal man, however, cannot understand this; to him such a proposition even seems absurd; and this is because he has too poor a conception of God, and because in our idea of the supreme felicity he finds nothing which he can handle, nothing which he can eat or drink, nothing, in short, which affects his sensual nature wherein he finds his chief delight, nothing, in a word, but lofty speculation and purity of mind. But they who are aware that there is nothing more excellent than understanding and integrity of mind conclude differently and more justly.

Thus do we explain that in which divine law especially consists, and also show what constitutes human law,—law having reference to social existence. Human laws, however, may have been sanctified by being specially revealed by

God, in which case they are properly referred to him. It is in this sense that the law of Moses, although not universal, but particular and adapted to the genius and preservation apart of a single people, may be called the law of God, or divine law; and, believing that this law was sanctified by prophetic light, I do not hesitate to speak of it as divine.

If, then, we turn to the nature of divine law, as it has just been defined, we shall find that it is, 1st, universal or common to all men; for we have inferred it from the whole nature of man; 2nd, that it does not require faith in historical narrative or historian. For since this divine natural law is conceived and understood on the sole grounds of human nature, it is as readily conceived to have existed in Adam as in any other man, to exist in one living among his fellow-men as in one passing his days in solitude and seclusion. Farther, no faith in history, however well attested, can bring our minds to a knowledge of God, or fill our souls with the love of him; for love here springs of intuitive knowledge, —knowledge of God derived from common ideas, certain of themselves and mentally understood, whence faith in historical records is not needed to enable us to attain supreme felicity. Faith in history, however, although of itself inadequate to impart to us a knowledge, and to fill us with the love, of God, may nevertheless be useful. The perusal of historical records, as they bear upon the social state and condition, may be extremely edifying, for, as we shall have better observed and more carefully studied the manners and customs and actions of mankind, so shall we have learned to live more guardedly in the world, and to accommodate our bearing and conversation, in so far as right and reason permit, to the peculiar genius of those around us, or with whom we have relations. 3rd, The divine natural law requires no ceremonial, i. e. no actions indifferent in themselves, and only called good because they are enjoined to us, or because they represent something good and held necessary to the soul's satisfaction,—or, if you please, no actions that exceed the grasp of the human faculties; for natural intelligence requires nothing which it does not reach and comprehend, but that only which can be pointed to as clearly good in itself, and is seen as a means to our happiness. But those actions which are good only from being enjoined, or from being symbols or representatives of some good thing, cannot improve our understanding; neither are they more than mere shadows, for they cannot be reckoned as the offspring or fruit of intelligence and integrity of mind. But it seems unnecessary to insist further on this head. 4th, Finally, we see the great reward of the divine law to be that law itself, in other words, the knowledge of God and the privilege of loving him in true liberty, in entireness and constancy of soul; whilst the penalty of being without it is subjection to the animal appetites, and inconstancy and tribulation of mind.

These points established, we have next to inquire, 1st, Whether by natural light or understanding we can conceive God as a law-giver or king prescribing laws to mankind; 2nd, What the Scriptures teach on the subject of natural light and natural law; 3rd, For what end rites and ceremonies were formerly established; and 4th, Of what import it is to know and to believe sacred history. In this present chapter we shall speak of the first two of these heads; of the two next we shall treat in the immediately succeeding chapters.

1. It is easy to come to a conclusion on the first head, from the nature of the will of God, which is not distinguished from his intelligence, save as regards our human capacity; in other words, the will of God and the intelligence of God are in themselves one and the same; they are only spoken of severally because of our ideas of the divine intelligence. For example, do we only conceive that the nature of the triangle is involved from eternity in the divine nature as an eternal truth, we then say that God possesses the idea or comprehends the nature of the triangle. But if we then imagine that the nature of the triangle is thus involved in the divine nature by the sole necessity of that nature, and not by the essential necessity and nature of the triangle, yea, that the necessity of the essence and properties of the triangle con-

ceived as eternal truths depend on the sole necessity of the divine nature and intelligence, and not on the nature of the triangle itself, then do we call by the title of will or decree of God that which we speak of as his intelligence. Wherefore, in respect of God, we affirm one and the same thing when we say that he from eternity has decreed and willed, or has understood, that the three angles of a triangle shall be equal to two right angles. Whence it follows that affirmations and negations in connection with God always involve eternal necessities and truths. If, for example, God said to Adam that he willed Adam should not eat of the fruit of the tree of knowledge of good and evil, it would imply a contradiction that Adam should have the power to eat of the fruit of that tree, and so it would be impossible that Adam should eat of it; for the divine decree must involve an eternal necessity, an eternal truth. But as Scripture tells us that God gave such a command to Adam, who nevertheless ate of the fruit, it is imperative on us to conclude that God only revealed to Adam the evil that would befall him if he ate of the fruit, but did not will that this evil should follow as matter of necessity.* Whence it came to pass that Adam understood the commandment given him not as an eternal and necessary law, but as an ordinance which reward or punishment accompanies, not of necessity, and from the nature of the act done, but in virtue, as it were, of the will and pleasure of a sovereign prince. Wherefore, the commandment in question is to be regarded as made in respect of Adam alone: it was a law only by reason of his defect of apprehension, and God stood to him in the relation of a legislator or prince to his people. For the same reason, viz. the want of apprehension (cognitionis), the Decalogue was law in respect of the Jews only, for, as they knew not the existence of God and eternal truth, when it was made known to them in the Decalogue that God existed and was alone to be worshipped, this must have been apprehended by them as a law in the social

---

* "Deum Adamo malum tantum revelavisse quod cum necessario sequeretur si de illa arbore comederet, at non necessitatem consecutionis illius mali."

sense; because, had God spoken to them immediately, not making use of physical media for his communication, they must then have apprehended the revelation made, not as a law in the human sense, but as an eternal truth. The same thing may be said of all the laws enunciated by the prophets in the name of God; they were never adequately apprehended as decrees of God, involving eternal truths and necessities. Of Moses himself, for example, it may be held, that though from the revelations made to him he saw how the people of Israel might be united in a certain country, and a separate community or empire established, and further, how the people might be disposed to obedience, yet that he did not perceive, neither was it imparted to him, that the means he made use of to accomplish the ends he had in view, were the absolute and best means for effecting his purpose. Moses had no adequate assurance even that, with the children of Israel united in common obedience within the promised land, the purpose contemplated would follow. Moses, in short, apprehended the revelations made to him not as eternal truths and necessities, but as precepts and institutes; and he, therefore, prescribed them as laws of God in the mere human sense, and so brought it to pass that God was conceived by the Israelites as a king, ruler, or legislator; as merciful, just, jealous, &c., though all these attributes belong to human nature alone, and ought not to be named in connection with the Divine nature. In this way, from this point of view, I say, are those prophets to be regarded who have uttered laws in the name of God. But Christ is an exception to this rule. Of him I hold we are to opine that he perceived things immediately, adequately, truly; for Christ, though he also appears to have enunciated laws in the name of God, was not so much a prophet, as he was the mouth of God: God revealed certain things to mankind by the mind of Christ immediately, as he had formerly made revelations mediately through angels (vide chap. i.), by articulate sounds, visions, dreams, &c. Wherefore it were as irrational to maintain that God accommodated his revelations to the opinions of Christ, as that he had formerly accommodated his revelations to the opinions of angels (i. e. of voices, visions, dreams, &c.), in order to impart to the prophets the things that were to be made known; an idea than which nothing more absurd can be conceived, especially when we know that Christ was sent as a teacher not to the Jews only, but to the whole of the human kind. It was not enough, therefore, that his ideas should be accommodated to Jewish views and opinions; they required to be in harmony with the opinions common to the whole of mankind, in other words, with absolutely true and universal ideas. And, indeed, when we say that God revealed himself immediately to Christ (i. e. to the mind of Christ), and not mediately as to the prophets by words and signs, nothing more is to be understood than that Christ perceived revealed things truly, adequately and in themselves, or that he comprehended them; for then is a thing really comprehended when it is perceived by the mind itself without the interposition of words or signs. Christ, therefore, perceived revealed things in themselves and adequately; so that if he ever prescribed them as rules or laws it was because of the ignorance and obstinacy of the people he addressed. Standing as the substitute of God, he accommodated himself to the capacity of the vulgar, and spoke more clearly than the prophets generally had done, though still somewhat obscurely, often teaching by parables, especially when he was addressing those to whom it was not yet given to understand celestial things (Matt. xviii. 10, *et seq.*). To those to whom it was given to know the mysteries of heaven, Christ undoubtedly taught eternal truths, not prescribing them as rules or commandments. In this sense he declared that he freed his disciples from the slavery of the law, all the while that he confirmed and established the law, engraving it deeply on their hearts. This truth Paul seems to point to in several places (Rom. vii. 6, and iii. 28); still he nowhere declares himself altogether openly on the matter, but speaks rather, as he says (Ib. iii. 6, 19), in a mere human manner. This, indeed, he shows sufficiently when he speaks of God as just, which is done by reason of the weakness of the flesh and to meet the views of the people, who always connect with the idea of God such qualities as mercy, grace, anger, jealousy, &c. In 1 Corinthians (iii. 1, 2) the language of Paul is at first plainly accommodated to the ideas of carnal men; for further on he teaches absolutely that the mercy and anger of God do not depend on the doings of men, but on the sole nature, in other words, the will of God. Previously, indeed, Paul has said that no man is justified by the works of the law, but by faith alone; whereby we are to understand the entire assent of the soul. And finally he says (Ib. viii. 9) that no man is blessed unless he have in him the mind of Christ, whereby he comes to know the laws of God as everlasting truths. Let us conclude, therefore, that it is only to meet the vulgar apprehension, or from defect of right understanding, that God is spoken of as just, merciful, jealous, &c., as though he were a king and lawgiver. God in reality acts and governs all things by the necessity of his nature, and his all-perfection alone: his decrees, his volitions, ever involve eternal truths, eternal necessities. So far the first point which I proposed to illustrate.

2. We now pass to our second head, and turning to the Sacred Volume we seek to know what is therein taught of natural light or understanding, and of divine law. At the very outset we encounter the history of the first man, and the narrative of God's command to Adam not to eat of the fruit of the tree of knowledge of good and evil. This seems to signify that God commanded Adam to do good, and to proceed under the guidance of the good in itself, and not as it is the opposite of evil; or otherwise, that he should seek good from the love of good, not from the fear of evil. For he, as we have shown, who does good from true knowledge and love of good, acts freely and with constancy of soul; whilst he who acts from fear of evil acts under constraint of evil as a slave, and as if he lived under the authority of another. The command which God gave to Adam (interpreted as above) may therefore be said to embrace the sum of the divine natural law. It accords absolutely with the dictates of the

whole of the natural light or understanding; and it would not be difficult, I apprehend, to explain the entire history or parable of our first parent on this basis. But I am not disposed to enter on the task; first, because I am not absolutely certain whether my interpretation agrees with the views of the writer of the Old Testament history or not; and next, because many do not admit that the history of Adam is a parable, but maintain that it is a narrative of actual events.* It will be better, therefore, that I go on citing other passages of Scripture as means of illustration of the position I have in hand, and I shall have recourse to those texts especially that were dictated by him who for strength of natural understanding excelled all the sages of his time, and whose sayings are held of equal worth with those of the prophets, I mean Solomon, whose wisdom and prudence are even more esteemed in Scripture than his gifts of prophecy and piety. In his Proverbs (xvi. 22) Solomon speaks of understanding as the true well-spring of life; and he makes misfortune to consist in foolishness only, in which sentence it is to be observed that by *life*, from the Hebrew word used, is to be understood true life, as plainly appears from Deuteronomy xxx. 19, 20. The fruit of understanding, therefore, consists in true life alone, and chastisement in deprivation of understanding only, a conclusion that accords entirely with what will be found set forth in our fourth position concerning the divine natural law. But that this fountain of true

---

* It is reasonable subject of regret that one so acute and learned as Spinoza should not have proceeded with his interpretation here, all the more as *The Fall* is the ground on which the whole dogmatic scheme of the Christian redemption as now understood reposes. It seems to be an element in man's nature to imagine things better and more happily constituted in times gone by than at the present hour—best of all, therefore, in times of the most remote antiquity; whence the idea of a primæval state of innocence and bliss. But natural science leads to other conclusions. Evolution, development, progress, not decline, is the history we read in the records of creation. Man, when he was called into being on this earth by his Almighty maker, *may have been as perfect* as we now find him, most probably *he was less perfect*, and very certainly he was *not more perfect* than he now is.—*Ed.*

life or understanding is that which alone gives laws to the wise is further plainly taught by our Sage, who says (Ib. xiii. 14), "The law of the wise is a fountain of life," which law, from the text quoted above, is seen to be understanding. Again, he teaches in the plainest terms (iii. 13) that understanding gives joy and true peace of mind to man: "Happy is the man that findeth wisdom, and the man that getteth understanding;" the reason being (ver. 16, 17) that "Wisdom gives length of days, and riches, and honour; her ways being ways of pleasantness and all her paths peace." The wise alone, therefore, according to Solomon, live in peace and equanimity, not as the wicked, whose minds are disturbed by opposing emotions, so that, as Isaiah has it (lvii. 20, 21), "They are like the troubled sea, for them there is no peace."

But what we have particularly to observe in these Proverbs of Solomon, inasmuch as our views are greatly confirmed thereby, are the sentiments contained in the 3rd verse of the second chapter, where we find these words, "If thou criest after knowledge and liftest up thy voice for understanding, . . . then shalt thou understand the fear of the Lord and find the knowledge of God; for the Lord giveth wisdom; out of his mouth cometh knowledge and understanding." By these words Solomon clearly declares, first, that wisdom or understanding alone teaches us that God is to be reverenced with knowledge and worshipped in a truly pious spirit; and, secondly, that wisdom and understanding flow from God, the only giver of these inestimable gifts. This truth we have ourselves insisted on when we showed that all our understanding and all our knowledge depended on the idea or knowledge of God alone, with whom they originate and by whom they are made perfect. Solomon proceeds immediately after (Ib. 9) to teach that this wisdom involves true principles of ethics and politics. "When wisdom entereth into thy heart," he says, "and knowledge is pleasant to thy soul, discretion shall preserve thee, understanding shall keep thee; then shalt thou understand righteousness and judgment and equity, yea every good path." Now all of this plainly agrees with natural science; for it is especially when we have come to a right understanding of things, and have tasted the pleasures of knowledge, that we perceive a universal system of ethics, the principles of true virtue, to be evolved.* Wherefore true happiness and the peace of mind it brings which satisfies natural understanding, even in Solomon's opinion, depends not particularly on the smiles of fortune, that is, on the favour of God, as things external are concerned, but on intrinsic satisfaction or virtue, which is God's favour as regards inward things, and is best assured and kept by watchfulness, counsel, and virtuous conduct. And here I must by no means pass by that passage of Paul in his Epistle to the Romans in which he says (i. 20), "For the invisible things of God from the creation of the world are clearly seen, being understood by the things that are made, even his eternal power and Godhead; so that they are without excuse, because, when they knew God, they glorified him not as God, neither were they thankful,"† &c.; words which very plainly proclaim that every one by his natural light may understand the power of God and his eternal divinity, from which may be known and inferred what things are to be sought after and to be done, what to be avoided. All are therefore "without excuse;" no one indeed can be entitled to plead ignorance for shortcomings here; though he might fairly do so were the question of aught supernatural, such as the passion of Christ in the flesh, his resurrection from the dead, &c. "Wherefore," continues the apostle (Ib. 24), "God gave them up to uncleanness through the lusts of their own hearts;" and so on to the end of the

---

* A universal system of morals must be based on the faculties proper to man under the guidance of the intellectual powers, the faculties man has in common with the lower animals being in subjection but not annulled.—*Ed.*

† This remarkable passage of the apostle, taken in the largest sense, seems to settle the question of verbal revelation or literal inspiration completely: Man and the universe around him are the true revelation of God to man. The mind of man, acting of itself and on the things beyond itself, and acted on in its turn by these, makes known the Being of God, and discovers the laws by which he has ordained that the universe and its parts shall be eternally and unchangeably ruled. Hence love, reverence, obedience, as duties of man to the Almighty.—*Ed.*

chapter, wherein he describes the vices of ignorance, which he specifies as its punishments, a conclusion in which he is plainly at one with Solomon in the passage already quoted, where the punishment of the foolish is declared to be their proper folly. It is not surprising therefore that Paul should hold evil-doers to be inexcusable, for as every man sows, so shall he reap; from evil, unless wisely corrected, evil necessarily springs, as from good follows good, if it be but joined to constancy of mind. Scripture therefore acknowledges and refers to the authority of our natural understanding and the divine law. And so I leave the subject I had proposed for discussion in this chapter.

CHAPTER V.

OF RELIGIOUS CEREMONIAL OBSERVANCE, AND FAITH IN HISTORICAL NARRATIVE. OF THE REASONS WHY RITES AND CEREMONIES ARE USEFUL, AND OF THOSE WHO FIND THEM NECESSARY.

IN the preceding chapter we have shown that the divine law, which renders mankind truly happy, and teaches the perfect way of life, was of universal application and common to all; indeed, we have so deduced it from the nature of man and shown it to be innate, written as it were on his heart and mind. But when we come to speak of Rites and Ceremonies, of those at least which in the Old Testament are declared to have been instituted for the Jews especially, and so accommodated to their state that they might be observed by the people at large, though not perhaps by every individual member of the Hebrew community, we see for certain that they do not belong to the code of the divine law, and that in themselves they contribute nothing of necessity, either to mental felicity or to virtuous life. They have reference, in fact, to the special election of the Jews; in other words, and as has been shown in our third chapter, to the mere temporal well-being of the body, and to the prosperity and peace of the Hebrew commonwealth; whence, save in connection with state-policy, they are inapplicable and of non-avail. If ordinances of this description consequently are classed in the Old Testament with the laws of God, this is only because they were instituted on the ground of revelation. But as reason, even of the most cogent kind, is not held of much account by the common run of Theologians, it will be satisfactory by the testimony of Scripture to confirm the points we have already demonstrated; and next, for the sake of greater clearness, to show both how and why ceremonies were of service in establishing and maintaining the empire of the Jews.

Isaiah has nothing more clearly expressed than that the divine law, taken absolutely, signifies that universal law which consists not in ceremonies, but in purity of life; for he calls upon his countrymen to listen to the divine law preached to them by him, which excludes feasts and sacrifices of every kind, but is comprehended in purity of soul and in virtuous action,—in succouring the helpless, &c. [Here are the noble words of the prophet,—"Hear the word of the Lord, ye rulers of Sodom; give ear to the law of our God, ye people of Gomorrah. To what purpose is the multitude of your sacrifices unto me? saith the Lord: I am full of the burnt-offerings of rams and the fat of fed beasts; and I delight not in the blood of bullocks, or of rams, or of he-goats. Bring no more vain oblations; incense is an abomination to me. Your new moons and your sabbaths and your appointed feasts my soul hateth: they are a trouble unto me; I am weary to bear them. And when ye spread forth your hands I will hide mine eyes from you: yea, when ye make many prayers I will not hear. Wash you, make you clean; put away the evil of your doings from before mine eyes; cease to do evil; learn to do well; seek judgment, relieve the oppressed, judge the fatherless, plead for the widow. Come now, let us reason together, saith the Lord."]

The testimony of the Psalmist is no less remarkable, when in Psalm xl. (7, 9), addressing God, he says, — " Sacrifice and offering thou didst not desire; mine ears hast thou opened; burnt-offering and sin-offering hast thou not required; I delight to do thy will, O my God; yea, thy law is within my heart." Here the Psalmist plainly reckons as law that only which is inscribed on his heart or mind, excluding ceremony and observance of every kind; these being mere institutions, not good of themselves, not written in the heart and understanding of man. Besides these there are other passages in Scripture which are to the same effect; but to have quoted the above two seems sufficient.

That ceremony and observance, moreover, are no aids to true happiness, but that they bear upon the temporal prosperity of the State, also appears from Scripture, which for ceremonial observance promises nothing but personal benefits and sensual delights; whilst for observance of the universal divine law, it assures us of true happiness. In the whole of the five books, commonly ascribed to Moses, nothing is promised but such temporal felicities as honour, renown, victory, riches, and health. And although scattered through these five books there are many things that concern morals, they are never propounded as universal moral precepts to be observed of all men, but only as commands especially adapted to the capacity and genius of the Hebrew people, and having an especial bearing on the interests of their State alone. For example, Moses does not as doctor or prophet teach the Jews that they are to do no murder, that they are not to steal, &c., but as a legislator and prince, or magistrate; for he does not commend these precepts by an appeal to reason, but adds pains and penalties to their infraction, which may, and indeed ought, to vary according to the genius of every nation, as experience proves. The command not to commit adultery, too, has reference alone to the advantages of the commonwealth and the rights of individuals. Had he intended to enunciate a moral precept, which should have a bearing not only on the conveniences or proprieties of public and private life, but on the true happiness of all, then would he have condemned not only the outward act but the frame of mind that led or consented to it, as Christ did, who taught universal moral doctrines only (vide Matt. v. 28*), and this is the reason why Christ

---

* "Ye have heard that it was said by them of old time, Thou shalt not commit adultery. But I say unto you, that whosoever looketh on a woman to lust after her hath committed adultery with her already in his heart."—*Ed.*

always promises spiritual rewards, not personal advantages as Moses does; for Christ, as I have said, was sent into the world not for the preservation of the temporal power of the Jews and the institution of legal formalities, but wholly and solely to teach the law of universal morality. In this view we readily understand that Christ came not to abrogate the law of Moses. He never attempted to introduce new laws into the republic; and in his moral teaching he was more careful of nothing than to distinguish between his precepts and the laws of the State. The grand cause of this solicitude appears to have been the ignorance of the Pharisees, who thought that he lived a good life who was zealous for the usages of the commonwealth or the law of Moses; which, as we have seen, bore reference only to the security and prosperity of the nation, and were not so much taught to the Hebrews as imposed upon them.

But let us return to our subject, and have recourse to Scripture for further assurance, that for ceremonial observance nothing is promised but personal advantages, whilst for obedience to the universal moral law peace of mind is the rich reward. No one among the prophets has taught this more clearly than Isaiah. In his 58th chapter, after condemning hypocrisy, he commends charity, the lightening of heavy burdens, to let the oppressed go free, to cover the naked, &c. "Then," he proceeds, "shall thy light break forth as the morning, and thy health shall break into bloom, thy righteousness shall go before thee, and the glory of the Lord shall gather about thee."* He next refers to the Sabbath, commending its careful observance, and as motive for doing so, promising reward in these words, "Then shalt thou delight thyself in the Lord, and I will cause thee to ride upon the high places of the earth, and feed thee with the heritage of Jacob thy father, for the mouth of Jehovah hath spoken it." The prophet therefore

---

* A Hebraism or mode of expression which refers to the time of death, aggregari ad populos suos, signifies to die.—Spinoza. The author's version is mainly followed in the above beautiful verse.—*Ed.*

for liberty bestowed and deeds of charity done promises health of mind with soundness of body in this life, and after death the glory of the Lord, whilst for ceremonials he has no higher reward to offer than security of power, temporal prosperity, and bodily well-being. In Psalms xv. and xxiv. there is no mention made of ceremonies, but only of moral precepts, for the reason that in these poems the only question is of true happiness, which is alone discussed there, although it is done in parable; for it is certain that by the holy hill of God, by his tents and the dwellers therein, we are to understand peace and purity of soul, and not the mountain of Jerusalem, nor the tabernacles of Moses, places which were not inhabited by any one, or were only served by those of the tribe of Levi. Further, all those sentences of Solomon, which I have referred to in the preceding chapter, for devotion to understanding and wisdom, promise true happiness, whereby the fear of God is at length understood, and the knowledge of God is revealed. That the Jews themselves, after the destruction of their power, were not held strictly to ceremonial observance is apparent from Jeremiah, who when he sees the desolation of Jerusalem to be imminent, and predicts it, declares that God only delights in those who know and understand that he is the Lord, who exercises loving-kindness, judgment, and righteousness in the earth; and who will punish the circumcised and the uncircumcised alike, who neglect his honour and glory (vide ix. 23, 24, 25), which is as much as if he had said that God, after the destruction of Jerusalem, would exact nothing, especially of the Jews, nor of their posterity, more than the observance of the natural law, which all mankind are bound to obey.

The New Testament amply confirms this view, for there, as has been said, moral doctrines only are taught, and for observance of these the kingdom of heaven is promised as the reward. In the New Testament, indeed, something is said of ceremonies after the gospel begins to be preached to other nations which lived under different systems of polity. Among the Jews themselves, the Pharisees remained the great sticklers for their ceremonial, retaining the whole or the greater part of it, rather, as it seems, through hostility to the new Christian sect than with any purpose or thought of being therefore particularly acceptable to God; for after the first destruction of their city, when the Jews were led captive to Babylon, as they were not then divided into sects, they forthwith neglected their ceremonies; and may indeed be said to have abandoned the whole of the law of Moses, suffering the code of their country to sink into oblivion, and beginning themselves to mix with the nations among whom they were domiciled. All this appears plainly from Esdras and Nehemiah.

It is not doubtful, therefore, that the Jews paid no more attention to the law of Moses after the destruction of their empire than they had done before its establishment; for whilst they lived among other nations, and before their departure from Egypt, they had no peculiar laws, observing no code but that of natural right, and doubtless conforming to the system of jurisprudence of the country in which they dwelt. As the patriarchs offered sacrifices to God, however, I presume that this was done to keep the flame of devotion alive in their souls, as they had been accustomed to sacrifices from the days of their youth. All, indeed, from the time of Enoch, were certainly habituated to sacrifices as the grand incentives to devotion [or means of making themselves acceptable to God]. The patriarchs, consequently, offered sacrifices to God, not in consequence of any divine command, or because taught to do so by the fundamental principles of divine or natural law, but in obedience to the uniform custom of their age; or, if they sacrificed because of any special command, this was no other than that of the law of the land in which they dwelt, and in which the same rite was observed, as we have shown in our third chapter, when speaking of Melchisedek.

And now I think I have sufficiently established my view of the significance of rites and ceremonies as regards the people on the authority of Scripture. But I have still to show in what way, and for what reason, the ceremonial of the Hebrews contributed to the establishment and support of their empire, and this I shall proceed to do as briefly as possible.

Society, a State, is not only most useful, as enabling us to live secure against the assaults of enemies, but is also advantageous, and even necessary, on many other grounds. Unless men were disposed to co-operate, to lend each other mutual assistance, the talent and the time necessary to his own convenient maintenance would be wanting to every one; for all are not alike fit for every kind of work, and no one suffices to provide everything most indispensable even to himself. The strength and the time, I say, would be wanting to him who alone and single-handed should propose to plough, sow, reap, grind, bake, brew, weave, stitch, &c., too many things to mention, but which are all most necessary to the support of life; and I have said nothing of the arts and sciences, which are all indispensable for the improvement of mankind, and for their comfort and well-being. We see those who live in a state of barbarism, and without a polity, passing miserable lives, but little raised in condition above the beasts of the field; and even they, wretched and unpolicied as they are, could not procure the few things they have without some kind of mutual assistance and co-operation. Were men constituted by nature so as to require nothing but that which right reason demands, society would require no laws, it would suffice then to teach men the true moral doctrine, to have them do of their own accord and free-will that which is truly good and useful.

But human nature is constituted very differently; all indeed strive after what they think will be advantageous to themselves, nowise, however, in accordance with the dictates of right reason, but mostly from mere desire, and swayed by those appetites and affections of the mind which never consider the future and the reasonableness of things. Hence it comes that no State could exist without authority and power at its head, and consequently without laws, which moderate or restrain human desires and passions, that were apt else to be uncontrolled. Human nature, however, will not long submit to any merely arbitrary or absolute control, and as Seneca, the tragedian, says, no one ever exercised violent authority long; moderation alone endures; for so long as men act from fear only, so long do they that which they most dislike, nor do they note the reason, the use, or the necessity of the thing done,—they have no care but to escape the penalties with which they are threatened. Men, indeed, under such a system of arbitrary control cannot but rejoice when misfortune befalls their ruler, even though they themselves should suffer with him; nay, they cannot help wishing him ill, and where they can they will not fail to inflict it. Men, again, can endure nothing less than to serve their equals, or to be governed by them. Finally, there is nothing more difficult than to take away liberties once conceded.

From these premises it follows:—First. Either that the whole community, if this were possible, should hold authority together, so that every one might be esteemed as serving himself, and none as serving his fellow; or if a few or one only be intrusted with the supreme authority, he or they ought to be something above the common level of humanity, or should at all events use every endeavour to persuade the vulgar that they are so. Secondly. The laws of the State, however constituted, should be such as that men shall be restrained, not so much by fear, as be led by the hope of some advantage which they greatly desire; for in this way every one will do his duty heartily and willingly. Lastly. Since obedience consists in this, that commands are carried out on the sole authority of the person commanding, it follows that where the authority belongs to all, and the laws are made by common consent, no one can be said to rule and no one to obey; and in a State so constituted, whether the laws are increased or diminished in severity, the people nevertheless remain equally free, seeing that it is not under the authority of another that they act, but in virtue of their own consent. It is very different where one alone possesses the supreme and absolute control; for all then is done on the sole authority of one, and unless the people have been educated in the persuasion that they are to depend entirely on the will and pleasure of the ruler, it may be difficult for him in case of necessity to institute new laws, or to abrogate privileges already conceded.

Having premised these general views, let us revert to the Hebrew Republic. The Jews, on their first exit from Egypt, being subjected to the laws of no other nation, felt themselves at liberty to institute their own system of jurisprudence, and to make new laws, to establish their authority wherever they could, and to take possession of territory whenever they were strong enough. But they never showed themselves less capable than when attempting reasonable legislation and self-government. The people were mostly barbarous in manners, every finer feeling blunted by long-continued and grievous slavery. The chief authority must therefore be intrusted to one whom all the rest should obey; one who should prescribe laws for the nation, and finally be the interpreter of his own decrees. Now Moses, more highly endowed than any of his contemporaries, as matter of course asserted, and readily obtained, this supremacy, persuading the people that he was divinely called, and proving his title to their obedience by many signs and wonders (Exod. xiv. and xix). On these grounds he based his system, and prescribed laws to the people; but he ever took especial care that they should do his bidding of their own free will, rather than from fear; a course which he was led to adopt by these two principal considerations, viz. the rebellious or contumacious temper of the people, which would not endure to be driven by fear alone, and the constant state of warfare in which by force of circumstances the Jews must live. Now for success in arms it is much more necessary to encourage the soldier by hope of honour and reward than to force him by threats of punishment to do his duty; for thus every one strives to shine by daring and magnanimity, rather than merely to escape observation or punishment by exposing himself as little as possible. Moses, therefore, was led to institute the Hebrew Republic on the basis of virtue and a divine mission, in order that the people might be induced to do their duty from devotion rather than from fear. Besides, he was abundantly bountiful in present temporal favours, and was lavish of promises for the future. Nor are his laws so severe as is often supposed, a fact of which any one may satisfy himself who carefully studies them, especially if he attends to all that is required before any one charged with an offence can be found guilty. Finally, that the people, who could not be left to the freedom of their own will, might depend entirely upon their ruler, Moses actually left nothing to the arbitrement of the Jews themselves, so long accustomed to slavery; everything was fixed by law, everything must be done in a certain definite way, depending entirely upon the will of the ruler: the Jew was not at liberty to plough, to sow, or to reap, in his own fashion, neither dared he to eat, to dress, to shave his head or his beard, to grieve or to rejoice, in short, to do any one thing, save in conformity with the orders and commands of the law. Nor was this all: he was ordered to have certain signs on his hands, on his forehead, and on the door-posts of his house, which should constantly remind him of the duty of obedience.

This, then, is the whole scope and tendency of the Hebrew ceremonial law. The people were to do nothing of themselves, but everything by the command of another. By all their actions, by all their thoughts, they were to confess that they were nothing of themselves, but the creatures of the ruler's will. From all this it clearly appears that ceremonial observances conduce in no way to true happiness, and that all those of the Old Testament, nay, the whole Law of Moses has no other purpose than the supremacy of the Jews, and consequently bears reference to nothing but mere personal advantages. As to the Christian ceremonial, such as baptism, the Lord's supper, feasts, public prayers, and the rest, if there be any more which are and always were common to the whole Christian community, supposing them to have been instituted by Christ or the apostles (and I am not quite certain that they were), still, these in themselves are nothing more than outward signs of the universal Church, not things that in any way conduce to true beatitude, or that have aught of sanctity in their nature. Wherefore I say that these ceremonies, although not instituted with a view to empire or state policy, but only in respect of the Christian society, are not generally imperative ; so that he who lives alone need in no way be bound by them, as he who lives under a dominion where the Christian religion is interdicted may ignore and abstain from them all, and yet live the good life that insures true happiness. We have an example of this in the Empire of Japan, where the Christian religion is prohibited, and the Dutch who dwell there are ordered by their East India Company's express commands to abstain from all outward religious observance. I do not deem it necessary to illustrate this matter further, though I could demonstrate its truth by many remarkable examples ; indeed, it would not be difficult to deduce the principle now insisted on from the pages of the New Testament itself, but I am induced to pass these by, my mind being bent on other matters. I therefore proceed to the second subject which was proposed for discussion in this chapter, viz. of the credibility of historical narrative, and the trust to be reposed in its authors. As this is one of the subjects to be investigated by natural light, I proceed thus :—

Whoever seeks to persuade or dissuade mankind of anything which is not evident of itself, is bound to state his proposition on acknowledged grounds, and by appeals to reason and experience to satisfy those he addresses ; that is to say, by reference to things that are appreciated by the senses, that happen in nature, or are comprised in self-evident intellectual axioms. But unless experience be such that it is clearly, distinctly understood, though it may convince mankind, still it cannot in the same degree affect the understanding, and disperse its clouds, as when the things taught are deduced from mathematical axioms, i.e. when they reach the mind by the sole power of the understanding. And this is especially the case when the question is of spiritual things, which do not in any way fall under the cognizance of the senses. But as, in deducing things from pure intellectual notions, a long concatenation of perceptions is mostly required, and in addition the most stringent precautions, the highest intellectual perspicacity, and the greatest reserve, all of which are rarely found in man, therefore are men more inclined to be taught by experience than to deduce and reciprocally to concatenate their perceptions from a small number of axioms; whence it follows that any one desiring to have his doctrine proposed to a nation, I do not say to the whole of the human kind, and who would be understood of all in all things, must be prepared to refer to experience for confirmation of his teaching, and be careful to accommodate his reasonings, and definitions of the things taught, to the capacity of the common people, who constitute the great mass of mankind; he must be chary in the use of concatenated reasonings, and of definitions intended the better to link his reasonings together; otherwise he will write for the learned only, in other words, he will be understood by a very small number out of the great mass of mankind.

But seeing that the whole of the Scriptures were first revealed for the use of the Hebrew nation at large, and subsequently of the whole human family, it was imperative that the things contained therein should be accommodated to the capacity of those to whom they were addressed, and that they should be referred to experience especially. Let us explain this point a little more fully. The things taught in Scripture that are of a purely speculative nature are principally these: There is a God, or Being who made all things, who with highest wisdom rules and sustains the world, and who carefully watches over those among men who live piously and honestly, but threatens the wicked with punishment, and distinguishes them from the good. And all its teaching to this effect, Scripture confirms by appeals to experience only in the histories of those whose laws and actions it records; it gives no definitions of the things taught; but in word and method accommodates itself to the capacity of common people. And although experience can give us no clear knowledge of any of these things, nor inform us what God is, in what way he sustains and governs all things, and takes care of man, still men may teach and illustrate so much as is necessary to enforce obedience, and as suffices to impress the minds of those addressed with devotional feelings.

These considerations I conceive enable us to speak assuredly of the kind of trust that is to be reposed, as well in the narratives contained in Scripture as in their writers. From what immediately precedes it evidently follows that such narratives were indispensable to the vulgar, whose capacity does not extend to a clear and distinct perception of things. He, again, who knowing these things denies them because he does not believe in the existence of God, nor that God watches over man and nature, is an impious person; whilst he who does not know them, and nevertheless by his natural light acknowledges the existence of God, and the other matters just touched upon, if in addition he lead a good life, may enjoy true happiness—ay, he may live much more happily spiritually than the vulgar believer, because, besides his right opinions, he has in addition clear and distinct conceptions in his mind. Lastly, he who is ignorant of these Scripture doctrines and histories, and who knows nothing of natural light, if he cannot properly be called impious, still is he barbarous, almost brutal, and without God's best gifts to man. But here it is to be observed, that when we say a knowledge of Scripture history is commonly very necessary, we are not to be understood as meaning all the histories contained in Scripture, but only those that are most remarkable, and of themselves, and without reference to any others, most obviously inculcate the doctrine we have insisted on, whereby the minds of men are most powerfully impressed. For were all the histories contained in Holy Writ required to prove its doctrines, and were no conclusion possible save on a general consideration of all these histories, then indeed would the demonstration and conclusion in regard to Scripture doctrines be impossible, not only for the people at large, but would also be absolutely beyond human capacity; for who could attend to such a multitude of histories, and to such a variety of circumstances and such diversities of doctrine, as present themselves in these histories? I, at all events, cannot persuade myself that the men who left us the Scriptures as we have them, possessed such amplitude of genius that they took in all the elements of such a demonstration, and still less that the doctrines of Scripture are not to be understood without listening to the domestic troubles of Isaac, the counsels of Achitophel to Absalom, the civil wars of Judah and Israel and other chronicles of this description, or that the Jews who lived in the time of Moses had more difficulty in comprehending the doctrines of their law than those who were contemporaries of Esdras. But of these topics I shall have more to say and at greater length by and by. The vulgar, we may meantime conclude, were only required to know those histories which were best calculated to lead their hearts to obedience and to piety. But the vulgar themselves are not sufficient judges of such matters; inasmuch as they are rather taken with narratives of wonderful and unlooked-for events than with the doctrines involved in history; and this is one grand cause wherefore, besides reading the Scriptures, pastors or ministers of the Church are particularly required to supply guidance and instruction in aid of the popular infirmity of understanding. But that we may not stray from our subject, nor delay to show what was especially proposed as the subject of this chapter, let us conclude that faith in the Bible histories, whatever these may be, forms no part of the divine law, that neither do these histories of themselves necessarily contribute to make men more virtuous or happy, nor are they of any use, save with reference to the moral doctrines they contain, those moral doctrines which are in fact the sole reason of the superiority of Bible over common history. The narratives of the Old and New Testament, in brief, excel ordinary narrative, and one narrative in them is more excellent than another, by reason of the wholesomeness of the truths therein contained, the salutary conclusions supplied. Wherefore, were any one to read the whole of the Bible histories, and to yield implicit faith to all their details, did he give no heed to the doctrines they were meant to inculcate, and amended not his life, he would be like one who read the Koran, or the romances of the poets, or the common chronicles of a country, with the attention which the vulgar commonly bestow on such matters. On the other hand, as has been said, he who was entirely ignorant of all Bible history, and nevertheless professed opinions salutary to himself and to others, and who above all led a good life, that man is truly blessed, and has indeed within him the spirit of Christ.

The Jews however thought very differently on this matter; for they maintain that sound moral views and a good life profit a man nothing, if embraced from natural reasons, and not as principles and practice prophetically revealed to Moses. Maimonides (Cap. viii. Regum, lege 11) dares openly to declare that "Every one who takes to heart the seven precepts,* and diligently follows them out, is to be reckoned among the pious of his nation, and the heir of the world to come; that is to say, if he adopts and practises what they enjoin because they were prescribed by God in the Law, and revealed to us by the mouth of Moses, though they were already precepts to the sons of Noah; but if he have been led by his reason to be what he is, he is not a true denizen, not one of the pious and learned of the nations." These are the words of Maimonides, to which Rabbi Joseph, son of Shem Tob, in his book entitled Kebod Elohim, or Glory of God, appends what follows: That "although Aristotle" (whom he thinks indited consummate principles of ethics, and whom he esteems above all other writers) "omits nothing that is within the scope of true ethics in his writings on this

---

* The Jews held that God gave to Noah seven precepts, which were alone to be observed by all nations, and to the Jews a great many more precepts in addition, that they might be made more blessed than the rest of mankind.

subject, although all the precepts he enjoins were carefully observed, this nevertheless would avail nothing towards salvation; because what Aristotle teaches is not embraced as a divine command prophetically revealed, but only as dictated by natural reason." But all these conclusions of Maimonides and Rabbi Joseph, son of Shem Tob, are mere figments, grounded neither on reason, nor to be found in Scripture, as any one who diligently reads it may readily convince himself. It seems, indeed, to be sufficient to mention such narrow views to have found their refutation. But it is no part of my purpose in this place to contend with writers who maintain that natural light can teach nothing salutary of the things that are essential to salvation; for they who permit nothing to themselves in the way of sound reason, can allow nothing to sound reason in another; and they who boast themselves above reason, only show themselves far below reason, which, indeed, their common mode of living would of itself sufficiently demonstrate. But I need not proceed further on this ungrateful track: I only add that we can know no man but by his works; and with Paul, I say, that for him who abounds in such fruits as love, joy, longsuffering, gentleness, goodness, faith, meekness, and temperance, the law is not ordained (vide Paul, Epistle to Galat. v. 22, 23), that that man, whether guided by simple reason or instructed by Scripture, is TRULY TAUGHT OF GOD, and is in every way blessed. Thus I conclude what I purposed to say on the divine law, and on rites and ceremonies.

CHAPTER VI.

OF MIRACLES.

As every science is called divine that is beyond the reach of ordinary intelligence, so are men inclined to see the hand of God in every event or phenomenon whose cause is commonly unknown. The vulgar, in fact, are persuaded that the power and providence of God never appear so manifestly as when something happens which is at variance with use and wont, especially if it interfere at the same time with their advantage or convenience. Nothing, for example, is thought to prove the existence of God so clearly as some presumed interruption of the regular course of nature; and it is on this account that they who seek to explain unusual events and phenomena by natural causes are very commonly regarded as guilty of calling in question the being, or at all events the providence, of God. So long as nature proceeds in its even and accustomed order, the vulgar think that God is doing nothing; and, on the other hand, they fancy that the powers of nature are suspended when God interferes. In this way two powers are imagined, distinct from one another, the Power of God and the Power of Nature, which last, however, is presumed to be influenced and ordered in a certain way by God; or, as is generally believed at the present time, which is created by God. But what is understood precisely by these two powers, God and Nature, is not explained; unless it be that God is conceived as a king and sovereign ruler, whilst Nature is imagined as a special subordinate force. The vulgar, therefore, give the title of a miracle or work of God to every extraordinary natural event; and partly from devotional feeling, partly from a spirit of opposition to those who cultivate natural science, they care not to inquire into the causes of phenomena, and will listen to nothing but that of which they are really most ignorant, and for which they therefore entertain the highest admiration. Now this mainly proceeds from men in general being without other reasons for adoring God, and referring all that happens to his will and pleasure, than by supposing natural causes abrogated, and the order of nature arbitrarily suspended. They only bow to the power of God, in short, when they believe the power of nature to be subjugated as it were by God.

When we inquire into the origin of such prejudices, we have to look as far back as the times of the primitive Jews. In order to convince the heathen nations about them, worshippers of visible deities, the sun, moon, stars, earth, air, water, &c., that such gods were weak and inconstant, and under the dominion of an invisible God, whom they adored, they narrated many wonderful miracles he had wrought; and, further, endeavoured to show that the whole of nature was ruled by him for their peculiar advantage. The system thus inaugurated laid such hold on the minds of men, that even to the present day each tribe or nation has not ceased from imagining miracles favourable to the conclusion that it was more acceptable to God than all the rest of mankind, and was, in fact, the final cause for which God at first created, and still continues to uphold, the world. Such vulgar folly arises from the circumstance that men in general have no sound conception either of God or of nature; that they confound the desires and imaginations of man with the desires of the Almighty, and figure nature in such small proportions as to believe that man is its principal part. But it is enough merely to hint at the opinions and prejudices of the vulgar concerning nature and miracles, and I therefore proceed to the consideration of the four principles which I here propose to myself to demonstrate, and in the following order: 1st, I shall begin by showing that nothing happens contrary to the order of nature, and that this order subsists without pause or interruption, eternal and unchangeable; I shall at the same time take occasion to explain what is to be understood by a miracle. 2nd, I shall prove that miracles cannot make known to us the essence and existence of God, nor consequently his providence, these great truths being so much better illustrated and proclaimed by the regular and invariable order of nature. 3rd, I shall prove by various examples, taken from Holy Writ, that Scripture, in speaking of the decrees and the will of God, and consequently of his providence, means nothing more than the order of nature itself, which necessarily results from his eternal laws. Fourthly and lastly, I shall discuss the proper manner of interpreting the miracles of Scripture, and insist on the main points which seem to require consideration in the narratives we have of these miracles. Such are the principal heads that form the argument of the present chapter; and they have an especial bearing upon the whole scope and purpose of this work.

1. With regard to my first position, it were almost enough to refer to my fourth chapter, on Divine Law, in which I have demonstrated that all that God wills or resolves involves the conception of eternal truth and eternal necessity. The intelligence of God not being conceivable as distinct from his will, as I have shown above, to say that God thinks or that God wills is to affirm one and the same thing. Consequently, the same necessity, in virtue of which it follows from the nature and perfection of God that he thinks a certain thing such as it is, this same necessity, I say, implies that God wills the thing such as it is. But as nothing is absolutely true save by divine decree alone, it is evident that the universal laws of nature are the very decrees of God, which result necessarily from the perfection of the

Divine nature. If, therefore, anything happened in nature at large repugnant to its universal laws, this would be equally and necessarily repugnant to the decrees and intelligence of God; so that any one who maintained that God acted in opposition to the laws of nature would at the same time be forced to maintain that God acted in opposition to his proper nature, an idea than which nothing can be imagined more absurd. I might show the same thing, or strengthen what I have just said, by referring to the truth, that the power of nature is in fact the Divine Power; Divine Power is the very essence of God himself. But this I pass by for the present. Nothing, then, happens in nature* which is in contradiction with its universal laws. Nor this only; nothing happens which is not in accordance with these laws, or does not follow from them: for whatever is, and whatever happens, is and happens by the will and eternal decree of God; that is, as has been already shown, whatever happens does so according to rules and laws which involve eternal truth and necessity. Nature consequently always observes laws, although all of these are not known to us, which involve eternal truth and necessity, and thus preserves a fixed and immutable course. Nor will sound reason ever persuade us to ascribe a limited power and efficacy to nature, and to conceive its laws as operative in a certain restricted sense only, and not universally; for, since the power and efficacy of nature are the power and efficacy of God, and the laws of nature are the ordinances of God himself, we must needs believe that the power of nature is infinite, and its laws of such extent that they reach and pervade all that is comprehended by the divine intelligence. Were they not so, what else could be inferred than that God had made nature so impotent, and given it laws and statutes so barren, that he is forced frequently to intervene anew if he would have these laws continued, and the frame of things upheld in conformity with his wishes,—a doctrine as remote from reason as can well be conceived.

* By nature here I do not understand the material universe only, and its affections, but besides the matter an infinity of other things.

From these premises, therefore, viz. that nothing happens in nature which does not follow from its laws; that these laws extend to all which enters into the divine mind; and, lastly, that nature proceeds in a fixed and changeless course; it follows most obviously that the word miracle can only be understood in relation to the opinions of mankind, and signifies nothing more than an event, a phenomenon, the cause of which cannot be explained by another familiar instance, or, in any case, which the narrator is unable to explain. I might say, indeed, that a miracle was that the cause of which cannot be explained by our natural understanding from the known principles of natural things. But as miracles were calculated for the vulgar apprehension, which ignores all knowledge of the principles of natural things, it is certain that the ancients regarded as a miracle that which they could not explain in the way in which they were wont to account for natural things, viz. by recurring to their memory for another similar thing which they were accustomed to regard without wonder; for the vulgar always think they understand a thing when they have ceased to marvel at it. The ancients, therefore, and almost all men, even to the present time, have had no other standard of a miracle but this; and there can be no question but that many things are related in Scripture as miracles which are readily to be explained on the known principles of natural things, as has been already suggested in Chapter II., when we spoke of the sun standing still in the time of Joshua, and retrograding in the days of Ahaz, of which I shall have more to say when I come to speak of the explanation of miracles, a subject which I promised to discuss in this chapter. But it is time I passed on to my second proposition, which was to show that from miracles we can neither obtain a knowledge of the existence nor of the providence of God; on the contrary, that these are much better elicited from the eternal and changeless order of nature.

2. The existence of God not being obvious of itself,* it

---

* We doubt of the existence of God, and consequently of all things, so long as must necessarily be inferred from ideas, the truth of which is so unquestionable that no power can be assigned or even imagined adequate to shake them. From the moment we conclude from these ideas that God exists, they ought to present themselves to the mind as beyond the sphere of doubt; for could we imagine that these notions could be changed by any power whatsoever, then should we doubt of their truth, and consequently of our conclusion as to the existence of God also, the effect of which would be that we should no longer feel certain of anything. And then we really know of nothing that agrees with nature or differs from it, save that which we have shown to agree with or to differ from these principles; wherefore, could we conceive that aught could happen in nature from any power (whatever this might be) which was repugnant to nature, this would also be repugnant to these primary notions, and so would have to be rejected as absurd; or else we should be forced to doubt of first notions (as we have just said), and consequently of God and of all conceptions whatsoever. Miracles, therefore, conceiving these as events contravening the established order of nature, are so far from proving to us the existence of God, that they would actually lead us to call it in question, seeing that without them we can be absolutely certain of the existence of God, as we truly are when we know that all things in nature observe a definite and unchanging course.

But suppose it is said that a miracle is that which cannot

---

we have only a confused, instead of a clear and distinct, idea of God. Just as he who does not know the nature of the triangle does not know that the sum of its angles is equal to two rectangles; in the same way, he who only conceives the Divine nature in a confused manner does not see that *to exist* belongs to the nature of God. Now, to conceive the Divine nature in a clear and distinct manner, it is necessary to attend to a certain number of extremely simple notions, which are called common notions, and with their assistance to connect the conceptions which we form of the attributes of the Supreme. Then only for the first time does it become evident to us that God exists necessarily; that he is omnipresent, that all we conceive envelopes the nature of God, and is conceived by its means; lastly, that all our adequate ideas are true. On this point the reader is referred to the prolegomena of my Tractate, entitled, "Principia philosophiæ Cartesianæ more Geometrica demonstrata."

be explained by natural causes; this may be understood in two ways: either that it has natural causes which cannot be investigated by the human understanding, or that it acknowledges no cause save God, or the will of God. But as all that happens, also happens by the sole will and power of God, it were then necessary to say that a miracle either owned natural causes, or if it did not, that it was inexplicable by any cause; in other words, that it was something which it surpassed the human capacity to understand. But of anything in general, and of the particular thing in question, viz. the miracle, which surpasses our powers of comprehension, nothing whatever can be known. For that which we clearly and distinctly understand must become known to us either of itself, or by something else which of itself is clearly and distinctly understood. Wherefore, from a miracle, as an incident surpassing our powers of comprehension, we cannot understand anything, either of the essence or existence or any other quality of God or nature; on the contrary, when we know that all things are determined and sanctioned by God, that the operations of nature follow from the essence of God, and that the laws of nature are eternal decrees and volitions of God, we conclude unconditionally that we know God and his holy will by so much the better as we have a better knowledge, a clearer comprehension, of natural things,—how they depend on God as their first cause, and how they exist and act according to eternal, changeless laws ordained by him. Wherefore, as regards our understanding, those events which we clearly and distinctly comprehend, are with much better right entitled works of God, and referred to his will, than those which are wholly unintelligible to us, although they strongly seize upon our imagination and wrap us in amazement; inasmuch as those works of nature only which we clearly and distinctly apprehend render our knowledge of God truly sublime, and point to his will and decrees with the greatest clearness. They therefore plainly trifle who, when they do not know a thing, fall back upon the will of God—a most ridiculous way of professing or excusing ignorance. Moreover, whatever other inference may be drawn from miracles, nothing, at all events, can be concluded from them in regard to the existence of God; for, inasmuch as a miracle is a limited act, and never expresses more than a certain limited power, it is certain that we can never from such an effect infer the existence of a cause whose power is infinite; we could at the most conceive a cause, the power of which was relatively greater. I say at the most, for a certain event might happen from many causes concurring to produce it, of which the immediate cause should be of less potency than the mass of concurring causes, though greater than that of each of them severally. But the laws of nature (as already shown), reaching to infinity, and being conceived by us as a kind of eternity, and nature in virtue of them proceeding in a certain and immutable order, they so far declare to us in an assured manner the Infinity, the Eternity, and the Unchangeable nature of God.

Let us conclude, therefore, that we can know nothing by miracles of the existence and providence of God; on the contrary, that these attributes are far better inferred from the regular and unchanging order of nature. In this conclusion I of course speak of miracles, as understanding by them nothing more than events which surpass, or are believed to surpass, the common comprehension of mankind. For if miracles be understood as interruptions or abrogations of the order of nature, or as subversive of its laws, not only could they not give us any knowledge of God, but, on the contrary, they would destroy that which we naturally have, and would induce doubt both of the existence of God and of everything else. Nor do I here recognize any difference between a phenomenon or event *contrary* to nature, and one *beyond* nature, a phrase by which some understand a phenomenon not repugnant to, but not producible by, nature; because as a miracle takes place not beyond but in nature, if it be held to be above nature, it must needs interrupt the order of nature, which we otherwise conceive to be, by the decrees of God, fixed, immutable, eternal. Did aught consequently take place in nature which did not follow from its everlasting laws, it would necessarily contravene the order which God has established in nature by the universal laws he has decreed for its government, and would thus subvert nature and its laws, and consequently lead to general scepticism and atheism.

From these views and reasonings I think I have sufficiently established my second proposition, and believe we may safely conclude anew that a miracle, whether contrary to nature or above nature, is a sheer absurdity; and therefore that by a miracle in Holy Writ we are to understand nothing more than a natural phenomenon which surpasses, or is believed to surpass, human powers of comprehension.

Before proceeding to my third position, viz. that we cannot know God from miracles, I gladly take occasion to confirm the above conclusions by the authority of Scripture, which, although nowhere openly teaching so much, nevertheless gives it clearly enough to be understood in many passages. Thus Moses teaches (Deut. xiii.) that a false prophet, although he work miracles, is yet to be put to death: "If there arise among you a prophet . . and giveth thee a sign or wonder, and the sign or wonder come to pass, saying, Let us go after other gods, . . thou shalt not hearken unto the words of that prophet; for the Lord your God proveth you, . . and that prophet shall be put to death." From this it plainly appears that wonders or signs could be worked by false prophets, and that men, unless duly imbued with a true knowledge and love of God, could be led with like facility under the guidance of miracles to worship false gods as to adore the true and only God. For in the same passage these words are added; "For Jehovah, your God, tempts you, that he may know whether you love him with all your heart and all your mind." And then, of what avail did miracles prove in giving the children of Israel reasonable ideas of God? When they had persuaded themselves that they were forsaken by Moses, they demanded visible gods from Aaron, and, oh shame! a calf was their idea of God; and this in spite of the multitude of signs and wonders they had seen. Asaph, the psalmist, too, although he had heard of so many miracles, doubted nevertheless of the providence of God, and had almost strayed from the right way, had he not at length acquired better notions of that wherein true happiness consists (vide Psalm xxxvii.). Solomon also, in the times when the Jewish nation was at the height of its prosperity, suspects that all things happen by chance (vide Eccles. iii. 19, 20, 21, and ix. 2, 3, *et seq.*). Lastly, almost all the prophets exhibit a very confused idea of God's providence, and are evidently at a loss to make the order of nature and the events that happen in the world agree with such ideas as they entertained. Nevertheless, the matter has always presented itself clearly enough to the philosopher who strives to comprehend it, not by means of miracles, but by forming clear conceptions of God and nature; to the philosopher who conceives true happiness to consist in virtue and peace of mind alone, and who studies to obey nature, not to make nature bend to him; inasmuch as he knows for certain that God governs nature in the way his universal laws compel, not in the manner the particular laws of man would require, and that thus God has regard, not to the human kind alone, but to the fabric of the world at large. It is therefore certainly proved from Scripture itself that miracles give no true knowledge either of God or of his eternal providence.

There is one thing, however, constantly repeated in the Scriptures, viz. that God showed signs and wonders, or wrought miracles, in order that he might become known to the Jewish people. Thus in Exodus (x. 2) we read that God deceived the Egyptians, and gave signs of himself to the children of Israel, that they might know he was the Lord. But it does not therefore follow that miracles were the means by which God taught this truth; it only shows that the Jews held opinions which led them to be readily persuaded by signs and portents; for in our second chapter we have satisfactorily shown that prophetic reasons, or reasons formed from revelation, are not formed from universal and common notions, but from the preconceptions and opinions, however absurd, of those to whom the matter was revealed, or whom the Holy Spirit desired to convince; a position which we have illustrated by many quotations, and also by the testimony of the Apostle Paul, who tells us himself that he was Greek with the Greeks and Jew with the Jews. Now although these miracles might satisfy Egyptians and Jews, in appealing to their prejudices, they could not give any true notion or knowledge of God; they could only lead to the admission that there was a God more powerful than anything known to them; and, lastly, that the Jews, with whom at this time all had gone most prosperously, were the especial objects of his care and protection, but not that God really cared for and protected all mankind alike; for this truth philosophy alone could teach. The Jews, consequently, and all who know nothing of the providence of God save from dissimilar states of human affairs and the unequal fortunes of men, have persuaded themselves that they were more acceptable to the Supreme Being than any other people, although they did not in reality surpass other nations in aught that constitutes true excellence, as we have shown at length in our third chapter.

3. I proceed to prove from Scripture that the decrees and commandments of God, and consequently his providence, are nothing more than the order of nature; that is to say, when Scripture declares this and that to have been done by God, or to be the will of God, nothing is to be understood but that the act was in accordance with the laws and order of nature, and not, as the vulgar believe, that nature for a season had ceased to act, or that its order had for a certain time been subverted. Scripture, I here observe, never directly teaches anything that does not bear immediately on its doctrines; for its purpose, as I have shown in connection with the divine law, is not to teach by natural causes, nor by merely speculative considerations. Thus, in the First Book of Samuel (ix. 15, 16) we are informed that God revealed to Samuel that he should send Saul to him; yet God did not

send Saul to Samuel in the way in which men are wont to send expressly one to another, for the visit of Saul to Samuel arose out of concurrent circumstances, thus—Saul was in search of the asses he had lost, as narrated in the preceding chapter of the book, and failing to find them, and even thinking of returning home without them, on the suggestion of his servant he sought out Samuel the seer, that he might inquire of him where he should discover his strayed cattle; from no part of the whole narrative does it appear that Saul received any special command from God to visit Samuel. In Psalm cv. 25 it is said that God changed the hearts of the Egyptians, so that they hated the children of Israel; but this was obviously a natural incident, as appears from Exodus i., where we find very sufficient reasons why the Egyptians oppressed the Jews and reduced them to slavery.* In Genesis ix. 13 God informs Noah that he would show himself in the clouds, and set his bow there, which is but another way of expressing the natural law by which the rays of the sun suffer refraction when they fall upon drops of water. In Psalm cxlvii. 18 the natural action of wind and heat by which hoar-frost and snow are melted is spoken of as the word of God, and in ver. 15 the wind and the cold are entitled the commandment and word of the Lord. In Psalm civ. 4, again, wind and fire are called the angels or messengers, and ministers of God; indeed, very many expressions of the same kind are met with in Scripture, all of which proclaim most distinctly that the words commandment, decree, and word of God, are often nothing more than expressions for the agency and order of nature itself. Wherefore there is no reason to doubt that everything related in Scripture happened naturally, though it is always referred immediately to God, because it is not the business of Holy Writ to teach by reference to natural

---

* And the children of Israel multiplied, and waxed exceedingly mighty; and there arose a new king over Egypt, and he said, "The children of Israel are more and mightier than we: let us deal wisely with them, lest they join unto our enemies and fight against us," &c.—*Ed.*

causes, but only to narrate events in such a way as shall most powerfully strike the imagination, constant recourse being had to the manner and style which best serve to arouse wonder, and consequently to impress the minds of the many with devotional sentiments.

If, therefore, some things be found in Scripture for which we can assign no reason, and which moreover seem to have happened contrary to the usual course of nature, this ought really to be no hindrance to us; we are still by all means to believe that what really happened happened naturally. The propriety of this conclusion is confirmed by the fact that special circumstances, although not always particularly dwelt on, are often connected with miracles, especially when the account of them is sung in poetic strains, which clearly proclaim that they were the effect of natural causes. For instance, when Moses wished the Egyptians to be infected with blotches and blains, he cast hot ashes into the air (Exod. ix. 10); the locusts also came upon the land through a natural command of God, namely, on the wings of an east wind which blew day and night; and they ceased their ravages or disappeared by the agency of a violent westerly gale (Exod. x. 14, 19). In the same way, by the command of God, or by means of a strong east wind which blew all night, a way was opened for the Israelites through the waters of the Red Sea (Exod. xiv. 21). Elisha, also, when he set about resuscitating the lad who was thought to be dead, bent over him repeatedly, until he had restored warmth to the child [and perhaps inflated his lungs], who then and at at length opened his eyes* (vide 2 Kings iv. 34, 35). So also in the Gospel according to John (ix.) we find certain circumstances related as preparatives to the healing of the blind man by Christ; and, indeed, through the whole of the Scriptures many things of the same kind occur, which all proclaim that miracles require something more than the mere mandate, as it is called, of God. Wherefore, we are to

---

* "And he (Elisha) lay upon the child, and *put his mouth to his mouth*, and the flesh of the child waxed warm," &c —*Ed.*

believe that, although the circumstances and the natural causes of miracles are not always fully related, nevertheless that none ever happened without their concurrence. This is very strikingly illustrated by what we find in Exodus (xiv. 27), where the whole statement is, that Moses "stretched forth his hand, and the waters of the sea returned to their strength in the morning." Here there is no mention of a violent wind as the agent of the phenomenon: but in the song of Moses (ib. xv. 10) we find these words: "Thou didst blow with thy wind, the sea covered them," the wind of God here being a very strong wind; but the agency is omitted in the narrative in order that the wonder might appear the more striking.

But some may perhaps insist that in Scripture a multitude of things can be pointed out which are altogether inexplicable by natural causes, as, for instance, that the wickedness or the piety and prayers of man may be the cause of rain and inundation, and of the fertility or barrenness of the earth; that faith can cure the blind, make the sick whole, &c. But I think that I have already sufficiently replied to this objection; for I have shown that the purpose of Scripture is never to explain things by their immediate causes, but only to present them in a sequence, and in a style calculated to arouse the devotional feelings of the multitude especially; and this is the reason why God and things in general are there often spoken of in what without irreverence may be styled a somewhat objectionable manner, the purpose aimed at being not to convince the reason, but to engage and influence the imagination. Suppose, for example, that the fall of a great empire were to be narrated in the sober style usual with historical and political writers, the people would be little moved by it; but a different effect would be produced if all were poetically depicted and referred to the immediate agency of God, as is most commonly done in Scripture. When the ground is said to become barren in consequence of the wickedness of mankind, therefore, or the blind are restored to sight through faith, such statements ought not to move us more than when we read that because of the sins of men God is angry or sorrowful, or repents him of the good he had promised and done, or is reminded of a promise he had made by a sign in the heavens, and very many things of the same sort, which are either mere poetical expressions, or narratives in conformity with the opinions and prejudices of the writer. Let us unhesitatingly conclude, then, that whatever of truth we find in the Scripture narratives of events, these uniformly came to pass in accordance with the laws of nature which necessarily govern all things; and when we meet with any incident there which may be demonstrated as opposed to the laws of nature, or which can in no way be reconciled with them, we may feel assured that it has been added to the sacred Scriptures by some sacrilegious hand; for whatever is against nature is against reason [and against God], and what is against reason is absurd, and therefore to be scouted.

4. I have now only to make a few remarks on the interpretation of miracles; or, rather, to resume the heads of what I have just said, and to illustrate them by one or two examples. What makes it the more necessary to do so is lest any one, by interpreting a certain miracle amiss, should rashly suspect that he had found something in Scripture which was repugnant to natural reason.

It is very seldom that men relate an event simply as it happened; that they mingle nothing of their own fancies or opinions with the narrative. When they see or hear anything new, indeed, unless especially on their guard against preconceived opinions, they mostly even perceive things quite otherwise than as they are in fact, especially if the matter in question is beyond the capacity of the listener or narrator, and still more if it interferes in any way with his interests or affections. From this it comes that in their Chronicles and Histories men are much more apt to give their own views and opinions than to narrate events as they actually happened; and so it turns out that the same incident related by two persons of dissimilar views often appears as if two different events were spoken of. It is, therefore, upon occasion not very difficult from the style and statements of a narrative to discover the opinions of the chronicler or historian. I could confirm these reflections by quotations from various philosophers, even, who have written the history of nature, as well as from the chroniclers of historical events; but I think this superfluous, and shall content myself with citing a single instance from Scripture, leaving the rest to the judgment and research of the reader. In the time of Joshua the Jews believed, as the vulgar do at the present time, that the sun was in motion and the earth at rest. They did not fail accordingly to accommodate to this opinion the account of the miracle which befell in the great battle against the five kings; for they have not said simply that the day on which the battle took place seemed longer than usual, but that the sun and moon stood still in their course, ceased from their motions. Now this manner of stating the event was obviously well calculated to impress the minds of the heathen of those times who worshipped the sun, with the conviction that this luminary was under the control of another more powerful divinity, at whose nod it could be made to pause in its course against all former experience. Partly on religious grounds, therefore, partly from preconceived opinions, the Jews apprehended and related the event of the long day during the battle with the five kings very differently from the way in which it occurred in fact.

To interpret the miracles of Scripture consequently, and to understand them from the narratives, it is absolutely necessary to be informed of the opinions of those who first witnessed or narrated them, and also of those who have left us an account of them in writing, and to make a cardinal distinction between the event in itself and the impression it may have produced on the minds of those who witnessed it. Without this precaution we should certainly confound the opinions and prejudices of witnesses and historians with events in themselves. Nor were this all, we should still be liable to confound things that actually transpired with things imaginary, or that were more prophetic representations conceived in dreams and visions. For in Scripture many things are narrated as realities, things which were indeed believed to be realities, which nevertheless were mere fanciful or imaginative representations; as, for example, when it is said that God, the Being of beings, "came down from heaven" (Exod. xix. 28, and Deut. v. 28), and that Mount Sinai "smoked because God descended upon it enveloped in fire;" "that Elijah was taken up into heaven in a fiery chariot drawn by fiery horses," &c. These are all but ideal representations, in conformity with the opinions of those who have transmitted them to us, and as they themselves received them, viz. as sober accounts of actual events. Every one, but a little raised above vulgar notions, is aware that God has neither right nor left, is neither in motion nor at rest, nor in one place more than another, but that he is absolutely infinite, and includes all perfections in himself. They, I say, know these things who judge after the conceptions of pure intelligence, and not as imagination influenced by external sense leads us to conclude, which the vulgar always do when they picture God to themselves as corporeal, as surrounded by regal pomp and state, with his throne established in the heaven of heavens above the stars, the distance of which from the earth is not conceived to be extremely great. To these and similar opinions many narratives in Scripture are plainly adapted, and are not to be accepted by the philosophical as accounts of things as they are in fact, or that actually occurred.

Another important point in the review of the Scripture miracles is this, that the figurative language of the Hebrews —their tropes and poetical expressions—be well understood; for whosoever loses sight of these will inevitably fasten many miracles upon Scripture which its writers never even imagined, and so not only mistake the manner in which signs and wonders actually occurred, but also proclaim his own ignorance of the sacred text. By way of example let us turn to Zechariah (xiv. 7). Speaking of the event of a certain approaching war, the prophet expresses himself thus, "It shall be one day which shall be known to the Lord, not day nor night; but at even time it shall be light." These words seem to involve a great miracle or mystery; and yet they signify nothing more than this,—that the battle should be doubtful through the whole of the day, its issue being only known to God, but that in the evening the victory would be won. It is in such enigmatical language indeed that the prophets were wont to speak and to write of the victories and disasters of nations. Isaiah, for instance, depicting the desolation of Babylon (xiii.), makes use of these words, "The stars of heaven and the constellations thereof shall not give their light; the sun shall be darkened in his going forth, and the moon shall not cause her light to shine." Now, I do not suppose any one imagines that all this happened literally when the Babylonian empire fell, any more than that which the prophet immediately adds, "For I will make the heavens to tremble, and remove the earth out of her place." In like manner, the same prophet (xlviii.), desiring to make it known to the Jews that they should assuredly return to Jerusalem from Babylon and not suffer from thirst on their journey, says, "And they thirsted not when he led them through the deserts; he caused the waters to flow out of the rocks for them; he clave the rock and the waters gushed out." The meaning of this is simply that the Jews found springs in the desert to slake their thirst—and springs do well-up in the desert at intervals;—for when the Jews returned to Jerusalem with the consent of Cyrus, it is certain that no such miracle occurred literally as that which the prophet describes. Very many things of the same kind are met with in the sacred writings,—mere modes of expressing themselves in use among the Jews, which I do not think it necessary to specify more in detail. I remark generally that the Hebrews were wont not only to embroider their statements with flowery or poetical language, but, further, that they almost always used devotional expressions. This is the reason why in Scripture we sometimes find the expression *bless* God for the contrary, as in

1 Kings xxi. 10, and Job ii. 9.* For the same reason the Jews referred everything to God, so that Scripture in parts seems to narrate nothing but miracles, even when speaking of the most natural occurrences. Examples of this system have been given in sufficient number above. We are to conclude therefore, when we find it said that God hardened the heart of Pharaoh, that nothing more is implied than that Pharaoh was firm and uncomplying; and when it is stated that God opened the windows of heaven, we are only to understand that a great deal of rain fell, and so on. Whoever regards these passages with an unbiassed mind, and remembers that many things are spoken of in the curtest terms, and without any of the accompanying circumstances, will find almost nothing in Scripture which can be shown to be repugnant to natural reason; and on the contrary, much which, although at the first blush appearing obscure, with a little reflection comes to be readily enough interpreted and understood.

I have thus, I think, said all I had it at heart to say on the subject of miracles. But before quitting it, and bringing the chapter to a close, I find one thing which I think ought to be mentioned, namely, that in discussing the subject of miracles I have proceeded otherwise than when treating of Prophecy. Of Prophecy I affirm nothing but what I could deduce from grounds revealed in Scripture, eliciting the chief points from principles cognizable by the natural understanding; and this I did of set purpose; because, of prophecy, when its statements went beyond the reach of our faculties and the question became purely theological, I could affirm, as I could know, nothing except from the revelations made. Here, consequently, I was forced to collate the prophecies, and from them to form certain dogmatic conclusions, which gave me a glimpse, in as far as this was to be had, of the nature

* This is as Spinoza has it, and as we presume it is in the original Hebrew, but in the margin of the Codex opposite the word *bless* stands the Variorum reading *curse* or *blaspheme*; and as in our English version we always have the marginal variation substituted for the textual word, so we have *blaspheme* in Kings and *curse* in Job. Vide some interesting observations of the Author on the marginal notes of the Hebrew codices in Chapter ix.—*Ed.*

and qualities of prophecy in general. But in regard to miracles, as the subject of our present inquiry is plainly philosophical, viz. whether we can admit the occurrence of anything in nature subversive of its laws, or that is not the effect of these laws, I required to do nothing of the kind; I have rather and intentionally striven to elucidate the subject upon principles familiarly known, and on grounds accessible to our natural understanding; I say I have taken this course of set purpose, for I could readily have explained miracle on a dogmatic basis entirely derived from Scripture. And that this may more plainly appear, I shall here yet further show that Scripture in several places affirms of nature in general that its course is fixed and unchangeable. In the 148th Psalm, for example (ver. 6), in Jeremiah (xxxi. 35, 36), and in Solomon (Ecclesiastes i. 10), it is clearly declared that there is nothing new under the sun. The sage, indeed, in further illustration of this truth (Eccles. i. 10, 11), proceeds to say that although occasionally something happens which seems new, still it is not new, "It hath been already of old time which was before us, whereof there is no remembrance, neither shall there be any remembrance of things that are to come with those that shall come after." Again, in chapter iii. 11, he says that "God hath made everything beautiful in his time," and immediately after he adds (ver. 14), "I know that whatsoever God doeth it shall be for ever; nothing can be put to it, nor anything taken from it;" all of which teaches most distinctly that the order of nature is fixed and immutable, that God was the same in all times, known and unknown to us, and that the laws of nature are so perfect and so fruitful that nothing can be added to, as nothing can be taken from, them, and, lastly, that miracles are only seen as something new because of the ignorance of man. These things then are expressly taught in the sacred Scriptures; but nowhere do they teach that anything happens in nature which contravenes its laws, or which might not follow from their agency; such views are therefore on no account to be connected with Scripture. Add to all this that miracles require causes and circumstances (as has been already shown), and do not proceed from that royal authority, to me inscrutable, which the vulgar connect with God, but from divine authority and decree; that is to say (as I have also made manifest out of Scripture), from the laws of nature and its unchanging order; and, finally, that miracles could also be performed by impostors, as we have it expressly declared in Deuteronomy (xiii.) and in Matthew (xxiv.). From all this it follows most obviously that [the events styled] miracles have been natural occurrences, and are therefore to be so explained as neither to appear new things, to use the words of Solomon, nor as things opposed to nature, but in such a manner, if this may in any wise be done, as shall assimilate them with natural things. It is with a view to assist every one in this course that I have brought together the few rules, derived exclusively from Scripture, which I have given for the study and interpretation of miracles. And here I beg to be allowed to say, that when I declare the teaching of Scripture in regard to miracles to be as I have stated it, I would not be understood as meaning to say that such things are there taught as principles needful to salvation, but only that the prophets regarded miracles in the same manner as we do; consequently, that it is permitted to every one to think on this subject in that way which shall seem to him best calculated to raise his mind to the worship of God, and lead him to embrace the principles of true religion with his whole heart and spirit. Such, in fact, was the view of Josephus, who ends the Second Book of his Antiquities in these words:

"The word miracle ought not to make us incredulous; why should not the men of old be believed who tell us of a path of safety opened through the sea, whether revealed to them by the will of God or followed in the natural course of things? Is it not confidently related by those who have written the life and deeds of Alexander that the Sea of Pamphylia opened a way, when there was no other left, for the King of Macedonia and those who were with him, when God willed to make use of this great commander to overthrow the

Persian Empire? Of these things, therefore (miracles), every one is to be left free to think as he pleases." Such are the words of Josephus, and his opinion of the necessity of belief in miracles.

If the reader will go on to read Mr Hume's masterly Essay on the subject here discussed, he will, however well disposed to be credulous, feel himself forced for ever to abandon all belief in miracles. The different lines of argument pursued by Spinoza and by Hume severally supplement each other, and seem to leave nothing more to be said on the subject. Miracles indeed have long disappeared from the world of Science; they only linger now among the uneducated—still, alas, in the only proper sense of the term, a very numerous body in the world! The uselessness of miracle as a means to any good end is as old as the Book of Genesis: "If there come a prophet among you and he *do signs and wonders*, if he say: Let us go after other gods,—that prophet shall be put to death." And to come nearer the present age of the world, we ask what matters it to us whether Christ walked on the Lake of Galilee or not? we are not influenced in our life and conversation by our belief or unbelief in the report of such an unnatural incident. But it is' of the last moment to us, and to mankind in all time to come, that we have the example of our Lord's blessed life, the prayer he taught his disciples, and the sermon he spoke on the mount.—*Ed.*

CHAPTER VII.

OF THE INTERPRETATION OF SCRIPTURE.

That the Scriptures are the word of God is in everybody's mouth; and it is also said that they teach true happiness, and point out the way of everlasting life to man. But the thing itself is plainly judged of very differently; for the generality of men seem to care for nothing less than to live according to the precepts of Holy Writ, and whilst some are seen eager to parade their own conceits for God's word, others, under pretext of zeal for religion, seem only solicitous to force the rest of the world to think as they do themselves. Theologians, I say, have hitherto shown themselves especially ingenious in extorting their own conceits and figments from the letter of Scripture, and in supporting their various conclusions by divine authority: they never proceed more rashly and with fewer scruples than when they set about interpreting the Scriptures. If they show anxiety about anything, it is not lest they should connect error with the Holy Spirit; but lest they themselves should be convicted of mistake, and so have their proper authority contemned. But did mankind feel that hearty conviction of the excellence of the Scriptures which they are ready enough to avow with their mouths, they would pursue a very different manner of living; their souls would not be disturbed by so many discordant passions, nor distracted by such ardent hatreds; neither would they make so many and such rash attempts to interpret Scripture and to produce novelties in religion. They would not venture to embrace as Scripture doctrine aught which was not most plainly set forth as such in Scripture itself. Then, too, would those sacrilegious men who have not feared to tamper with Scripture in many places, have withheld their hands from such wickedness. But vanity and audacity have gone so far that religion is made at length to consist less in obeying the decrees of the Holy Spirit than in adopting and defending the commentaries and conclusions of men; the effect of which is, that instead of teaching charity and good-will, religion becomes the vehicle of hatred and discord in the world, and all under the name and pretext of zeal for sacred things. With such ills superstition, moreover, has been associated,—superstition which teaches men to despise reason and nature, and only to admire and respect that which these alike ignore. It is not to be wondered at therefore if some, whilst striving to excite a greater reverence and respect for Scripture, have actually explained it in such a way as to make its precepts seem repugnant both to common sense and nature. This is the reason why such profound mysteries have been supposed to lurk in Holy Writ, and why, in searching after these, to the entire neglect of useful truths, many have plainly lost their way, have ascribed their own delirious dreams to the Holy Spirit, and expended their strength and ingenuity in defending absurdities. For even thus does it fare with man: That which he conceives by pure intelligence, that he defends by reason and understanding; and that which he imagines by the affections of his mind, that does he justify by temper and passion.

That we may not get entangled in this maze, that we may keep our minds free from theological prejudices, and not adopt the imaginations of man as divine truths, we shall now proceed to treat of the true method of interpreting Scripture, and of commenting upon it; for without this we can know nothing certainly of what Scripture or the Holy Spirit would teach. Now on this point, in few words, I say that the proper method of interpreting Scripture does not differ from the proper method of interpreting nature, but agrees with it almost in every particular. For, inasmuch as the way of interpreting nature consists especially in bringing together, in arranging and contrasting, the facts of natural science, from whence, as from assured data, we arrive at general conclusions and definitions; so also in interpreting Scripture it is necessary to co-ordinate its simple statements and histories, and from them, as from fixed data and principles, to come to legitimate conclusions in regard to the meaning and purpose of the authors of the narrative. Whoever proceeds in this way, taking particular care to assume no other principles nor data in his interpretations than those which are contained in Scripture itself, may advance without fear of mistake, and even discuss matters which are beyond our comprehension, as well as those which we appreciate by our common faculties.

But that this may be clearly seen, not merely as the safe way, but as the only way, and as agreeing entirely with the method of interpreting nature, it is to be observed that Scripture most commonly treats of matters which cannot be deduced from the principles supplied by natural intelligence; for by much the larger portion of the Bible is made up of histories and revelations; and the histories are principally of miracles, that is, they are narratives of extraordinary and unusual events in nature, accommodated to the opinions and prejudices of the writers; whilst the revelations, as we have shown in Chapter II., are in conformity with the opinions and lights of the prophets who propound them, and, indeed, they very frequently transcend human capacity altogether. Whence it follows that the interpretation of all these things, i. e. of almost everything contained in Scripture, is to be sought from Scripture alone, even as the interpretation of nature is to be derived from nature. As to the moral doctrines which are also comprised in the Bible, although these may be demonstrated from common or natural notions, still, the demonstration that Scripture teaches in a particular way must not be sought for by natural light, but must be derived from the words of Scripture itself. If, indeed, and without prejudice, we would test the divineness of Scripture, we ought to be assured out of itself that its teaching is of sound moral doctrine; for in this way only can its divineness be demonstrated; just as we have already shown that certainty of the true prophet was especially derived from an assurance of his manifesting a mind and temper solely disposed to goodness and truth, so much being imperative before faith could be put in his words. But it is impossible to have any assurance of the divinity of God from miracles, as has been already shown; for miracles were also performed by false prophets. Wherefore, the sole sufficient test of the divineness of Scripture lies in the excellence of the precepts it declares, in the fact that it teaches true virtue. Now that it does so can only be shown from itself. Were it otherwise, we should indeed be much to blame in adopting Scripture as our guide, and in speaking of it as of divine origin. The knowledge of Scripture, therefore, is to be wholly and solely derived from its own pages. Scripture, however, never gives definitions of the things of which it speaks, any more than does nature itself. Wherefore, whatever the conclusions formed in regard to natural things, they are to be drawn from the different narratives that occur in Scripture, in regard to each individual thing. The universal rule in interpreting Scripture, then, is, never to ascribe as Scripture doctrine aught which we do not most plainly find set forth in its narratives. It will now be our business to inquire as to what we should expect Scripture history to be, and of what things it should principally speak.

1. Scripture history necessarily includes the nature and properties of the language in which it is written, and in which its authors were wont to speak. From these, under the guidance of common usage, we should be enabled to investigate the various senses in which each word, phrase, or expression is employed. And as all the writers, both of the Old and New Testament, were Jews, it is certain that a knowledge of the Hebrew tongue is above all things necessary, not only to the understanding of the books of the Old

Testament, which are written in this language, but also of those of the New Testament, which, although promulgated in other languages, nevertheless have the strong impress of Hebrew peculiarity upon them.

2. The matter treated in each book being noted and reduced under distinct heads, an immediate and connected view of every passage that treats of the same thing is obtained; and the passages which are of doubtful or obscure meaning, or which contradict one another, are to be indicated:—I call clear or obscure those passages which of themselves, or from the context, are either readily or with difficulty understood; for our business here is with the meaning only of the passages in question, nowise with their truth. Wherefore it is of prime necessity, whilst investigating the sense of Scripture, that we be not pre-occupied with our own reasonings, based though they may be on an adequate knowledge of natural things. I say nothing here of our prejudices, lest we confound the true sense of the text with natural truths; the sense of Scripture being to be made out from the words of the text itself, or by legitimate ratiocination upon them alone, no ground of induction being admitted but that which Scripture itself contains. That this position may be the more clearly understood I shall illustrate it by an example. The views of Moses when he says that *God is fire*, and that *God is jealous*, are plain enough so long as we regard the meaning of the words only; and these expressions I therefore place in my category of plain things, although in regard to truth and reason they are most obscure. Still, although the literal sense of the words is repugnant to natural reason, unless they be also clearly opposed to the principles and fundamentals of Scripture, this sense, viz. the literal sense, must be retained; and, on the contrary, if the expressions, literally interpreted, are seen to disagree with the principles derived from Scripture, although entirely accordant with reason and natural light, they must be interpreted otherwise or taken metaphorically. That we may truly know therefore whether Moses believed God to be fire or not is by no means to be inferred

from this, that such an opinion agrees with, or is repugnant to, reason, but solely from the other expressed opinions and views of Moses. Now, as Moses in many places pointedly declares that God has no likeness to anything which is in heaven or earth, we must needs conclude that the words quoted are to be explained metaphorically. But as we are bound to depart as little as possible from the literal sense, in any case, we are first to inquire whether the words in the single phrase *God is fire* may not have another sense than the literal one; that is, whether the word *Fire* ever signifies anything else than fire, the effect of combustion; and if it were found, from the uses of the Hebrew tongue, that the word which is equivalent to fire is not employed in any other sense, then were the phrase *God is fire* not to be interpreted in any way that is not repugnant to reason; but, against everything else in harmony with reason, the interpretation of literal fire would have to be adopted. Again, supposing that even this could not be done in conformity with the usages of the language, then would the different interpretations be found irreconcilable, and we should be forced to suspend our judgment in regard to the true meaning of the phrase. But when we find the word *fire* also used to signify anger and wrath (vide Job xxxi. 12), then are the views of Moses readily reconciled, and we legitimately conclude that the two phrases, *God is fire* and *God is jealous*, embody one and the same meaning. Moreover, as Moses clearly teaches that God is a jealous God, and nowhere informs us that God is without passions or affections of the mind, we readily conclude that Moses himself believed, or at all events desired to teach, what he says, although the opinion expressed is in our apprehension repugnant to reason. For, as I have already shown, we are not at liberty to twist the sense of Scripture into conformity with the dictates of our reason and our preconceived opinions, but the interpretation of the whole Bible is to be derived from itself alone.

3. Finally, Scripture history ought to comprise an account of all the books of the prophets that have come

down to us, the life, manners, and culture of the author of each particular book: who he was, on what occasion, at what time, to whom, and, lastly, in what language he wrote; and then the fortune of the several books should be made known, viz. how and in what way each was first received, and into whose hands it fell; next, how many different versions of it are extant, by whose advice it was received among the number of the sacred books, and, lastly, how the books, all of which are now acknowledged as sacred, were gathered together into one body. All these things, I say, are to be expected in a history of the Hebrew Scriptures. For, in order that we may know what matters are propounded as laws and what as moral precepts, it is proper that we should know something of the life, manners, and occupation of their authors; besides, we the more readily explain the words of any one, as we are the better informed in regard to his genius and acquirements. Then, it is well to know the occasion on which, and the age and nation to which, writings are addressed, in order that we may not be led to confound eternal and universal decrees with such as are temporary only, or of limited applicability. It is important, further, to be informed of the other particulars just enumerated: that, besides the books themselves, and the authorities for their acknowledgment, we should know whether they may not have been tampered with by unscrupulous hands; or at all events whether errors may not have crept into them, and whether the text have been revised and corrected by men sufficiently skilful and perfectly worthy of trust. All of these things are most necessary to be known, lest, carried away by blind impulse, we come to embrace whatever is obtruded upon us, instead of that only which is certain and of vital import.

Even after we have secured and solidly established this history of the Scriptures, when we have certainly set down nothing as prophetic doctrine which does not follow from the narrative, or may not be clearly inferred from it, then it will be time for us to gird ourselves up for inquiry into the purposes of the prophets and the Holy Spirit. But for this end method and order are required similar to that which we employ in interpreting nature from its history. For, as in inquiring into natural things we endeavour above all to discover those which are most general, which are common to nature at large, viz. motion, attraction, gravitation, &c., and their laws, which nature always observes and by which she always acts, and from these proceed step by step to other less general laws, so also in Scripture history, that is first to be ascertained which is most general, which is the basis and foundation of the whole superstructure, and which finally leads to the special eternal law commanded by the prophet and most necessary to all mankind; such a law or doctrine as this for example,—that there is One omnipotent and eternal God, who alone is to be worshipped, who rules over all, who cares for all, and especially regards those who worship him in truth, who love their neighbours as themselves, &c. These and other similar precepts are so clearly taught in Scripture that there never was man yet found who questioned the sense of the passages in which they are contained. But as to what God is, in what respect he sees all things, and provides for all things, &c., on these, and like matters, Scripture does not professedly teach anything as eternal doctrine. On the contrary, it has been already shown that the prophets themselves were not agreed on such topics; so that nothing in regard to them is to be assumed as the doctrine of the Holy Spirit, although natural light would often of itself suffice for coming to satisfactory conclusions.

This most general or universal doctrine of Scripture being satisfactorily determined, we then proceed to search for other doctrines less general, which still bear reference to the common usages of life, and which are derived as offshoots from the grand doctrine; such as the outward manifestation of the true virtues [charity, meekness, justice, temperance, &c.], which are only called into action with the occasion given. When any obscurity or doubt presents itself in connection with these less general precepts of Scripture, it is to be cleared up or resolved by reference to the universal doctrine; and, again, when any contradiction is encountered, the occasion, the time, and the writer are then to be passed in review before any conclusion is come to. Thus, when Christ says, "Blessed are the mourners, for they shall be comforted," the text tells us nothing as to who the mourners were, nor for what they grieved; but when he afterwards teaches that we are to be solicitous about nothing save only the kingdom of God and his righteousness, which he declares to be the highest good (vide Matt. vi. 33), it follows that he understands those only who mourn for the kingdom of God and his righteousness, neglected of men; for these only can they grieve who love nothing but the divine rule and equity, and openly contemn all other things, the gifts of fortune. So also must we interpret that passage wherein Christ desires him who is struck on the right cheek to turn the left also to the smiter; had Christ given such a command as a legislator he would have gone counter to the law of Moses, which certainly gives very different advice. Wherefore we are to inquire as to the time at which, and the persons to whom, Christ spake. Now we find that Christ then spoke not as a legislator who lays down laws, but as a doctor or teacher of precepts, whose grand purpose was not to inculcate external observance, but to improve the mental state of mankind. And then he uttered the words quoted to men oppressed, to members of a corrupt state, where justice was little heeded, and whose ruin he saw was imminent. We find Jeremiah using very similar language under somewhat similar circumstances when prophesying the first destruction of Jerusalem (vide Lament. iii.). Wherefore, seeing that Christ and the prophets only taught in such terms in seasons of oppression and public distress; that such precepts are nowhere in Scripture propounded as laws; that Moses, who did not write in times of disaster and oppression, but laboured to found a prosperous commonwealth, and who, though he condemns hatred and revenge against a neighbour, nevertheless inculcated equal pains for equal damage done, an eye for an eye, a tooth for a tooth, &c., it follows most clearly, from the very fundamentals of Scripture, that the teaching of Christ and Jeremiah on the endurance of wrong and giving way to the wicked in all things, was only intended for times of oppression, when justice was despised, and nowise for citizens in a well-regulated state, where justice is respected, and where every one who feels a regard for right brings his wrongs before the judge (vide Levit. v. 1), not from any feeling of revenge (Ib. xix. 17, 18), but that he may assert the supremacy of justice and the laws of his country, and give no countenance to the evil-disposed in their wickedness. And this agrees in every respect with natural reason. It were easy for me to adduce many other instances confirmatory of the principles I am now advocating; but I think these may suffice to illustrate my views, and to show the utility of the method of interpretation which it is my especial purpose at present to enforce.

Hitherto I have only spoken of the interpretation of such passages of Scripture as bear upon the common concerns of life, and which must therefore be held as more easy of investigation; about these, indeed, there has never been any controversy among Bible commentators. Other matters occurring in Scripture, however, which are purely speculative, cannot be so easily set at rest; the way here becomes narrower, for inasmuch as the prophets differ among themselves on speculative things, and their narratives are mostly accommodated to the prejudices of the age in which they were written, we are by no means at liberty to interpret obscure passages of one prophet by clearer passages of another, unless it most obviously appears that the two writers entertained one and the same opinion. Of the way in which the opinion of the prophets in such cases is to be discovered from Scripture, I shall proceed to say a few words as necessary to our subject. Now, here, as in preceding instances, we must begin with universals in the first degree; inquiry above all is to be made from the clearest announcements of Scripture as to what constitutes prophecy or revelation, as to that in which it especially consists; next we are to learn what a miracle is, and so in succession arrive at more common things; then we come down to the opinions of each prophet, and from these we reach at length the meaning of each particular prophecy, history, and miracle. Of the precautions to be taken, lest in this course the views of prophets and historians be confounded with the purpose of the Holy Spirit and the truth of the thing itself, we have already spoken in the proper place, and illustrated our remarks by numbers of examples; wherefore I do not now hold it necessary to say more on the subject here. I will but add, in connection with the *sense of prophecy*, that our method only enables us to investigate that which the prophets saw or heard, but not what they desired to signify or represent by their hieroglyphics; this indeed may be conjectured, but cannot be certainly deduced from the fundamentals of Scripture.

We have thus discussed the method of interpreting Scripture, and have at the same time shown that it supplied the sole and certain way of ascertaining its true meaning. I confess, however, that they, were there any such persons in existence, would be still more certain of the meaning of Scripture who had received a definite traditional explanation of its text from the prophets themselves, as the Pharisees think they have, or who had a pontiff who could not err in his interpretations, as the Roman Catholic Christians boast that they have. Still, as we could not really be certain either of this Pharisaic tradition, nor of the pontifical authority, so could we found nothing decisive upon either of these; for the earliest Christians, and the most ancient sects of the Jews, denied the existence of any such traditional interpretation, and recognized no such infallible authority. And then, when we look to the long series of years (I say nothing of other things) over which the traditions extend, which the Pharisees have received from their Rabbins, who carry them back to the time of Moses, we find they can have no foundation in fact, as I shall show at length in another place. Such tradition indeed would be suspicious under any circumstances; and although according to our method of proceeding we are obliged to suppose one of the traditions of the Jews to be uncorrupted, to wit, the signification of the words of the Hebrew language which we receive from them, still, whilst often feeling grave doubts of the events narrated, we feel none about the meaning of the words in which they are described, for usage never yet changed the signification of a word, though it has frequently altered the sense of a phrase. To change the meaning of a word, indeed, were very difficult, for whoever should attempt to do so would have to explain the word in the new sense from every writer who had used it in its old and usual signification; and then the vulgar in their every-day intercourse use and preserve language as well as the learned, whilst the learned are mostly interested in the meaning of ornate discourses and of books. So that whilst it is easy to imagine the learned to have altered or corrupted the sense of some passage in a rare book, they cannot have touched the meaning of a single word within it; add to this, that if any one had a mind to change the meaning of a common word he could scarcely hope to secure the observance of the change by posterity, or cause it to meet with acceptance in every-day conversation and writing. From these, and other like considerations, we readily conceive that it could never enter into the mind of any one to corrupt a language, though it might very well happen, and has very often happened, that the meaning of an author has been altered by tampering with his expressions, or by misinterpreting his language.

Since the method of investigation we have propounded, then, appears to be the true and only one—the entire method being founded on the principle of seeking a knowledge of Scripture from Scripture itself—it may be assumed that what Scripture will not supply towards enabling us to obtain a knowledge of its meaning, is plainly to be despaired of. And here I think it advisable to consider some of the difficulties which inhere in the method I have proposed, as well as what more were to be desired, in order that by its means we should arrive at a thorough and certain knowledge of the sacred writings. The first great difficulty connected with our method arises from the consummate knowledge of the Hebrew tongue, which its due application implies. But whence is this now to be obtained? The ancient masters of the Hebrew tongue have left nothing to posterity on the elements and principles of the language; we, at all events, have little or nothing of theirs—no dictionary, no grammar, no syntax. The Hebrew nation has lost all that it ever had of the elegances and ornaments of life (nor is this wonderful, after such long ages of depression, disaster, and persecution), and has preserved nothing but a few fragments of its language and its literature; almost all the names of fruits, trees, birds, beasts, fishes, &c., and much besides, have perished. Then the meaning of many nouns and verbs which are met with in the Bible is either wholly unknown or is subject of dispute. With all this, when we apply ourselves to study the syntax of this language, a matter of so much moment, and seek to discover the idioms and modes of expression peculiar to the Hebrew people, we find that time, the consumer, has blotted them almost all from the memory of man. We shall not therefore always be able, as we should wish, to determine the precise meaning of every passage which the common uses of the language would permit, and we shall come upon many sentences which, although expressed in words extremely well known, are nevertheless of meaning most obscure, and are sometimes even incomprehensible.

To these difficulties, which spring from the impossibility of having a perfect history of the Hebrew language, must be added those that arise from the constitution and nature of the language itself, which occasion so many ambiguities that it is impossible to find such a method as shall assuredly teach us how to investigate the true sense of all the expressions of Scripture.* Besides the causes of ambiguity common to and

* I should say, *impossible for us* who are not accustomed to the Hebrew language, and who have lost the secret of its syntax.

inherent in all languages there are certain others, peculiar to the Hebrew, from which many extraordinary difficulties arise, and on the nature of which it is proper that I should say something.

1. In the first place, doubt and obscurity are often produced in the Bible from this, that the letters of the same organ are used reciprocally one for another. The Jews divide the letters of their alphabet into five classes, in consonance with the five instruments or organs of the mouth which subserve articulation, viz. the lips, the teeth, the tongue, the palate, and the throat. For example, *Alpha*, *Ghet*, *Ghain*, *He* are called gutturals, and without any distinction, any at all events known to us, are used one for another. *El*, again, which generally signifies *to*, *towards*, is often used for *hgal*, which commonly means *above*, and *vice versâ*, whence it comes that the whole of a sentence is often rendered of doubtful import, or made to look as if it had no meaning at all.

2. A second source of ambiguity exists in the numerous meanings that are attached to the Hebrew conjunctions and adverbs. For example, *vau* serves indifferently for conjunction and disjunction, and signifies *but*, *because*, *then*, and *however*. *Ki* has seven or eight significations, *wherefore*, *although*, *if*, *when*, *inasmuch*, *as*, *because*, *combustion*, &c., and so almost of all particles.

3. The third source of doubt, and it is a very fertile one, consists in this, that in the indicative mood, verbs want the present tense, the preterite imperfect, the preterpluperfect, the future perfect, and various other tenses of most common use in other languages; in the imperative and infinitive moods, verbs have nothing but the present, and they are altogether without the subjunctive. And although all these defects in moods and tenses may be met and supplied, often with extreme elegance, by certain rules easily deduced from the structure of the language, still the older writers neglect them entirely, and make use indifferently of the future for the present and the past, and contrariwise of

the preterite for the future; moreover, they assume the indicative for the imperative and subjunctive,—all, as may be conceived, not without an endless amount of doubtful meaning as the consequence.

Besides the three causes of obscurity now noted in the Hebrew language, there yet remain to be mentioned two others, each of much more moment than all the rest. The first of these is, that *the Hebrew has no vowels;* the second, that *it is without spaces between the words and sentences, and has no accents to indicate the proper pronunciation;* and although these two deficiences, viz. the vowels and signs of accentuation, are wont to be supplied by *points*, it is impossible that we should acquiesce in the sufficiency of these, inasmuch as they are the invention and resource of men of these later times, whose authority can have no weight with us. The ancient Hebrews wrote without points (i. e. without vowels and accents), as appears from the most ample testimony. The moderns supplied vowel-points and accents, as it seemed good to them that the Bible should be interpreted; wherefore they are to be regarded as mere interpolations of yesterday, and deserve no greater faith, as they have no higher authority, than the lucubrations of ordinary commentators. They who are ignorant of this cannot understand how it comes that the author of the Epistle to the Hebrews (xi. 21) should have interpreted the text he quotes from Genesis (xlvii. 31) very differently from the way in which it presents itself in the pointed and accented Hebrew text,—as if the apostle had to learn the sense of Scripture from the punctists! To me these persons appear to err, and not the apostle; and that the discrepancy may be seen to have arisen solely from the deficiency of vowels in the language, I lay both versions before the reader. The punctists with the assistance of their points, read: "And Israel bowed himself upon the bed's head," but the author of the Epistle to the Hebrews reads, "Jacob worshipped, leaning on the top of his staff;" reading מַטֶּה *mate*, instead of מִטָּה *mita*, a difference due entirely to the use of a vowel point. Now as in the original narrative it is Jacob's age only that is in question, not his death, which is not spoken of till the next chapter, it seems more probable that it was the narrator's intention to say that Jacob leant upon the head of the staff, which the aged so commonly use for their support, than that he bowed himself upon the head of his bed. In this example, it has not been so much my purpose to reconcile the version of the apostle with the text of Genesis, as to show how little faith is due to our modern points and accents, and thus to prove that he who would interpret Scripture conscientiously is bound to have these in doubt, and to inquire for himself at the fountain-head.

Resuming the thread of our subject, the glimpses now given of the constitution and nature of the Hebrew language will enable every one readily to conceive that so many doubts and difficulties must arise as to make any method of investigation incompetent to resolve them all. For it is in vain to expect that the meaning of every passage can be ascertained by its collation with others; (and we have shown that in general this was the only way of eliciting the true sense from among the many senses which each particular passage will often bear when considered textually.) Such a collation of passages, however, cannot, save by chance, serve for the illustration of any particular passage, inasmuch as none of the prophets wrote with the express view of explaining either his own or another's writings; and then we cannot conclude as to the mind and meaning of one prophet from the mind and meaning of another; unless perchance it be in regard to matters bearing upon ordinary life and conversation, as we have already shown; for when the question is of speculative things, or when miracles and histories are narrated, we can come to no conclusion whatever. I could, moreover, readily show by examples that there are many passages in Scripture which are absolutely inexplicable; but I prefer to pass these by for the present, in order that I may proceed with my business of showing still further wherein the true method of interpreting Scripture is itself defective, and with what other difficulties it is beset.

Another difficulty in following out our method arises from its requiring a particular account of all that has ever happened to the books of Scripture. Now of this we for the most part know nothing. Of the authors, or, if you please, writers, of many of the books, we either know almost nothing, or we entertain grave doubts as to the correctness with which the several books are ascribed to the parties whose names they bear, as I shall immediately show. Then, we neither know upon what occasion nor at what time those books were indited, the writers of which are unknown to us. Further, we know nothing of the hands into which the books fell; nor of the codices which have furnished such a variety of readings, nor whether perchance there were not many other variations in other copies. But of the great importance of information on all these points I have already spoken briefly in the proper place, where however I have on purpose omitted certain considerations which must now come under review.

If we have a book under perusal containing many incredible or incomprehensible statements, written, too, in language sufficiently obscure, of whose author we know nothing, neither anything of the time in which or the occasion on which he wrote, we shall certainly mostly strive in vain to master the true meaning of the text. For all these matters unknown, we can in nowise know either what was or what might have been the purpose of the author. With all preliminaries known, on the contrary, we could then so rule our thoughts, that, preoccupied by no prejudices, we should ascribe neither more nor less than of right belongs to the author, or to him on whose account he wrote, and should think of nothing but that which the author may have had in his mind, or which the time and the occasion of writing seemed to require. So much, I think, will be admitted by all. It very often happens indeed that we read histories in different books, which in many respects resemble one another, but of which we form very dissimilar estimates, according to the opinion we entertain of the writers, or of the purpose of their writing. I know that formerly I read in a certain book of a hero named Orlando, who was wont to fly through the air on the back of a winged monster over various regions of the earth, slaughtering vast numbers of men and giants, with other fantastical recitals of the same sort, all plainly absurd and inconceivable when tested by reason and understanding. In Ovid, again, I have read a similar history, of which Perseus is the hero; and in the Books of Judges and Kings we have the history of Samson, who alone and unarmed [save with the jaw-bone of an ass] slew thousands of men; and of Elijah, who flew through the air, and at length went up to heaven in a fiery chariot drawn by fiery horses. These, I say, are all obviously tales of the same character; nevertheless we form very different estimates of each of them: for of the first, we say the writer had no purpose but to indite vanities for our amusement; of the second, that he had a political aim in view; and of the third, that the matter is sacred, and all this for no other reason than because we entertain different opinions of the writers of the several narratives. It is certain therefore that some knowledge of the authors whose writings contain matter obscure or incomprehensible is essentially necessary to the right understanding of their works. For the same reason, moreover, and that we may choose the proper reading from among a great variety of readings of extremely obscure productions, it is necessary that we know in what copies the several readings are found, and whether there be not others extant of still higher authority.

Another difficulty which we find in interpreting certain books of Scripture on this plan lies in this, that we have not these books in the language in which they were originally composed. The Gospel according to Matthew and unquestionably also the Epistle to the Hebrews were written, as all agree, in Hebrew; but the Hebrew version is now nowhere extant. Of the language in which the Book of Job was written great doubts are entertained. Aben Ezra affirms in his commentaries that it was translated from some other language into Hebrew, and that this is the cause of its obscurity. Of the Apocryphal books I say nothing, for they are of very different authority.

Such are the difficulties that attend upon the system of attempting to interpret Scripture from its own contents, difficulties which I esteem so great, that I have no hesitation in affirming that after all the true meaning of many passages will either entirely escape us, or be but vaguely conjectured. Still it must be observed that these difficulties are only especially felt when we have to investigate the opinions of the prophets upon matters incomprehensible, and which can only be imagined, and not upon things which can be appreciated by the understanding, and of which a clear conception can be formed; for the things which are readily appreciated from their own nature can never be put so obscurely, but that they are readily enough understood,* according to the proverb which says, A word is enough to the wise. Euclid, for example, who only wrote of extremely simple and perfectly intelligible matters, is easily understood of every one in his own language; for to be certain of the meaning here, it is not indispensable to have a perfect knowledge of the tongue in which the author wrote; a very ordinary and almost puerile proficiency suffices; neither do

* By things appreciated by their own nature I do not understand those only that are demonstrable in a rigorous manner, but those also which our mind can embrace with moral certainty, and which we conceive without amazement, though it be impossible to demonstrate them. Every one conceives the propositions of Euclid before he has read the demonstration of their truth. In the same way we at once apprehend historical narratives whether they refer to the past or the present, provided they be but credible,—the institutions of nations, their legislators, their manners, &c.—such things I call conceivable and clear, although no mathematical demonstration of them can be given. I call inconceivable, on the contrary, all hieroglyphics to which no meaning can be attached, and such historical narratives as it is impossible to credit. It may be remarked, however, that there are many of these narratives where our method admits of critical investigation being called in with a view to discover the intention of the writer.

we here find it requisite to study the life and manners of the author, nor are we interested in knowing in what language he wrote, in what age he lived, to whom he addressed himself, &c.; neither do we see it necessary to inquire into the fortune of the books, nor their various readings, nor how nor by whose advice they were accepted as genuine. Saying so much of Euclid, the same is to be understood of all who have written of things appreciable in themselves; and so let us conclude that the meaning of Scripture on all matters of moral doctrine is easily and certainly to be ascertained from itself. For the principles of true piety are expressed in the most familiar words, inasmuch as they are common to all, as there is nothing more simple or more easy of apprehension, and as the conditions to salvation and true happiness consist in purity of life and peace of mind. Now, as we only entirely acquiesce in those things which we clearly understand, it follows most obviously that we can be perfectly certain of the meaning of Scripture in all things salutary and needful to conduct of life and peace of mind; wherefore there is no reason why we should be very anxious about the rest; for as this cannot, for the most part, be embraced by the reason and understanding, it is really more matter of curiosity than of importance.

And now I think I have exposed the true method of interpreting Scripture, and sufficiently explained my views of its value. I do not doubt but every one will see that this method requires nothing save natural light or understanding; for the nature and excellence of natural light consists especially in this, that it leads by legitimate deduction from things known or assumed as known to a knowledge of things obscure or unknown; nor is there any other concession which our method of inquiry demands. And although we admit that it does not suffice for coming to definite conclusions on everything that is contained in the Bible, this does not arise from any deficiency in the method itself, but from this, that the way which it points out as the right and safe one has never been regularly trodden by scholars; so that, with the lapse of time, it has become overgrown, entangled as it were, and almost impassable, a fact which I think sufficiently indicated by the difficulties I have myself pointed out to the course along it.

We have now to examine the opinions of those who differ from us in our view of the proper method of searching the Scriptures. And the first adverse opinions we shall touch upon are of those who maintain that natural light is of non-avail in interpreting Scripture; that for this end a supernatural illumination is imperative, the nature of which I must leave to their own explanation. I, at all events, can only conjecture that in terms more obscure than are in common use, they have been willing to confess with the rest of the world that they often doubted of the true meaning of many parts of Scripture; for if we attend to the explanations they offer, we find nothing supernatural about them, nothing indeed but mere conjectures. The explanations of the supernaturalists indeed are often found identical with those of the critics, who ingenuously avow that they have no guide but their natural understanding, and arrive at their conclusions by entirely human means, viz. long, painful, and laborious research. They who say that natural light does not suffice for this, speak unadvisedly; for the difficulty of interpreting Scripture arises in nowise from any deficiency of human capacity, as we have already shown, but wholly from the carelessness (I will not say malice) of mankind, who neglected the history of Scripture when they might have secured and verified it; and also from this, that all (unless I deceive myself) confess the supernatural light to be a divine gift, intrusted to the faithful only. The prophets and apostles, however, were wont to preach not to the faithful alone, but to infidels and impious persons also, who were nevertheless apt enough to understand the meaning of the words addressed to them: had it been otherwise the prophets and apostles would have reserved their teaching for infants and children, and not have addressed grown men endowed with reason; in vain would Moses have prescribed his laws, could they only have been understood by the faithful, who in fact require no law. They who have recourse to supernatural light for understanding the discourses of the prophets and apostles, plainly show themselves to be without natural human light; and I am therefore very far from conceding to such the possession of any supernatural and divine gift.

Maimonides, I must here admit, was of a very different opinion from mine; for he thought that every part of Scripture admitted of various and even contrary interpretations, and maintained that we could never be certain of the truth of any one of these, unless we knew that the particular part, interpreted as proposed, contained nothing which either did not entirely agree with reason, or which was seen to be completely repugnant to reason, for if the passage in its literal sense were found wholly repugnant to reason, although clearly enough expressed, he thought that the sentence required to be otherwise than literally interpreted. This idea he distinctly enunciates in the second book of his MORE NEBOUCHIM, where he says: "Know that we do not shrink from saying that the world existed from all eternity, because of the texts on Creation which are met with in Scripture. For the texts which teach that the world was created, are not more numerous than those which speak of God as corporeal; nor do we feel ourselves precluded from explaining the passages that speak of the *creation* of the world, even as we have explained those that refer to God as *corporeal* and shown him to be incorporeal; nay, it were perchance found much easier to explain the texts referring to creation, and to show the world eternal, than we found it, with the Scriptures before us, to remove the idea of corporealness from the blessed God. But I am moved by two reasons neither to believe in the eternity of the world, nor to seek to demonstrate its eternal existence. 1. Because it can be clearly demonstrated that God is incorporeal, and it is necessary to explain away all the passages whose literal sense is repugnant to this demonstration; for it is certain that they must admit of another explanation besides the literal one. But the eternity of the world admits of no demonstration, so that it is not requisite to force the Scriptures, and to explain them in conformity with an opinion, to the opposite of which, swayed by some particular reason, we might rather incline. 2. Secondly, because to believe that God is incorporeal is not repugnant to fundamental law, &c., whilst to believe that the world is eternal, in the sense understood by Aristotle, destroys the law from its foundation." Such are the words of Maimonides, and from them the consequence we have spoken of evidently follows: Had he satisfied himself from his reason that the world was eternal, he would not have shrunk from twisting and interpreting Scripture in such a way as at length to make it appear to teach the thing he thought. He would indeed have become perfectly certain that Scripture, although everywhere openly disclaiming any such conclusion, intended to teach the eternity of the world; and so he would have remained uncertain of the true meaning of Scripture, however clearly expressed, so long as he remained in doubt of the truth of a fact, or had not made up his mind on the subject. For so long as the truth of a thing is not ascertained, so long do we remain ignorant as to whether the thing agrees with or is repugnant to reason; and consequently also we do not know whether the literal sense be verily true or false. Could such an opinion be shown to be well founded, I should concede unreservedly that we needed another than our natural light for the interpretation of Scripture. For of all that is found in Scripture almost nothing can be deduced from principles acknowledged by natural light (as we have already shown). The truth of the things there set forth could not therefore be ascertained by the light of nature, from which consequently nothing could be known of the true sense and meaning of Scripture. To determine this another light beyond that of nature would be required. Whence it would follow, if the opinion in question were correct, that the vulgar, as for the most part they either ignore demonstrations, or do not appreciate them, could know nothing of Scripture save from the explanations of critical philosophers. And were it once to be supposed that these could not err in their interpretations, they would constitute a new authority in the Church, a new order of priests or pontiffs, which the vulgar would be more disposed to laugh at than to respect. Now although our method of investigation requires a knowledge of the Hebrew language, a study to which the vulgar are not likely ever to betake themselves, still this is no valid objection to our plan; for the vulgar among the Jews and Gentiles, to whom the prophets and apostles of old addressed themselves, understood the language, and followed the meaning of their teachers, though they may not have appreciated the reasons of the things taught, which, according to the opinion of Maimonides, they ought also to have known in order to understand the preaching and writing of the prophets and apostles.

It does not follow therefore as a consequence of our method that the people at large should be obliged to acquiesce in the conclusions of interpreters; for I show a people conversant with the language of the prophets and apostles, which they could, therefore, interpret for themselves; but Maimonides cites no community conversant with the causes of things from whom a knowledge of Scripture meanings might be attained. And as to the commonalty of the present time, we have already shown that all things necessary to salvation, although their causes may be unknown, are nevertheless easily appreciated in every language, they being of sufficiently common and familiar import. And here, though it may not be the case when causes are in question, the vulgar are competent and sufficient judges. In other respects—in matters not bearing upon life and conversation—the vulgar and the learned are on the same level.

But this opinion of Maimonides appears to require some further investigation. First, he supposes that the prophets agreed among themselves on all subjects, and that they were consummate philosophers and theologians, for he will have it that their conclusions are always drawn from the truth of things absolutely, an idea which we have shown in our second chapter to be without any foundation in fact. Next, he supposes that the sense of Scripture cannot be learned from Scripture itself, for the absolute truth of things is not apparent from Scripture, inasmuch as Scripture demonstrates nothing, neither does it teach the things of which it speaks by definitions and references to their first causes; wherefore, according to Maimonides, neither could its true meaning be ascertained from itself, nor were this even to be sought for in the text. But that these notions are erroneous appears also from the matter of our present chapter, in which we have shown both by reason and example that the sense of Scripture can not only be known from itself alone, but that it can be determined from no other source, when matters accessible to natural understanding are spoken of. Maimonides finally supposes that we are at liberty even to deny and explain away, or to twist and torture, the literal sense of the words of Scripture, although most obvious and express, into something else in consonance with our prejudices and preconceived opinions. Such licence, besides that it is diametrically opposed to all we have demonstrated in this chapter and elsewhere, must needs be seen by every one as equally rash and inadmissible. But were we even to grant Maimonides such excessive liberty of interpretation, wherein would it serve him? In nothing assuredly; for the matters that are not susceptible of demonstration, and that form the greater bulk of the Scriptures, could not be investigated satisfactorily on such grounds as he proposes, nor could they be explained and interpreted by such rules as he lays down. By pursuing our own plan, on the contrary, we find that we are able to explain and confidently to discuss many things that are obscure, as has been already proven, both on the ground of reason and of fact; whilst those parts that are by their nature easily intelligible are at once interpreted from the context alone. The method proposed by Maimonides therefore is obviously useless; and when we see that by its means all the certainty of the meaning of Scripture which the mere reading of the text affords, and which indeed follows from any other mode of interpretation, disappears, it is seen to be totally inadmissible. We therefore denounce the method which Maimonides proposes for the interpretation of Scripture as useless, noxious, and absurd.

With regard to the traditional interpretation of the Pharisees, we have already said that it is not in harmony with itself; and of the Roman pontifical system, I say, it requires clearer evidence for its authority than any I can discover. I therefore reject it for this and no other reason. For if the Scriptures now present to us the same matters with the same certainty as they did formerly to the Jewish high priests, I should not be disturbed by the fact that among the Roman pontiffs there had been found more than one heretical and impious man; because we know that among the Jewish high priests of old heretical and impious men were also encountered, men who obtained the office of high priest by sinister means, in spite of which they were nevertheless invested by the command of Scripture itself with the supreme power of construing the law (vide Exodus xvii. 11, 12, and xxxiii. 10, and Malachi ii. 8). But as the Roman pontiff can show no such authority for the right he assumes, his power is questionable; and lest any one, misled by the example of the Hebrew high priest, should think that the Roman Catholic religion also required a pontiff, it is to be noted that the laws of Moses were the laws of the country, the ground of public right, and necessarily required some public authority for their preservation; for had every one been at liberty to interpret the laws of the State in his own arbitrary way, there would soon have been no true republic; its fabric would have been dissolved, and public right converted into private right. But it is altogether different with regard to religion; for inasmuch as it consists much less in outward acts than in simplicity and purity of soul, it has nothing whatever to do with public right and power. Purity and probity of soul are founded on no power of law, on no public authority:—no one can be compelled by law or constraint to follow the path of true happiness. To pursue this, pious advice, friendly and fraternal counsel, good education, and, above all, a well-balanced and liberal mind, are indispensable. Since therefore the indefeasible right of thinking independently on all subjects, even on religion, belongs to every one, and as it is impossible to conceive any reasonable man divesting himself of this right, the full and perfect title and authority to judge religion independently, and consequently to explain and interpret Scripture for himself, belongs of right to every man. The privilege of administering the laws and pronouncing final judgments on public affairs is lodged with the magistrate, for no other reason than that it is the public right of which he is the guardian and expounder; and in like manner is the right of judging and interpreting religion lodged with each individual man, because it is his own peculiar and private business. There is a great deal wanting therefore to satisfy us, when from the authority of the Jewish high priest to interpret the laws of his country, it is inferred that the Roman pontiff is also by right possessed of authority to interpret the Christian religion to the whole world. On the contrary, we much more readily arrive at the conclusion, from the nature of religion, that every one can best do this for himself. And herein we believe that we see another proof of the excellence of the method we have proposed for arriving at a knowledge of the Scriptures. For assuming as we do that the supreme right to interpret the Bible belongs to every one individually, we conclude that the standard of interpretation should be nothing but the natural light or understanding which is common to all, and not any supernatural light, nor any extrinsic authority; for the task ought not to be so difficult as only to be practicable by the most learned philosophers, but should be found within the scope of the common genius and capacity of mankind, as it is by the plan which we have proposed; for we have seen that the difficulties which still attach to it are owing to the carelessness of men, and do in nowise belong to the nature of the subject itself.

CHAPTER VIII.

OF THE PENTATEUCH, AND THE BOOKS OF JOSHUA, JUDGES, RUTH, SAMUEL, AND KINGS. THESE BOOKS ARE NOT AUTOGRAPHS. ARE THEY THE WORK OF ONE OR OF SEVERAL WRITERS? AND IF OF ONE, WHO WAS HE?

In the preceding chapter we have treated of the grounds or principles on which a knowledge of the Scriptures should be based, and have shown that a faithful history of their contents must underlie everything else. But this, although of prime necessity, the ancients almost entirely neglected; or if they wrote anything on the subject, it has perished in the lapse of time. The greater part of the grounds or first principles of historical Scripture knowledge is therefore wanting or lost to us; a misfortune that might have been endured, had later writers confined themselves within proper bounds, transmitted the little they had received or discovered with good faith to their successors, and abstained from coining novelties out of their own brains, whereby it has come to pass that the history of the Hebrew Scriptures is not only defective, but is so full of errors that it is now impossible to reconstruct it free from all imperfection. It is within the scope of my undertaking, however, to seek to amend the fundamentals of Scripture knowledge, and not to rest content with getting rid of a few of the more common prejudices of theologians. I only fear that I attempt this task at too late a date, for things have now gone so far that men will not readily suffer themselves to be corrected in their conclusions, and especially persist in hugging pertinaciously whatsoever has come down to them in the name of religion. Save with a very few, therefore, there seems little room left for reason to enter, so completely has prejudice blinded the mind and understanding of the mass of mankind. I shall nevertheless try to do something in this direction, not turning my back upon the labour, since there is no apparent reason for despairing of a certain measure of success. And that I may proceed regularly, I shall begin with the prejudices commonly entertained in regard to the writers of the sacred books, and speak first of the author of the Pentateuch.

Moses is believed by almost every one to be the author of the Pentateuch, i. e. of the Books of Genesis, Exodus, Leviticus, Numbers, and Deuteronomy. So pertinaciously did the Pharisees cling to this belief, that they held every one a heretic who ventured to think otherwise, and this is the reason why Aben Ezra, a man of a liberal spirit and no mean erudition, and who, so far as my reading extends, was the first to animadvert upon this prejudice, has not thought fit to open his mind freely on the matter, but only to hint at it in words so obscure, as to be generally unintelligible. These, however, I for my part shall not fear to render plain by placing the whole subject in the broadest light. The words of Aben Ezra, which occur in his commentary on Deuteronomy, are these:—
"Beyond Jordan * * * provided thou understandest the mystery of the Twelve; * * also that Moses wrote the Law whilst the Canaanites were in the land, * * * it will be revealed on the mountain of God. * * * Then also behold his bed, his bed of iron; * * then knowest thou the truth."
Now in these few and disjointed words does Aben Ezra indicate his opinion that it was not Moses who wrote the Pentateuch, but some other person who lived long after him; and lastly, that the book which Moses wrote was not any one we now have under his name, but another. To shadow forth these particulars, Aben Ezra in the above passage shows,—First, that the preface to Deuteronomy could not have been

written by Moses, inasmuch as he did not pass the Jordan. 2nd, He gives us to know that the book written by Moses was inscribed on the circle of a single altar (Deut. xxvii. and Joshua viii. 37, &c.), which, according to the accounts of the Rabbins, was composed of not more than twelve stones; whence it follows that the book of Moses was much less extensive than the Pentateuch; and this I interpret as the meaning of our author when he speaks of the mysterious twelve, unless perchance he refers to the twelve maledictions, which are contained in the chapter of Deuteronomy quoted, and which he may have opined were not contained in the Book of the Law, inasmuch as the Levites, besides the words of the law, are ordered by Moses regularly to recite these curses on disobedience, in order that the people might be reminded of and better bound by their oaths to observe the commandments of the Lord. Or it is possible that Aben Ezra may have referred to the last chapter of Deuteronomy, which consists of twelve verses exactly, and relates the death of Moses. But I need not pursue this point further. 3rd, Our author's next clause consists of the words of Deuteronomy (xxxi. 9), "And Moses wrote this law, and delivered it," &c., words which cannot be from Moses himself, but are plainly those of another writer, giving an account of the life and writings of the great Hebrew prophet. 4th, Our author in his third clause refers to Genesis xii. 6, where the historian relating how Abraham came into the land of Canaan, adds,—" And the Canaanite was then in the land," the "*then,*" *at that time,* plainly excludes the time when the narrative was written; whereby we see that the history must have been composed after the death of Moses, and when the Canaanites had been driven from their country and no longer possessed the land; only under such a state of things could such language have been used. Aben Ezra in his comment upon the passage, "The Canaanite was then in the land," remarks,— "It would appear that Canaan, the grandson of Noah, took the land then possessed by his tribe the Canaanites, from some other occupant; but if this were not so, there must then be a mystery concealed in the matter, and he who divines what this is, had better keep silence." The meaning is, that if Canaan invaded the country, the sense requires us to read, —"The Canaanite was *then* in the land," as referring to a former state of things, when it was inhabited by another tribe or nation. But if Canaan was the first who colonized the country (as it seems to follow from Genesis x. that he was), then the text excludes the present time, i. e. the time of the writer, which consequently could not have been that of Moses, in whose days the Canaanites possessed the land; and this is the mystery about which Aben Ezra recommends silence to be kept. 5th, Aben Ezra observes that in Genesis xxii. 14, a mountain in the land of Moriah is called the Mount of the Lord, a title however which it had not till after it was devoted to the building of the temple. But the choice of Mt Moriah for this purpose had not been made in the time of Moses, who, instead of presuming to select a spot for this purpose, prophesies that God would one day choose a place for himself, which should be called by the name of the Lord.* 6th, Our author intimates that in chapter iii. of Deuteronomy we find these words, in connection with the history of Og, King of Bashan,—" For only Og, King of Bashan, remained of the remnant of the giants; behold, his bedstead was a bedstead of iron; is it not in Rabbath of the children of Ammon? nine cubits was the length thereof, and four cubits the breadth of it, after the cubit of a man." The parenthesis here clearly proves that he who wrote this portion of Scripture lived long, very long after Moses, for such a style of narrative belongs only to one who speaks of things of the most remote antiquity, and who uses remnants of things past as testimonies to the accuracy of his narrative. In all likelihood this iron bed of Og, King of Bashan, was only discovered in the time of David, who subdued the city of

* It is not Abraham, but the narrator, who gives the name of Mountain of God to Mount Moriah. For it is said in the passage, that the place which is called at this time, " Revelation shall be made on the Mountain of God," was named by Abraham, " God shall advise."

Rabbah, as we find it narrated in the Second Book of Samuel (xii. 30). But it is not in this place only that we discover the writer of the Pentateuch interpolating the words of Moses, for he says a little further on (Deut. iii. 14),—"Jair the son of Manasseh took all the country of Argob unto the coasts of Geshuri and Maachathi, and called them after his own name, Bashan-havoth-jair, unto this day." These words, I say, are added by the historian to explain the words of Moses which he had just given. "And the rest of Gilead, and all Bashan being the kingdom of Og, gave I unto the half-tribe of Manasseh, all the region of Argob with all Bashan, which was called the land of giants." The Jews, contemporaries of this writer, were aware without doubt which were the towns of Jair, of the tribe of Judah, but they did not know the name of the jurisdiction of Argob, nor of the land of giants, whereby he was forced to tell them what the places were which in former ages had been so entitled, and at the same time to give a reason why they were designated by the name of Jair, of the tribe of Judah, and not of Manasseh (vide Chronicles ii. 21, 22). Thus do we explain the enigmatical passage of Aben Ezra, and quote the texts of the Pentateuch which support our interpretation of its meaning.

But Aben Ezra has neither noticed all nor even the principal passages of those books, which, as of still greater importance, require attention from us. For example and firstly: The writer of the books of the Pentateuch not only continually speaks of Moses in the third person, but moreover testifies to many things concerning him. Thus he uses such phrases as these, "God said to Moses;" "God spake with Moses face to face;" "Moses was the meekest of men" (Numb. xii. 3); "Moses was wroth against the leaders of the host" (Ib. xiv. 14); "Moses a divine man" (Deut. xxxiii. 1); "And Moses, the servant of God, died; never was there a prophet in Israel like unto Moses." In Deuteronomy, on the contrary, where Moses himself explains the law to the people he speaks and relates his deeds in the first person; thus he says, "God spake to me" (Deut. ii. 1, 17, &c.); "I prayed to God," &c. It is only by and by, towards the end of the book, that the historian, after having given the words of Moses, proceeds with his narrative in the third person,— how Moses delivered such and such a law (which he has just explained) to the people; how he had admonished them; and how at length his life had come to an end. All of which things, viz. manner of speaking, testimony, and entire context, clearly indicate that these books were not written by Moses but by another. 2. It is also to be particularly observed that in this history it is not only narrated how Moses died and was buried, and how the Jews mourned for him for thirty days, but over and above all this we have a comparison instituted between him and all the prophets who lived after him, "Never was there a prophet in Israel," we are informed, "like unto Moses, whom God knew face to face." Now, testimony such as this could not be delivered by Moses of himself; nor yet by any one who followed him closely, but necessarily by some person who lived long ages after him; a view that is confirmed by the tense in which the historian speaks, which is always the preter-past—" never was there," "never did there exist a prophet," &c. And then when mention is made of the place of his sepulture, we are told in the present tense that "no one *knows*, not even unto this day." 3. It is further to be remarked that certain places are mentioned by names which they did not bear in the time of Moses, but by others which they acquired subsequently; as, for example, where Abraham pursued the enemy even to *Dan* (Gen. xiv. 14), a name which the city did not obtain till long after the death of Joshua (Judges xviii. 29). 4. The historical narrative is sometimes carried on beyond the time of Moses. Thus, in Exodus we learn that the children of Israel were fed with manna for 40 years, until they came to peopled territory, until they reached the borders of the land of Canaan; that is, until the time of which we read in the Book of Joshua (v. 12), and also in that of Genesis (xxxvi. 31), in which we find these words, "These are the kings who ruled in Edom before a king reigned over the children of

Israel." Here the historian undoubtedly informs us that the Idumeans were ruled by kings before David subdued them, and established governors over the country* (vide 2 Samuel viii. 14).

From the whole of this it is as clear as the noonday light that the Pentateuch was not written by Moses, but by one who lived many ages after him. And then when we inquire for the books which Moses himself wrote, as they are referred to in the Pentateuch, we make sure from these references that they were other than any of the five books now generally ascribed to him. 1st, it is known from Exodus (xvii. 14) that Moses by God's command wrote "the war against the Amalekites;" where or in what book however we do not learn from the chapter just quoted; but in Numbers (xxi. 12) we find a book quoted which is entitled "The wars of God," in which, without doubt, was comprised the history of this war against the Amalekites; and, further, the account of all those encampments which we are told in Numbers (xxxiii. 2) Moses himself described. We have intimations of another of Moses' books in Exodus (xxiv. 4, 7), entitled, "The book of the Agreement," which he read to the Israelites when they first entered upon their covenant with God. But this book or epistle could have contained little more than the commandments or laws of God, which are given in the Book of Exodus (xx. 22, to xxiv.), as no one will deny, who reads the passages referred to above with impartiality and any soundness of judgment; for there we find it stated that Moses, as soon

---

* From this time the Idumeans ceased to have kings until the reign of Jeroboam, during which they separated from the Jewish Empire (2 Kings viii. 20). Their government was administered during this period by Jewish governors, who stood to them in stead of their ancient kings; this is why the governor of Idumea is entitled King in Scripture (2 Kings viii. 9).

Here the question arises as to when the last king of Idumea began to reign; was it before the accession of Saul? or is the question in this chapter of Genesis of the Idumean kings before the conquest of the nation? on this point there is reasonable room for doubt; but as to those who would include Moses in the list of Hebrew kings, Moses who established an entirely sacred empire, altogether different from a monarchical government, I should say that they cannot intend such a proposition to be taken seriously.

as he saw the minds of the people suitably disposed for the alliance with God, proceeded to commit to writing the discourses and the laws which God had imparted to him, and then, having first performed certain ceremonies, with the dawn of day he read the conditions of the compact about to be made in presence of the whole assembly of the people, who doubtless understood, as with one accord they assented to them. From the shortness of the time employed in reading, then, as well as from the nature of the compact to be concluded, it follows that the Book of the Agreement could have contained little beyond what has just been stated. It is certain, lastly, that in the fortieth year after the Exodus from Egypt, Moses explained all the laws he had propounded (Deut. i. 5), and bound the people anew to their observance (Ib. xxix. 14), and finally that he wrote a book which contained commentaries on the law; and this new compact (Deut. xxxi. 9) it was which was entitled, "The book of the Law of God." This book Joshua subsequently augmented with an account of another covenant by which in his day the people bound themselves again, and for the third time, to Jehovah (vide Josh. xxiv. 25, 26).

But, as we have no book extant containing the exposition of the law and second covenant of Moses, or the same book with the covenant of Joshua appended, it must needs be acknowledged that the book has perished; or we must consent to talk foolishly with the Chaldean paraphrast Jonathan, and torture the words of Scripture into the shape we desire; this Jonathan, indeed, is one of those who would rather corrupt the text of Holy Writ than confess his ignorance; for he translates the Hebrew words which signify "And Joshua wrote these words in the Book of the Law of God" into Chaldean, which interpreted read thus, "And Joshua wrote these words and preserved them with the book of the law of God." What shall be done with those who see nothing in Holy Writ but what they wish? And what is this but to ignore Scripture and forge a new and a vain thing? We for our part conclude that this Book of the Law of God, which

Moses wrote, was not the Pentateuch, but another book altogether, which the author of the Pentateuch introduced in what seemed to be its proper place in his own compendious work;—a conclusion that is borne out by everything that precedes, as it will also be by all that is to follow. Thus, when it is related in the place of Deuteronomy just cited, that "Moses wrote a book," the historian adds that Moses delivered it to the priests, and commanded them besides that they should read it at certain stated times to the whole people; a circumstance of itself sufficient to prove that the book in question was much less bulky than the Pentateuch; for it could be gone through at one meeting, so as to be understood by all the people. Nor is this to be passed by unnoticed, that of all the books which Moses wrote he especially commanded this one of the second covenant, and the song (which he wrote subsequently for the whole people to learn by heart), to be religiously preserved and guarded. The first covenant was held to bind none but those who were actually present; the second was to be esteemed imperative upon all, and even upon posterity (vide Deut. xxix. 14, 15); wherefore he ordered the book of this second covenant to be religiously preserved for future ages, for whom the song or canticle is also especially designed. Since, therefore, it is not ascertained that Moses wrote any other than the books above referred to, and as he himself directed no other book but that on the law with the canticle to be religiously preserved for the sake of posterity, and, lastly, as there are many things in the Pentateuch which could not possibly have been written by Moses, it follows that no one in his right mind can uphold Moses as the author of the Pentateuch. He who should do so would have to contravene every principle of right reason.

But here some one perchance may ask, Whether Moses, besides these books, did not commit the laws to writing when they were first revealed to him? that is to say, whether for the long period of 40 years he wrote down none of the laws he bore about with him in his memory, except those few which I have said were contained in the original covenant? To these questions I reply, that although I admit it to be consonant with reason to believe that Moses when he received the laws also wrote them down, I deny nevertheless that we are therefore at liberty to affirm that he did so; for we have shown above, that we are to take nothing for granted on such subjects save and except that only which meets us in Scripture, or which by legitimate inference can be deduced from its teaching, but not from anything else, though this may seem in harmony with the soundest reason. Add to this, that even reason does not force us to come to such a conclusion. For the council perchance communicated the edicts of Moses to the people in writings which the historian afterwards gathered together, and inserted in due order in the life of Moses. So much for the five books ascribed to Moses; let us therefore proceed to examine the remaining books we have indicated.

The Book of Joshua is readily shown on similar grounds not to be his autograph, but certainly the production of another, who bears witness concerning him, viz. that his fame extended over all the earth (vide vii. 1); that he omitted nothing of all that Moses commanded (viii. 35, xi. 15); that he grew old, and called together a general assembly of the people of Israel; and that he died. Some particulars are even added of events that happened after the death of Joshua. We are told, for instance, that the Israelites continued to worship God so long as the old men who had known Joshua lived (xxiv.). In the 16th chapter we are informed that " they " (Ephraim and Manasseh) " drove not out the Canaanites that dwelt in Gezer; but the Canaanites dwell among the Ephraimites unto this day, and serve under tribute." This is the same fact which is related in the Book of Judges (i.), and the expression " unto this day " also shows that the writer is speaking of matters that had happened long ago. The same thing may assuredly be said of the text of chapter xv., where we have an account of the sons of Judah (ver. 15), and the history of Caleb (ver. 14). The circumstance of the two tribes and a half who built an altar beyond Jordan seems also to have happened after the death of Joshua (vide xxii. 10, *et seq.*), inasmuch as there is no mention made of Joshua throughout the transaction: the people alone deliberate about carrying on the war, send ambassadors, expect the answer to be brought back by them, and finally approve of it. To conclude: from the 10th chapter (ver. 14) it follows unquestionably that the Book of Joshua was written many ages after the death of its reputed author, for here we are informed that "there was no day like that, before it or after it" (when the sun and moon stood still at the command of Joshua), "that the Lord hearkened* unto the voice of a man." If Joshua ever wrote any book, therefore, it must have been that which is referred to immediately before the passage just quoted (ver. 13), under the title of the Book of Jasher [and this is lost to us].

As to the Book of Judges, I do not think that any person of sane mind could persuade himself that it was written by the Judges of Israel themselves; the Epilogue, indeed, of the whole history, which we have in the 2nd chapter, shows clearly that it was written by one person only. Then, as this writer often reminds his reader that "in those days there was no king in Israel," there can be no doubt of the book having been composed subsequently to the times when the Jews were ruled by kings.

The Books of Samuel need not detain us, when we find the history carried on long after his death. I only add that the books were certainly written long after the age of Samuel; for in the First Book (ix. 9), the writer admonishes us parenthetically that, "Beforetime in Israel, when a man went to inquire of God, thus he spake, Come, let us go to the seer: for he that is now called a Prophet was beforetime called a Seer."

Upon the Book of Kings still less need be said, as out of themselves we learn that they were composed from the books

---

* In Spinoza's version the word is *obeyed*—and he notes it particularly. —*Ed.*

of the doings of Solomon (xi. 5), the Chronicles of the Kings of Judah (Ib. xiv. 19, 29), and the Chronicles of the Kings of Israel.

Let us conclude, therefore, that all the books which we have just passed under review are apographs — works written ages after the things they relate had passed away. And when we regard the argument and connection of these books severally, we readily gather that they were all written by one and the same person, who had the purpose of compiling a system of Jewish antiquities, from the origin of the nation to the first destruction of the city of Jerusalem. The several books are so connected one with another, that from this alone we discover that they comprise the continuous narrative of a single historian. Thus, as soon as he ends the life of Moses he passes to the history of Joshua—"And it came to pass when Moses, the servant of the Lord, was dead, that God said to Joshua," &c. Joshua dead, again, by the same transition and conjunction, the historian begins with the Judges,—"And it came to pass, after Joshua was dead, that the children of Israel required of God," &c. With this book, as a kind of appendix, the short book of Ruth is connected thus, "And it came to pass in those days, when the Judges judged in Israel, that there was a famine in the land," &c. In like manner, the First Book of Samuel ended, the writer proceeds to the Second Book; but the history of King David not being concluded there, he adds on the First Book of Kings, and the narrative requiring more space still, the Second Book. The context, finally, and the order of the histories, also indicate that they are all the work of one writer, who commences his task with a certain fixed and definite scope, beginning with an account of the origin of the Hebrew nation, and next describing in regular sequence the times and occasions on which Moses announced the law and prophesied to the Jews. Next he tells how, led on by the predictions of Moses, they invaded the Promised Land (Deut. vii.); how, when they had conquered this, they forsook the laws of Jehovah (Deut.

xxxi. 16), whence many sore disasters followed (Ib. ver. 17), how they next desired to choose themselves a king (Ib. xvii. 14), who, as he observed or neglected the law, brought prosperity or disaster on the people (Ib. xxviii. 36, *et seq.*), until he reaches the conclusion,—the destruction of the Jewish Empire, as it had been foretold by Moses. On other subjects which have nothing to do with the establishment of the law, the writer either keeps silence altogether, or he refers the reader to other historians. The whole of these books, therefore, lead to one end, viz. to enforce the sayings and edicts of Moses, and, from the course of events, to demonstrate their sacredness. From these three points taken together, then, viz. the unity and simplicity of the argument of all the books, their connection or sequence, and their apographic character, they having been written many ages after the events they record, we conclude, as has just been said, that they were all written by one historiographer. Who this was, however, cannot be so readily shown, although from certain concurring, and by no means trifling, circumstances, I am led to suspect that Ezra was the man. I say I am led to Ezra as the writer. Thus, when the historian, whom we now know to have been alone in the work, has brought his narrative down to the time when Jehoiachim recovered his liberty, he adds that he himself had sat at the king's table all his life, but whether this were the table of Jehoiachim or of the son of Nebuchadnezzar is not certain, for the sense of the passage is doubtful. Whichever it was, it follows nevertheless that the books in question could have been written by no one before Ezra. Now Scripture bears testimony to no one but Ezra, who flourished at this time, whose studies were likely to have led him to investigate and illustrate the law of God, and who was a writer skilled, as we are informed Ezra was, in the law of Moses (vide Ezra vii. 6, 10, 11). I cannot, therefore, conceive any one but Ezra to have been the writer of these books. In the testimony to the accomplishments of Ezra just referred to, we see that he not only gave his mind to the study of the laws of God, but that he also illustrated or commented on them; and in Nehemiah (viii. 9) we find these words, "They read the annotated book of the law of God, and gave their mind to it, and understood the Scripture."* Now, as the whole or the greater part of the law of Moses is comprised in the Book of Deuteronomy, and much additional matter is there interpolated with a view to its better comprehension, I conjecture that the Book of Deuteronomy is the identical book of the law of God, written fairly out, annotated, illustrated, and explained by Ezra, which was then read. But as there are many things interpolated in the Book of Deuteronomy by way of parentheses, for the better understanding of the text, I shall give two instances of the sort, with the commentary of Aben Ezra upon them. Thus, in chapter ii. verse 12, we find these words, "The Horites dwelt in Seir beforetime; but the children of Esau drave them out, and destroyed them out of sight, and dwelt in their stead, as Israel did in the land of his inheritance which God gave him." This passage is inserted as an explanation of the earlier verses of the same chapter, where Israel, after compassing Mount Seir many days, is instructed to turn northward, and to pass the territories of their brethren, the children of Esau, then dwelling in Seir, the district which had fallen to them by lot as an heritage, but of which the children of Esau had only obtained possession by invading it, and expelling the Horites who dwelt in the land before them; exactly as the Israelites after the death of Moses had fallen upon and exterminated the Canaanites, and then taken possession of their lands. The words of Moses are also interpolated parenthetically in verses 6, 7, 8, and 9, of the 10th chapter. Every one must see that the 8th verse, which begins thus, "At that time the Lord separ-

* The word *annotated*, or interpreted, is omitted in the English version. Spinoza's version seems much the better of the two. The English is as follows: "So they read in the book of the law of God distinctly, and gave the sense, and caused them to understand the reading."—*Ed.*

ated the tribes of Levi, to bear the ark," &c. &c., and ends with these words, "unto this day," must necessarily refer to verse 5, and not to the death of Aaron, which appears to be mentioned for no other reason than that Moses, in the history of the golden calf which the people worshipped, had said (vide ix. 20) that he had prayed to God for Aaron. He then proceeds to explain that God, at the time Moses speaks of, elected the tribe of Levi to himself, that he might show the reason of the election, and why the Levites were called to no share of the inheritance; and this done, he goes on with the thread of his narrative in the words of Moses. Add to what precedes, the preface of the book, and the places where Moses is mentioned in the third person, besides numerous passages which cannot now be detected by us, but which doubtless were added in order that the men of the writer's time might the more readily understand the narrative, I say that had we the Book of the Law as Moses wrote it, I do not doubt but we should find many discrepancies, both in the expressions, in the order, and in the reasons for the commandments. For when I compare the decalogue of the Book of Deuteronomy with that of Exodus (where the history of the decalogue is expressly given) I find discrepancy between the two, in these important particulars,—The fourth commandment is not only delivered differently, but is, further, much more prolix in its details; and, more important still, the reasons assigned for the commandment differ *toto cœlo* from those given in Exodus; lastly, the order in which the tenth commandment is here explained is also different from that observed in Exodus. I am of opinion, therefore, that all this, as well as much more in other places, is the work of Ezra, because he laid himself out to explain the law of God to the men of his own time. I am further of opinion that the Book of Deuteronomy, as it has come down to us, is Moses' Book of the Law of God, illustrated and explained by Ezra. I am, moreover, disposed to conclude that this was the first book written by Ezra of all that came from his hand; and for this reason,—that it contains the laws of the country, which are the most requisite to be known by the people; and also because this book is not connected with the one which precedes it by any conjunction, as all the others are with their antecedents, as has been shown. Deuteronomy, on the contrary, begins abruptly thus, " These be the words which Moses spake," &c. Having achieved this first work, the purpose of which was to make a knowledge of the laws accessible to the people, I believe that Ezra then set about the task of narrating the entire history of the Hebrew nation, from the creation of the world to the destruction of Jerusalem, in which larger undertaking he inserted this Book of Deuteronomy in its proper place. Perhaps he was led to call the first five books of his history by the name of Moses, because in them especially are comprised the incidents in the life of the great prophet: the leading personage gives his name to the narrative. For the same reason the sixth book is entitled the Book of Joshua, the deeds of this leader forming its principal burden; the seventh is the Book of Judges, the eighth the Book of Ruth, the ninth and tenth of Samuel, and, lastly, the eleventh and twelfth of Kings, though neither Joshua, the Judges of Israel, Ruth, Samuel, or the Kings, had any part in the composition of the books that pass by their names. But whether Ezra put the finishing hand to his work, and completed it as he may have wished, is matter of so much interest that we shall discuss the subject in the next chapter.

Surely the following remarkable passages from 2 Esdras (xiv. 20, *et seq.*) ought to be quoted here. Esdras speaks, " Behold, Lord, I will go as thou hast commanded me, and reprove the people which are present, but they that shall be born afterward, who shall admonish them? The world is set in darkness, and they that dwell therein are without light; *for thy law is burnt, therefore no man knoweth the things that are done of thee.* But if I have found grace before thee, send the Holy Ghost into me, and *I shall write all that hath been done in the world since the beginning, which were written in thy law,* that men may find thy path. And he answered me, saying, Go, &c., and prepare me many box trees [tablets for writing], and take with thee five which are ready to write swiftly; and I shall light a candle of understanding in thine heart, which shall not be put out till the things be performed which thou shalt begin to write. * * * And my mouth was opened, and shut no more. The Highest gave understanding to the five men, and they wrote the wonderful visions of the night that were told," &c. The Ezra of the Canon and the Esdras of the Apocrypha are certainly one person. The narratives in the books under these names accord in the main.—*Ed.*

CHAPTER IX.

OF THE SAME BOOKS OF THE OLD TESTAMENT. DID EZRA PUT THE FINISHING HAND TO HIS WORK? ARE THE MARGINAL ANNOTATIONS OF THE HEBREW CODICES TO BE CONSIDERED AS VARIORUM READINGS OF THE TEXT?

How much the preceding disquisition on the actual writer of the first twelve books of the Hebrew Scriptures aids us in understanding them appears sufficiently from the passages quoted in support of the views advanced. Without some such guide as we have attempted to supply, indeed, these books must remain an enigma to every one.

But, besides the writer, there remain many other things in the books themselves which demand animadversion, although superstition would persuade us to avert our eyes from too curiously scrutinizing their contents. Among the number of interesting subjects of inquiry is the one wherefore Ezra—whom I shall continue to speak of as the writer or compiler of the earlier books of Scripture, until another is discovered with better pretensions to the authorship—did not, as he certainly did not, put the finishing hand to the work he undertook? Ezra did little, in fact, but gather materials from other earlier writers, and then, without much examination or any care for arrangement, set down the results of his labours in a simple style; and it is in this inartificial and undigested state that the narrative compiled by him has been transmitted to posterity. What cause prevented Ezra from revising his work I am at a loss to conjecture, unless perchance it were a sudden or premature death. But that the matter is as I have stated it seems abundantly demonstrated by the few fragments of the earlier Hebrew historians that have come down to us. For the history of Hiskiah, from the 17th verse of chapter xviii. of the Second Book of Kings onwards, is derived from the narrative of Isaiah; and the whole of what is said about Hiskiah in Isaiah, is contained in the Chronicles of the Kings of Judah, the same incidents being found narrated, with trifling exceptions, in the same words in both. From any diversity here, however, nothing more can be inferred than that there were different versions extant of the narrative of Isaiah, unless, indeed, it be imagined that there is some mystery lurking under the fact of the identity mentioned. Again, the last chapter of the Second Book of Chronicles is comprised in the last chapter of Jeremiah; and, further, the 7th chapter of the Second Book of Samuel is contained in the 17th chapter of the First Book of Chronicles; but the words in several places are encountered so singularly altered, as to make it evidently appear that these two chapters were derived from two different copies of the history of Nathan. Lastly, the genealogy of the Kings of Idumea which we have in the 36th chapter of Genesis is met with in the very same words in the 1st chapter of the First Book of Chronicles, although it is agreed that the author of this book derived the particulars he narrates from other historical records, and not from any of the twelve books which we here ascribe to Ezra. There is no reason to doubt, therefore, that if we had those historical records, the fact would be immediately ascertained to be as represented; but these ancient documents having all perished, we have no resource but critically to study the histories that have come down to us, to scrutinize their order and connection, the various repetitions in their course, and, finally, the discrepancies in the reckonings of years, in order that we may form a judgment of what remains.

We shall now, therefore, proceed to consider the chief of these matters, beginning with the account of Judah and Tamar, which the historian in the 38th chapter of the Book of Genesis enters upon in these terms: "Now it came to pass at that time, that Judah went down from his brethren." "At that time" necessarily here refers to some other time than that in which the historian is immediately speaking; but of the precise time referred to we have no means of judging.* For from the time when Joseph was carried into Egypt to that when the Patriarch Jacob also proceeded thither with the whole of his family, we can reckon no more than 22 years; for Joseph, when he was sold by his brethren, was 17 years of age, and when released from prison by order of Pharaoh he was 30; if to the difference between these two numbers, 13, we add the seven years of plenty and the two years of dearth, we have 22 years. But in this space of time no one can conceive that so many events could have happened as we find recorded; viz. that Judah begat three children one after another by one wife, whom he had just then espoused; the eldest born of whom, when his age permitted, took Tamar to wife; but he dying, a second brother espoused the widow; and he also dying, Judah himself had knowledge of Tamar, and by her had twins, one of whom, within the interval mentioned, married and had children. Such a series of events is plainly impossible within the time specified in Genesis, and must therefore have occurred at some other time; Ezra, our historian, however, gave the story of Judah

---

* That this passage can only refer to the time when Joseph was sold by his brethren is made evident by the context, but the same thing may be concluded from the age of Judah, who was then 22 years old at the most, taking as basis for the calculation the history of him which has just been given. From chap. xxix. of Genesis, last verse, it appears that Judah was born in the 10th year of Jacob's servitude to Laban, and Joseph in the 14th year. Now we know that Joseph was 17 years old when he was sold by his brothers, so that Judah was not more than 21. They, therefore, who pretend that the long absence of Judah from the house of his father occurred before the sale of Joseph try to deceive themselves, and their anxiety for the Inspiration of Scripture only brings it into question.

and his sons and Tamar, as he found it, without examining the matter very particularly, or making sure that it accurately fitted in with the other circumstances with which it was connected. But this is not the only tale that is derived from different records or traditions; the entire history of Jacob and Joseph appears to be similarly derived, so little do the several parts of it agree with one another. Thus, in the 47th chapter of Genesis it is recorded that Jacob, when first presented by Joseph, his son, to Pharaoh, was 130 years old; from which if 22 be taken, which he passed in sorrow on account of the loss of Joseph, and 17 for Joseph's age when he was sold by his brethren, and, lastly, seven which he served for Rachel, Jacob is found at a very advanced age, viz. 84, when he took Leah to wife; on the contrary, Dinah could scarcely have been seven when she was violated by Sechem; and Simeon and Levi, again, scarcely 12 and 11 when they ravaged a city and put all the inhabitants thereof to the sword.

But there is no occasion here to pass the whole of the Pentateuch under review; any one who but observes that in these five books precept and narrative are jumbled together without order, that there is no regard to time, and that one and the same story is often met with again and again, and occasionally with very important differences in the incidents, —whoever observes these things, I say, will certainly come to the conclusion that in the Pentateuch we have merely notes and collections to be examined at leisure, materials for history rather than the digested history itself. Nor is it only to the Pentateuch that these remarks apply; the seven books which remain, down to the destruction of Jerusalem, have the same character, and are made up or put together in the same way. Who can fail to see, for example, that from verse six of the 2nd chapter of Judges the writer is drawing from another record, in which the deeds of Joshua are also set forth, and from which the very words employed are probably derived? Our historian, after having in the last chapter of Joshua given an account of the death and burial of this great captain, and in the 1st chapter of Judges promised that he would next speak of what came to pass after Joshua's death, instead of doing so and going on with the thread of his story, connecting the incidents which he now begins to relate with those that had gone before, starts afresh, as it were, and repeats the tale of the death and burial of Joshua. In like manner are the 17th and 18th chapters of the First Book of Samuel taken from another record; in which a cause is assigned for David's frequenting the palace of Saul very different from the one mentioned in the 16th chapter of the same book; for we do not see that David went to Saul summoned to his presence on the recommendation of his servants (as we have it stated in the 16th chapter), but that David, having been casually sent by his father to his brothers in the camp of Saul, and having engaged and slain the Philistine giant Goliath in single combat, the fame of the deed reached the king's ears, and the youthful victor was consequently brought before him. I suspect also that in the 26th chapter of the same Book of Samuel the writer narrates from another source the same incident which he had already recorded in the 24th chapter. But I pass on to the consideration of the time which must have elapsed between one important event and another in the history of the Hebrew nation.

In the 6th chapter of the First Book of Kings it is said that Solomon built the temple in the 480th year after the Exodus; from the narrative of events, however, we conclude that a much longer period must have elapsed, for we have it stated that,—

	YEARS
Moses led or governed the people in the desert	40
Joshua, who lived 110 years, according to Josephus and others, governed for a period of	26
Chusan Rishataim ruled during	8
Othniel, son of Cenaz, was judge during	40
Eglon, King of Moab, held sovereign sway for	18
Ehud and Sangar were judges for	80
Jachin, King of Canaan, had sovereign sway for	20

	YEARS
The people were afterwards at peace for	40
The people were under the dominion of the Medes	7
In the time of Gideon liberty was recovered for	40
The sway of Abimelech lasted	3
Tola, son of Pua, judged	23
Jair judged	22
The people were under the sway of the Philistines and Ammonites	18
Jephtha judged	6
Absan the Bethlemite	7
Elon the Sebulonite	10
Abdan the Pirhonite	8
The people were again subject to the Philistines	40
Samson* judged	20
Eli judged	40
The people were again subject to the Philistines till liberated by Samuel	20
David reigned	40
Solomon reigned before the building of the Temple	4
The sum of which is	580

To this number, moreover, must be added the years during which the Hebrew republic flourished after the death of Joshua, until it was subdued by Chusan Rishataim, which I believe to have been many; for I cannot persuade myself that immediately after the death of Joshua all who had seen the marvels wrought by him had died at once, nor that their successors by a single casualty could have been led to bid adieu to the law, nor, from the height of virtuous courage, could have sunk into the slough of vice and indifference, nor, finally, that Chusan Rishataim could with a word have enslaved them. Now since each of these events must have required almost an age to itself, there can be no doubt but that verses 7, 9, and 10, of the 2nd chapter of the Book of Judges comprise the history of very many years which are passed over in silence. There are further to be added the years during which Samuel was judge, the number of which

---

* Samson was born after the Jews had fallen under the dominion of the Philistines.

is not given in Scripture. Still further must be added the years of Saul's reign, which I have not mentioned in the preceding enumeration, because from his history it is not sufficiently ascertained how many years he did reign. It is said, indeed, in chapter xiii. verse 1 of 1 Samuel, that Saul reigned for two years, but the text here is defective; and from the history itself we learn that he reigned during more than the number of years specified. That the text is truncated, no one acquainted with the merest rudiments of the Hebrew language can doubt; for it begins thus,—" Saul was [* * *] years old when he began to reign; and he reigned two years over Israel."* Who does not see that the number of the years of Saul's age when he came to the kingdom are wanting here? But that a considerable number must be admitted is obvious from the narrative of events. For in the 7th verse of the 27th chapter of the same book we find that David dwelt among the Philistines, with whom he had sought refuge on account of Saul's anger, for one year and four months; all that happened, therefore, must have taken place according to this reckoning in no longer an interval than eight months, which I think no one will insist upon as probable. Josephus, indeed, at the end of the sixth book of his Antiquities, amends the text thus,—" Saul therefore reigned during the life of Samuel for eighteen years, and after the death of Samuel for two years more." The entire history of chapter xiii., however, agrees in nothing with what has gone before. At the end of chapter vii., for example, it is related that the Philistines had been so severely handled by the Israelites, that during the life-time of Samuel they had not dared to encroach upon the territories of the Jews; but here, in this 13th chapter, we are told that the Israelites were invaded by the Philistines (Samuel being still alive) and reduced to such extreme poverty

* " Annum natus erat Saul cum regnaret, et duos annos regnavit supra Israelem." This is the author's rendering of the Hebrew text. Our English version reads thus :—" Saul reigned one year; and when he had reigned two years over Israel, he chose him two thousand men," &c., a mode of getting over the difficulty for which there is no authority.—*Ed.*

and misery that they were not only without the arms necessary for their defence, but without the means of making them. I should however expend a vast amount of labour to little purpose were I to attempt so to reconcile the various tales that are told in this First Book of Samuel, as to make it appear that they were all arranged and written by one historian. I therefore return to my subject. The years, then, during which Saul reigned have to be added to the computation given above. Lastly, I have not included the years of the Hebrew anarchy because they are not given in Scripture. I say then that I do not know in what interval of time the events related from the 17th chapter to the end of the Book of Judges may have happened. From what precedes however it follows most clearly that no true reckoning of years can be derived from the histories themselves, nor that these histories can be regarded as accounts of the same or of corresponding events; they are often very dissimilar, or are even mutually opposed. Hence we conclude that they have been collected from a variety of sources, and transmitted to us in a crude and undigested condition.

Nor does there appear to be less discrepancy between the Chronicles of the Kings of Judah and the Chronicles of the Kings of Israel; thus, in the Chronicles of the Kings of Israel it is said that Jehoram, son of Achab, began to rule in the second year of the reign of Jehoram, son of Jehoshaphat (2 Kings i. 17); but in the Chronicles of the Kings of Judah we read that Jehoram, son of Jehoshaphat, began his reign in the fifth year of the reign of Jehoram, son of Achab (Ib. viii. 16). And whoever will be at the pains to collate the narratives of the Book of Chronicles with those of the Book of Kings will discover many similar discrepancies, which I do not think it worth while to criticize, still less the comments of various writers who have attempted to reconcile these narratives with one another. The Rabbins seem to me to be absolutely insane, and the commentators whom I have read to dream, so constantly do they contrive purely imaginary solutions of difficulties, at the cost not infrequently of plainly corrupting the text of the narrative. To give a single instance,—when in the Second Book of Chronicles we read that Ahaziah was forty-two years old when he began his reign, we are informed that the years here are to be reckoned from the reign of Omri, not from the birth of Ahaziah. Now if it were possible to show that such was the purpose of the author of the Book of Chronicles, I should not hesitate to add that he knew not what he said. In this same way and manner are many other imaginations set before us, which, were they well founded, would lead me to say, unhesitatingly, that the ancient Hebrews were both ignorant of their mother tongue and violated the plainest rules of historical narrative. I should further add that neither rule nor reason was to be acknowledged in interpreting the Scriptures, but that every one was to feel himself at liberty to invent and interpolate whatever he chose.

Should it be thought, however, that I here speak in terms too general, and on grounds insufficient, I entreat the objector to show us anything like distinct arrangement in these writings, such as historians in the present day might imitate with advantage. If such a one, whilst explaining and reconciling facts, (keeping all the while with due closeness to the text; having respect to the genius of the Hebrew tongue, and proper regard to the manner in which the narratives are connected,) succeeds in so presenting matters that his system of interpretation may be generally followed, to that man, I say, I will freely give my hand, and take him for my Magnus Apollo, my guide; for I confess that, however anxiously and long I have myself inquired, I have been unable to discover anything like a guiding principle out of the labyrinth of difficulties I encounter. I add, further, that I set down nothing here which I have not long and seriously meditated; and although from my youth I was imbued with the common opinions concerning the Scriptures, I have been compelled in my manhood to abandon those, and to espouse those views which I promulgate in this place. But there is no reason why I should detain the reader with such matters, or seek to push him upon a desperate undertaking; it was right however that I should propose the thing in order to manifest my own mind more clearly; and I now proceed to speak of the other matters which I think deserve to be considered in connection with the fortune of these books.

Now it is to be observed that, besides the peculiarities which have been already discussed, the books of the Old Testament have by no means been so very carefully preserved by those into whose hands they fell successively, but that blemishes have crept into them. Even the more ancient scribes have animadverted upon various doubtful readings, and on several imperfect or truncated passages besides; and very certainly they have not noticed all of these that occur. But whether the imperfections are of such magnitude as to throw serious obstacles in the reader's way I shall not stay to question; for my own part, I regard them as of lighter moment, to those at least who read the Scriptures with unbiassed judgment; and this much I can safely affirm, that I have not met with any error, nor any variety of reading in connection with the moral doctrines, which would thereby be rendered either obscure or doubtful.

But many will not allow that error or mistake has crept into any part of Scripture whatsoever. They maintain that God, by his special providence, has preserved the whole Bible incorrupt; the various readings of the text that are extant they declare to be signs of inscrutable mysteries; so are the asterisms which occur in the middle of 28 paragraphs of Scripture;[*] nay, they contend that there are great arcana connected with the tops of the Hebrew letters! But whether all this have been said from simple foolishness, or idiot piety, or from arrogance and malice, to make it appear as though they were the sole depositaries of the mysteries of God, I know not; but this I do know and aver, that I have met with nothing that savoured of mystery in their writings, but only with puerile imaginations. I have, moreover, read the works of some of the more recent cabalistic triflers, whose

[*] Vide end of this chapter for an explanation of this.—*Ed.*

folly I can never sufficiently admire. But that errors, blemishes, mistakes, as said above, have crept into Scripture, no one possessed of sound judgment can in my opinion deny who reads the passages referring to Saul, which I have already quoted (1 Samuel xiii. 1), and the 2nd verse of the 6th chapter of the Second Book of Samuel, where we find it stated that "David arose and went with all the people that were with him from Baale of Judah, to bring up from thence the ark of God." Every one must see that here the place to which they went, namely, Kirjath-jearim, whence the ark was brought, is omitted.* Nor do I think it can be denied that the 37th verse of the 13th chapter of the Second Book of Samuel is confused and truncated : " And Absalom fled and went to Talmai, the son of Ammihud, King of Geshur. And David mourned for his son every day. So Absalom fled, and went to Geshur, and was there three years." In the same way, I know that in former times I noted various other passages, which at this moment do not occur to me.

With regard to the marginal annotations constantly met with in all the Hebrew codices, I think no one can question their having reference to various or doubtful readings, who attends to the fact that most of them are connected with, or have arisen from, the great similarity which many of the Hebrew letters bear to one another. The resemblance of כ Kaf to ב Bet, י Jod to ו Vau, ד Dalet to ר Res, &c., cannot be overlooked. Thus, in the Second Book of Samuel, the penultimate verse of the 5th chapter in the common version reads,—" when thou hearest," opposite which in the margin stands,—" where thou hearest." In the 22nd verse of the 21st chapter of Judges we

---

* Kirjath-jearim is also called Bahgal of Judah, which has led some critics to believe that the words Bahgal-Jehudah was the name of a town ; but this is an error, since Bahgal is in the plural. If the text of Samuel be compared with that of Chronicles (xiii. 6), it will be seen that David did not depart from, but that he went to, Bahgal. Had the author of the Book of Samuel wished to indicate Baale of Judah as the place whence David carried away the ark, he must, in order to speak Hebrew, have expressed himself in this wise,—" And David rose up, and departed from Bahgal of Judah, and carried away from thence the ark of God."

read,—" When their fathers or their brethren come to us," the marginal note supplies the "to complain" [which is adopted in the English version]. In the same manner many things have arisen from the use of the letters which are styled quiescent,—letters which are for the most part slurred, or scarcely indicated in speaking, and which in Hebrew are taken indifferently one for another. For example, in Leviticus xxv. 30 it is written,— "The house that is in the walled city shall be established to him," &c.; in the margin, however, the reading is,—"that is *not* in the walled city."

Now although these things are clear enough of themselves, it is nevertheless necessary to reply to the views of certain Pharisees, who try to persuade themselves and us that the marginal readings of the Hebrew Scriptures have a mysterious meaning, and were attached by the writers of the books themselves to their completed works. The first of these assumptions, to which indeed I pay little attention, is derived from the custom or practice followed in reading the Scriptures. "If," they say, "these marginal notes are appended on account of a variety of readings, the best of which posterity have not been able to decide on, whence comes it that the marginal word is the one which in reading the Scriptures is constantly employed? Why, say they, has the sense which the writer desired should be adopted been noted in the margin? The text, on the contrary, should have been found as it was meant to be read, the correct reading and proper sense not noted in the margin." The second of the Pharisees' reasons, which seems to have a certain speciousness about it, is derived from the nature of the thing itself. The defects and errors of the text they say cannot have been introduced of set purpose, but have crept by accident or inadvertence into the codices, and that this is the case appears from various considerations. In five different places, for example, in the Bible, the Hebrew word for girl, or young woman, is met with, and in each of these, with a single exception, the letter ה He, against all grammatical rule, is omitted; in the margin, however, the defective aspirate is regularly supplied. Now shall the error here be set down to the score of the writer or writers of the Bible? By what fatality could it have happened that the pen slipped as often as it had to write the Hebrew word for young woman? The error in the text could easily and without misgivings have been corrected, in conformity with a simple and definite grammatical rule. Since, therefore, these readings have not occurred from chance or accident, since such obvious errors have not been simply corrected, the Pharisees conclude that they were introduced by the first scribes of set purpose, and that they have a certain significance. But it is easy to reply to such assumptions, for the argument they derive from the custom among the Jews of using the marginal words in *viva voce* exercises, whilst they continue to employ the textual one in writing, causes me no difficulty : perchance the superstitious observance referred to has arisen because both readings being esteemed equally good or passable, it was thought proper always to write one, and always to read the other, in which way both would be preserved. It was doubtless thought presumptuous, in a matter of so much moment as a phrase in Holy Writ, to come to any positive determination, whereby something false might be taken for the uncertain truth, and they therefore escaped the dilemma of seeming to prefer one version to another by regularly writing the one and constantly reading aloud the other. It is note-worthy, however, that the marginal readings are not inscribed on the sacred rolls [from which the reading takes place in the Synagogue], because perchance it was willed that things, although correctly set down in the text, should nevertheless be otherwise read in public, namely, as they were noted on the margin, and so it came to be universally ruled that when the Bible was read aloud the marginal words or phrases should be delivered.*

But all the marginal annotations of the Bible can by no means be regarded as varia, or doubtful readings ; there are many which have come down from remote antiquity that do

* In the English version of the Bible the marginal readings seem to have been constantly adopted as the text.—*Ed.*

not fall under such a category; and I shall therefore proceed to show why the scribes were induced to preserve both classes of annotations. Now many of the marginalia contain explanations of obsolete words, and sometimes they are substitutions of more delicate for coarser words, which the improved taste or manners of the times did not permit to be uttered in public; for the old writers were not wont to beat about the bush in courtly phrase, but to call things by their most common names. When times of greater refinement arrived, however, expressions that were used without a thought of their indelicacy by a former generation begun to be regarded as obscene; to avoid these without altering the text of the sacred volume itself a marginal note supplied the word or words that were required as substitutes in the open lecture; and so the sensitiveness of the public in regard to the integrity of the text was respected—the written word remained, the spoken phrase did not offend the ear. Whatever the motive for the practice of using the marginals in reading the Scriptures may have been, it certainly was not because the words in these contained the true readings, or that all interpretation was to be made in conformity with them. For, besides that the Rabbins in the Talmud often differ from the masoretic writers, and have other readings which they approve, as I shall soon show, there are, over and above all these, other things in the margin, which seem to be less in consonance with the genius of the Hebrew language. In the Second Book of Samuel, for example (xiv. 23), it is written, "In that the king hath fulfilled the request of his servant;" a construction which is regular, and agrees with that in verse 15 of the same chapter; but opposite to it stands the marginal variation, "of thy servant," which does not agree with the person of the verb that is used. So, again, in the last verse of the 16th chapter of the same book it is written, "As if a man had inquired at the oracle of God," and opposite in the margin stand the words, "who had inquired," &c., the "who" supplying the nominative to the verb; which, however, is not judiciously or properly done, for the common custom in this language is to assume impersonal verbs in the third person singular of the active verb, as is perfectly well known to grammarians. In like manner, numerous other marginal notes are met with which can in no way be preferred to the words of the text.

Besides doubtful readings, the scribes noted obsolete words; for there can be no question but that in the Hebrew, as in other tongues, time and later usage rendered many words obsolete or antiquated ; and these being found in the Bible by the more recent scribes, who marked everything, as has been said, they were annotated in order that the reading might be given before the people in accordance with usage and custom. This is the reason why the word *nahgar* is noted wherever it occurs, because more anciently it was of common gender, masculine or feminine. So, too, the metropolis of the Jews was written Jerusalem—not Jerusalim. The same thing has to be said of the pronouns *himself* and *herself*, later writers having turned the *Vau* into *Jod* (a change that is of frequent occurrence in Hebrew) when they wished to indicate the feminine gender; but this was not done by the ancients, who were not accustomed to distinguish the masculine from the feminine except by the vowel sounds. Thus of the anomalies of certain words, some belong to the ancients, some to the moderns, and, lastly, the ancients in their day often used the paragrammatic letters with singular elegance. All of these points I could illustrate by many examples; but I am unwilling to trespass longer on the patience of the reader. If any one inquires, however, how I came to know what I have stated above? I reply that I often met the words and particulars which have been indicated in the most ancient of writings—in the Bible itself—and that the only reason for words and phrases becoming antiquated and obsolete is their disuse by successive writers; in other languages, as well as in the Hebrew, although long ago dead, obsolete words are nevertheless recognized. But, some one may still insist, since I admit that the greater number of the marginals refer to doubtful readings, and ask how it happens that there are never more than two variations to one word or phrase? why not occasionally three or more? And, again: that as some things in the text are so plainly repugnant to grammatical rule, which are duly corrected in the margin, it is not to be believed that the scribes could have hesitated as to which was the correct version. But it is easy to answer these queries and suggestions. To the first I say that the readings were often many more than those we find noted in our codices. In the Talmud there are many which are neglected by the Masoretes, and these often differ so much from one another that the superstitious corrector of the Bamberg Bible confesses in his preface that he found it impossible to reconcile them. He says, "Here I know not what to answer, unless it be to repeat what I have already said, viz. That it is the wont of the Talmudists to contradict the Masoretes." Wherefore, I cannot admit the assumption that there never were more than two variants to one place; although I readily concede—nay, I believe—that no more than two are ever found in any one codex, and this for two reasons: 1st, Because the main cause of the various readings is not more than two-fold in its nature; being due in the first place to the resemblance of one Hebrew letter to another; and it is, in fact, an ever recurring question, when there is any room for doubt, whether ב *Bet* or כ *Kaf*, ו *Jod* or ו *Vau*, ד *Dalet* or ר *Res*, &c., is the proper letter to be used; and as these are among the most constantly employed in the language, it frequently happens that either indifferently will make tolerable sense with the context. Then, whether the syllable should be long or short is determined by the quantities of those letters which we have spoken of as quiescent or slurred. Add that all marginals do not refer to doubtful readings; many, we should say, had been appended from conscientious motives, and, as has been said, for the sake of explaining obsolete or antiquated words. 2nd, Another reason wherefore the readings are limited to two, I conceive may have been connected with the scarcity of MSS.; few scribes could be supposed able to command the use of more than one or two, or three at most, to transcribe from. In the 6th chapter of a Hebrew book entitled ".Tract of the Scribes" no more than three MSS. are mentioned, which are said to have been discovered in the time of Ezra,—the scribes indeed maintain that the marginalia were all added by Ezra. However this may be, if there were three codices extant, we can readily imagine that in any one place two of these always agreed; and, on the contrary, it could not be held otherwise than very strange had three copies only of the same book given three different readings of a great number of passages. That copies of the Hebrew Scriptures became excessively rare after the time of Ezra will cease to be matter of wonder to whosoever reads the first chapter of the First Book of Maccabees, or the seventh chapter of the Twelfth Book of Josephus's Antiquities. It is rather wonderful, after the long and terrible persecution the Jews endured, that they should have been able to preserve anything whatsoever; a truth which I think no one will be inclined to question who reads with the slightest attention the history of their sufferings. We therefore seem to see causes enough why no more than two variants are preserved of any passage; and in this fact we find no support for those who infer that the Bible in the noted passages is intentionally written obscurely, and covers certain important mysteries.

With regard to certain passages written so incorrectly as to outrage the usages of verbal composition in all times, and which ought therefore to have been corrected absolutely, and not noted in the margin, I have nothing to say; nor can I divine what sentiment of respect withheld the hand of the scribe from setting them right. Perhaps it was through scrupulousness, and a desire to transmit to posterity these ancient writings as they themselves had received them, and to note the discrepancies of the originals as various readings rather than as matters of doubtful import; nor, indeed, have I myself spoken of them as doubtful, but because I have in truth found almost all of them to be so, and have often been puzzled to conclude which reading was to be preferred.

In addition to all these doubtful different readings, the scribes have further noted many defective or truncated places—gaps in the middle of paragraphs, &c.—the number of which is given by the Masoretes at twenty-eight; I am not aware whether they connect anything mysterious with this number or not. The Pharisees, however, religiously preserve certain spaces in their transcripts of the Scriptures. I give a single example as an illustration. Thus we find the 8th verse of the fourth chapter of Genesis written as follows, "And Cain said to his brother Abel . . . . . and it came to pass whilst they were in the fields that Cain," &c.* The blank space is left at the point where we might have expected to learn what Cain said to his brother. In this way the spaces left by the scribes, besides those we have made the subject of particular remark, are twenty-eight in number; though many of the passages where they occur would not really appear truncated were the interposed spaces omitted.. But of such matters enough.

* In the English version, where difficulties seem to be very commonly made smooth, the omission in the verse quoted would not be noticed were it not pointed out. It is as follows, "And Cain talked with Abel, his brother: and it came to pass," &c.—*Ed*.

CHAPTER X.

OF THE REMAINING BOOKS OF THE OLD TESTAMENT.

I PASS on to the remaining books of the Old Testament. Now of the two Books of Paralipomena (1 and 2 Chronicles) I have nothing certain or important to say, except that they were written long after the time of Ezra, and perhaps, even, after the restoration of the temple by Judas Maccabeus; for in chapter ix. of the First Book the historian informs us "what families first dwelt in Jerusalem" (the "first" here referring to the time of Ezra), and in the 17th verse he gives the names of the gate-keepers, two of whom are also mentioned by Nehemiah (xi. 19). This of itself suffices to show that the books were written long after the rebuilding of the city. Of their actual writer, however, of the authority that is due to them, of their utility and doctrine, I have nothing to say. Indeed, I cannot sufficiently wonder how these books came to be received as sacred by those who severed the Book of Wisdom, of Tobit, of Esdras, and the rest, which are styled Apocryphal, from the canon of Holy Writ. My purpose here, however, is not to uphold the authority of these writings; I am content to leave them as I find them regarded by the world at large.

The Psalms were also collected and divided into five books during the epoch of the second temple; for Psalm lxxxviii., according to the testimony of Philo, was produced whilst

King Jehoiachim was still detained a prisoner in Babylon, and Psalm lxxxix. when he had obtained his liberty; and I believe that Philo would not have said what he has done had it not been the received opinion of his age, or had he not had the information from some one worthy of trust.

The Proverbs of Solomon, I believe, were also collected about the same time; or, at least, in the time of King Josiah; for, in the 25th chapter, verse 1, we read, "These are also proverbs of Solomon, which the men of Hezekiah, King of Judah, copied out." And here I cannot keep silence on the daring of the Rabbins, who would have excluded this book, with Ecclesiastes, from the Scripture canon, and placed it beside those other writings whose absence we have but now regretted. And rejected these books would assuredly have been, had they not been found to contain several passages in which the law of Moses was commended. It is indeed greatly to be lamented that most excellent and holy things should have depended on the choice of such men as the Jewish Rabbis who settled the canon of the Old Testament. I am grateful to them, however, for having been pleased to communicate these books to us at all; although I cannot refrain from doubting whether they transmitted them with entire good faith,—a point on the discussion of which I am indisposed to enter. I therefore proceed to the Books of the Prophets.

When I examine these writings attentively, I find that the prophecies which they contain were collected from other books, and are not always set down in the same order as they were delivered by word of mouth or in writing by the prophets themselves; neither do they contain all the prophecies that were uttered, but those only that could be gathered up here and there. These books consequently cannot be regarded as more than fragments. Isaiah, for instance, began to prophesy during the reign of Uzziah, as the narrator himself declares in the 1st verse of the 1st chapter of the book. But when we turn to Chronicles (2nd Book ch. xxvi. 22) we find that Isaiah not only prophesied at the time mentioned, but had further narrated, in a book now lost, the whole of the transactions of King Uzziah's reign. What we have of Isaiah, however, is taken, as has just been said, from other writings, especially from the Chronicles of the Kings of Judah and Israel. Add to this that the Rabbins maintain that Isaiah prophesied in the reign of Manasseh, by whom he was finally put to death; and although they probably relate fables here they seem still to have believed that the whole of the prophecies of Isaiah were not extant.

The Prophecies of Jeremiah, in like manner, which are narrated historically, are taken from various chronologers; for besides that they are accumulated without arrangement, no respect being had to times, we find the same tale variously repeated oftener than once. Thus, in the 21st chapter we have an explanation of the cause of the prophet's alarm, in the circumstance that he had foretold the devastation of the city to Zedekiah, who had consulted him. The narrative breaks off suddenly here; for chapter xxii. is occupied with the declamation of the prophet to Jehoiachim, who reigned before Zedekiah, and to whom he foretells an approaching captivity. Next in disorder, in chapter xxv., we have those things that were revealed to the prophet before this time, viz. in the fourth year of the reign of King Jehoiachim; then, those that concerned the first year of this king's reign, and so on, no order in the incidents or the times being observed, prophecies accumulated pell-mell on one another, until at length, in chapter xxxviii. (as if the fifteen intervening chapters had formed one great parenthesis), we are brought back to that which the writer had begun to relate in the 21st chapter. The conjunction which we find at the beginning of the 38th chapter plainly refers to verses 8, 9, and 10 of chap. xxi.; but strangely enough the alarm of Jeremiah is here described in very different terms, and the cause of his long imprisonment in the porch of the prison is told quite otherwise than in chap. xxxvii. These references suffice to show that the prophecies of Jeremiah are scraps collected without arrangement from different historians; on no other supposition can the state of confusion in which they exist be understood.

The other prophecies contained in the remaining chapters, where Jeremiah speaks in the first person, appear to be derived from the volume which Baruch wrote at the dictation of Jeremiah himself, for, as we learn from chapter xxxvi. 2, it only contained so much as was revealed to the prophet from the time of Josiah to the fourth year of the reign of Jehoiachim, from which date indeed this book begins. From the same volume, also, all that is contained between the 2nd verse of the 45th chapter and the 59th verse of the 51st chapter appears to be derived.

That the Book of Ezekiel is nothing more than a fragment is clearly indicated by its introductory verses; for who does not see that the conjunction with which it begins refers to matters that have gone before, and is the bond between these and what is to follow. Nor is it the conjunction only that leads to this conclusion; the whole of the context supposes other writings: for the thirtieth year, from which this book commences, shows the prophet in the course of proceeding with his narrative, not beginning it, as he himself indeed shows parenthetically in verse 3, where he says,— "The word of the Lord came expressly* unto Ezekiel, the priest, the son of Buzi, in the land of the Chaldeans," &c., as if he had said, the words of Ezekiel thus far refer to other things, which were revealed to him before this thirtieth year. And then Josephus (Antiq. book x. ch. ix.) relates how Ezekiel had foretold that Zedekiah should not see Babylon; a particular which we do not find mentioned in the Book of Ezekiel as we have it; on the contrary, we there read (chap. xvii.) that Zedekiah should be taken captive to Babylon.†

---

* *Sæpe, often*, in Spinoza's version.—*Ed.*

† No one therefore would have imagined that the prophecy of Ezekiel was in contradiction with that of Jeremiah; whilst this suspicion must take possession of every one who reads the account of Josephus. The event proved that both prophets had spoken the truth.

Of Hosea it cannot be said for certain that he wrote more than we find in the book which passes under his name. Still I cannot help wondering that we have not more from his hand, seeing that he prophesied for upwards of 84 years, according to the testimony of the writer of the book. Of this at least we are sure generally, that neither do the books we have contain the whole of the prophecies pronounced, nor does the collection of prophetical books that has come down to us contain all of the same sort that were written. Of all the prophets who discoursed during the reign of Manasseh, and of whom there is a general notice in 2 Chronicles (xxxiii. 10, 18, 19), we have absolutely nothing; neither have we everything of the twelve minor prophets. The only prophecies of Jonah which we have, for example, are those he delivered to the Ninevites, though it is known that he also prophesied to the Israelites, on which see 2 Kings xiv. 25.

The Book of Job, and Job himself, have been the subject of much controversy among writers. Some have been of opinion that Moses wrote the Book of Job, and that the whole history is no more than an allegory. This is the conclusion of the Rabbins in the Talmud, and is that favoured by Maimonides in his work entitled More Nebuchim. Others, again, regard the book as true history, they believing that Job lived in the time of Jacob, and took his daughter Dinah to wife. But Aben-Ezra, as I have already had occasion to say, in his commentaries on this book concludes that it is a translation from another tongue into Hebrew, a conclusion which I could well desire had been better supported than it is, for then we should be able to infer that the Gentiles also had their sacred books.* I, therefore, leave the question in

---

* This sentence would lead us to conclude that Spinoza was unacquainted with the sacred books of the great Eastern Nations—the Vedas of the Hindoos and the Zends of the Persians. The Vedas indeed were only made known to scholars in very recent times; but the Zendavesta must surely have been familiar to learned persons in the time of Spinoza. The learned Th. Hyde published his Historia Religionis veterum Persarum in the life-time of Spinoza, as we believe.—*Ed.*

doubt; but venture to add that in my opinion Job was a Gentile, of great constancy of mind and purpose, who had first lived in affluence, then fallen into singular adversity, and had finally recovered his prosperous position. Ezekiel (xiv. 14) mentions Job along with other pious men, and I believe that his various fortunes and his constancy of mind under affliction afforded frequent occasion for discussing God's providence; and, as I further opine, the occurrence of such contingencies in the life of man as prosperous and adverse fortune gave the author of this book the hint for the composition of his dialogue; for the treatment and the style of the Book of Job do not appear to connect themselves with a man in sickness and sorrow and with ashes on his head, but rather with one meditating at his ease in his study. With Aben-Ezra, therefore, I am disposed to believe that the book is a translation from another tongue; for it contains allusions to the poetry [and mythology] of the Gentiles, as where the father of the gods twice calls a council, and Momus under the name of Satan carps with the greatest license at the decrees of God, &c.* But these are mere conjectures, without any sufficient foundation.

I proceed to the Book of Daniel. This book, from chapter viii. onwards, unquestionably contains the writing of Daniel himself, but whence the preceding seven chapters were derived I know not, though we may suspect, from the whole book, with the exception of the 1st chapter, having been written in Chaldee, that the source was the Chaldean chronologies. Could this only be clearly established, it would be a remarkable testimony to the assurance that the Scriptures are sacred only in so far as the things signified in them are understood, and not in so far as the language or

* The reader will call to mind the bold and almost profane way in which Goethe introduces his demon Mephistopheles into the heavenly council. Faust is Job in another shape, Mephistopheles is Satan,—as Faust represents the nobler and better, Mephistopheles the lower and more sensual, element in man's nature. It is in the Book of Job that we first meet with Satan, or the devil, a personage of whom the early Hebrews, the people of Elhoim and of Jehovah, knew nothing. —*Ed.*

style of composition is regarded; and that all books which teach and narrate things good and true, in whatever language written, by men of whatever nation composed, are equally and alike sacred. This much at all events may be noted, that these chapters of Daniel were written in Chaldee, and are nevertheless held of like sanctity with the rest of the Bible.

With the Book of Daniel the First of Ezra is so intimately associated that it is readily seen to be the work of the same writer, who goes on to narrate in succession the affairs of the Jews from the epoch of the first captivity. With the Book of Ezra, again, I do not hesitate to associate that of Esther; for the conjunction with which this book begins can refer to nothing else; nor is it to be believed that Esther is the book which Mordecai wrote; for in chapter ix. (20, 21, 22) we have some notice of Mordecai himself, and of the Epistles he indited, and their contents; and in the 31st verse of the same chapter we learn that Queen Esther confirmed by an edict the arrangements for the feast of the Purim (feast of lots), and that this edict was written in a book; that is to say, as it reads in Hebrew, in a book known to every one of the time. This book, however, Aben-Ezra confesses, and with him all are bound to confess, has perished, with so many others. Lastly, the historian refers for other particulars of the reign of Mordecai to the Chronicles of the Persian Kings. There can be little doubt therefore of this book having been the production of the same pen which wrote Daniel and Ezra, and in addition Nehemiah,[*] which is often entitled the 2nd Book of Ezra. Four of these books consequently—Daniel, Ezra, Esther, and Nehemiah—we affirm to be the work of one writer; but

[*] That the greater part of the extant Book of Nehemiah is taken from the work which the prophet himself composed, appears from the testimony of the transcriber (vide ch. v. 1). But further, there is not the least doubt that all, from the beginning of chap. viii. to verse 26th of chap. xii., and also the two last verses of chap. xiii., which are a kind of parenthesis added to the words of Nehemiah, have been supplied by the actual writer of the book which bears the name of Nehemiah.

there is not room even for conjecture as to who he was. If we would ask whence he, whoever he was, who wrote these books derived the particulars of the histories they contain, it is to be observed that the prefects or princes of the Jews of the second temple (like their kings in the time of the first) retained scribes or historiographers in their service, whose business it was to write their annals or chronologies. The chronologies or annals of the kings are quoted everywhere in the two Books of Kings; but those of the princes and priests of the second temple are first referred to in the Book of Nehemiah (xii. 23), and next in Maccabees (book i. ch. xvi. 24). And without doubt these annals formed the book of which mention has just been made, in which the edict of Esther and the writings of Mordecai were contained, and which, with Aben-Ezra, we have said is now lost. From this lost book, therefore, all that is comprised in the four books above cited was in all probability derived; for no other is referred to by their author, and we know of none besides of public authority. That the books in question were not written either by Ezra or Nehemiah appears from this, that in Nehemiah (xii. 10, 11) we have the genealogy of the high priest Jeshua continued to Jaddua, the sixth pontiff, who went to meet Alexander the Great, the Persian power being then almost destroyed (vide Joseph. Antiq. book ii. ch. viii.); Philo Judæus, indeed, in a book of the time, calls Jaddua the sixth and last high priest under the Persians. In the same chapter of Nehemiah we have these words,—" in the days of Eliashib, the Levites Joiada and Johanan and Jaddua were recorded priests, &c., to the reign of Darius the Persian .. in the book of the chronicles;" and I have no idea any one will believe that Ezra or Nehemiah enjoyed such longevity as to have outlived 14 kings of Persia; for Cyrus was the first who gave the Jews permission to rebuild the Temple, and from Cyrus to Darius, the 14th and last king of Persia, more than 230 years are reckoned. Wherefore I do not doubt but that the books in question were written long after Judas Maccabæus had restored the worship of the

Temple, a conclusion to which I am led besides by the fact that about this time certain spurious books of Daniel, Ezra, and Esther were produced by some evil-disposed person, who might have been of the sect of the Sadducees; for the Pharisees, to the best of my belief, never acknowledged the authenticity of these books. And although some fables are found in the book entitled the 4th of Ezra, which we also encounter in the Talmud, these are not therefore to be ascribed to the Pharisees; for except the utterly foolish among them, there is none who does not admit that these fables were interpolated by some ignorant trifler. My own idea is, that the interpolations were made by an enemy, in order to render the traditions of the Pharisees ridiculous in the eyes of the world. Another reason for the appearance of the Books of Daniel, Ezra, Esther, and Nehemiah at the particular time specified may have been to show the people the prophecies of Daniel fulfilled, and in the midst of so much misery to strengthen them in piety, and in the faith of better times to come.

Into these books, however, notwithstanding their recent date, unless I greatly deceive myself, many errors have crept through haste and inadvertence in the transcribers. In them, as in the other books of Scripture, we discover many of the marginal notations, of which we have already spoken at length, and several places besides in so imperfect a state that it is impossible to account for them save by supposing carelessness. But I must first speak of the marginalia of these books. Now, if, we are to concede to the Pharisees their assumption that these annotations are of like antiquity with the text, then it were necessary to say that the writers themselves, if perchance there was more than one writer, noted the particular passages they have done, in consequence of not finding the chronologies whence they had their data over-accurately written; and although some things were clearly errors, still they did not venture to correct and amend the venerable MSS. from which they transcribed.

But I need not again enter on this subject, or describe it in its particular application at greater length than I have already done, I therefore proceed to the mistakes that are not noted in the margin. And I say, first, that I know not how many have found their way into the 2nd chapter of Ezra; for in verse 64, the sum of all whose genealogies are severally enumerated in the body of the chapter is given as 42,360; yet if the particular items be added together they will be found to amount to no more than 29,818. There is, therefore, an error here, either in the total or in the items. But the total probably is correctly given, because doubtless it was stored in the memory of every one as something remarkable, and the several smaller numbers were not likely to be so well retained; had any mistake been made in the sum-total, it would have been patent to every one, and must immediately have been corrected. And this view is confirmed by what we find in Nehemiah (vii. 5), where this chapter of Ezra is referred to under the title of a Register of Genealogy, and where the sum-total agrees exactly with that of Ezra, though the particular numbers differ widely, some of these being more, some less, but together making no greater a sum than 31,089; whence there can be little doubt that many mistakes have glided into the secondary or partial sums in the books both of Ezra and Nehemiah. The commentators, however, who have endeavoured to reconcile these obvious incongruities have one and all feigned and fashioned to the extent of their ingenuity; and whilst fancying that they added to the excellence of the Scriptures, they did in fact but bring the writers of the Bible into contempt, making them appear as if they neither knew how to express themselves in their mother tongue nor how to arrange what they had to say. To me, indeed, they only seem to render obscure what is plain enough in Scripture; for, indeed, were it everywhere permitted to proceed in the manner they have done, there were no text in the whole Bible on the sense of which doubts might not be raised. But I need not detain my reader long with such topics; for I persuade myself that were any historian to permit himself the liberties which Bible critics devoutly concede to the Scripture writers, they would be among the first to challenge his method, and to laugh him to scorn. And if they think that he blasphemes who declares that Scripture is in any part erroneous, I ask by what name I am to call those who fasten what they please upon Scripture? who so prostitute the sense of the sacred historians that they seem to babble and confound everything? who finally deny the most plain and obvious meanings of Holy Writ? For what is there clearer in Scripture than that Ezra, with his associates in the genealogical epistle comprised in the second chapter of the book that goes under his name, intended to enumerate separately or in divisions all who proceeded to Jerusalem, although he includes among them not only all those whose genealogies he knew, but those also whose descent was unknown to him. What I ask is plainer than that Nehemiah simply transcribes or describes this Genealogical Register in his seventh chapter? They who explain these things otherwise do in fact but ignore the plain sense of Scripture, and so take from its authority. They think it pious, forsooth, to reconcile or accommodate one part of Scripture with another! a childish piety in verity, that blurs the light with darkness, reconciles the true with the false, and taints the sound with the rotten. Let me not, however, be supposed to brand as blasphemers those who have had no purpose to lead astray—for truly to err is human. I return to my subject.

Besides the errors which must be acknowledged in the sums of the Genealogical Registers, both of Ezra and Nehemiah, there are many mistakes in the names of families, many especially in the genealogies, in the historical accounts, and, I apprehend, in the prophecies themselves. The prophecy of Jeremiah, for example (xxii.), concerning Jechoniah, cannot be made to tally in any way with the histories we have of him towards the end of the Second Book of Kings, and in chapter iii. of 1 Chronicles (17, 18,

19), the last verse of which especially appears insurmountable. Neither do I see with what propriety the same prophet could inform Zedekiah, after he had seen his sons slain before him, and had his own eyes put out, that he should die in peace (vide Jerem. xxxiv. 5). Were we to be guided by the event in interpreting this prophecy, the names would have to be changed, Jechoniah being substituted for Zedekiah. But this were perhaps taking too great a liberty with the text, and I am content to leave the point incomprehensible as I found it, the rather because if there be an error here it must be ascribed to the author, not regarded as a mistake of the scribe.

As to the other matters which I have pointed out as requiring elucidation, I do not think of entering on them; this could only be done by being wearisome to the reader, and it is the less called for as they have all been made the subject of particular commentary by others. The Rabbi Selomo is constrained by the many contradictions in the genealogies to break out in these words, "Ezra" (the author, as he believes, of the two books of Paralipomena or Chronicles)—"Ezra calls the sons of Benjamin by other names, and traces their descent by different lines from those we have in the Book of Genesis; and that he speaks of the greater number of the cities of the Levites by other names than those in Joshua arose from his finding discrepancies in the originals whence he drew his information." A little further on he continues, "If the genealogy of Gibeon and others be found twice or even oftener described differently, this has arisen from Ezra having met with many different genealogical registers, in extracting or copying from which he followed the reading of the greater number; but when the number of discordant genealogies was equal on each side, then he copied both accounts." In this passage the Rabbi yields the point in dispute about the origin of these books of Scripture, admitting that they were derived from originals, and were put together carelessly, without due regard to the accuracy of the narrative. It may be said, indeed, with justice, that commentators, when they strive to reconcile discordant passages, do nothing more for the most part than point out the causes of the mistakes; for I do not imagine any one in his senses believes that the sacred historians wrote in such a way as incessantly to contradict themselves.

But some, perchance, will here interpose, and say that I plainly destroy the authority of Scripture by what I advance, for thus may the whole body of the Bible come to be suspected as corrupt. But I have shown, on the contrary, that comfort may be taken from this: that the clear and pure parts will not be twisted into agreement with the obscure and faulty parts, and so corrupted; and that it is not reasonable, because certain parts are found erroneous, that all should be made objects of suspicion; for no book in this world was ever yet found without faults. But I ask, shall it therefore be said that any book was ever written that is entirely faulty? certainly not; especially when the language used is simple and perspicuous, and the purpose of the writer is manifest.

I here bring to a close what I had to say on the books of the Old Testament, and presume to conclude from all which precedes, that before the time of the Maccabees there was no canon of Holy Writ extant; but that the books we have were selected from among many others by and on the sole authority of the Pharisees of the second temple, who also instituted the formula for the prayers used in the Synagogue.* Whosoever, therefore, should seek to demonstrate the authenticity and authority of the Hebrew Scriptures, must be held bound to show on what authority each of their books severally rests. It is not enough to prove the divineness of one to conclude that therefore all the others are divine. And then it were imperative to show that the council of the Pharisees could not err in their selection of the books they admitted; and this I think no one will ever be able to demonstrate. The

* The grand Synagogue which decided the canon of Scripture did not assemble till after the subjection of Asia to the Macedonian power. To its authority the Pharisees always refer when they invoke what they call their Traditions.

reason that especially induces me to affirm that the Pharisees alone selected the books of the Old Testament and placed them in the canon of the Sacred Writings is this, that in the 2nd verse of the last chapter of Daniel I find a prophecy of the resurrection of the dead, a contingency which the Sadducees denied. The opinion of the Pharisees on this point is clearly indicated in the Talmud; in the second chapter of which we read as follows: "Rabbi Jehuda, surnamed Rabi, said that certain learned persons wished to suppress the Book of Ecclesiastes, because its words are opposed to the words of the law (of Moses, understood). Now why was it not suppressed? because it begins according to the law, and ends according to the law." He says further: "They also desired to exclude the Book of Proverbs," &c., and concludes thus: "I name the name of Neghunja, Son of Hiskias, from gratitude; because but for him the Book of Ezekiel would have been suppressed, its words being held contrary to those of the law." From these extracts we can see plainly that a council of the men learned in the law determined what books were to be received as sacred, and what to be rejected as of no sanctity. He, therefore, who would be certain of the authority of the whole of the Scriptures, let him enter into council anew and require the title of each of its books to the place it occupies.

And now it were in order that I proceeded to examine the books of the New Testament in the same manner as I have reviewed those of the Old. But as I hear that this is being done by men versed in science and skilled in languages, and as I myself have not so accurate a knowledge of the Greek as might tempt me to undertake the task, and lastly, as we are without copies in the original tongue of the books which were written in Hebrew, I do not mean to enter upon it in detail, but shall content myself with touching upon those points only that fall most immediately within the scope of my undertaking.

CHAPTER XI.

DID THE APOSTLES WRITE THEIR EPISTLES IN THE CHARACTER OF APOSTLES AND PROPHETS, OR MERELY AS TEACHERS? OF THE OFFICE OF THE APOSTLES.

No one who reads the New Testament can doubt of the apostles having been prophets. But as the Old Testament prophets did not always speak from revelations made to them, but on the contrary did so very seldom, as has been shown at the close of Chap. I., we may be permitted to doubt whether the apostles wrote their Epistles as prophets, from revelation and by the express command of God, like Moses, Jeremiah, and the rest, or whether they wrote as private and learned persons merely. This inquiry is the more necessary, seeing that Paul in his First Epistle to the Corinthians (xiv. 6) indicates two kinds of preaching, one from revelation, another from knowledge; wherefore I say it is doubtful whether in their Epistles the apostles prophesy or teach. Now when we look to the style of these writings we find it altogether foreign to that of prophecy. The prophets were in the constant habit of insisting that they spoke from the decrees of God: "Thus saith the Lord," "Thus saith the Lord of hosts," "The voice of the Lord came," &c., are phrases of incessant recurrence. Nor was this style adhered to only in the public assemblies; it was followed in the Epistles which contained revelations, as we see in the one of Elijah to Jehoram (vide 2 Chron. xxi. 12), where we have the words, "Thus saith the Lord God." But in the letters of the apostles we meet with nothing of the kind; on the contrary, Paul expressly declares to the Corinthians that he speaks according to his own opinion (1 Cor. vii. 12). It is certain, indeed, that in many places expressions which betray hesitation of mind, and a perplexed manner, are met with, as when he says, "Therefore we conclude "* (Rom. iii. 28); "For I reckon" (Ib. viii. 18), and many other passages of the same uncertain kind. Besides such phrases, other modes of expression, as remote as possible from the authoritative tone of prophecy, are encountered in the writings of Paul, as when he says, "But I speak this by permission, not of commandment," "I give my judgment as one that hath obtained mercy of the Lord to be faithful" (Ib. vii. 25), with many more. It is to be observed also that when he says in the chapter just quoted that he has, or has not, the command of God to say what he does, he does not mean a precept or command of God specially revealed to him, but only the doctrine which Christ taught to his disciples in his Sermon on the Mount. Further, if we pay attention to the manner, as well as the matter, in which the apostles deliver the evangelical doctrine in their Epistles, we shall see that it differs widely from that of the prophets. The apostles frequently reason, so that they appear to discuss and dispute rather than to prophesy. The prophets under the old law, on the contrary, never reason, their utterances are mere dogmas and decrees, because in them God is always intro-

---

* The translators of Scripture render the Greek word *logidsomai* by *I conclude*, and insist that Paul takes this word in the same sense as *sullogidsomai*. But *logidsomai* has the same meaning in Greek as the Hebrew word which signifies I opine, I think, I judge, a sense which is in perfect accord with the Syriac version. The Syriac version, in fact (if indeed it be a version, which is extremely doubtful, for we neither know the time when it appeared nor the translator, and because Syriac was the common language of all the Apostles), — the Syriac version, I say, translates this text of Paul by a word which Tremellius explains very satisfactorily by the phrase, *We think then*. The word *rahgion*, in fact, which is formed from the cognate verb, signifies opinion, thought; and as *rahgava* is used for the will, it follows that the word in question, *mitrhaginam*, cannot signify anything but we will, we think, we are of opinion.

duced as the speaker, who reasons not, but by the absolute authority of his nature decrees. The calling of the prophets did not consist with reasoning; for whosoever attempts to confirm dogmatic decisions by reasoning, in so doing submits them to the arbitrament of every one. And this Paul by his reasonings does in fact; for he says to the Corinthians (2 x. 15), "I speak to you as men of understanding, judge ye what I say." The prophets, however, did not apprehend the things they revealed by their natural powers, that is to say, by the force of their understanding, as I have shown in Chapter I. And although in the Pentateuch we discover certain conclusions arrived at by inference, still, if due attention be given to the passages where these occur, it will be seen that they cannot in any way be taken as peremptory arguments. Thus, when Moses says to the Israelites (Deut. xxxi. 27), " If whilst I lived among you ye were rebellious against God, much more rebellious will ye be when I am dead." This is certainly not to be understood as if Moses by reasoning wished to satisfy the Jews that after his death they would necessarily depart from the worship of the true God: for the conclusion would be false, as may be shown from Scripture, the Israelites having continued faithful to Jehovah during the lives of Joshua and the Elders, and later, indeed, during the ages of Samuel, David, Solomon, &c. These words of Moses, consequently, are to be regarded as a mere moral locution, wherein he foretells rhetorically, and in colours heightened by his imagination, the future lapse of the people from the worship of the Lord God. The reason, however, why I do not say that Moses spoke the words above quoted of himself, and to make his prediction look more probable, is this, that in the 21st verse of the chapter just cited we are informed that God himself communicated the fact to Moses in different words. But there was no need by special reasons to make the prediction and decree of God more certain to Moses, though there may have been a necessity why he should more vividly picture the event in his imagination; and this he could do in no better way than by throwing into the future the present rebellious spirit of the people, a spirit which he had so often experienced in times past. In this way, I apprehend, are all the arguments of Moses scattered through the Pentateuch to be understood; they are not derived from the sanctuary of reason, but are mere modes of expression, whereby he announced the decrees of God more pointedly, whilst he himself conceived them more vividly. I would not, however, be held to deny from revelation that the prophets could show themselves possessed of argumentative powers; I only affirm that the more logically they reason, the more closely does the matter they reveal assimilate with what is natural; and it is especially from the absolute dogmata, or decrees, or opinions they utter that the prophets are to be distinguished as having had supernatural knowledge. Therefore was it that Moses, the greatest of the prophets, never made use of legitimate reasoning; whilst the lengthy arguments and deductions of Paul, such as are found in the Epistle to the Romans, can in no way be conceived as coming from supernatural inspiration. The mode of address, as well as the style of discussion, employed by the apostles in their Epistles, therefore, clearly proves that these were not written from revelation and by divine command, but entirely from their own natural understanding and experience, and that they contain nothing more than fraternal admonitions mixed with certain politenesses or urbanities (which the old prophetic authority utterly repudiates), as where Paul applies a little of the unction of flattery to his correspondents: "And I myself," he says, "am persuaded of you, my brethren, that ye also are full of goodness, filled with all knowledge," &c.; and then he goes on to excuse his own boldness in writing to them as he does: "Nevertheless, brethren, I have written the more boldly unto you, in some sort as putting you in mind," &c. (vide Epis. to Rom. xv. 14, 15). We may besides infer so much, from this: that we nowhere read of the apostles being commanded to write, but only to preach wherever they went, and to confirm their sayings by signs; for the actual presence of the apostles and the exhibition of signs were absolutely necessary to convert the nations to the religion of Christ, and to confirm them in the faith, as Paul himself says expressly in the Epistle to the Romans (i. 11): "For I long to see you, that I may impart unto you some spiritual gift, to the end ye may be established."

But here it may be objected, that in the same way we may conclude the apostles did not even preach as prophets; for when they went preaching here and there they did so, not like the prophets of old, by the express command of God. In the Old Testament we read of Jonah going to Nineveh to preach or prophesy, and at the same time of his having been sent expressly thither, when it would be revealed to him what he was to say. So also it is related at great length of Moses, how he went into Egypt as the messenger of God, and, at the same time, what he was to say to the people of Israel and to Pharaoh, and what signs and wonders he was to do, in order to win them to have faith in his mission. Isaiah, Jeremiah, Ezekiel, were all expressly ordered to preach to the Israelites. And none of the prophets ever preached anything which the Scripture does not declare to have been received from God. But it is only on very rare occasions that we read in the New Testament of anything of this sort, when the apostles went preaching in different places; on the contrary, indeed, we find express intimation of their having themselves selected one place or another as the scene of their labours. Paul and Barnabas went so far as to quarrel about their helpers, and to part company, taking different fields of operation from those originally intended. "Barnabas determined to take with them John, surnamed Mark, but Paul thought not good to take him with them; . . . and the contention was so sharp between them that they departed asunder one from another" (Acts xv. 37, 38, 39). They sometimes also attempted in vain to go where they desired, as the same Paul testifies in the 13th verse of the 1st chapter to the Romans, where he says, "Oftentimes I was purposed to come to you, but was let hitherto;" and in the last chapter of the First

Epistle to the Corinthians he expresses himself thus, "As touching our brother Apollos, I greatly desired him to come unto you with the brethren, but his will was not at all to come at this time; but he will come when he shall have convenient time." From such expressions, from the discussion between the apostles referred to, and from the fact that Scripture never testifies to any command of God that they should go and preach in this place or in that, as it does in the case of the old prophets, I must conclude that the apostles preached and taught, not as prophets, but simply as teachers.

But we readily solve this question when we attend to the different vocations of the prophets and the apostles. The former were not commanded to preach and prophesy to all nations alike, but only to some in particular, and required an especial mandate to each. But the apostles were called to preach to every people without exception, and to convert all to the faith. Wherever they went, therefore, they fulfilled the general command of Christ, nor was there any necessity that what they were to preach should be revealed to them before proceeding on their mission; even when brought before the judgment-seat on account of their teaching they were admonished to take no thought of how or what they were to speak, "for it shall be given you in that same hour what ye shall speak" (vide Matt. x. 19). Let us conclude, therefore, that the apostles received those things only by special revelation which they preached at once *viva voce* and confirmed by miracles (see what has been said in the beginning of Chapter II.); but that what they taught in writing or by word of mouth without sign or miracle as witness to their mission, was taught of their own natural knowledge (vide 1 Cor. xiv. 6); nor do we hesitate at all in this conclusion; for all the Epistles begin with a testimony to the apostolate of the writer, and, as I shall immediately show, to the apostles was given, not only the power to prophesy, but also the authority to teach. For this reason let us admit that as apostles they wrote their Epistles, and therefore presented the credentials of their apostolate to those whom they addressed; perhaps, too, that they might the more readily conciliate the reader's favour, and arouse his attention, they desired above all things to testify that they were the same men who had made themselves known to the faithful by their preaching, and had shown by many a wonderful sign that they taught true piety and the way of eternal life. For whatever I find in those Epistles concerning the calling of the apostles, and the holy and divine spirit which animated them, I see refers to their discourses; with the exception always of those places in which the Spirit of God and the Holy Spirit are taken as synonymous with a mind at ease, happy, and dedicated to God (on which topics see what has been said in Chapter I.); for example, where Paul in his First Epistle to the Corinthians (vii. 40) says, "But she is happier after my judgment, if she so abide, and I think also that I have the Spirit of God;" here the context plainly shows that the apostle by Spirit of God means his own mental state, as if he had said, "The widow who wills not to marry a second time is happy according to my view, who live a bachelor, and esteem myself happy." There are other passages of the same kind which I think it superfluous to cite in this place.

Since, then, we conclude that the Epistles were written with the aid of natural light alone, we have still to inquire how the apostles were in a condition to teach of natural knowledge things that transcend it. But if attention be paid to what is advanced in Chapter VII. of this work, we shall find no difficulty in settling this point. For although the things contained in Scripture often greatly exceed our power of comprehension, we can still securely speak concerning them, provided we admit no other principles of interpretation besides those which are derived from Scripture itself; and it was in this very way that the apostles were wont, from the things which they saw, heard, and received by revelation, to arrive at conclusions, which at fitting times they communicated to the people. Then, although religion, as it was preached by the apostles, in simple narratives of the history of Christ, does not fall under the domain of reason proper, its sum and substance consisting mainly in moral precepts, like the whole of the doctrine of Christ, it may nevertheless be readily apprehended by the natural powers. And, again, the apostles did not require supernatural light so to accommodate to vulgar capacity the religion they had already confirmed by miracles as to make it willingly received by all; nor did they require anything of the kind to enable them each in the way he judged best to admonish mankind of their duties, which indeed was the end and aim of the Epistles.

And here it is further to be noted that the apostles received not only the power of preaching the history of Christ as prophets, i. e. of confirming their teaching by miracles, but also authority to inculcate what they taught in such ways as to each seemed best, in order to confirm their converts in piety and virtue. Both of these gifts are clearly indicated by Paul in his Second Epistle to Timothy (i. 11), when he says, "Whereunto I am appointed a preacher, and an apostle, and a teacher of the Gentiles;" and again, in the First Epistle to the same (i. 7), "Whereunto I am ordained a preacher and an apostle (I speak the truth in Christ, and lie not), a teacher of the Gentiles in faith and verity." These passages, I say, clearly indicate both kinds of authority: that of the apostle and that of the teacher; and in the Epistle to Philemon (verse 8th) we have a further assurance of the authority he has to admonish whosoever and whensoever he pleases, for he says, "Wherefore, though I might be much bold in Christ to enjoin thee that which is convenient, yet for love's sake," &c. Here it is to be remarked, that had Paul received the command of God to proceed as prophet, and as prophet to teach, then would he not have felt himself at liberty to change God's commandments into entreaties. Wherefore it is necessary to understand that when he speaks of the liberty of admonishing he speaks as a teacher and not as a prophet.

Still it does not follow with sufficient clearness that the apostles were at liberty to choose the mode of teaching which each of them thought the best, but merely that they were not prophets only, but also teachers in virtue of their office of apostles,—unless, indeed, we call in reason to our aid, and declare that he who has the authority to teach has also the authority of choosing the manner of teaching he prefers. But it will be more satisfactory to explain the whole subject from Scripture, from which indeed it clearly appears that each of the apostles chose his own way of teaching. Thus Paul in his Epistle to the Romans says (xv. 20), " Anxiously striving to preach not where the name of Christ was invoked, lest I should build on a another's foundation (*alienum fundamentum*)."* Had all the apostles, however, followed the same manner of preaching, and built up the Christian religion on the same foundation, Paul would have had no reason to speak of the foundations of another apostle as *strange* or *foreign* (*alienum*), inasmuch as they would have been the same as his own. But as he uses the word strange we must needs conclude that each of the apostles raised his religious superstructure on a different foundation ; and that they in their capacity of doctors or teachers were affected in the same way as doctors or teachers in the world at large, each of whom has his own method of teaching, which he always prefers when instructing the uneducated, or those who have not begun to study the arts and sciences (not even the mathematics, of the truth of which no one doubts) under any one else. And then, in perusing the Epistles with some attention, we see that the apostles agree sufficiently as to the substance of their religion, but differ considerably as to the fundamentals. For Paul, to confirm the brethren in the faith, and to show them that salvation depends on the grace of God alone, taught that no one could be glorified because of his works, that no one could be justified by his good deeds, but only because of his faith, (Epist. to Rom. iii. 27, 28).

* The version of Spinoza is followed here. The English version could only by a kind of force be made to furnish a text to our author's immediate remarks. —*Ed.*

Still more in the same direction is implied in the whole of St Paul's doctrine of election or predestination. But James, on the other hand, teaches that justification is of good works, and not of faith alone (Epist. gen. of James ii. 24) ; and, casting aside all those reasonings and disputations of Paul, he declares that the whole of religion consists in a few simple elements. And there can be no question but that from this diversity of foundation selected by each of the apostles for his religious edifice, endless disputes and schisms arose, whereby the Church, even in the time of the apostles, was sorely shaken, and by which it will continue to be torn to the end of time, till such time, at all events, as religion, separated from theological and philosophical speculations, is reduced to the few simple doctrinal truths which Christ taught to his disciples. Such a thing, however, was impossible to the apostles, because the gospel was still unknown to the world;* and so, lest the novelty of their doctrines should shock the ears of the multitude too much, they did what they could to accommodate their teaching to the genius of their age, and built upon the foundations then best known and most commonly admitted (vide 1 Cor. ix. 19, 20). We therefore see none of the apostles philosophizing to the same extent as Paul, whose vocation it was to preach to such nations as the Greeks and Romans, who were more or less familiar with philosophy ; whilst the other apostles, who preached to the Jews, contemners of philosophy, accommodated themselves to their state and temper, and taught religion stripped of all philosophical speculation (vide Epist. to Gal. ii. 11), &c. How happy would our own age be, could we see religion freed from every kind of superstition !

* The earliest in point of time of the New Testament writings are some of the Epistles. The Gospels are long posterior in date to these—60, perhaps 100, years, or more; the three first probably different versions of one original, the fourth derived from other sources, and the composition of a Platonist.—*Ed.*

CHAPTER XII.

OF THE TRUE COVENANT OF THE DIVINE LAW; WHY THE SCRIPTURES ARE CALLED SACRED, AND WHY THEY ARE SAID TO BE THE WORD OF GOD. THE HEBREW SCRIPTURES, IN SO FAR AS THEY CONTAIN THE WORD OF GOD, HAVE COME DOWN TO US UNCORRUPTED.

They who hold the Bible as it is, to be the hand-writing of God, sent from heaven to man, will doubtless exclaim that I am guilty of the sin against the Holy Ghost, in concluding that it is in parts imperfect, corrupt, erroneous, and inconsistent with itself; that we have but fragments of a much greater mass of hieratic writings; and finally, that the original of the covenant which God made with the Jews has perished. Yet I cannot but think, if these persons will only consider the subject calmly, that they will cease from their clamour. For the voice of reason and the declarations of the prophets and apostles alike proclaim that the eternal word and covenant of God—The True Religion—is divinely inscribed on the heart and mind of man, and that this is the true covenant, this the bond on which God has set his seal and impressed the idea or likeness of his divinity.

Religion was delivered to the first Jews as a written law, because in those early times they were treated as children. Both Moses and subsequently Jeremiah, however, foretold to them a time to come when God would write his laws in their hearts (Deut. xxx. 6; Jeremiah xxxi. 33). The Jews therefore, and especially the Sadducees, were the only parties truly interested in contending for the law inscribed on tables of stone; they who have the law written in their hearts and minds are nowise interested in the dispute. Whoever duly considers this will find nothing in what precedes that is repugnant to the word of God or true religion, or that tends in any way to weaken its hold upon man; on the contrary, they will find nothing that does not rather strengthen true piety; as indeed has already been shown at the close of Chapter X. Were this not so, I should have determined to hold my tongue; yea, to escape difficulties, I should have preferred admitting that all sorts of unfathomable mysteries were locked up in Scripture. But as from such concessions superstitions the most intolerable and other grave inconveniences have arisen, of which I have made mention in my introduction to Chap. VII., I have thought that I could by no means keep silence. Religion requires no superstitious trappings, but is much rather shorn of its native beauty when meretriciously tricked out.

It may still be said, however, that though the divine law be written in the heart and mind of man, Scripture is nevertheless the word of God; and so that it is no more admissible to say of Scripture, than it were of the very word of God, that it is imperfect and corrupt. Now for my part, I rather fear that they who speak in this way incline to set themselves up for saints, and to turn religion into superstition, nay, that they come at length to fall down and worship an idol composed of ink and paper for the true word of God. Of this I feel assured, that I have said nothing unbecoming of the sacred Scriptures, in so far as they are the word of God; that I have advanced no proposition which I have not been prepared to support by the most cogent reasons; and I can therefore positively affirm that I have uttered no word that is irreverent, or has even a smack of impiety. I own, indeed, that some profane persons, to whom religion is a load, may pretend to derive a license for their irregular lives from my observations, and thence conclude that the Scriptures are everywhere and alike corrupt and imperfect, and are therefore of no authority in the conduct of life. It is impossible in any contingency to escape false inferences; according to the proverb that nothing however right can be said but it may be twisted to wrong by an evil construction; and they who are disposed to indulge in sensual pleasures are never at a loss to find an excuse for their doings. It is, indeed, distressing to believe that they who formerly held the originals of our sacred writings in their hands, who had the ark of the covenant in their keeping, the very prophets and apostles of old, were no more trustworthy than the rest of the world; but it must be owned that all, Jews as well as Gentiles, were always found alike: true virtue has in all ages been extremely rare. To remove scruples, however, I shall now proceed to show, 1st, in what sense Scripture as a dumb thing can be called sacred and divine; 2nd, what that is contained therein is truly word of God, and not comprised in any set number of books; and, lastly, I shall show that the doctrines of Scripture, in so far as they are necessary to obedience and salvation, cannot have been corrupted. These points established, every one will be able to see that I have said nothing against the word of God, and nowhere given scope or license for impiety.

That which is intended for piety and the practice of religion is called sacred and divine; but it is so only so long as men use it reverently: devoted to impious purposes, that which was before sacred and divine forthwith becomes profane and accursed. For example, a certain place was by the patriarch Jacob called Beth El, the house of God, because there he worshipped God revealed to him; but by the prophets the very same place was called Beth-aven, the house of iniquity, because there the Israelites, at the command of Jeroboam, were wont to sacrifice to idols (Amos v. 5, and Hosea x. 5). This other example shows the same thing very clearly: words have a certain signification by use and wont, and if they are so arranged according to their familiar uses as that men in reading them are moved to devotion, then will these words be sacred, as will a book written with words so disposed. But if these words fall into disuse by the lapse of time, so as at length to convey no meaning to the reader, or the book they compose falls into almost entire disuse, either through malevolence or because it is no longer wanted, then will the words and the book be useless, and have no sanctity. Lastly, if the same words are otherwise disposed, or if by usage they have come to bear another and a contrary meaning, then will the words and the book, which before were sacred, become impure and profane. From which it follows that nothing beyond the mind absolutely, or in respect of itself only, is either pure or impure, sacred or profane. This proposition is illustrated by many parts of Scripture. To quote one or two: Jeremiah (vii. 4) says that the Jews of his times falsely called the temple of Solomon the temple of God; for, he proceeds to explain, the title "temple of God" could only be properly applied so long as it was entered by men who worshipped him in truth, and who did justly; but frequented by homicides, idolaters, and other wicked persons, then was it rather a den of transgressors. Scripture nowhere informs us as to what became of the ark of the covenant, which I have often wondered at; this only seems certain, that it perished, or was consumed with the temple, although there was nothing held so sacred or so much reverenced by the Jews. For this reason, therefore, Scripture also is sacred, and its doctrines are divine, so long only as it moves mankind to piety towards God; but if it comes to be almost entirely neglected, as it was at one time by the Jews, it is nothing more than ink and paper; it may then indeed be profane, and obnoxious to corruption; and if under such circumstances it is corrupted or perishes, it is a false phrase to say that it is the word of God which is corrupted or perishes: in the neglect of its precepts it has ceased to these men to be the word of God, even as in the time of Jeremiah it was incorrect to say that the building which perished in the flames was the temple of the Lord. Thus therefore does he address the transgressors of his day:

" Wherefore do ye say, We are skilful, or that the law of God is with us? In vain was the law set forth, in vain the pen of the scribe!" that is to say: you deceive yourselves, though the Scriptures be among you, when you say you have the law of God, after having roused his wrath by your wickedness. So also, when Moses broke the first tables of the law, he by no means cast the word of God from his hands in anger, for who can imagine this of Moses, or believe it possible as regards the law of God? but merely the stone tables, which, although sacred before, because on them was inscribed the covenant whereby the Jews were bound in obedience to Jehovah, nevertheless lost all sanctity after the people had violated the compact by worshipping a calf. In the same way, and for the same reason, the tables of the second covenant, as well as the ark of the sanctuary, could be said to perish. It is not therefore wonderful that the original writings of Moses are no longer extant, nor that the Scriptures we possess, of which we have spoken in preceding chapters, should only have reached us in the state we find them, when the original of the divine covenant, the most sacred of all things, has totally perished. Let them cease, then, to accuse us of impiety, who have not breathed a murmur against the word of God, who have been most careful not to alter or corrupt it; let them rather turn their anger, righteous, if anger ever can be righteous, against the ancients, whose wickedness and neglect profaned the ark, the temple, the law of God, and subjected the sacred things confided to them to change and corruption. If, finally, in consonance with what is said in the Second Epistle to the Corinthians (iii. 3), they desire to be "declared the epistle of Christ, written not with ink, but with the spirit of the living God; not in tables of stone, but in fleshy tables of the heart," let them cease to worship the letter, which kills, and show themselves more eager after the spirit, which gives life everlasting.

I have thus, I think, sufficiently explained in what sense Scripture is to be held sacred and divine. But I have still to show what is properly to be understood by the Hebrew phrase *Dabar Jehovah*, translated, word of God, or word of the Lord. The word *dabar* has, however, several significations besides word; it means discourse, edict, and thing. We have already shown in Chap. I. how in Hebrew a thing is said to be of God, or is referred to God, and from this it will easily be understood what is intended in Scripture, when the words, the sayings, the commands of God are mentioned. It is therefore unnecessary to repeat what has already been said on this point; neither is it necessary to recur to what has been advanced in Chap. III. on Miracles. It will be enough here to recall the matter to the reader's attention, in order that what I am now about to say may be the better understood; namely, that the expression *word of God*, when any subject is matter of discourse other than God himself, properly signifies that divine law of which we have spoken particularly in Chap. IV.; in other words, that universal or truly Catholic religion, proper to the whole human family, of which Isaiah speaks (ch. i. 16 *et seq.*), which he says consists not in ceremonies, but in charity and holiness of life and mind, and which he entitles indifferently word and law of God. The expression word of God, again, is used metaphorically for the order of nature and fate, or necessary sequence in creation (which, in fact, depends on and follows the eternal decrees of the divine nature); and especially for so much of this order and succession as the prophets foresaw, and this because they did not perceive future events as the effects of natural causes, but as the special behests or decrees of God. Further, the phrase is employed for the command of a prophet, in so far as it has been conceived in virtue of his peculiar prophetic power, and not by the force of his natural understanding, and this happened especially from the prophets having been accustomed to regard God as a law-giver, as has been shown in Chap. IV. Scripture consequently is entitled Law of God, from these three causes: 1st, because it teaches absolute religion, of which the everlasting God is the author; 2nd, because it relates predictions of future events as decrees of God; 3rd, because they who were its authors mostly taught in virtue of a certain peculiar gift, not in virtue of their natural understanding, and commonly introduced God as the utterer of their revelations. And although there are many other things in Scripture which are mere matter of history, and conceptions of our common natural capacity, still the title is derived from the preponderating characteristic of the Bible writings. In this way do we readily perceive how God is to be understood as the author of the Bible. It is because of the absolute religion which is taught therein, not because it is a collection of books which God desired to communicate or did verbally communicate to man. Thus also do we understand why the Bible is divided into the books of the Old and New Testament, because of the prophets having been accustomed before the coming of Christ to preach religion to the Jews as the law of their native country, and in virtue of a covenant made in the time of Moses. After the appearance of Christ in the world, however, the apostles preached religion as an universal law to all mankind, and in virtue of the Passion of Christ alone. But this does not imply that there is any diversity in the doctrines of the Old and New Testament; nor that they are the instruments of two special covenants; nor, finally, that the universal religion, which is also the most natural religion, is anything new, save and except to those who know it not before. "It was in the world," says John the Evangelist (i. 10), "and the world knew it not."

Though we had fewer books, then, both of the Old and New Testament, than we possess, we should not therefore be without the word of God, by which, as already said, we understand the true or absolute religion; even as we do not think that we are without God's blessed word because we are without many other most precious writings, such as "The Book of the Law," which was wont to be religiously preserved in the temple as the instrument of the covenant between God and the Jews, to say nothing of the "Book of the Wars," "The Chronologies," and many more, from which those books which we now possess, and which compose the Old Testament, were extracted and put together. This view is confirmed by many other considerations : 1st, Because the books of both the Testaments were not written by an express command for all ages at one and the same time ; but fortuitously, as it were, for certain individuals, and as the time and their peculiar mental constitution required. This is plainly indicated by the vocation of the prophets, who were called to admonish the wicked of their age ; so is it also in the Epistles of the apostles. 2nd, Because it is one thing to understand Scripture and the minds of the prophets, and another to comprehend the mind of God, i. e. to comprehend the very truth of a thing in itself, as follows from what has already been said in Chap. II., which treats of The Prophet. The same distinction we have shown requires to be made in regard to the narratives and the miracles (vide Chapter VI.) ; but no such thing can be said of the parts in which true religion and true virtue are discussed. 3rd, Because the books of the Old Testament are a selection from among a great number, and were finally put together and approved by a council of Pharisees, as has been shown in Chapter X. The books of the present New Testament, in like manner, were assumed into the Canon by certain councils, by whose decrees, also, numerous other books were rejected as spurious, which were nevertheless held sacred by many. The members of these councils, however, were not prophets, but merely doctors and learned persons, though it is proper to admit that they had the word of God as a standard in making their selection : before approving the books they chose they necessarily had a knowledge of the word of God. 4th, Because the apostles wrote not as prophets, but as teachers, and chose their own mode of teaching, having regard doubtless to the state and capacity of those they were called upon to instruct ; whence it follows that there must be many things in the writings of the apostles which, as regards religion, might be dispensed with. 5th, Because, lastly, we have four evangelists in the New Testaments. And who can believe that God desired to narrate and in writing to communicate to man the history of Christ four several times? And although some things are contained in one Gospel which are not in another, and one often aids in understanding another, we are not therefore to conclude that everything in the four Evangels is needful to be known, and that God elected four different men to write distinct narratives in order that the history of Christ might be better understood. The several evangelists seem to have preached their Gospel in different places, and each to have written what he had preached in a simple style, that he might himself relate the history of Christ, and not with any view to explaining the narratives of the others. If, indeed, by the mutual collation of the four Gospels we do come to understand some passages better than we did before, this is rather fortuitous than necessary, and occurs in respect of a few passages only, which, had they remained obscure or unintelligible, the history would still have been equally perspicuous, and mankind not the less instructed.

Thus do we show that Scripture can properly be called the word of God in respect of the absolute religion, of the universal divine law alone which it proclaims. But we have now to show that in so far as it is the word of God, Scripture is neither mendacious, nor imperfect, nor corrupt. Now I call that mendacious, corrupt, and imperfect, which in writing and construction is so faulty that the sense is by no means to be made out by taking the language in any of its accredited significations, or when the meaning is not to be had from the text alone; for I would not be supposed to affirm that Scripture, in so far as it contains the divine law, always makes use of the same literal apices, of the same letters, and, finally, of the same words (matters which I leave to the Masoretes and those who superstitiously worship the letter of Scripture), but only that the sense, in regard to which alone can any writing be spoken of as divine, has come down to us uncorrupted, although the words in which it was originally embodied may be supposed to have been altered many times. This, as has been said, takes away nothing from the divineness of Scripture; for it would have been equally divine had it been written in other words or in another language. That in this sense we have received the divine law uncorrupted, no one, I think, can doubt. For from Scripture we learn, without any kind of difficulty or ambiguity, that its sum is this,—to love God above all, and our neighbour as ourselves. Now there can be no error here. This is no sentence set down by a hasty and careless pen; and did Scripture elsewhere teach aught different, it were necessarily to be regarded as corrupt; for divine and neighbourly love is the foundation of all religion, and this ignored, the whole fabric falls to pieces. Such Scriptures would not be those of which we make question here, but a totally different production.

It remains established therefore that Scripture has always taught this doctrine, and that here no error has crept in to corrupt the sense of the text. Such a thing would have been immediately apparent to all; nor could any attempt even have been made to alter the sense without detection. Since, then, this fundamental principle is to be held established, it follows of necessity that all which rests on it or which without dissidence flows from it, is also to be held fundamental and assured;—such as that God exists; that he is omniscient, foreseeing all; that he is omnipotent; and that in virtue of his eternal decree it is well with the good but ill with the wicked, and that our salvation depends on his grace alone. Such, in brief, is the teaching of the whole of Scripture; otherwise everything else it contains were vain and without significance. Nor are the other moral precepts of Holy Writ to be regarded as less free from taint, seeing that they all obviously rest on the broad foundation of love of God and love of our neighbour. The commands to do justly, to succour and assist the poor and oppressed, to do no murder, not to commit adultery, not to covet our neighbour's goods, &c., —these are precepts which the wickedness of man could never corrupt, and of which no length of time can lessen the excellence. Anything fallen away or taken away from such precepts would again immediately spring up or be supplied from the universal foundation on which they all rest, and especially from that precept of CHARITY which is everywhere so strongly insisted on both in the Old and in the New Testament.* Add, that though there is no crime the most heinous which has not been committed by man, still there is no one who, to excuse his guilt, has attempted to destroy the laws, or to present as an eternal and wholesome precept that which is impious and pernicious. For we see mankind so constituted by nature, that no one—be he king or be he subject—ever does any baseness, but he tries to surround his deed with such circumstances and excuses as tend to make it appear that he has done nothing against justice and propriety.

Let us conclude, therefore, absolutely that the whole of the universal divine law which Scripture teaches has come down to us in its original, genuine, and uncorrupted state. Besides this, however, there are other things which we cannot doubt have been handed down to us in perfect good faith. Under this head I class the ground-work of the Scripture histories, these having been familiarly known to all. The common people of the Jews in former ages were wont to sing the antiquities of their nation in their psalms. The heads of the things done by Christ, and the story of his passion, were also speedily spread over the whole of the Roman Empire. Wherefore it is not to be believed, unless the majority of the people had come to such an understanding, which is a thing incredible, that the grand facts of this history have been transmitted to posterity in another shape than that in which they were first made known. Whatever, therefore, is suspicious in Scripture, or incorrect, or false, can only be so as regards the other matters of which

---

* "Though I speak with the tongues of men and of angels, and have not charity," says the apostle Paul (1 Cor. xiii.), "I am become as sounding brass or a tinkling cymbal. And though I have the gift of prophecy, and understand all mysteries, and all knowledge; and though I have all faith, so that I could remove mountains, and have not charity, I am nothing."—*Ed.*

it treats, viz. the circumstances of this or that narrative, prophecy, or miracle; in narratives calculated to arouse the devotional feelings of the people, or to disconcert the philosophers; or, lastly, in speculative matters, after they had begun to be introduced into religious discussions by schismatics, in order that each might find support for his own conceits in Holy Writ. But it matters little to the soul's state whether such things are in great or in small measure. This I shall proceed to show in the next chapter, although I believe, from what has just been said, as well as from Chapter II., that it has been already demonstrated.

CHAPTER XIII.

SCRIPTURE TEACHES NOTHING THAT IS NOT EXTREMELY SIMPLE. IT REQUIRES NOTHING BUT OBEDIENCE, NOR TEACHES AUGHT OF THE DIVINE NATURE THAT MEN, BY FOLLOWING A CERTAIN RULE OF LIFE, MAY NOT IMITATE.

In the Second Chapter of this treatise we have shown that the prophets had a peculiar faculty of imagination only, and no special gift of understanding; that God had revealed to them no mysteries of philosophy, and that he had accommodated himself to their pre-conceived opinions. In Chapter the Fifth we showed that those things only were taught and delivered in Scripture which could be easily understood by all; that it did not proceed in the way of axiom and definition to deduce and concatenate things, but announced in simple terms what was to be said, and, in order to secure faith, appealed to experience, to miracles, and the records of history, the style and phraseology being such as were best calculated to fix the popular attention (vide Chap. III. and the points demonstrated under section 3). Finally, in Chapter the Seventh we have shown that the difficulty of understanding Scripture lay in the language alone, not in the sublimity of the argument. In addition to which, let it be remembered that the prophets preached not to the learned only, but to the Jews indiscriminately, and that the apostles were wont to hold forth in the synagogues, then the places of common resort for all classes of the people.

From these facts it follows that the doctrine of Scripture contains no sublime speculations, no philosophical problems, but simple things only, that may be apprehended even by the dullest. I cannot therefore sufficiently wonder at the ingenuity of those of whom I have spoken above, who see such deep mysteries in Scripture that no human tongue is competent to explain them; and who have on the strength of this assumption introduced so much philosophical speculation into religion that the Church assumes the aspect of an academy, and religion that of a science, or rather of a controversy. But why should I wonder at seeing the men who boast of having supernatural light unwilling to yield in knowledge to the philosophers who have only their natural understanding for their instructor? I should be surprised, indeed, did I find them teaching anything new as matters even of mere speculation which had not been already well worn by the handling of the Gentile philosophers (whom they nevertheless accuse of blindness); for when those pretended mysteries are scanned a little closely they are found to resolve themselves into Aristotelian, Platonic, and other philosophical conceptions, which a fool might be supposed to find in his dreams more readily than a reasonable man in the Holy Scriptures. In speaking thus I would not be held to declare without any reservation that Scripture contains nothing of a speculative nature; in the preceding chapter, I have referred on the contrary to certain matters of this kind, even as fundamentals in Scripture doctrine; I only mean to maintain that they are few in number and sufficiently simple; and I shall now proceed to show wherein they consist, and how they are to be determined. And this will be easy for us, since we have ascertained that Scripture was not intended to teach the sciences; whence we may see that it is obedience only which is required from man, and that stubbornness and contempt, not ignorance, are condemned. Now since obedience to God consists in the love of our neighbour (for he who loves his neighbour, to the end that God may be glorified, according to Paul in his Epistle to the

Romans (xiii. 8), fulfils the law), it follows that in Scripture no other science is recommended save that which is necessary to mankind, in order that by obeying God in conformity with the precept of neighbourly love they may show themselves obedient to him, as in ignoring it they must necessarily prove themselves contumacious, or at all events without the discipline of reverential submissiveness. The other speculative matters which do not bear immediately in this direction, those about God, or that refer to the knowledge of natural things, do not touch Scripture in fact, and so are to be distinguished and separated from revealed religion. But although these things are readily perceived by every one as has been said, nevertheless, as on them depends the entire judgment in matters religious, I am in the mind to enter more fully upon the subject and to explain it thoroughly. To which end it is before all things requisite to show that an intellectual or accurate conception of God is not given, like obedience, as a gift in common to all the faithful; and next, that that knowledge which God by the prophets requires of all men, and which every one is held bound to possess, is nothing but the knowledge of his divine justice and mercy, qualities which are readily demonstrated from Scripture. For, 1st, it follows most obviously from Exodus vi. 2, where God, to show the singular grace showered upon Moses, says to him, "I was revealed to Abraham, to Isaac, and to Jacob, as El Sadai, but by my name Jehovah I was not known to them."* For the better understanding of this text it is to be observed that El Sadai in Hebrew signifies God who suffices, because he gives to every one what suffices him; and although Sadai is often taken for God absolutely, there is no question but that El, the proper earliest title of the Supreme, is everywhere understood. Then it is to be observed that no name for God but Jehovah is ever found in Scripture where the absolute essence of God without

---

* Spinoza's version is followed here of necessity, the English version for *El Sadai* giving *God Almighty*, a rendering which goes far to destroy the meaning of the passage.—*Ed.*

reference to created things is indicated. The Jews therefore contend that this is the only proper name of God, the other words by which he is designated being mere appellatives; and it is a truth that the other names of God are such substantives or adjectives—attributes, in short—which seem appropriate to God when he is viewed in relation to created things, or is manifested by their means. EL, or with the letter *ha* added, ELOHA, signifies nothing more than the powerful, as already said, and is not appropriate to God save as signifying pre-eminence; in the same way as when we speak of Paul *The Apostle*. *El*, therefore, indicates the grand attributes of God as we conceive them; *El*, the powerful, the great, the awful, the just, the merciful, &c. The word, again, is often found in the plural *Elohim*, with the singular sense, and then it implies all the attributes of God collectively; this form is very frequent in Scripture. But as God informs Moses that he was not known to the patriarchs by his name of Jehovah, it follows that they knew no attributes of God that explain his absolute essence, but only his influences, his promises,—in other words, his power, in so far as it was made manifest by visible things. Now God does not say to Moses that the patriarchs knew him not by his name of Jehovah, in order to accuse them of any infidelity or unworthiness; on the contrary, it was to laud their faith and belief, who though they had not the singular knowledge of him possessed by Moses, yet believed firmly in his promises, and did not, like the great prophet, in spite of his more sublime ideas of God, doubt or question the divine word:—they never objected to God like Moses, that instead of the promised safety he had brought the Jews into greater misery than before. Since then the patriarchs were ignorant of the proper name of God, and God informs Moses that this was so in order that their simplicity and faith might be commended, and that the singular favour shown to Moses might at the same time be commemorated, it follows, most obviously, as we have stated above, that men at large are not held to know the attributes of God by a commandment, but that to do so is a gift peculiar to some only among the faithful. Is it worth the pains to prove this truth by further Scripture testimony? Who does not perceive that the divine conception exists not with equal force and clearness in the minds of all believers? and that no one can be wise at the word of command, any more than he can continue to live or to be? Men, women, children, all alike can obey upon command, but they cannot equally be wise. But if any one should say that it was by no means necessary to know the attributes of God, but simply and without demonstration to believe, this were to jest; for invisible things, which are objects of the mind alone, can be seen by no other than those inward eyes which appreciate the force of demonstrations; they, therefore, who have not these, see absolutely nothing of such things, and all they hear said of them touches their mind no more than the words of a parrot or an automaton touch the bird or the machine which articulates without sense or reason.

Before I proceed further, however, I feel bound to give a reason why in Genesis we constantly find the patriarchs using, and speaking in, the name of Jehovah, which seems plainly in contradiction with what has just been said. But if attention be had to what is stated in Chapter VIII. it will be found easy to reconcile the one statement with the other. In our 8th chapter we have shown that the writer of the Pentateuch speaks of things and places by different names from those they bore in the times long gone by, of which he is giving an account; he uses the titles that were best and most familiarly known in his own day. God, therefore, in Genesis is said to have been known to the patriarchs by the name of Jehovah, not because this name was really communicated to them, for it was not, but because the word is of all words the most holy to the Hebrews. This explanation I believe to have been necessary, seeing that in our text from Exodus it is said expressly that God was not known to the patriarchs by his name of Jehovah; and further, because in another passage of Exodus (iii. 13) Moses asks to know the name of God, which, had it been known at all, would surely have been known to the leader of the people. Let us conclude, then, that the faithful patriarchs of old did not know the proper name of God, and that knowledge of God is in virtue of a gift, not of a commandment.*

Let us now proceed to the second head of our subject, and show that God sought no other knowledge of himself from man by the mouths of the prophets than that of his divine justice and charity; a knowledge, in other words, of such

* Any but the most cursory reading shows the earlier portion of the Book of Genesis to be derived and compiled from at least *two* different sources. The first chapter and the three first verses of the second chapter form a whole; a grand simple history of creation; and in the English version the Great First Cause is here always simply designated God. This by biblical scholars has been spoken of as the *Elohistic* portion of Genesis. From the 4th verse of chapter ii. the history of creation is again entered on, and more particularly as regards man. Here the simple word *God* gives place to the more elaborate *Lord God.* What is interesting to observe also is this,—that in the first the grand and undoubtedly by much the more ancient history of creation, the gift of the vegetable kingdom to man, is *without reservation :* " And God said, Behold, I have given you *every herb* bearing seed which is upon the face of all the earth, and *every tree* in the which is the fruit of a tree yielding seed ; to you it shall be for meat." It is only in the second or *Jehovistic* account, as it has been called, that we find the *reservation of the tree of the knowledge of Good and Evil.* Further, in the grand old Elohistic account, God creates man in his own image, " *male and female created he them.*" In the more modern history man is at first single, and the Lord God discovers that " it is not good for the man to be alone," and resolves " to make an help meet for him ;" and then follows the tale of the rib from which woman was fashioned, and all this in connection with the name of him who said, " Let there be light, and there was light," and as if sex had not been an universal, and therefore primary and eternal, decree of the Almighty. It is in this *romance of creation,* too, that the tale of the serpent occurs : " Now the serpent was more subtil than any beast of the field which the Lord God had made." " And he *said* unto the woman," &c., as if articulate speech were not the apanage of man alone, the creation of an order of faculties of which we do not find a trace so low in the scale of being as reptiles. All this portion of the Bible can in no wise be taken literally,—it is fancy, poetry, allegory, of which various interpretations have been given ; among others it has been said that man has lived without care through the summer half of the year; but then comes autumn with its fruits, and ushers in the winter half, the astronomical sign of which is the serpent or dragon, &c. The relations of astronomy to mythology are most fully and ably treated by M. Dupuis in his learned work entitled, 'Origine des Cultes,' 6 vols. 8vo. Paris. Subsequently the Elohistic and Jehovistic elements are greatly jumbled together, yet not always so but that each can often be detected by its own characteristics.—*Ed.*

attributes of God as men by a certain rule of life may readily imitate; and this indeed is expressly taught by Jeremiah; for speaking of Shallum, son of King Josiah, he says (xxii. 15), "Did not thy father eat and drink, and do judgment and justice, and then it was well with him? He judged the cause of the poor and the needy; then it was well with him: was not this to know me? saith the Lord." Nor is the meaning less clear of what is said in chapter ix. 24: "But let him that glorieth glory in this, that he understandeth and knoweth me that I am the Lord, which exercise loving-kindness, judgment, and righteousness in the earth; for in these things I delight, saith the Lord." The same sentiments are, besides, found in Exodus (xxxiv. 6, 7), where God, in answer to Moses, who desires to see and to know him, reveals no other attribute but such as shows forth his divine justice and mercy. Lastly, what is said by John cannot be passed by without notice in this place, although we shall have occasion to speak of it by and by at greater length; for as no one has seen God, he interprets or explains God to be Love or Charity, and concludes that he indeed knows and possesses God who has charity in his heart.

We therefore see that Moses, Jeremiah, John, all alike make a knowledge of God to consist in a very few principles, which every one may be held bound to know and observe, the sum and substance of which is this: That God is all righteous, and all merciful, and the sole exemplar of the true life to man. Scripture gives no express definition of God; nor does it prescribe any attribute besides those just mentioned as necessary to be known and imitated. From all of which we conclude that the intellectual conception of God, involving considerations of the nature of the Supreme as he is in himself, which man is incapable of imitating by any course of life, and which he cannot therefore take as an example to be followed, has nothing whatever to do with the institution of a perfect rule of life, with faith and with revealed religion; and as a consequence of this it is plain that men may go wrong in regard to it in every way without sin.

It is not therefore to be wondered at that God should have accommodated his revelations and modes of revelation to the imaginations and preconceived opinions of the prophets, and that the pious have frequently entertained different opinions of God, as we have shown by numerous examples in our second chapter. Again, there is no reason for wondering that God is constantly spoken of so improperly in Scripture, and that eyes, ears, hands, feet, senses, a mind, and proportions, are ascribed to him, to say nothing of such mental emotions as anger, jealousy, mercy, &c.,— or that he is pictured as a sovereign or judge, seated on a royal throne in heaven, with Christ on his right hand, and the heavenly host around. All this is mere condescension to the capacity of the vulgar, whom Scripture strives to make not learned but obedient. The common run of theologians, however, have concluded, that whatever they saw by their natural understanding which did not accord with higher conceptions of the divine nature was to be interpreted metaphorically; and that whatever transcended their capacity was to be taken quite literally. But if everything of this kind that is found in Scripture were necessary to be interpreted and understood metaphorically, then were Scripture written not for the rude and unlettered populace, but for the most learned and philosophical only among men. And what is more; if it be impious to conceive and believe those things of God which we have thus far set forth in all purity and simplicity of mind, then ought the prophets to have been especially careful to avoid such phrases, and in respect of vulgar weakness to have spoken expressly of the attributes of God in such a way as to make them readily appreciable and retainable by ordinary men; but this they have nowhere done. We are therefore by no means to believe that opinions, abstractly considered, and without reference to deeds, have anything either of piety or impiety in themselves; let it rather be said of any man that he is good or bad, as he is moved by his opinions to obedience and purity of life, or otherwise is led to licentiousness of conduct and rebellion against God's decrees: he who, believing the truth, yet shows himself contumacious, is a sinner, as he who believing falsehoods yet leads a good life is pious and good. The true knowledge of God comes not by command, as we have shown, but is a divine gift; and God asks nothing more of man than recognition of his divine justice and mercy, which leads not to science, but is indispensably necessary to obedience to his eternal laws.*

---

* For what doth the Lord require of thee, but to do justly, to love mercy, and to walk humbly with thy God? (Micah vi.)—*Ed.*

CHAPTER XIV.

OF FAITH, THE GROUNDS OF FAITH, AND THE DISTINCTION BETWEEN FAITH AND PHILOSOPHY.

To have a right conception of the nature of faith, it is especially necessary to know that Scripture was adapted to the capacity, not of the prophets only, but of the thoughtless and inconstant Jewish people, no one of whom with the slightest attention could misunderstand it. Whoever accepts indiscriminately as the universal and absolute doctrine of God all that is comprised in the Scriptures, however, does not exactly know what is adapted to common apprehension; neither can he escape confounding vulgar opinion with divine doctrine, or producing the comments and conceits of man for sacred commands, and abusing the authority of Scripture. Who does not see this as the grand cause why sectarians urge so many conflicting opinions as articles of faith, which they never fail to confirm by texts of Scripture? Whence indeed it has passed into a proverb in the Low Countries, "that there is never a heretic but he quotes Scripture for his views: *geen ketter sonder letter.*" For the sacred books of the Jews were not written by one hand, nor even in the same age; but by several men of diverse genius and in different centuries; between the first and last of whom almost two thousand, and perchance many more, years intervened. We would not however accuse those sectaries of impiety because they accommodate Scripture to their views, inasmuch as Scripture itself in former times was accommodated to the common apprehension; every one therefore may be held free to adapt it to his opinions [provided he change nothing of its spirit], if by doing so he sees that he can give a more entire consent, and yield a more full obedience, to all that regards God's justice and mercy. We, however, charge those with violating the great law of charity who refuse to concede the same liberty to others which they arrogate to themselves, who condemn and persecute as enemies to God all, though leading most peaceable and virtuous lives, who do not think as they do themselves, and, on the contrary, exalt those as the elect of God who are of their opinion, though they be [often of doubtful lives and] always of weak understanding. Nothing, as I believe, can be more wicked than such conduct, nothing conceived more detrimental to the general weal.

With a view to determine the limits within which each member of the community may be held at liberty to think as he chooses in matters of faith, and, though thinking differently from others, may still be reckoned among the number of the faithful, I shall now proceed to inquire concerning faith, and essay to determine the grounds on which it rests. This will be the business of the present chapter, and I shall at the same time be careful to distinguish between faith and philosophy, which indeed is the main purpose of my whole work. To proceed with order, then, let us recur to the grand intent of the Scriptures at large, which will give us a true standard of faith. Now we have seen that the purpose of Scripture was solely to teach obedience. This I hold to be undeniable. For who does not see that either Testament is nothing from beginning to end but a doctrine and discipline of obedience? and that all the Scripture teaching has no other end but to induce mankind to obey of their own free will? Moses did not attempt to convince the Israelites by reasoning, he bound them by covenants, by oaths, by benefits conferred; and then he constrained the people to respect the laws by threatening pains and penalties for their infraction, whilst he held out the prospect of reward for their faithful observance. All such means are plainly not means of knowledge or instruction, but only of obedience. The Gospel doctrine, again, makes mention of nothing but simple faith, viz. to believe in God, and to worship him in sincerity and truth; in other words, to obey and to serve him. I do not think it necessary here to heap together texts from Scripture to demonstrate so plain a proposition. As to what every one is to do in order that he may obey God, this is most clearly set forth in many parts of Scripture; and indeed it is comprised in very brief terms, he is to love God with all his heart, and his neighbour as himself. In this is comprehended the whole of the law; and it is unquestionable that he who loves God and his neighbour is obedient indeed, and blessed according to the law, whilst he who neglects this divine precept is rebellious and in sin. Lastly, it is admitted by all that Scripture was written and published for the behoof, not of the learned alone, but of all kinds and degrees of men; not for this age or for that, but for all times, whence it follows most assuredly that we are bound by the Scriptures to believe nothing more than is necessary to carry out the divine command of Godly and Neighbourly love. This command, therefore, is the sole rule and measure of a catholic faith; by this alone are the dogmas which all must embrace to be determined.

But this being so obvious, and all else resting on, or flowing legitimately from, so plain a principle, it may well be asked how it has happened that so many dissensions have arisen in the Church? and whether there may not be other causes for these besides those which have been mentioned in the beginning of Chapter VII.? These same causes, in fact, oblige me in this place to discuss the mode and principle of determining the dogmas of a catholic faith on the foundation assumed; for unless I did so, and established the matter in conformity with certain rules, I should deservedly be held to have advanced my subject but little, inasmuch as every one, under pretext of something needful to obedience, might then assert the liberty of introducing what he pleased, especially when there was any question concerning the divine attributes. That I may present the whole subject in order, I shall therefore begin with a definition of faith. Now faith, on the grounds assigned, is nothing but this,—To entertain such thoughts of God as, if wanting, obedience to him is withheld; and, obedience given, adequate thoughts of God are implied.* This definition follows so plainly from what has been already demonstrated, that it seems to require no explanation. Nevertheless, I shall enlarge upon a few particulars which follow from it. 1. Faith of itself is not salutary, it is only so in respect of the obedience it implies; or, as James says (Epist. Gen. ii. 17), "faith being alone, if it hath not works is dead." It follows that he who is truly obedient necessarily has a true and saving faith; for obedience conceded, faith, as we have said, is necessarily conceded also. This the apostle just quoted goes on to declare (Ib. 18), where he says, "Show me thy faith without thy works, and I will show thee my faith by my works." John also writes (1st Epist. iv. 7, 8), "Every one that loveth (God and his neighbour) is born of God, and knoweth God; he that loveth not, knoweth not God; for God is love." From which it follows again that we can adjudge no one faithful or unfaithful except by his works. That is to say, if his works be good, although he differs in the articles of his creed from other believers, he is to be accounted faithful; as, on the contrary, if his deeds be evil, though he may assent to the words of the truly pious, still is he an infidel. For obedience given, faith is necessarily given, and faith without works is dead, as John also expressly teaches (Ib.13), where he says, "Hereby

---

* Nempe nihil aliud sit (fides) quam a Deo talia sentire quibus ignoratis tollitur erga Deum obedientia, et hac obedientia posita, necessario ponuntur. The reader may possibly make a translation of this definition which he likes better than the one given above. For our own part, and without circumlocution, we should define Faith to be: such conceptions of the power and wisdom of God as insure obedience to his will declared in his eternal laws.—*Ed.*

know we that we dwell in him and he in us, because he hath given us of his spirit," by spirit, here, charity or love being understood; for he had just said that God was love; and plainly concludes from his adopted principles that he who has the spirit of God truly within him has also charity. John, indeed, as he says that no man hath seen God, concludes that no man knows or conceives God save through the feeling of love towards his neighbour, that no one can appreciate any other attribute of God but this of love, in so far as man is capable of the sentiment. These views, though not peremptorily or dogmatically announced, nevertheless exhibit the ideas of this apostle with sufficient clearness. But we learn more of them when we go back to his 2nd chapter (3, 4), where we find these words, "And hereby do we know that we know him if we keep his commandments. He that saith I know him, and keepeth not his commandments, is a liar, and the truth is not in him." From these texts, yet again, it follows that they are Antichrists indeed who persecute honest men, men who love justice and charity, because they differ from them in speculative opinions, and hold not the same articles of a dogmatic creed with themselves. They who love justice and mercy thereby show themselves true believers, as we know from Scripture, and he who persecutes the true believer is Antichrist. It follows, in conclusion, that to faith, absolutely true are less indispensable than pious dogmas, that is to say, dogmas or precepts that move the mind and heart to obedience. And although among these there may be many which have not a shadow of truth, provided that he who accepts them is unconscious of this, he does not rebel against them, as he would necessarily do were he better informed; for how were it possible that one who studies justice and mercy should go on adoring God as a conjuror, were he aware that such a practice was absurd in connection with reasonable ideas of the divine nature? Men, however, may err through simplicity of mind; and Scripture, as we have seen, condemns not ignorance but disobedience only—indeed, this follows from the mere definition we have given of faith, all the elements of which must be sought in the broad foundation we have adopted, and in the whole purpose of the Scriptures, unless we would mix up our own imaginations with the sacred teachings. Now these do not require dogmas that are absolutely true, but such only as are needful to obedience and to strengthen the mind in neighbourly love, in which sense alone can any man be said to be in God, and God in him, as the Apostle John has it.

Since, therefore, the faith of every man is to be held good and profitable, or the contrary, as it conduces to obedience or to disobedience, and not as it is in itself either true or false, and no one questions the great diversities that occur in the general dispositions of men,—that all cannot by their nature alike agree in all things; that opinions affect men in different ways, what moves one to piety and devotion moving another to laughter and contempt,—it follows that into the constitution of a catholic or universal faith no dogma must enter which can be the subject of controversy among reasonable and just men. As in the nature of things, then, that dogma which to one is pious and profitable is to another impious and profitless, therefore are all dogmas to be judged by their effects, by the works they produce, by the lives and conversation to which they lead.*

To the universal faith, therefore, belong those dogmas alone which obedience to God absolutely demands, and which, neglected, obedience is absolutely impossible. Of all other articles of faith, every one as he best knows himself, and as he finds these calculated to confirm him or otherwise in godly and neighbourly love, may be allowed to think as he pleases. Were such a course followed, there were no room left, mo-

* To find a standard of moral and religious truth has long been a desideratum. Spurzheim, the most philosophical of the phrenologists, proposed the following,—" The absolutely true in morals and religion is that which is in harmony with all the faculties proper to man, the faculties he has in common with the lower animals being in subjection." This we apprehend is unimpeachable. Vide Essai philosophique sur la nature morale et intellectuelle de l'homme, par G. Spurzheim. Paris, 1815. An admirable work.—*Ed.*

thinks, for controversy within the bosom of the Church. Nor shall I now shrink from specifying the heads of AN UNIVERSAL FAITH, which are also the fundamental dogmas of Scripture. They are these: THERE IS A SUPREME BEING, WHO DELIGHTS IN JUSTICE AND MERCY, WHOM ALL WHO WOULD BE SAVED ARE BOUND TO OBEY, AND WHOSE WORSHIP CONSISTS IN THE PRACTICE OF JUSTICE AND CHARITY TOWARDS OUR NEIGHBOUR. All else that enters into the religious conception is readily deduced from these grand principles. In a more extended shape, the Elements of the Universal Faith may be presented thus:—

1. GOD, the Supreme Being, the just, the merciful, exists, and is the example of the true life. He who knows not God, or believes not that God exists, cannot obey him, nor know him as his judge.

2. GOD is one. No one doubts but this belief is absolutely necessary to the highest devotion, admiration, and love of God; for devotion, reverence, and love arise from the idea of supreme excellence in one over all.

3. GOD is omnipresent, and all things lie open before him. Were aught believed to be hidden from God, or he were held not to see all, doubts might arise of the impartiality of his justice, which governs all, or his justice might even be denied.

4. GOD has sole dominion and right in all things. Uninfluenced by aught beyond himself, he acts and wills of his own sovereign pleasure and peculiar grace; for all are bound to obey him, he to obey none.

5. The worship of GOD consists, and obedience to him is shown, in justice and charity alone, in other words, in the love of our neighbour.

6. All who obey and worship GOD in this way are saved; whilst they who live under the empire of sensuality are lost. If this be not firmly believed by men, there is no reason why they should prefer obedience to God to indulgence in sensual pleasures.

7. Lastly, GOD forgives those who repent of their

transgressions. There is no man who has not sinned; were not God clement and forgiving, therefore, all might despair of their salvation; nor were there else any sense in believing that God is merciful. He, however, who believes that God in the plenitude of his grace and mercy forgives erring man, and who is moved thereby to greater love and reverence towards the Supreme, he indeed knows Christ according to the spirit, and Christ is in him.

Now no one can deny that all these things are indispensably necessary to be known, in order that men may without exception obey God, in conformity with the prescription of the law already explained; for were anything taken from them, obedience were also taken away. As to what God is, —God the divine exemplar of the true life to man—whether he be spirit, fire, light, mind, &c., has nothing to do with faith, nothing with the reason why and way in which God is the pattern of the true life to man, nothing with our conception of him as just and merciful, nothing with the question as to how all things are and act by him, and we consequently have understanding through him, and through him know what things are truly just and good. On such points every one is at full liberty to think for himself. Again, it is of no moment, as regards faith, whether God is believed to be Omnipresent according to his essence or according to his power, whether he governs all things of his free will or by natural necessity, whether he prescribes laws in the manner of a sovereign prince, or decrees them as eternal truths; whether man yields obedience to God of free will, or by the necessity of a divine command; lastly, whether the reward of the good and the punishment of the bad are natural or supernatural in kind. It matters not as respects faith, I say, how these and other such questions are understood and answered; provided always that no conclusion be come to which gives a greater licence to sin, or lessens the sense of obedience due to God. Wherefore every one must be held at liberty to accommodate such dogmas to his natural capacity, and to interpret them unhesitatingly in such wise as to him seems good, but ever so as that he can embrace them willingly, and obey God with his whole heart and understanding. For as we have already seen that in former times the principles of faith were revealed and written in harmony with the capacities and opinions of prophets and people, so now is every one held bound to accommodate his faith with his opinions, in order that he may cleave to it without mental repugnance, without hesitation or reserve; for we have shown that faith required, not so much absolute truth, as piety or submissiveness, and that it is only good and salutary by reason of the obedience it secures; consequently, that no one is really in the ranks of the faithful, save and except he be found among the obedient. It is not the man, therefore, who shows the best reasons for his faith who necessarily has the best faith, but he who shows the noblest works of justice and charity. And here I leave it to the decision of every one to say how salutary is such a doctrine, how necessary to the common weal, that men may live in peace and unity together, and that the causes of crime and disorder may be taken away.

But before proceeding further, I have to take up the objections that were incidentally alluded to in Chapter I., and of which the consideration was deferred, when speaking of the intercourse of God with the Israelites on Mount Sinai. Now although the voice which the Israelites heard could give these men no philosophical or mathematical assurance of the existence of God, it was sufficient to excite them to reverence God as they had already conceived him, and to induce them to obey his commandments; which indeed was the end and aim of the manifestation. For God willed not to teach the Israelites the absolute attributes of his essence (he revealed none of these on the occasion), but to soften the hardness of their hearts and lead them to obedience. He therefore assailed them not with reasons, but with the din of a tempest, and spoke to them in thunder and lightning (vide Exodus xx. 20).

It now only remains for me to show that between faith and science, or between theology and philosophy, there is no affinity and nothing in common. This, I think, no one will deny who considers for a moment the scope and foundations of these two departments of human knowledge, which indeed differ *toto cœlo;* the scope of philosophy being nothing but truth, that of faith again, as we have abundantly shown, nothing but piety and obedience. And then, the foundations of philosophy are common ideas, and must be sought for in nature alone. Of faith, however, the foundations are laid in history, in language, and must be sought in Scripture and revelation only, as has been already shown in Chapter VII. Faith therefore accords to every one the fullest liberty of philosophizing, and of coming to what conclusions he pleases about the nature of things and ideas, without any charge of sin; accounting him only as heretical and schismatic who teaches views that lead to hatred, anger, strife, and disobedience; and, on the other hand, regarding him only as among the number of the faithful who, according to the measure of his powers and purposes, persuades to and practises justice and charity.

To conclude, as the subject with which I have just been engaged is the main part of all I proposed to myself in this treatise, I am anxious before proceeding further to entreat the reader most earnestly to read over the two last chapters again, and again and again to weigh and ponder their contents. I trust he will then be convinced that I have not written with any purpose of producing novelties, but with a wish to correct imperfections, and to amend erroneous views, in which I venture further to hope he will allow I have sometimes been successful.

One of the remarkable differences between the Old and the New Testament dispensations is the different emphasis that is laid in each on the principle of *Faith* or *Belief*. In the Old Testament the words *belief* and *believe* occur but very rarely, and are scarcely used to mark a *principle.*—Belief indeed is scarcely once enjoined as *a duty* in its pages. In the New Testament, on the contrary, we have *belief, believe, believing,* among the words of most frequent occurrence.

Belief and unbelief, however, are wholly general and relative terms, and the mental acts they indicate have neither merit nor demerit in themselves—there may be as much demerit in belief as merit in unbelief, and *vice versâ*. In the

CHAPTER XV.

THEOLOGY DOES NOT ASSIST REASON, NOR DOES REASON AID THEOLOGY. OF THE GROUNDS OF OUR BELIEF IN THE AUTHORITY OF THE SACRED SCRIPTURES.

They who do not know how to distinguish between philosophy and theology dispute whether Scripture should be aidant to reason or reason helpful to Scripture; that is to say, whether the sense of Scripture ought to be made to harmonize with reason, or reason be made to bend to Scripture. Of these two views one is taken by the sceptics, who deny the certainty of reason, the other by the dogmatists. That both grossly err, however, is apparent from what has already been said. And, indeed, whether one opinion or the other be adopted, either reason or Scripture must of necessity be abused. We have shown that Scripture does not teach philosophy, but piety; and that the whole contents of the Bible are accommodated to the capacity and preconceived opinions of the vulgar. He, consequently, who would make Scripture harmonize with philosophy will have to fasten many things on the prophets which they did not imagine even in their dreams, and will often have to interpret their meaning much amiss. He, on the other hand, who attempts to make reason and philosophy the hand-maids of

modern world of science especially, we *know* or we *do not know* as regards things positive, we *believe* or *disbelieve* in reference to things doubtful.—*Ed.*

theology will find himself forced to recognize the prejudices of the vulgar of old as divine things, and with these to fill and obscure his understanding; so that both—this with, and that without, reason—will seem to rave.

The first among the Pharisees who openly maintained that Scripture should be harmonized with reason was Maimonides (whose opinion we have reviewed in Chapter VII., and refuted by many arguments), and although he enjoyed a great reputation among them as a writer, still the greater number of his co-religionists disagree with him in this, and cast themselves at the feet of a certain Rabbi Judah Alpakhar,* who, anxious to avoid the error of Maimonides, falls into another opposed to it. This Rabbi maintained that reason ought to be aidant, and, indeed, subordinate, to Scripture. He does not think that anything in Scripture is to be understood metaphorically because the literal sense is repugnant to reason, but only because it is at variance with Scripture itself, i. e. with precepts or dogmas elsewhere clearly expressed. He therefore lays it down as an universal rule, that whatever Scripture teaches dogmatically, and affirms in express words, is, on its sole authority, to be received as absolutely true; that no dogma is to be found in the Bible which directly contradicts another, but only seems to do so inferentially, the manner of speaking in Scripture often appearing to suppose something contrary to that which is taught in fact; and for this reason only are such texts to be interpreted as metaphorical. For example, Scripture teaches clearly that God is One (Deut. vi. 4). Nowhere is it found directly affirming that there are several Gods; though there are many places in which God speaks of himself, and where the prophets speak of God, in the plural number. Here a peculiar manner of speaking only is to be supposed; the purpose of the language not being to declare that there are several Gods. Wherefore all such passages are to be explained metaphorically; to wit, not because it is repugnant

---

* I remember formerly to have read the letter of R. J. Alpakhar, in which the matters quoted are contained among the letters addressed to Maimonides.

to reason to suppose that there are more Gods than one, but because Scripture itself directly affirms that there is only one God. So, also, because Scripture directly affirms (as our Rabbi thinks) that God is incorporeal (Deut. iv. 15), are we, on the authority of this passage alone, and not of reason, to be held to believe that God is without body, and consequently, on the sole authority of Scripture, are all the passages in which God is spoken of as having hands, feet, back parts, &c., to be explained metaphorically, the mere mode of speaking in these making it appear as though God were corporeal.

Such is the opinion of this writer, who, inasmuch as he desires to explain the Scriptures by the Scriptures, I much commend; but I am astonished that a man endowed with reason himself should seek to destroy it. It is true, indeed, that Scripture is to be interpreted by Scripture so long as the question is of the sense of the language, and the meaning of the prophets; but, having found the true sense, it is then indispensable that judgment and reason be summoned to approve of the conclusions attained. But if reason when opposed to Scripture is nevertheless to be completely subjected to it, I ask whether this is to be done knowingly, or ignorantly and as if stricken with mental blindness? If blindly, then indeed we act foolishly and without judgment; but if knowingly, then do we accept on the sole authority of reason that Scripture, which, to be consistent, we should reject when it is opposed to reason. And I ask, who can receive or adopt into his mind anything against which reason rebels? For what is it mentally to deny anything, but that reason disclaims it? And, truly, I cannot sufficiently express my amazement that there should be found men in the world eager to disparage reason, and to subject this greatest of gifts, this divine light, to the dead letter which human malice may have corrupted; who think it no sin to speak against the mind of man, this table on which the true covenant of God is writ, to call it corrupt, and blind, and lost; but who esteem it the greatest wickedness to call in question the mere sign and symbol of the Word of God! These persons, forsooth, think it pious and proper to trust nothing to their own judgment, but impious and reprehensible to doubt of the good faith and judgment of those who have transmitted the Sacred Books of the Jews to us! But this is sheer folly, not piety. And I ask, What are they anxious about? What do they fear? That faith and religion are not to be vindicated unless men agree to ignore all experience and bid adieu to reason? If they do indeed think so, they rather fear than trust the Scriptures. But far from us be the thought that religion and piety should be subordinated to reason, or reason be subjected to religion, and that each may not assert its own right, pursue its own course in perfect concord with the other. Of this point, however, I shall speak by and by; for here I have, above all things, to examine the rule laid down by this Rabbi Alpakhar.

He, as I have said, would have us, without question asked, embrace as true, or reject as false, all that Scripture affirms or denies; and, again, he maintains that Scripture never in express words contradicts affirmatively or negatively in one place what it affirms or denies in another. How rashly both of these assertions are made no one who has inquired can be ignorant. For, passing by the fact, which he has not noticed, that Scripture is made up of many books, written at different times for different generations of men by different authors, I say the Rabbi Alpakhar ventures the statement he makes entirely on his own authority, Scripture saying nothing of the kind; that he ought to show all the places which are only inferentially contradictory to be susceptible of a ready metaphorical explanation from the nature of the language, or by reason of the place where they occur; and, lastly, that he should be held bound to prove that Scripture has reached us wholly uncorrupted.

Now I ask, in the first place, whether we are to be compelled to embrace as true, or reject as false, all that Scripture contains which is repugnant to reason? Perhaps, however, he might here reply, that Scripture contains nothing that is repugnant to reason. I, on my part, insist that in Scripture it is expressly affirmed and taught that God is jealous (ex. gr. in the Decalogue itself; in Exodus iv. 14; in Deuteronomy iv. 24, and in many other places); and I say this is repugnant to reason. Nevertheless, the Rabbi Judas Alpakhar would have us receive the assertion as true —ay, and if we can find anything in Scripture which implies that God is not jealous, this would have to be explained metaphorically, and held to mean nothing of the sort. Again, Scripture says expressly that God descended on Mount Sinai (Exod. xix. 20 *et seq.*), ascribes to him other motions in space, and nowhere expressly teaches that God does not move; this, therefore, would have to be received by all as true; and because Solomon says that God is infinite—that the heaven of heavens cannot contain him (1 Kings viii. 27),— although he does not affirm expressly, though it follows by inference, that God does not move, this must necessarily be so explained that it shall appear not to take away the faculty of locomotion from God. So, also, heaven would have to be assumed as God's dwelling-place and throne, because it is expressly affirmed so to be in Scripture. In the same way, there are very many expressions in conformity with the opinions of the prophets and the vulgar which reason and philosophy, but not Scripture, declare to be false or mistaken, although all must be supposed to have been true in the opinion of their authors, by whom reason and philosophy were little regarded.

Our Rabbi, in conclusion, affirms falsely that one passage contradicts another by inference only, not directly. Thus Moses affirms directly that "God is fire" (Deut. iv. 24), and he as directly denies that God has any resemblance to visible things (Ib. iv. 12); now, did our Rabbi rule, this would not be to deny directly, but only by inference, that God was fire; let us concede therefore that God is fire—but no, let us rather escape from such stuff, lest with him we seem to talk idly, and proceed to other more pregnant instances for his confutation. Thus, Samuel in one passage (1 Sam. xv. 29) denies that God ever "lies or repents;" and Jeremiah in another (Jer. xviii. 8, 10) affirms that God repents him of the good and evil he intended. What? are not these two texts directly opposed to each other? Which of the two would our Rabbi explain metaphorically? Both are universal, both are contradictory; what one positively affirms, the other as positively denies. In obedience to his own rule, therefore, he would be bound at once to adopt each as true, and again to reject each as false. And, then, what signifies it that one place contradicts another not directly, but only by consequence, if the consequence be clear, and the circumstances of the place, and the nature of the subject, will not bear a metaphorical interpretation? And that there are many such passages in the Bible has been amply shown in more than one chapter of this treatise—in the Second Chapter, for example, where the diverse and contradictory opinions of the prophets were presented, in Chapters IX. and X., where, in especial, the striking contradictions that occur in the several histories were discussed, so that I have no occasion to repeat myself or to quote further instances in order to show what absurdities follow from the rule of interpretation suggested by the author quoted, or the erroneousness and inconsiderateness of his opinions. Wherefore we declare the views as well of this writer, as of Maimonides, to be untenable, and maintain unshaken the position, that theology is neither subject or subordinate to reason, nor reason subject to theology, but that each reigns supreme in its own proper sphere; the sphere of reason being truth and knowledge, whilst that of theology is piety and obedience; the power of reason not extending so far as to be able to determine that men by obedience only, without any knowledge of things, may be saved; whilst theology asks nothing, prescribes nothing, but obedience, and neither wills nor avails aught against reason. For the dogmas of faith, as we have shown in the preceding chapter, are determined by theology only in so far as is requisite for obedience; but the definite comprehension of these, as regards their truth, &c., it leaves to the decision of reason, which indeed is the light of the soul;

that without which nothing is conceived but dreams and vain fancies.

And here I take occasion to say that by theology I understand revelation, in so far as it shows the aim which Scripture has in view (namely, the way and manner of obedience, or the principles of true piety and true belief); in other words, that which is properly called the word of God, and which consists not in any certain number of books called sacred (vide Chap. XII). Theology, in this sense, if its precepts and rules of life be regarded, will be found to agree with reason; and, if its end and aim be kept in view, to differ in nothing from what reason dictates; so that it is of universal application, common to all. In so far as the body of Scripture is concerned, we have already shown in Chapter VII. that its meaning was to be ascertained from its history solely, not from the general history of nature, which is the foundation of philosophy alone. Nor ought we to be discouraged if, after having investigated the true meaning of Scripture in this way, we find it here and there in contradiction with reason; for, whatever of this sort may be found in the Bible, or that man without detriment to charity may ignore, that we certainly know does not touch theology or the Word of God, so that on these matters every one may think as he pleases without sin. Let us conclude definitively, therefore, that neither is Scripture to be made to conform to reason, nor is reason to be subjected to Scripture.

But since the very foundation of theology, viz. that man is blessed or saved by obedience alone, cannot be demonstrated by reason to be either true or false, we may be asked reproachfully wherefore we believe in it? If we embrace it without reason, like blind men, we therein act foolishly, and without discretion. If, on the contrary, we seek to determine this foundation by reason, theology thereby becomes a part of philosophy, and not to be severed from it. To these suggestions, however, I reply that I have shown definitively that this fundamental dogma of theology is not to be investigated by means of the natural understanding; at all events, that no one has yet been found who could demonstrate it in this way, and that revelation therefore became essentially necessary. We may use our judgment, nevertheless, in order that what is revealed may be embraced with moral certainty at least. I say, with moral certainty, for we cannot look to have any higher assurance than had the prophets, to whom the revelation we possess was first made, and whose assurance was moral only, as has been shown in Chapter II. of this Treatise.

I think, therefore, that they err egregiously who seek to prove the authority of Scripture by means of mathematical formulas or demonstrations. For the authority for the Bible rests on the authority of the prophets, so that it can be supported by no more powerful arguments than those by which the prophets of old were wont to persuade the people of their title to be heard; our own assurance of the same can indeed rest on no other foundation but that on which the prophets rested their assurance and authority. Now we have found the whole certainty of the prophets to repose on these three things: 1. A clear and lively imagination; 2. Signs or miracles; 3. lastly and chiefly, A mind disposed to justice and goodness. The prophets built on no other foundations than are supplied by these, and so could not demonstrate their authority by any other means, either when in former times they addressed the multitude by word of mouth, or hold intercourse with us now in written characters. As to the first principle—viz. that they imagined vividly, this could only be known to the prophets themselves; so that our whole certainty of revelation must and ought to rest on the remaining two, viz. signs and doctrine. And this was expressly taught by Moses, for he bids the people obey the prophet who shows a true sign in the name of God; whilst he orders the false prophet, although he prophesies in the name of God, to be put to death (Deut. xxviii.). He also condemns him to death who seduces the people from the true religion, although he should confirm his discourse by signs and portents (Deut. xiii.). Whence it follows that the true is to be distinguished from the false prophet by doctrine and miracle together: he who shows doctrine and miracle Moses declares to be a true prophet, and him the people are ordered to believe without fear of being led astray; as they, again, are declared to be false prophets and worthy of death who prophesy falsely, though they speak in the name of God, or who teach false gods, though they work miracles.

We therefore only feel ourselves bound to believe Scripture, or the prophets, on the ground of their doctrine confirmed by signs. For since we find the prophets commending charity and justice above all things, and aiming at nothing else, it is impossible to imagine that they spoke of evil purpose. They certainly taught of upright mind, and to make men blessed through faith and obedience. And, inasmuch as they confirmed this excellent doctrine by signs in addition, we satisfy ourselves that they spoke not idly, that they did not rave whilst they prophesied; a conclusion in which we are the more confirmed when we find that they taught no moral precept which does not agree entirely with reason; for it is not little that the word of God, as spoken by the prophets, entirely agrees with the very word of God speaking in us. And on this point, I say, we have the same assurance from the Bible which the Jews of old had from the mouths of their prophets; for, as we have shown above (Chap. XII.), in so far as doctrine and the chief elements of their history are concerned, the Scriptures have come down to us unchanged. This position we assume as the ground of the whole of our Theology and Scripture belief; and although it is not susceptible of a mathematical demonstration, still it may be acknowledged with the entire concurrence of reason and understanding. For it were mere folly to refuse to receive that which has been confirmed by the testimony of so many prophets; which is a source of so much comfort to weaker souls; from which such good results ensue to the commonwealth; and which moreover can be believed without danger or detriment to any, on the sole ground that it is not susceptible of mathematical demonstration. As if, indeed, in the sagest conduct of life we admit nothing as true which might be called in question on any pretext of doubt; or as if most of our doings were not sufficiently, and some of them wholly, uncertain.

I confess, indeed, that they who think philosophy and theology mutually contradictory and subversive, who maintain that each ought to be expelled from the other's domain, and that one or other is to be bid adieu to, they, I say, do not without good reason endeavour to lay a solid foundation for theology, and even strive to find a mathematical demonstration of its principles. But who, save a desperate and insane person, would rashly choose to bid good-bye to reason, to despise the arts and sciences, and to deny the certainty of rational conclusions? At the same time, it is impossible absolutely to excuse those who call reason to their aid in rebutting reason, and who strive by means certain to make it seem uncertain. When they seek by mathematical demonstrations to show the truth and authority of theology, indeed, and to take away the authority of reason and the natural understanding, they only bring theology under the dominion of reason, and seem plainly to suppose that the authority of theology would be without lustre unless illumined by the natural light of reason. On the other hand, if they boast that they acquiesce entirely in the internal testimony of the Holy Spirit and call reason to their aid, for no other cause than on account of unbelievers, and with a view to convincing them, still no credit were to be given to their assertions, as we could easily show that they only speak from passion or vain-gloriousness. For from the preceding chapter it follows conclusively, that the Holy Spirit gives no testimony save through good works; wherefore Paul himself in his Epistle to the Galatians calls these "fruit of the Holy Spirit" (Gal. v. 22), and this is nothing, in truth, but that contentment and acquiescence of heart and understanding which spring from good deeds done. Of the verity and certainty of things, however, which are solely matters of speculation, no spirit save reason supplies any testimony, reason, which, as we have already shown, asserts the empire of truth for itself. If, therefore, any one declares himself possessed of any spirit but that which gives him certainty of truth, he boasts idly, and speaks from the promptings of his feelings only; or else he seeks refuge in sacred things from the fear he has of being exposed by philosophers and held up to public contempt; but in vain, for at what shrine shall he be well received who assails the majesty of reason?

But I make an end of this discussion, for I seem to myself to have made out my case, which was to show how philosophy was distinct from theology, and that wherein each principally consisted; that neither was subordinate, but that each held sway in its own sphere without prejudice to the other; finally, as occasion presented itself, I have shown the absurdities, inconveniences, and evils that have followed from confounding these two elements, and not keeping each entirely distinct from the other. Before proceeding to another part of my subject, I desire again and distinctly to express my opinion of the value and necessity of the Sacred Scriptures to man. These I estimate very highly; for as we do not perceive by the light we bring with us into the world that simple obedience is the way of life, whilst revelation alone by the singular grace of God teaches this, which we could not learn by our reason, it follows that the Scriptures have been a great source of comfort to mankind: all without exception may obey, but there are very few indeed who, under the guidance of reason, could attain to habits of virtue; so that without Scripture we might despair of the well-doing of almost all mankind.

CHAPTER XVI.

OF THE FOUNDATIONS OF A COMMONWEALTH. OF THE NATURAL AND CIVIL RIGHTS OF INDIVIDUALS; AND OF THE RIGHTS OF THE GOVERNMENT OR RULING AUTHORITY.

Thus far our aim has been to separate philosophy from theology, and to proclaim the title to free thought and free discourse which these alike concede to all. It is now time to inquire how far this liberty of opinion and of speech extends in a well-ordered state. To discuss this subject with due order and regularity we must inquire into the foundations on which a commonwealth reposes, and first of the natural rights of individuals, without present reference to general polity and religion.

By right and institution of nature I understand nothing more than the rules of nature prescribed to individual things, whereby each is determined to existence and action in a certain specific manner. For example,—fishes are determined by nature to live in water, and the great to devour the small. Fishes therefore possess the water by the highest natural right, and by the same do the great live on the small. For it is certain that nature, considered absolutely, has unlimited rights within the bounds of possibility; in other words, the right of nature is as extensive as its power. The power of nature, however, is only another phrase for the power of God, who has the first and highest right to all and over all. But as the power of nature at large is nothing more than the aggregate power of every individual thing in nature, it follows that each individual thing has the highest right to all it can compass or attain, and that the rights of individuals are coextensive with their power. And as it is the highest law of nature that every individual thing should seek to continue in the state appropriate to it, and this with reference to itself alone and to nothing else, it follows that every individual has the highest right to its state, i. e., as I have said, to be and to do as its natural constitution determines. Nor do we here recognize any difference between man and the rest of the beings of creation; nor between the man endowed with reason and the man who knows nothing of reason, nor between the sane in mind and the insane or fatuous. For whatsoever does anything acts by the laws of its nature or by the highest right, because acting as it is ordained to do by nature, and incapable of acting otherwise. Wherefore, among men, so long as they are considered to be living under the empire of nature alone, he who as yet knows nothing of reason, or who has not yet the habit of virtuous conduct, lives with perfect right by the laws of mere appetite, even as he lives by the laws of highest right who regulates his life in conformity with the dictates of reason. In other words, as the wise man has the highest right to all that wisdom commands, or to live according to the laws of reason, so the foolish or ignorant man has entire right to live according to the laws of appetite. And this is what the Apostle Paul teaches when he acknowledges no sin before the promulgation of the law; that is to say, so long as men lived under the empire of nature they were not living in sin.*

* Epist. to Rom. v. 13. Might not Paul's teaching as well as our author's here be fairly received with reservation? Right and wrong surely precede law, and are its cause. He sinned in the deed who smote his brother, not because it came to be written, "Thou shalt not kill." Have we not in fact the *highest authority*, that of the *Master*, for this view? "Ye have heard that it was said by them of old, Thou shalt not commit adultery; but I say unto you, That whosoever looketh on a woman to lust after her hath already committed adultery in his heart." (Matthew viii. 27, 28.)—*Ed.*

The natural right of every man therefore is determined by appetite and power, not by sound reason. For all are not constituted by nature to act according to the rules of reason. On the contrary, all are born ignorant of everything; and before they can know the true rule of life, and acquire virtuous habits, a great part of their lives must already have passed. Meantime, nevertheless, they are held to live, and, as much as in them lies, to preserve their state of being. But this they must do by the sole impulses of appetite or desire; for nature gives nothing else as a guide to the natural man, not conferring the power of living by the rules of sound reason. Men are therefore no more bound to live by the rule of absolute right than is a domestic cat to live by the laws of a lion's nature.

Whatever any one, regarded as under the empire of nature only, deems useful to himself, therefore, whether led to do so by right reason or by an impulse of appetite, that he desires by a supreme law of nature, and it is lawful for him by force, by cunning, by entreaty—in short, in any and every way, to obtain possession thereof, and to hold as an enemy whoever opposes him in the satisfaction of his desire.

From the above it follows that the law or institute of nature, under which all are born, and for the most part live, prohibits nothing but that which no one desires, and no one can desire; and that it does not absolutely gainsay dispute and difference, anger and hatred, stratagem and wile, nor indeed anything to which passion persuades. And this is not to be wondered at; for nature is not comprised within the narrow limits of the laws of reason, which are of service to man only and are meant for his sole guidance in conduct, but embraces an infinity of other matters which have respect to the eternal order of creation at large, in which man is a mere atom. By the necessity of nature, for instance, every individual thing is constituted to exist, and to act in a certain determined manner, so that whatever appears to us evil or absurd, does so because we know things partially only, and are ignorant of the order and concatenation of nature at large; and because we would direct all in conformity with our reason, although that which our reason calls evil is not evil as regards the order and rule of nature generally, but only as regards the law of our proper nature.

That it is advantageous for man to live according to the laws and special precepts of reason which, as has been said, are only intended to be useful to him, cannot be questioned. There is no one who does not desire to live in peace, in safety, and free from fear, which, however, were impossible so long as every one was permitted to do as he pleased, and so long as no greater authority was given to reason than to such passions as hatred and revenge; for no one can live amidst enmities, hatreds and wiles otherwise than anxiously; and there is no one who will not use his best endeavour to escape from their influence. Again, if we reflect that men live very wretchedly who live without mutual aid, and, without the requisite culture of reason, as has been shown in Chapter V., we perceive most clearly that to live in comfort and security it is indispensable for men to combine together, and to agree that the right which each had from nature individually should be had collectively,—that each should cease to live for himself alone by force and appetite, but that everything should be determined by the will and consent of the community. This, however, would be attempted in vain if all only willed to follow the dictates of appetite (for by the laws of appetite every one is drawn his own several way); every one must be firmly resolved, and indeed be bound, to govern himself in all things by the dictates of reason alone (which no one ventures openly to gainsay, lest he appear to have lost his understanding), to restrain his appetites or affections when these persuade to aught hostile to the interests of others, and to do nothing to another which he would not have done to himself, and, lastly, to defend the rights of others as if they were his own.

Let us now inquire how this compact is to be arranged and entered on so as to be definite and enduring. For it is a general law of human nature that no one neglects what he esteems to be good unless in the hope of a greater good, or the fear of a greater evil; nor does any one brave an evil save to escape a greater evil, or in the view to achieve a greater good; that is to say, he elects what he thinks the preferable of two good things, or the least detrimental of two evils. I say expressly that the thing or course chosen appears more or less good or bad to the party electing, not that the thing or the course chosen is in itself either better or worse than that which is shunned. This law I hold to be so firmly fixed or impressed on the nature of man that it is to be placed among the eternal truths which no one can ignore. But from this it necessarily follows that no one can honestly promise to forego his natural rights, and that no one would keep such a promise if made, unless it were in the fear of some greater evil or the hope of some greater good. To make this point more clear, let it be supposed that a robber compels me to promise that I will surrender to him my property in a place which he chooses to name. Now, although my natural right is determined by my power alone, as I have already declared, it is certain that if I can escape from this robber by guile or stratagem, promising him everything he asks, it is lawful for me of my natural right to do so. Or, again, suppose that for no fraudulent purpose, but inconsiderately, I have promised some one to abstain from meat and drink for twenty days, and by and by I see that I have made a foolish promise, which I cannot keep at all, or could only keep with great detriment to myself, inasmuch as by natural right I may choose the less of two evils, I am at perfect liberty to break such a promise, and to hold my engagement as though it had never been made. This, I say, may be done by natural right, whether I see that I promised rashly and amiss on the ground of right reason or of mere opinion; for whether I see what I promise to be good or bad, right or wrong, as I greatly dread evil I strive in every way by nature's ordinance to avoid it.

From these premises we conclude that a contract can

have no force save by reason of its usefulness; this taken away, the contract is at the same time cancelled and made null and void. For this reason, too, is it in vain to attempt to bind parties in perpetuity, unless especial measures are taken to make a greater amount of damage than of advantage to follow from a breach of the compact to the party or parties contracting. And this consideration ought to weigh greatly in the institution of every state. If all indeed were led by reason, and knew the vast advantages, not to say the necessity, of a sound system of civil polity, there would be none who would not detest guile in every shape, none who would not strive with their whole might to preserve that highest blessing, a well-ordered state, in the assurance that they themselves would have their ample reward in peace and security of life. But men, alas! are very far from always yielding obedience to the dictates of reason; each is mostly governed by his desires only, and avarice, envy, vain-glory, hatred, &c., often engross the mind so entirely that there is no room left for reason to enter. Wherefore, although men are generally ready enough to promise fairly, and to plight their word for their good intentions, still no one can be sure of another's truth unless there be something added to the promise; inasmuch as every one by natural right may act deceitfully, and may not consider himself bound to stand by his engagements unless led to do so in the hope of a greater good or the fear of a worse evil. But, as we have already shown that natural right, in so far as the individual is concerned, is solely determined by the power which each severally possesses, it follows that so much of this power as he transfers to another, whether perforce or voluntarily, so much of his natural right does he necessarily cede to that other, and that he who possesses supreme power has also supreme right, which he may enforce by all the strength of the law. Now this power the government or chief magistrate will only retain so long as the means of enforcing what is willed is retained. In other words, a ruler holds his authority by a precarious tenure, and no one more powerful than himself will be bound, unless he so pleases, to obey him.

In this way, then, without the smallest infringement of natural right, may a state be instituted, and all agreements kept with the most perfect faith, that is to say, if each individual transfers the whole of the power he has of himself to the community of which he is a member, which then comes to possess supreme natural right in everything—in other words, the supreme authority which every individual, whether willingly or from fear, will then be bound to obey. A state or community thus constituted is called a democracy, which is then defined as a general assembly of men, holding collectively the highest right to all which each possessed individually. Wherefore it follows that the supreme authority itself is bound by no law, whilst all are bound to obey it in whatsoever it ordains; for to this, whether tacitly or expressly, must all consider themselves pledged when they have transferred their common natural right to a collective supreme power. Should the individual members of a democracy therefore desire severally to preserve any particular right to themselves, they must take especial care that they also preserve the power to defend it; for if they have not taken measures of precaution of this kind, and a stand cannot be made upon the right in question, without a division being created in the state, and it may be without its existence being imperilled, then have they subjected themselves unconditionally to the ruling authority, and they have nothing for it but obedience. And this being so, and when reason and necessity alike enforce submission, it follows that unless we would be accounted enemies of the commonwealth, and set ourselves against reason, which is persuading with all its might to the support of the supreme authority, we are bound to obey the commands of the highest power, although to us they may appear absurd; for reason also bids us in a strait to choose the less of two evils. Add to this, that the danger of having to submit unconditionally to the will and authority of another is then very imminent; for we have seen that ruling powers have the right to command whatever they please, so long as they possess the power to enforce their commands, or are, in fact, the head of the state; for if they once lose their power of compelling obedience, they at the same time lose their power of commanding, which then falls to those who have been strong enough to acquire it. It only happens very rarely therefore that the highest powers in a state exert their authority very absurdly; for it is especially incumbent on them, on the mere ground of self-interest, and that they may retain possession of power, to consult the common good, and order all things by the dictates of discretion and right reason. No one, as Seneca says, rules long who rules by violence. And then, absurdities are less to be apprehended in a democracy; for it is next to impossible that the majority of an assembly, especially if it be numerous, should yield to one foolish person, or agree to any foolish or pernicious thing. Besides, as the very basis and aim of a policied state are escape from the empire of brute passions, and the restraint of mankind within the bounds of reason and propriety, in order that they may live together in peace and harmony—I say, if the foundation be disturbed, the whole superstructure necessarily falls. The duty of the supreme power or government, therefore, is to provide for these things, and the duty of subjects is to obey, to execute the commands of the chief authority, and to acknowledge as law and right that only which this declares to be so.

In speaking thus, however, some may suppose that I am turning subjects into slaves; for they may think that he is a slave who only moves at the command of another, as he is a freeman who lives and acts of his own free will. But this is not absolutely so; for he who is mastered by his appetites, and who can neither comprehend nor do what is truly for his good, is the greatest slave of all; as he is the true freeman who lives in all things conformably to reason. Action by command, in another word, obedience, does not therefore imply the abrogation of liberty in every sense, and he who obeys is not necessarily a slave. It is the motive or purpose of the action that constitutes him bond or free: if the end of the action be for the behoof of the party commanding, not of the agent, then is the agent a slave and useless to himself; but where the advantage of the community at large, and not of the ruler, is the aim, as it is in a republic or constitutional state, then is he who obeys no slave, but subject only to the laws of his country, as that commonwealth is the freest whose laws are founded in the highest right and reason. In such a state every one who so wills may be truly free, for there may he live in conformity with the dictates of reason.* In the same way are children not to be accounted slaves though they be held bound to obey the commands of their parents; for the commands of parents are presumed to have an especial bearing on the advantage of their children. We therefore recognize a great difference between slave, son, and subject, words which may be severally thus defined: *slave*, one who is held to obey the commands of a master, these commands having reference only to the advantage of the party commanding; a *son* does what is advantageous to himself on the command of his parent; a *subject*, lastly, does what is useful to the community, and therefore to himself, by obeying the commands of the supreme power in the state.

Thus briefly do I present the foundations of democratic authority, of which I desired to treat in particular, both because it seems to me the most natural form of government, and to accord best with the liberty which every individual has by nature. In a democracy no one transfers his natural

---

* In whatever social state man may find himself, he may be free. Man is free, in fact, in so far as he acts in conformity with reason. But reason (observe that this is not Hobbes's theory) counsels peace, and peace is only possible along with obedience to a common law. The more reasonably a man governs himself, therefore, the more free is he; and the more faithful he is to the common law the more obedient is he to the decrees of the governing power or sovereign whose subject he is.

rights to another in such wise that he shall never be consulted on any matter of public interest, but to the majority of the community whereof he is a member. And for this reason, all in the democratic form of civil polity, as in the natural state, remain equal. Again, I was anxious to treat of this form of government expressly, because it assists me most in my purpose of showing the advantages which accrue from liberty in a commonwealth. I shall therefore pass by the several other forms of government without notice; nor, indeed, is it requisite that we should particularly consider these, their origin, institution, &c., such matters following from what is special in each taken in connection with what has just been said of democracy. As a general thesis the question may be put thus: whosoever possesses the supreme power, whether one, a limited number, or all, has the right to command whatever he wills. Moreover, he who, whether voluntarily or upon compulsion, transfers to another his right of self-defence, abandons to this other his natural title to independent action, and thereby becomes bound to obey him in all things, so long as he—king, council, parliament, people —keeps possession of the supreme authority, which was the foundation of the right of transference. On this subject I do not think it necessary to say more.

Having now shown the foundation and the right of the supreme power in a policied state, it will be easy to ascertain wherein private right consists, what constitutes a wrong, what is the meaning of justice and injustice in civil affairs, to determine who is a confederate or ally, who an enemy, and, lastly, to show wherein the crime of treason consists.

By *Private Civil Right* we can understand nothing but the liberty enjoyed by every one to maintain himself in his estate and condition, a liberty which is guaranteed by decrees of the supreme power in the state, and is defended by its authority alone; for, having transferred his right to live according to his own will and pleasure to another, in other words, the right and power of self-defence which he originally possessed, he is held bound to live by the rule prescribed to him by this other, and to defend himself under his guidance.

Wrong is done when a citizen or subject suffers an injury in person or estate from another, contrary to his civil rights or the decree of the supreme authority. Wrong cannot be conceived, save in a social sense state; it cannot properly occur as between the supreme authority and a subject, everything being lawful to the ruling power, but only between private persons, who are held bound by law not to injure one another.

Justice comes of that frame of mind which gives to every one what belongs to him by civil right. *Injustice*, again, follows from a disposition to withhold or to take from another what properly belongs to him by right and law. Partiality and impartiality are equivalent terms for unjust and just, for he who is intrusted with the authority to determine differences between citizens is held to have no respect of persons, but to regard all as equal, and to defend the rights of every one with like zeal and conscientiousness, neither bending to the rich nor treading on the poor.

Confederates are the men composing two or more distinct states, who for mutual defence, to escape the perils of war, or for any other reason of presumed utility to themselves, enter into a compact not only not to injure one another, but to lend each other mutual aid and assistance in case of need, each all the while retaining its individual independence. This treaty or compact remains in force so long as the motive which led to its being entered into—whether fear of danger or prospect of advantage—continues to be felt, for no engagement is ever made, save in the hope of some benefit, or from the fear of some evil. If the ground of the compact be taken away, the compact comes to an end of itself, as is proved by every-day experience. For, though different states often enough agree not to injure one another, still each will strive to the extent of its ability to prevent its neighbour from becoming more powerful than itself. Nor are the terms of a treaty ever much regarded unless actions prove in conformity with these; if promises to aid and be useful are not kept [or if 'kept to the ear, are broken to the hope'], then deceit and injury are apprehended, and not without reason; for who but a fool, ignorant of the rights of ruling powers, would trust to the mere words and assurances of one possessed of supreme authority, armed with the power to do as he pleases, and to whom the glory and advantage of his own nation must be the supreme law! When with these we connect moral considerations, we shall see that no one who holds the chief authority could without guiltiness keep promises that would prove injurious to the interests of the state he rules. Whatever promise he may have made which he sees involves injury to the community over which he presides cannot be kept unless he breaks faith with his subjects, and this he is especially bound to observe; this indeed it is customary for rulers to engage themselves by solemn oaths to observe.

An *Enemy* is one who lives beyond the bounds of a state, and behaves in such a way as shows that he does not acknowledge its authority either as confederate or as subject; for it is not hate or animosity that makes an enemy of a state, but right; and the right of the state in regard to him who does not recognize its authority by treaty or contract is the same as it is in regard to him who brings damage upon it; wherefore, the state may compel him by every means at its command either to join it as a confederate or to comply with its behests as a subject.

The crime of *Treason*, lastly, occurs only among the subjects of states who by tacit or express agreement have transferred the whole of their rights to the ruling power; and he is said to be guilty of this crime who attempts in any way to seize the sovereign authority for himself, or to transfer it from the possessor to another—I say, who makes the attempt, in this case; for were the matter not subject to adjudication till after the fact, the state would mostly intervene too late, and when the supreme authority had already been successfully usurped or transferred. I add, that I speak unconditionally of any attempt on any pretext whatever to seize the supreme power, myself acknowledging no difference in the guilt, whether advantage or disadvantage accrue to the commonwealth at large from the act of usurpation; for in whatever way, on whatever pretext, this is attempted or accomplished, it is equally treason to the state, and he who is guilty of the deed is justly condemned. This done in war, is allowed by all to be properly done. He, for example, who does not hold the post assigned to him, but of his own motion either retreats or attacks the enemy, without the command of the General-in-chief, although it were advisedly and even successfully done, is still held liable to be put on his trial, and even to be condemned to death for disobedience of orders,—for having failed in his oath, in fact, and usurped the right and authority of his commander. That citizens are absolutely bound by the same rule, however, is not seen so clearly by all, although the reason for obedience is the same in each case. For, since the commonwealth should be watched over and directed by the supreme authority alone, and citizens are absolutely engaged to yield this right, if any one, of his own mere motion and without the order and concurrence of the supreme power, takes it upon him to originate or to meddle in any business, although advantage may certainly accrue from it, nevertheless he violates the right of the ruling power; he commits treason, and is properly condemned and cast for punishment.

It still remains for me to vindicate what has been affirmed a little above, viz. that it is not openly contrary to revealed right to maintain that one who lives in the natural state without the use of his reason, agreeably to the laws of appetite, lives in conformity with the laws of the highest natural right. For, as all alike, whether in possession of their reason or not, are bound by the divine command to love their neighbour as themselves, it seems impossible to live according to the laws of mere appetite and not do injury or injustice to others. To this objection, however, if the natural state only be regarded, we can readily find an answer; for the natural state, both in itself and in time, is anterior to religion. No one knows by nature that he owes any obedience to God; this knowledge follows from no reason, but can only be enforced upon every one by revelation confirmed by signs. Wherefore, until revelation was given to man, no one could be held bound by the divine law of which he was necessarily ignorant. Consequently, the natural state is by no means to be confounded with the religious state, but is to be regarded as without religion and law, and therefore without sin or crime, as we have already said, confirming our conclusion by reference to the authority of the Apostle Paul.* Nor do we only conceive the natural state with reference to its ignorance, and its antecedence to the revelation of the divine law, but with reference to the liberty in which all are born. For if men were held by nature to the observance of divine law, or if divine right were natural right, it would have been superfluous for God to have entered into a covenant with man, and bound him by a bond and an oath. Wherefore, it must be acknowledged unconditionally that divine right began from the time when the Jews, engaged by an express compact to obey God in all things, when they abandoned their state of natural liberty, as it were, and transferred this their

---

* When Paul says that men have no refuge in themselves, he speaks after the manner of man, for in the ninth chapter of the same Epistle in which he uses such language he teaches expressly that God shows mercy to whom he pleases, and hardens the wicked at his will, and that the reason why men are inexcusable is not that they have been admonished beforehand and have then followed their own devices, but that they are in the hands of God like clay in the hands of the potter, who of the same material makes one vessel to honour and another for vulgar uses.—*Auth.*

Vide our note, page 271. Before man had revelation he could not of course be bound by its decrees. But religion very certainly is no effect of revelation—revelation adds nothing new to human nature. The religious is an original element in the constitution of man; he has it immediately from the Almighty; and revelation is rather an evidence of its existence than its cause. All the tribes or nations with whom the Jews came in contact had their gods and their religious systems, and certainly not by revelation. The natural state of man, therefore, is not irreligious. No savage tribe is without some form of religious idea.—*Ed.*

birthright to God; precisely as we have said is done in the civil state. Of these matters, however, I shall treat more at length in a subsequent chapter.

But here it may still be said that ruling powers as well as subjects are bound by the divine law, whilst we have declared that the supreme authority in a state did not part with its natural rights, and that to it all things within the range of its power were lawful. To remove this difficulty, which arises not so much from any reason of state as from considerations of natural right, I say, that in the state of nature every one is bound to live by revealed right, on the same grounds as he is held bound to live by the dictates of reason, viz. because it is advantageous and necessary to his well-being that he do so: if he wills not so to live, he refuses at his peril. Thus is one in the natural state held to live in his own proper way, not in obedience to the commands of another, neither acknowledging any earthly judge nor fearing any avenger in right of religion. And I affirm that the supreme power in the state retains the right of so living; that whilst it may take counsel with others, it is itself bound to acknowledge none as a judge, none save itself as avenger of any right infringed; unless, indeed, it were a prophet expressly sent by God, and who attested his mission by unquestionable signs. Nor even then were it the man whom the sovereign power might be held bound to acknowledge as judge, but God himself. But if the sovereign authority refuse to obey God in his revealed will, it must do so at its peril, as there is neither natural nor social law to restrain it, social law or right depending entirely, as we have seen, on the decree of the supreme authority, as natural right depends exclusively on the laws of nature, which are ordered not in accordance with religion only, which aims at the benefit of man alone, but in accordance with nature universally, that is to say, with the eternal decrees of God.*

* The doctrines of Spinoza, in this chapter, will be approved by no Englishman. They are only compatible with a despotism; and the political sin against the Holy Ghost that is unpardonable, is the intrusting one man with

This truth seems to have been conceived, although obscurely, by some who maintain that man may sin against the revealed law of God indeed, but not against his eternal decree, whereby he has predestined all things. But if any one should now ask, What if the supreme authority should command anything against religion, and against the obedience which has been engaged to God by solemn covenant? Is the divine or the human authority to be obeyed? Here I only say in reply, that God is to be obeyed above all when we have a certain and unquestionable revelation of his will. But inasmuch as men are wont to err egregiously in religious matters, and as disputes and differences of great moment arise through diversity of capacity and temper—a truth to which experience amply testifies,—it is certain that if no one is held bound by law to obey the supreme power in matters which in his opinion belong to religion, then the right of the chief authority in the state would depend on the several judgments and dispositions of the individuals which compose it. For no one would be held bound by that which he deemed contrary to his belief, or perchance his superstition, and so all under this pretext might assume a licence for irregular conduct of every kind. But as on this plea the rights of the state would be annihilated, it follows that it must be competent for the supreme authority (with which both by divine and natural right lies the responsibility of upholding and defending the commonwealth) to determine, in virtue of the trust confided to it, the religious system which all shall be held bound to observe. Should they who possess the supreme power in the state be heathens, either no compact is to be made with them, but every extremity rather is to be endured; or if an agreement have been come to, and the rights of the community have been transferred to them, as by this the people will have abandoned their right

absolute power. It is curious to find purely speculative views leading the son of a refugee from the spirit of despotic persecution, himself the denizen of a country which had suffered so much from the abuse of Right by Might, to deliver himself in the way our author does in this chapter.—*Ed.*

of defending either themselves in their persons or their religious principles, there will then be nothing for them but to submit and keep faith with their rulers, save always in the case in which God by a certain revelation has promised his help against a tyrant, or when he has excepted one by name from the obedience due by subjects. Of all the Jews dwelling in Babylon, we only find notice of three young men with such faith in the protecting power of Jehovah that they refused to obey the commands of King Nebuchadnezzar. All the rest, with the single exception of Daniel, whom the king himself adored as a prophet, compelled by the strong hand of power, obeyed, believing probably that they were given over by the will of God to the king, who held his authority immediately from on high. Eleazar, on the contrary, desiring to give his countrymen an example of constancy, inasmuch as his country was still something more than a name, encouraged them to suffer everything with him rather than consent to transfer to the Greeks their rights and their independence, rather than bow down and swear fealty to the gods of the heathen. Such an example, indeed, has been frequently presented to the world. They who bear sovereign sway in Christian states, moreover, have not hesitated, for their advantage and greater security, to form alliances with Turks and heathens, and have required their subjects settled or about to settle in heathen countries to assume no greater liberty, either in civil or spiritual things, than was conceded by treaty, or than the barbarous authorities permitted. Of such an arrangement we have a notable example in the intercourse between the Dutch and Japanese, of which mention was made above.

CHAPTER XVII.

INDIVIDUAL RIGHT IS NEVER WHOLLY ABANDONED TO THE RULING POWER IN A STATE. OF THE HEBREW REPUBLIC IN DIFFERENT PERIODS OF ITS EXISTENCE, AND OF THE CAUSES OF ITS DECLINE AND FALL.

THE idea developed in the preceding chapter concerning the right of the supreme power in a state over all, and of the natural rights of individuals transferred to it, although agreeing in many respects with experience, still remains entirely theoretical in various particulars. Theory and practice, however, may here be brought to assimilate very closely. No one, for example, could ever so completely transfer his power, and consequently his rights, to another as to cease himself from feeling as a man; nor was there ever any sovereign power in the world that could dispose absolutely, and at its will and pleasure, of everything belonging to the state and the people. In vain were a subject commanded to hate him who had done him service, to love him who had done him an injury, to feel no offence at unworthy usage, not to desire escape from solicitude about his personal safety, and many other things of the same kind, which follow of necessity from the constitution of human nature. So much I think is clearly demonstrated by experience; for never have men so entirely abandoned their rights, so effectually ceded these to another, that they themselves came no longer to be considered and feared by him to whom they were confided, and who by this confidence was raised to the sovereign power in the state; so true is it that despotic rulers have mostly lived in as much fear of their subjects, though stripped of their rights, as of foreign enemies. Would men indeed so completely divest themselves of their natural rights, as thenceforward to have no will or choice left save as he or they who held the supreme power commanded, then truly might governors rule tyrannically and cruelly with impunity. But I think that no man in his senses would ever consent to strip himself of all natural right and power: every one, under all circumstances, must still reserve something of these, which consequently will not depend on another, but belong to himself in peculiar.

To have a proper understanding of the extent of the right and power of the highest authority in a state, it must however be observed that the right of a ruler does not exactly consist in this,—that he can force subjects through fear to obey his commands, but in this absolutely,—that his commands are obeyed. For it is not the reason or motive for the obedience yielded, but the obedience itself, which gives the sovereign authority its right and power of command. Whether subjects obey from fear of punishment or hope of reward, from love of their country, or moved by any other affection or impulse, they still resolve of their own proper motion to obey, and in so doing act in conformity with the decrees or commands of the highest power in the state. Whatever a subject does, consequently, that harmonizes with the commands of the sovereign power, whether he be moved by love or driven by fear, or disposed by love and fear at once, or by respect, a feeling composed of fear and admiration, or, in short, by any other motive, he then acts not of his own right alone, but by the right also of the supreme power. This position is greatly confirmed by the fact that obedience bears reference to an internal mental condition rather than to an outward act; so that he is truly most under the authority of another who obeys all his commands with hearty good will; as he bears the most absolute sway who reigns in the hearts of his subjects, and he who is greatly feared by his subjects is a tyrant in his state, and mostly lives in dread of those over whom he is set. Then, although it is impossible to command the mind like the tongue, still are the minds of subjects in some sense under the control of the sovereign power, which can generally and in various ways bring it to pass that the great majority of those over whom it exercises authority shall like, dislike, and do whatever it desires. And although this takes place by no direct command of the supreme power, it is nevertheless very commonly done, as experience proves, by the influence of its authority. Wherefore, without any violence to their reason, we conceive men believing, loving, hating, despising, &c., on the sole authority of their rulers, without themselves having been primarily moved by any feeling of love, hate, or contempt.

Now although in this way we perceive the right and authority of a government to be sufficiently ample, still it never happens that so much power is given as to enable those who hold it to assert an absolute and arbitrary right to all they desire. This I think I have already demonstrated with sufficient clearness. But to show in what way and by what means a state might be established that should prove permanent I have said does not fall within the scope of my present undertaking. Still, that I may attain the end I have in view, I shall here indicate what was formerly taught in this direction by divine revelation to Moses; and then I shall pass in rapid review the history and successes of the Jews, in order that we may gather from these what may be allowed by rulers to subjects for the sake of adding to the security and extending the power of the state.

That the safety of the commonwealth mainly depends on the faith of subjects, on their courage and constancy of purpose in carrying out the orders of the ruling powers, is sufficiently proved both by reason and experience. But it is not so readily seen by what means subjects are to be induced to repose unswerving faith and trust in their rulers. All alike, rulers and ruled, are men, indisposed to labour, greatly disposed to sensual indulgence. They who have had much experience of the fickle and uncertain temper of the multitude have almost despaired of humanity; for men are not governed by reason and the higher sentiments, but by appetite and affection alone. Always inconsiderate, they are easily led by their greediness and their love of indulgence; arrogant, each thinks that he alone knows all, and desires to arrange everything in his own way; selfish, he judges this and that to be just or unjust, right or wrong, as he believes it to square or not to square with what he thinks his interest; vainglorious, he despises his equals, and refuses to be guided by them; envious, he grudges to others greater honour and better fortune than fall to himself; vindictive, he desires evil to others and rejoices when it happens,—but enough, it is needless to go further; for all know full well what crime and wickedness discontent with the present and desire of change have produced; what blind rage and the prospect of escape from hateful poverty have led mankind to do, and how entirely mere personal considerations engage and influence men's minds. To foresee and forestall disturbance in a state from such causes, to leave no room for disorder to creep in, so to arrange matters that every one, whatever his temper and disposition, shall prefer the public good to his private advantage, this is the task undertaken, this the work to be achieved by the patriot ruler. From sheer necessity much has mostly been done to secure these great ends; matters, however, I think have scarcely yet been so satisfactorily arranged but that governments have still been in even greater danger from their own citizens than from foreign foes, and have feared unfriends at home fully as much as enemies abroad. Of the truth of this position let the great Roman Republic supply the proof. Invincible by enemies from without, it was often vanquished and miserably oppressed by its own citizens, never more cruelly perhaps than in the civil war of Vespasian against Vitellius (vide Tacitus, Histor. lib. iv.). Alexander, again, as we learn from Quintus Curtius (lib. viii.), was less eager for fame among his enemies than for the good report of those he ruled over; for he thought his power more at the mercy of his subjects than of hostile nations, and upon one occasion when anxious about his position he entreated his friends in this wise,—"Do you but preserve me from domestic intrigue and privy conspiracy, and I can meet the dangers of the battle-field without fear." Philip held himself safer in the fight than in the theatre: he had often escaped the hands of open enemies, but from the hands of his own people hostile, he thought there could be no escape. And, indeed, if the fate of despotic rulers be inquired into, it will be found that more have fallen by the hands of their subjects than of their enemies (vide Qu. Curtius, lib. x. § 6). For this reason, and to make themselves more secure, we see that kings in times gone by who usurped their state have often endeavoured to persuade the world that they derived their origin from the immortal gods. They presumed that if they could but make their subjects regard them not as equals, as mortals like themselves, but as gods, they would more readily suffer themselves to be ruled, and prove more submissive in all things. Thus Augustus Cæsar persuaded the Roman people that he was descended from Æneas, the son of Venus, and was therefore to be ranked among the divinities; he consequently ordered that temples should be raised in his honour, that his bust, in the guise of one of the gods, should be there enshrined, and that divine honours should be paid to him by a body of priests attached to his service (Tacit. Annal. lib. i.). Alexander, for his part, ordered that he should be saluted as the son of Jove. But this appears to have been done from policy, not from vanity, as is proved by his answer to Hermolaus: "It was enough to move laughter," he is reported to have said himself, "when Hermolaus wished me to rebel against Jupiter, by whose oracle I had been acknowledged: Is the decision of the gods in my power? Jove himself had saluted me by the name of son; and after the deeds I had done it surely was not amiss in me to accept the title. I would that the Indians also believed me to be a god; for reputation does much in war, and falsehood believed will often stand instead of truth" (Qu. Curtius, lib. viii. § 8). In these few words does the great conqueror show his own sense of the divinity that was imputed to him by the ignorant populace, and at the same time indicate his reasons for suffering himself to be addressed as a god. Cleon, in his oration, defends what had been done. After sounding the praises of Alexander extravagantly, he has recourse to all his art in persuading the Macedonians to support the king in his enterprise, and thus passes on to the advantages of the course he advocates: "The Persians," he says, "worship their kings as God, not from piety only, but also led by policy to do so, for majesty is the guardian of state security. He would," he continues, "prostrate himself upon the bare ground as the king passed to his meals, and the by-standers, and especially all prudent persons, would do the same" (Qu. Curtius, lib. viii. § 5). But the Macedonians were sharper-witted than Cleon thought, and not to be won in this way. Nor indeed are any above the rank of mere barbarians to be so openly deceived or seduced into submitting from respectable subjects to be made slaves of, useless to themselves. It is not so difficult however to persuade many persons that royalty is something sacred; that kings are God's vice-gerents on earth; that they reign by the grace of God, not by the suffrage and consent of man, and are upheld and protected by a special providence. Many other devices of the same sort have been imagined by monarchs for the security of their persons and the increase of their authority; but these I pass by, and proceed to what I have said I had particularly in view, viz. the things to these ends that were taught to Moses by divine revelation.

We have already seen in Chapter V. that after their exodus from Egypt the Jews were bound by the laws of no other nation, but were free to institute new laws of their own, whilst at the same time they assumed the right to invade and occupy such territories as suited their wishes or convenience. For after their escape from the intolerable Egyptian oppression, when they were bound by no compact to any authority, but had resumed their natural rights, and every one was in a condition to consider whether he should keep these to himself or cede them to another, they by the advice of Moses, in whom all at that time had implicit confidence, resolved to transfer their natural rights to no mere man, but to yield them wholly to Jehovah alone. This, without long deliberation, but with one accord and with much clamour, they engaged to do, promising implicit obedience to all God's commandments, and engaging to acknowledge no law but that which he by his divine revelation should constitute as right. Now this engagement of the Jews to Jehovah, or this transference of their rights to him, was effected in the same way as we have above conceived it to be accomplished in ordinary society, when men resolve to cede their natural rights to a sovereign ruler or ruling power. The Jews, in fact, gave up their natural rights to Jehovah in terms of an express agreement (vide Exodus xxiv. 7), voluntarily binding themselves by an oath to the faithful observance of its terms on their part, not compelled by force nor terrified by threats to do so. And then, in order that the agreement might be duly ratified and determined, Jehovah took no measures with them until they had had proofs of his wonderful power, by which alone they had hitherto been led and preserved, and by which alone they could hope to be protected in time to come (Exod. xix. 4, 5). For it was the belief that they could be saved by the protecting might of Jehovah alone, which led them to transfer to him the whole of that natural right of self-defence which they perhaps had previously believed they possessed of themselves, and with this the whole of their other natural rights. Jehovah alone, therefore, was sovereign over the Jews, and was properly entitled their king, as the Jewish empire was rightly called the kingdom of God. By an extension of this idea the enemies of the Jews were regarded as the enemies of God; and the citizen who attempted to usurp the supreme power was guilty in the act of treason to the rights of the realm, to the divine majesty, to the authority and decrees of Jehovah.

In the Hebrew state, consequently, the civil polity and religion, which consists essentially, as we have shown, in obedience to God, were one and the same. The dogmas of the Jewish religion were not doctrines, but declared rights and commandments; piety was accounted justice, impiety was injustice and crime; he who fell off from the state religion ceased to be a citizen, and for this cause alone was looked upon as an enemy; as he who died for his religion was held to have died for his country, and between civil right and religious profession no distinction whatever was made. On these grounds the ancient Hebrew state might truly be called a theocracy: its subjects were bound by no law save that revealed by God. All however was rather based on opinion than on reality; for the ancient Hebrews did in fact retain in their own hands the absolute right of ruling, as I shall immediately show by an analysis of the way and manner in which their state was administered.

Inasmuch as the Hebrews ceded their natural rights to no one among themselves, but all equally, as in a democracy, transferred these to Jehovah, and with one voice proclaimed that whatsoever God commanded without an express mediator, that they would do, it follows that by this arrangement all remained individually equal,—with like title to consult God, to receive and interpret laws,—in a word, to share in the administration of affairs. For this reason it was that all at first approached Jehovah of themselves that they might know his commands. But in their earliest interview the people were so much alarmed, and heard the voice of God speaking with such terror and amazement, that they thought the end of all things had come. Full of their fears, therefore, they besought Moses anew, saying, "Behold, the Lord our God hath showed us his glory and his greatness, and we have heard his voice out of the midst of the fire; we have seen this day that God doth talk with man, and he liveth. Now, therefore, why should we die? for this great fire will consume us; if we hear the voice of the Lord our God any more, then we shall die.... Go thou near and hear all that the Lord God shall say, and speak thou unto us all that the Lord God shall speak unto thee, and we will hear it and do it" (vide Deut. v. 24 et seq., and xviii. 15 et seq.). By this it is obvious that the Israelites annulled their first covenant with Jehovah; they transferred their title to consult him immediately, and to interpret his commandments for themselves, to Moses, who accordingly became the sole giver and expounder of the divine law, and consequently the supreme judge of the people, over whom no one else had authority. Moses, in fact, now stood to the children of Israel in the place of Jehovah; he alone possessed the supreme authority; he alone enjoyed the privilege of consulting Jehovah, of delivering the divine responses to the nation, and of enforcing obedience to these. The people had now engaged to be obedient, not to what God commanded them immediately to do, but to what God commanded Moses should be done. Moses, I have said, stood alone in his high authority; for if any one in his life-time presumed to prophesy aught in the name of God, although a true prophet, still he was accounted guilty, and a usurper of the supreme power (vide Numb. xi., xii.);* and here it is worthy of remark, that although the people had elected

* In this passage two men are said to have begun prophesying in the camp, whom Joshua proposed to arrest. Now he would not have done so had every Hebrew possessed the right of communicating the commands of God to the people without the permission of Moses. Moses, however, saw fit to leave these men unmolested, and he even spoke reproachfully to Joshua for having advised him to use his sovereign authority at a time when this authority had become such a burthen to him that he would rather have died than gone on to exercise it alone. "Enviest thou for my sake?" says Moses to Joshua. "Would God that all the Lord's people were prophets, and the Lord would put his spirit upon them." That is to say: would to heaven that the right to consult God, and, insomuch, the authority of government, was relegated to the hands of the people! Joshua, therefore, made no mistake in regard to the rights of Moses, but in regard to the occasion or season for the exercise of these rights, and this was the reason why Moses spoke reproachfully to him; precisely as at a later period David did to Abishai, when recommended by him to put Shimei to death, though guilty of treason (vide 2 Samuel xix. 22, 23).

Moses, they could not of right elect a successor to him. For in transferring their right of consulting God to Moses, and promising unconditionally to receive him instead of the divine oracle, they plainly lost their title to do so. He whom Moses chose they were bound to receive as elected by God. Had Moses chosen a successor, one who, like himself, possessed the whole administrative power—the right of consulting God in the tabernacle, and consequently the right of instituting and abrogating laws, of resolving on war and making peace, of sending ambassadors, of appointing judges, of choosing a successor, and of administering all the offices that appertain to a sovereign ruler—then the constitution of the state would have been purely monarchical. Nor would there have been any difference, in fact, save that a monarchy is usually said to be governed by the grace or will of God, which is not conspicuously manifested, whilst the Hebrew monarchy under Moses was ruled and governed, or was ordered to be ruled and governed, in a certain way by the decrees of God immediately and openly revealed to him. This difference, however, does not lessen the right and authority of the ruler in any respect; on the contrary, it rather increases them. In other matters, and particularly as regards the people, whether in a monarchy as usually constituted, or in that of the Jewish nation, they are alike subject in each, and uninformed of the divine decree; for in each all depends on the will of the monarch; and what is right or wrong is what he decrees to be one or other; nor are the people, because they believe that the sovereign commands nothing that is not revealed to him by God or by the command of God, the less, but, on the contrary, the more under the hand of authority. Moses, however, as said, chose no successor, but left the state to be so administered by those who came after him that it could neither rightly be called a democracy, an aristocracy, nor a monarchy, but a theocracy. For the right of interpreting the laws and of communicating the decrees of God was confided to one, and the right and authority of administering the affairs of the state was confided to another (vide Numb.

xxvii. 21). To make this matter more plain, I shall here give a succinct account of the whole administration of affairs in the ancient Hebrew state.

First, the people were commanded to build a house which should be, as it were, the palace of Jehovah, that is, of the sovereign power of the state; and this was to be done, not at the cost of any one, or of any number, but of the whole people, in order that the building in which God was to be consulted should be a common right or property. The Levites were the chosen administrators within this royal hall of audience, and Aaron, the brother of Moses, was made the chief among them, the second in authority as it were from Jehovah, the king, and Aaron's sons were to be regarded as his legitimate successors. Aaron, therefore, or the chief priest, as nearest to God, was the highest interpreter of the divine laws, the deliverer to the people of the responses of the divine oracle, and the intercessor with God for the nation. Now, had an officer with such powers possessed an equal right of civil command, there would have been nothing wanting to constitute him an absolute monarch. Of this right of civil command, however, the priest of the temple was deprived; indeed, the whole tribe of Levi was forbidden to take any part in the common affairs of life (to say nothing of the civil administration), whereby they might earn a livelihood; it was ordained that they should be maintained by the rest of the community, in order, as it was said, that they might be held in the higher honour by the multitude, as being solely devoted to the service of Jehovah.

Next, the militia, chosen indifferently from the remaining twelve tribes, were commanded to invade the territory of the Canaanites, and to divide these into twelve parts for allotment among themselves. For this business twelve chiefs were selected, one from each tribe, to whom, along with Joshua the captain and Eleazar the high priest, was given authority to divide the land of Canaan into twelve equal parts, and to distribute these by lot. Joshua, again, was chosen commander-in-chief of the militia or armed force, and to him alone was conceded the right in new or untried circumstances of consulting Jehovah; but he was to do so, not as Moses had done, alone in his tent or in the tabernacle, but by the medium of the chief priest, by whom only the answers of God were to be received. Once received, however, Joshua had absolute authority to proclaim the decrees of God, and to enforce obedience to them. He had also the right to advance and distinguish those whom he chose and as many as he chose, from among the militia, to send ambassadors, &c.,—in a word, the whole of the war administration lay with Joshua, as commander-in-chief of the army. No one, however, could legitimately succeed to this important office; nor could a successor be chosen in any other way than immediately by God, when the necessities of the nation seemed to require the appointment. Otherwise, all affairs of peace and war were administered by the chiefs of the tribes, as I shall immediately show.

Lastly, all males from the age of twenty to sixty were required to take arms, so that the army was the people, the people were the army, which swore fealty to no commander or high priest, but to their religion, or their God, Jehovah. The army, consequently, was called the host or ranks of God, and God himself among the ancient Hebrews was styled the Lord of Hosts. This was the reason why the ark of the covenant was always borne in the midst of the army during great battles, on the issue of which depended the fate of the nation for good or for evil. In the presence, as it were, of their king and ruler, it was presumed that the people would bear themselves with greater bravery, and put forth all their strength.

From the ordinances delivered by Moses to his successors we gather that he chose functionaries or administrators, not rulers of the state. He gave to no one the right of consulting God alone, and in such places as he pleased; and, consequently, he gave to no one the authority which he himself possessed of ordaining and abrogating laws, of decreeing peace or war, of electing ministers of the temple as well as of the state, which are all acts belonging to one who holds supreme or sovereign authority. The chief priest himself had the right, indeed, of interpreting the laws, and of delivering the responses of Jehovah; not, however, as Moses had done, whensoever he chose, but only when asked to do so by the commander-in-chief of the host, the supreme council of the state, or those in authority. On the other hand, the commander-in-chief of the host and the council could consult God when they chose; but they could only receive the answers he deigned from the high priest; wherefore, the sayings of God in the mouth of the high priest were not commandments, as they were in the mouth of Moses, but only responses delivered to Joshua and the council; however, they at length acquired the force of commandments and decrees. The chief priest, who received the responses of God immediately, had neither any military nor any civil authority; and they, on the contrary, who possessed lands of right could not of right institute laws. Again, the chief priests, both Aaron and his son Eleazar, were elected by Moses; Moses being dead, however, no one possessed the right of electing a pontiff, but the son legitimately succeeded the father in his office. The commander of the army was also chosen by Moses, and not by the high priest. The chief command was first assumed by Joshua in virtue of a title delivered immediately by Moses; but after the death of Joshua the high priest elected no one in his place; nor did the chiefs of the tribes consult God anew concerning a commander; each chief in the militia of his own tribe, and those of the tribes all together, met in council on the military affairs of the nation, they having resumed the right of supreme command which had been conferred on Joshua. It is obvious, indeed, that there was no necessity for a commander-in-chief, except when the different tribes had to combine their forces against a common enemy; a state of things which happened most remarkably under Joshua, when the several tribes had not yet determinate settlements, and all territory was held by common right. But when the whole of the tribes had become possessed of lands by right of successful war, and things were no longer held in common, there was no need of a general commander-in-chief, inasmuch as the tribes now stood to each other in the relation of confederates rather than of fellow-citizens,—they were so at least in respect of territorial divisions; in respect of God and religion, indeed, they were still fellow-citizens; but in regard to any right which one tribe had over another, they were strictly confederates, almost in the same manner (if abstraction be made of the common temple) as the members of the high and mighty confederation of the estates of the Netherlands. For a partition of a common thing is but an arrangement whereby each participant henceforth holds his own share distinctly and alone, the others interested ceding the rights they formerly had over that part to the possessor. For this reason did Moses choose chiefs of tribes; in order that after the division of the country each chief might have the particular care of the portion of territory belonging to his tribe and its immediate affairs, viz. the privilege of consulting Jehovah on the concerns of the tribe by the medium of the high priest, of commanding its militia, of founding and fortifying towns, of establishing judges in each city, of attacking the enemies of the tribe, and of administering all its concerns absolutely and without control, both in peace and in war. Nor was the chief to acknowledge any judge except Jehovah, or him whom the Lord God sent expressly as a prophet. Any chief who fell away from Jehovah was to be regarded by the rest of the tribe no longer as one of themselves, but as an enemy who had broken faith with them, and was to be dealt with accordingly. Instances in point are recorded in Scripture. Thus, after the death of Joshua, the children of Israel themselves, and not the now commander-in-chief, consulted Jehovah, and having been informed that Judah should first invade the territories of the Canaanites, this tribe entered into an agreement with Simeon to unite their forces and make war in common on the enemy, without including the other tribes in their arrangements, but leaving each of these to make war single-handed on the inhabitants of its allotment (Judges i. 1 *et seq.*). This was accordingly done, and with success; but instead of exterminating all, old and young, who stood in their way, according to orders, these tribes took the remnants of the original population under their protection, and received as subjects as many as chose to submit; an act of clemency for which they were afterwards severely censured by an angel sent by Jehovah for the purpose. In the narrow and selfish policy of Judah and Simeon the other tribes seem to have found no cause of offence. But against Benjamin, which had offended the whole Jewish people, and so loosened the bonds of good understanding that none of the confederates could again feel sure of hospitality among them, a war of extermination was raised; and after three battles Benjamin was finally defeated, and the whole tribe, innocent and guilty alike, involved in indiscriminate slaughter,—a deed that gave rise to late but unavailing repentance.

What has just been said of the rights of each particular tribe is sufficiently confirmed by these examples. But some may here ask by whom the chiefs of the different tribes were chosen? On this point, however, I regret that I am unable to gather anything certain from Scripture. I conjecture, nevertheless, that as the tribes were divided into families, whose heads were chosen from the elders of these, he who was senior among the elders succeeded of right to the place of chief. Thus Moses chose seventy coadjutors from among the elders, who with himself formed a supreme council; and they who had the administration of affairs after the death of Joshua are called Elders in Scripture. Lastly, nothing is more frequent among the Hebrews than by the title Elders to imply Judges.

These particulars I think worthy of attention, though I am aware that they give nothing in the way of certainty to my conjecture. Let it suffice for me to show that no one after the death of Moses united in his single person all the functions of supreme ruler; for as the whole authority of the state did not rest with any one man, nor with a single council, nor with the people collectively, but some things were confided to one tribe, others to other tribes, and others still were administered of equal right by the rest, it follows, most obviously, that the constitution of the Hebrew state from the death of Moses was neither monarchical, nor aristocratic, nor democratic, but, as I have said, it was theocratic; 1. because the royal palace was a temple, and in their common interest in this alone were the whole of the tribes constituted fellow-citizens; 2. because all the citizens were required to swear fealty to the Lord God their judge, to whom alone they promised absolute obedience in all things; and because the commander-in-chief of the nation, when there was occasion for such an officer, was chosen, not by themselves, but by Jehovah. This Moses expressly declares in the name of God in Deuteronomy (xix. 15), and the fact itself is testified to by the election of Gideon, Samson, and Samuel; so that there is no reason to doubt but that the other faithful leaders were also chosen in the same way, although this does not appear in their histories.

These matters premised, it is time that we saw what influence this constitution of the state had in securing moderation on the part both of rulers and the ruled, so that these were not rebels and those were not tyrants.

They who rule, or possess authority, whatever iniquity they perpetrate, still strive to give their acts a colour of justice, and endeavour to persuade the people that all they do is well and honestly done; and in this they easily enough succeed, when the entire interpretation of the laws lies with them. For it is not doubtful but that rulers derive the greater part of the power they possess to enforce their wishes, and to do what their appetites dispose them to do, from themselves if they are sole interpreters of the laws; as, on the other hand, they lose the greater part of their arbitrary power if the right of interpreting the laws lies with another, and the administration of the law is at the same time so public that no one is in doubt about what is done. Now from the constitution of the ancient Hebrew state it is manifest that a principal cause of maladministration was taken from the ruler by the interpretation of the law being confided to the Levites alone (Deut. xxi. 5), who had no share with the rest of the tribes in the general administration of affairs, but derived their whole income, or subsistence, and social position from the impartial interpretation of the laws. And then the whole people were commanded to assemble in a certain place every seven years, to be instructed by the high priest in the laws of their country, every man being ordered in addition to read and re-read with his utmost attention the Book of the Law. (Deut. xxxi. 9, and vi. 7.) The chiefs therefore for their own sakes, and if they wished to be honoured of the people, were bound to be careful that everything was done according to the prescribed forms familiarly known to all; for by this alone could they hope to be reverenced as vicegerents of God, and ministers of his supreme authority.

By opposite conduct they could not escape the hatred of the people, which is usually theological, i. e. unmitigated, in its character. To this end, to restrain within proper bounds the unbridled lusts of their chiefs, there was this important circumstance in addition, viz. that the militia was composed of the people at large, no one from the age of twenty to sixty being exempt from service, and the chiefs were not authorized to have in the ranks any foreign mercenaries. This, I say, was of the greatest moment, for it is certain that princes can only play the tyrant and oppress the people by means of a soldiery kept in pay by themselves, and they dread nothing more than the freedom of the citizen soldier, by whose bravery and endurance, and willing expenditure of his blood, the liberty and glory of the state have been achieved. On this account it was that Alexander, about to engage in the second war against Darius, laid to heart the counsel of Parmenio received through Polyspercon, and began to mingle foreign elements largely with his native army. Quintus Curtius informs us (lib. iv. 3, 13) that Alexander, having shortly before had occasion to censure Parmenio sharply, could not venture to reprimand him again, nor to trench on the liberties of the Macedonians, which he greatly disliked, until after he had raised the numbers of his mercenaries by means of prisoners drafted into his service much beyond the strength of his Macedonian troops. Then only did he venture to show the haughtiness of his disposition, hitherto repressed and kept within bounds by the privileges of the better class of Macedonian citizen soldiers. If, therefore, we see the freedom of the citizen controlling chiefs and princes who are wont to arrogate to themselves the whole credit of victories won in states where the human element alone is considered, how much more must it have availed in the Hebrew state, where the soldiers fought not for the honour of their chief but for the glory of the Lord, and only engaged in battle when the favourable answer of Jehovah had been received!

We are further to consider that as the chiefs of the Jewish tribes were bound together by the tie of religion alone, any one who showed signs of backsliding, or who actually fell away from his faith, was held an enemy by all the rest, and lawfully coerced and put down.

Still further, there was the fear of a new prophet springing up; for any one of pure life, showing by certain accredited signs that he was possessed of the gift of prophecy, by this alone proclaimed his title to the highest command; in the same way precisely as Moses had been chosen chief, the supremacy accruing in the name of God revealed to him immediately, not as with the chiefs of tribes by the medium of the high priest, who consulted and proclaimed the will of Jehovah. And there can be no question of the ease with which a prophet could carry the people with him when they were oppressed, and by trifling signs persuade them to whatsoever he chose; as, on the other hand, if the administration were properly conducted, the chiefs could always arrange matters so that the prophet remained answerable to them, and at their mercy. For they had the power of inquiring whether he were of blameless life and conversation or not, whether the signs he showed were certain and sufficient, and, finally, whether what he proclaimed in the name of God harmonized with the accredited doctrine and known laws of the nation; and in case the signs were not sufficient, or the doctrine propounded were new, the chiefs had the power to condemn the false or reputed false prophet to death. On the other hand, the prophet approved by the chiefs was received on their authority and testimony alone.

4. It is to be observed, 4thly, that the chief did not stand higher in respect of rank than the rest of the nobility, but that the administration of affairs was intrusted to him solely by reason of his age and his virtuous life.

5. Lastly, it is to be noted that the chiefs, and the militia generally, could not be held as more disposed to war than inclined to peace; for the militia, as has been said, was entirely composed of the citizens or people; and the affairs both of peace and war were administered by the same men: he who in camp was a soldier, in the city was a burgher; the leader in the field was judge in the hall of justice; the commander-in-chief of the host was chief in the state. No one therefore could wish for war for the sake of war, but rather for the sake of peace, and the maintenance of the common liberties; and the chief was especially careful to avoid the proposition of all novelties, in order not to place himself in opposition to the high priest, or make his own dignity as civil ruler clash with the dignity that belonged to the chief of the national religion. So much for the means and motives that tended to keep the chiefs within the bounds of their authority.

Let us now proceed to inquire into the means whereby the people were kept obedient. And here we have not far to search, for the fundamental principles of the Hebrew commonwealth proclaim them clearly, the most superficial study sufficing to show that these were all calculated to engender such a love of their country in the minds of the citizens that everything the most difficult seems easy in contrast with the idea of hoping to excite treasonable feelings among such a people. For after they had transferred their rights to Jehovah, and satisfied themselves that their empire was the empire of the Lord God, that they themselves were the sons of God, and all other nations his enemies, on which account they cherished the most inveterate hatred against them,—and that this feeling was held laudable and pious may be seen in Psalm cxxxix. 21, 22,* especially,—the Jews, as a people, could have a greater abhorrence of nothing than to swear fealty to the foreigner; neither could they conceive any wickedness so great, nor any act so worthy of execration, as betrayal of their country, in other words, of the kingdom of the God they adored. The Jews even held it sinful to dwell beyond the boundaries of their country, conceiving that the worship of God could be performed nowhere but in their native land; the soil they trod at home was alone holy, the rest of the earth was impure and accursed. Wherefore, David thus complains when brought before Saul, because he had been forced to dwell for a time in exile: "If those that moved thee against me be men, let them be accursed, for they have hindered me from walking in the heritage of God, but said to me, Begone, and worship other gods." And this was the reason—and it is worthy of especial notice—why no Hebrew citizen was ever condemned to exile; he who had committed a crime deserved punishment indeed, but he was not to be made an outcast and infamous. The love of the ancient Hebrew for his country, therefore, was not simple love; it was piety, it was religion, which, as well as contempt and hatred of other nations, was cherished by the daily religious service, and so fostered that it became a second nature. For the daily worship of the Jews was not merely different from, but was opposed to, that of every other people, whereby they became altogether singular and distinct from other nations. From the daily denunciations of the heathen, a persistent hatred of them was necessarily engendered; and nothing takes firmer hold of the mind than a feeling of this kind; for it is a hate sprung of the highest devotion, believed to be peculiarly pious and entirely acceptable to God; and then there was not wanting that most common cause of aggravated dislike, namely, a hearty reciprocation of the uneasy feeling of

---

* "Do I not hate them, O Lord, that hate thee? . . . I hate them with a perfect hatred: I count them mine enemies."—*Ed.*

hatred; for nations hated and contemned always return the compliment paid them with interest.

Now the vast influence which such conditions as these,—freedom of civil government, love of the people for their common country, absolute dominion asserted over subjugated tribes or nations, hatred of these not only allowed, but enjoined and held praiseworthy, the habit of accounting every foreign people enemies as matter of course, singularity of rites and customs, &c.—the vast influence, I say, which these various particulars exerted, in producing that wonderful constancy which distinguished the ancient Hebrew in enduring and in daring when the interests of his country were at stake, is demonstrated both by reason and experience. Never, whilst Jerusalem stood the holy city of the children of Israel, would they quietly endure the rule of the stranger, so that Jerusalem came to be designated the rebellious city (vide Ezra iv. 12—15). The Jews of the second empire, indeed, which was but a shadow of the first, when the high priests had usurped the seats of the leaders, were not subdued by the Romans without the greatest difficulty, a fact which Tacitus attests when he says,—"Vespasian had brought the Jewish war to an end, with the exception of the siege of Jerusalem, which was found a work of great and long-continued difficulty, by reason rather of the stubbornness of the people and the strength of their superstition than any abundance of provisions and other necessaries which they possessed as means of holding out." (Histor. lib. ii.)

But besides these things, the worth of which is matter of opinion only, there was something else in the Hebrew state altogether peculiar, and of the most enduring character, by which the people must have felt themselves withheld in the most powerful manner from all thought of revolt or secession, namely, the consideration of advantage, or interest, which is the pith and marrow, the life and soul of all human action; and this, I opine, had a very prominent place in the constitution of the Jewish commonwealth. Nowhere else in the ancient world did the citizens hold their possessions by so secure a tenure as in Jewry, where the meanest subject possessed a portion of land of the same extent as the greatest chief, and each was proprietor in perpetuity of his portion; for were any one compelled by poverty to sell his inheritance, on the return of the year of jubilee he must needs be put again in possession, restitution must be made; the law, in short, was definite that no man could be forced to alienate his land. And then, poverty could have been more tolerable nowhere than in the ancient Hebrew state, where neighbourly charity was practised without stint, as an act of piety towards God their king, and as a means of rendering him propitious. The Hebrew citizen, therefore, within the limits of the state could scarcely find himself otherwise than well and comfortable, although abroad he was open to the most unworthy usage, and to every insult and indignity. The feeling, indeed, that he had no equal abroad, that he had God alone for a master at home, that charity towards and love of his fellow-citizen was true piety, contributed not a little to the general hatred entertained by other nations for the Jew; and the reciprocation of this on his part, whilst it proved a powerful motive for keeping him in his own country, was another reason for shunning all causes of contention and avoiding civil war. In addition to this there was the discipline of perfect obedience in which the Jew was educated. All his actions to the minutest tittle were regulated by the prescriptions of the law; he was not at liberty to plough as he pleased; he could only do so at certain seasons, in certain years even, and with the same sort of cattle in the yoke; neither could he sow or reap, save at times and seasons foreordained,—in short, the life of the ancient Hebrew was a ceaseless round of obedience and observance, to which habit must have given the air of freedom rather than of constraint; whence also it followed that no one craved things forbidden, but only those that were commanded; and, to conclude, at certain seasons of the year the Jew was held bound to give himself up to ease and enjoyment, and this not to satisfy his own inclination, but to show hearty obedience to the commands of Jehovah. Three times in the course of every year the Jew was the guest of Jehovah (Deut. xvi.); the seventh day of every week was a day of rest on which he did no kind of work; and besides this sabbath, other times were indicated, on which merriment and conviviality were not merely permitted, but positively enjoined; nor do I imagine that anything could have been devised more calculated to incline men's minds to general obedience than this especial ordinance; for nothing takes such strong hold of the mind as the joy and gladness that spring from devotion, that is, from love and admiration joined. Nor was the Jew liable to be wearied and disgusted by repetition and familiarity, for the days of festival only recurred occasionally, and the services appropriate to each were different. To these various considerations must be added that extreme reverence for the Temple which distinguished the Jew, engendered by the peculiarities of his religious rites, as well as by the ceremonies he was bound to observe, and which were always most religiously observed before venturing to present himself within the sacred precincts; even at the present day it is never without the greatest horror that the Jew reads of the wickedness of Manasseh, who dared to set up an idol in the temple of the Lord. Nor was the popular reverence for the volume of the law preserved within the innermost sanctuary any less. In such a state of things, popular discontent and distaste were never to be feared; for no one dared to form or express any opinion of his own on divine matters; all alike were held bound to give unreasoning assent and obedience to whatever was commanded by divine authority, as received in responses within the temple, or as written and contained in the laws established by God. Thus, briefly, but I trust satisfactorily, have I explained the grand features of the Jewish Polity.

I have still to inquire into the causes whence it came that the Jews so often departed from their law, why they were so frequently subdued, and how their empire was at last totally overthrown. Some one will probably say here, that it was because of the obstinacy and stiffneckedness of the people. But this is puerile, for why were the Jews more stubborn than other nations? Was it from their nature? Nature, however, does not create a nation, but only individuals, who are only associated into nations by specialities of language, of laws, and of manners; and diversities in laws and manners can only arise because each nation has a genius of its own, is peculiarly circumstanced, and entertains certain singular prejudices. If, therefore, it were necessary to concede that the Jews had proved themselves more rebellious than the rest of mankind, this must be imputed to some vice in their laws, or in their manners and customs. Now this is true in fact; and had God willed that the Hebrew nation should have lasted longer as a power upon earth, he would have established their rights and laws on another basis, and instituted a different rule of administration. What, indeed, can we say but that the Jews began to excite the anger of their God against them, not, as Jeremiah says (xxxii. 31), from the time when the foundations of Jerusalem were laid, but from the first promulgation of the laws which governed them. To this Ezekiel bears witness when he says (xx. 25), "Wherefore, I gave them statutes that were not good, and judgments whereby they should not live, and I polluted them in their own gifts, in that they caused to pass through the fire all that openeth the womb, that I might make them desolate, to the end that they might know that I am Jehovah." To understand these words, and the cause of the subversion of the Jewish dominion, aright, it is to be observed that the intention at first was to make over the whole of the sacred offices to the first-born of all the tribes, and not to the Levites in peculiar (Numb. viii. 17); but, subsequently, when all but the Levites had bowed down and worshipped the golden calf, the first-born at large were rejected as defiled, and the Levites chosen in their stead (Deut. x. 8), a change on which the more I reflect the more disposed I am to break out in the words of Tacitus, and to say that at this time God's purpose was not to protect but to punish the children of Israel. Nor can I sufficiently express my amazement that such rage should have been found in the divine mind; or that laws, which always imply a purpose to secure the honour, safety, and general well-being of a nation, should have been delivered by Jehovah with an intention to revenge himself upon the Jewish people, whereby law ceases to be law, i. e. a means to the safety of the state and the individuals composing it, but rather appears as a snare, as a code of pains and penalties for sins induced. For all the gifts which the people were required to bestow on the priests and Levites in order that the first-born might be redeemed, a money price being set on every head rescued from the fire,* and, finally, the exclusive institution of the Levites to the priesthood, were so many memorials of the persistent defilement and rejection of the people at large. The Levites, too, must always have found something to find fault with among the mass of the nation. Among so many thousands there were doubtless occasional heretical theologians discovered, men with peculiar views [always objects of suspicion to a priesthood], and, on the other hand, the people must have been not indisposed to watch narrowly the lives and conversation of the Levites, who after all were mere men, and, as always happens, to impute the failings or improper conduct of one among them to the whole body; whence continual discontent and complainings. Moreover, there was the hardship of maintaining a set of men, unseen and in idleness, and not related to the rest of the nation by blood, especially in times when grain was dear. What wonder, then, if in seasons of leisure, when miracles had ceased, and there were no men of mark and likelihood as leaders, that the popular mind, fretful and grudging as it mostly is, began to feel weary of a worship,

* There can be no question of the redemption clauses in the thirteenth chapter of Exodus being interpolations. In verse 12, Jehovah's claim to every male that opened the matrix among men, and the firstlings of beasts, is absolute; in verse 13 there is question of redemption. In verse 15 the reasons for this requisition of Jehovah are given, and they plainly admit of no exception, so that the last clause of this verse must also have been interpolated. Any redemption is obviously inconsistent with the text of Ezekiel quoted above. See further, Numb. iii. 13.—*Ed.*

divine indeed in itself, but to them become an object of suspicion through its ministers, and their own nothingness in its offices,—what wonder, I say, if the people desired some change in their religious system, and that their leaders, always intent on keeping the supreme command in their own hands, gave way to the people in this, in order to secure them to themselves and detach them from the priesthood, yielded a ready ear to their complaints, and favoured the introduction of new forms of religious worship? Had the state been constituted in conformity with what was the original intention, all the tribes would have been confirmed in equal rights and honours for ever, and everything would have gone on smoothly and securely. For who would have felt inclined to question the sacred rights of his blood relations? who have been found indisposed to contribute to the support of his near kindred, his parents, his brothers? who to dispute their interpretation of the law, or to look for other than true responses through them from the oracle of God? The several tribes would certainly have felt themselves much more closely united, had all been held alike in every respect, had all especially had equal rights in the administration of the religious system of the nation. There would even have been nothing to fear had the election of the Levites to the sacred function had any other ground than anger and revenge. But, as we have seen, the Jews had aroused the anger of their God, who, to repeat the words of Ezekiel, polluted them in their own gifts, causing them to pass their firstborn through the fire to make them desolate.* These surmises are amply confirmed by the facts of Jewish history: as soon as the people began to have a little leisure in the wilderness, many, and these not men of the common order, were found to complain of the preference shown the Levites, and from this to hint that Moses did not deliver his decrees

* Is it possible that such words could ever have proceeded from the Supreme, supposing him for a moment invested with personality, and making use of human speech? Has this text been duly considered by those who maintain that the Hebrew Scriptures are the very word of God?—*Ed.*

from the divine dictation, but of his own arbitrary fancy: had he not preferred his own tribe to all the others, and given the office of high priest as an eternal inheritance to his brother? Wherefore the people approached Moses tumultuously, insisting that all were alike holy, and that he himself was raised against right over the heads of all. Nor could Moses appease the multitude on this occasion by any ordinary means; he was forced to have recourse to a miracle in sign of his own trustworthiness, whereby all the discontented were exterminated. But this only led to a new rebellion of the whole people, who believed that they had been destroyed by no judgment of Jehovah, but by the device of Moses. Nor was the tumult allayed till a terrible pestilence had so broken the spirit of the nation that they who survived would rather they had died than been spared. It might be said, therefore, that the rebellion ceased, rather than that concord was restored, as Scripture itself testifies, for Jehovah, whilst he predicts to Moses that after his death the people would fall away from the worship of the true God, proceeds to say, "For I know their imagination which they go about even now, before I have brought them into the land which I sware." And immediately afterwards Moses himself says to the people, "For I know thy rebellion and thy stiff neck; behold, while I am yet alive with you this day ye have been rebellious against the Lord, and how much more after my death" (Deut. xxxi. 21, 27). And all this, indeed, happened, as is well known. Whence proceeded great changes, great licence in all things, luxury and idleness, whereby everything began to go from bad to worse, until after the nation had been several times subdued and enslaved, they entirely broke with the divine institution, and clamoured for an earthly king, desiring a royal palace, not the temple, as the seat of their government, and that the several tribes should continue to be fellow-citizens or subjects in their respect for the sovereign, not for the divine law and high priest of Jehovah. But out of this were engendered abundant materials for new seditions, from whence ensued at length the collapse and fall of the Hebrew dominion. For what can sovereigns bear less than a precarious tenure of authority, and an imperium in imperio? They who from a private station were first chosen to fill the throne might be content with the degree of dignity and power to which they had been raised; but when their sons had attained to the same eminence by right of succession, everything must have begun to change. The whole mind of the prince was then given to centring all power in himself, which for the most part he had not, so long as the right of legislation lay, not with the civil ruler, but with the high priest, who was at once the guardian of the law deposited in the ark of the temple, and its interpreter to the people. The first kings among the Jews were bound by the laws like subjects, not raised above them; neither could they legally abrogate old, nor institute new, laws having equal authority with the old. Again, as the law of the Levites forbade kings equally with subjects, as unclean and profane, to meddle with sacred things, and further, as the whole security of the kingly power virtually depended on the pleasure of another, viz. the high priest, who was regarded as a prophet, it is obvious that there was a power in the state greater than that of the king, who therefore, and necessarily, reigned precariously. Of this we have evidence on several occasions. With what freedom, for instance, does Samuel the priest address and order Saul the king, and how readily for a single transgression does he transfer the kingdom from Saul to David! It was to get the better of this state of things that the kings consented to rear temples to other gods, where there should no longer be Levite priests to be propitiated and consulted, and then they sought out those who prophesied in the name of God, that they might have prophets of their own to oppose to the true prophets of Jehovah. With all their striving, however, they never completely attained their wishes. For the prophets of Jehovah, prepared for all contingencies, were ever on the look-out for favourable times; they had still their eye on the successor in power, whose authority is always precarious whilst the memory of the former king endures. They could easily then, on their sacred authority, induce an inconsiderate or a piously-disposed and virtuous king to vindicate the divine right to the chief authority, or at all events to a share of it. But the prophets could never effect much in this way, for although they might get rid of a tyrant from among them, there were still causes at work why they only obtained a new one at the cost, perchance, of the life of many of the people. Whence came no end of discord and dissension and civil war, whilst the causes why violence was done to the right divine always remained the same, and indeed could not be removed, save with the total destruction of the empire.

We have now seen how religion came to be introduced into the Hebrew commonwealth, and in what way this empire might have been eternal if the rightful anger of the lawgiver had suffered it to continue. But as this was not permitted, the Jewish empire necessarily came to an end at last. And here I speak of the first empire only; for the second was scarcely a shadow of the first, the state being then governed by the laws of the Persians, whose subjects the Jews had now become; and when they had regained their liberty the priests usurped the right of election to the sovereign authority, and so ruled absolutely; whence the great anxiety shown by the priesthood at once to rule and exercise the pontificate. But it is not important to say more of the second or restored Jewish empire. Whether the first, as we conceive it capable of indefinite duration, were worthy of imitation, or whether it were pious to attempt as far as possible to imitate it, will appear in the following chapter. For the present I would only beg attention to the conclusion which I derive from all that has just been said, viz. that divine right, or right founded on religion, is based on the covenant made between Jehovah and the children of Israel, without which there had been nothing but natural right; consequently that the Jews were religiously bound to one another only, and that the dispensation under which they lived has no bearing upon other nations who were not parties to the agreement.

CHAPTER XVIII.

OF CERTAIN POLITICAL AXIOMS DERIVED FROM THE CONSTITUTION OF THE HEBREW REPUBLIC AND THE HISTORY OF THE JEWISH PEOPLE.

ALTHOUGH the Hebrew state, as exhibited in the preceding chapter, might have been perpetual, still it could not now be imitated; nor indeed were it desirable that it should. For he who would transfer his rights to God must come to an express understanding and agreement with God, as the Hebrews did of old: not only were his own consent, but that of the Supreme, requisite to make the contract complete. But God has made it known to mankind by the apostles that covenants with him are no longer implemented with ink, nor engraved upon stone tables, but are written by his holy spirit on the heart. And then, such a polity as that of the ancient Hebrews might perhaps have been found adapted to them in their state of isolation in Judea, without commerce or communication with the rest of the world, but would never suffice for those nations who must of necessity hold commercial intercourse with others: the constitution of the Hebrew state could have met the wants of only a small number of nations. Nevertheless, although not to be commended in everything, it had still much that is most worthy of being noted, and which perchance it might be found advantageous to imitate. As it is not my purpose, however, to treat expressly of the Hebrew republic, I shall pass by the greater number of its distinguishing peculiarities, and only pause upon those that seem to fall within the scope of my undertaking. And first I shall show that the election of a chief ruler, possessing the highest attributes of government, is not inconsistent with the idea of a divine kingdom.

After the Jews had transferred their rights to Jehovah, we see that they also delivered the supreme authority into the hands of Moses, who thus acquired the sole right of instituting and of abrogating laws in the name of God; of choosing the ministers of the religious rites; of judging, teaching, inflicting punishment,—in short, of ruling absolutely in all things.

Again, although the ministers of religion were the interpreters of the laws, still it was not within their province to sit in judgment upon the people, nor to excommunicate any one; these high functions belonged exclusively to the judges and chiefs elected by the community (Josh. vi. 26, Judges xxi. 18, and 1 Samuel xiv. 24). Besides these important points, if we consider the successful career of the Jews, and consult their histories, we shall find other particulars very deserving of attention; for instance, 1st, that there were no religious sects among them until after the chief priests under the second empire had acquired the power of issuing decrees, of transacting the business of the state, and, with a view of making their authority perpetual, had arrogated to themselves the rights of sovereign princes, and even hinted a wish to be called kings. The reason of this is obvious; for in the first empire no decree could derive a title from the high priest; he having no authority to issue decrees, but only to deliver the responses of Jehovah to questions proposed by the chiefs or councils of the tribes. In these times, therefore, the high priests could have had no desire to promulgate new commandments; their duty and business lay in the administration and defence of ancient decrees and familiar institutions; for in no other way could they preserve their own privileges and immunities against the jealousy of the chiefs but by keeping the laws uncorrupted. But after they had acquired the power of meddling in the business of the state, and had associated princely with their proper pontifical duties, each began to seek for fame and reputation, not only in the sphere of his religious duties, but beyond these, and wherever he could connect his name with affairs of state; hence the manifest desire of determining everything by pontifical authority, and of constantly issuing decrees on such subjects as new ceremonies and new articles of faith, which they desired should be held no less sacred, nor of less authority, than the laws of Moses. From this it came to pass, by and by, that religion declined into a sort of spasmodic superstition, and law became corrupted against all sense and reasonable interpretation; to which must be added the circumstance, that whilst the priesthood were paving the way to the seat of civil power in the beginning of the restoration, they assented to everything that could win the people to their party; approving of acts done by them, although most reprehensible, and twisting Scripture into agreement with all their immoralities. To this unworthy conduct Malachi testifies in the most pointed manner; inveighing against the priests of his day, he designates them as contemners of the name of God, and proceeds in these words: "The priest's lips should keep knowledge, and the people should seek the law at his mouth; for he is the messenger of the Lord of hosts. But ye are departed out of the way; ye have caused many to stumble at the law; ye have corrupted the covenant of Levi, saith the Lord of hosts" (ii. 7, 8), and so he goes on to accuse them of arbitrarily interpreting the laws, and of having no respect to God, but of being swayed only by personal considerations. It is certain, however, that the priests could never walk so warily but that they were challenged in their innovations by some of the more clear-sighted and forward of the people, who, subsequently increasing in boldness, contended that no laws were binding save those only that were written; and that no other decrees which the Pharisees, who were mostly sprung of the common people, entitled traditions of the patriarchs, were in any wise to be observed. However this may have been, it is still certain that the flattery of the priesthood, the corruption of religion and the laws, and the incredible increase in the number of these, gave frequent and grave occasions for difference and disputation, of a kind too that could never be composed or concluded; for when men fall out on the score of their superstitions, which they then designate their religion, and the civil power abet any party, it is impossible to bring them to a reasonable understanding; they necessarily fall off from one another, and become divided into sects which mutually hate and, with the opportunity given, persecute one another.

2. It is worthy of remark that the prophets, mere private individuals, by the freedom of their admonitions, warnings, chidings, and denunciations, seem rather to have excited than improved the people, who would have yielded and been corrected had they been addressed by their king or chiefs. The prophets, indeed, were often insufferable even to good and pious kings, by reason of the right they arrogated of adjudging this and that as pious or impious, and even of reproving with their tongue the sovereign himself who ventured to do aught, whether of a public or a private nature, in opposition to their judgment. King Asa, who by the testimony of Scripture appears to have ruled justly, put Hanani the prophet into prison because of the freedom of his criticisms on the treaty which Asa had concluded with the King of Syria (2 Chron. xvi). Besides this, there are other instances which plainly show that religion took more damage than benefit from such liberty; to say nothing of the fact that disastrous civil wars arose out of the assertion by the prophets of their right to speak as they pleased.

3. It also deserves to be noted that so long as the people kept the supreme authority in their own hands, only a single civil war arose, which was soon entirely put an end to, when the victors were so tender of the vanquished that they took care of them in every way, and restored them to their former rights and privileges. But after the people had changed the

first form of their government to a monarchy, and were ruled by kings, there was scarcely any end of the civil wars that ensued, in which battles so bloody were joined that the accounts we have of their atrocity almost surpass credibility: in one battle we read of 50,000 of the Israelites slain by the Judeans or Jews; and in another, on the contrary, the Jews were slaughtered in vast numbers by the Israelites (the precise number of the slain is not given in Scripture). In this battle the King of Judah was taken prisoner, the walls of Jerusalem were almost entirely demolished, and the Temple itself was despoiled of all its treasures, as if to show that the victors set no bounds to their rage. Laden with the spoil of their brothers and satiated with their blood, the Israelites finally consented to receive hostages, and leaving the king in his now desolated empire, they sheathed the sword, feeling secure, not of the good faith, but of the weakness of Judah. No great number of years having elapsed, and the Judeans having by this time recruited their strength, we find them again at war with the Israelites, in which these last were again the victors, and slew, as it is stated, 120,000 of the Judeans, leading besides into captivity as many as 200,000 of their women and children, and bearing away an immense booty. Worn out by these and other sanguinary wars, which only receive a passing notice in Scripture, the Hebrew nation at large was so much weakened as by and by to become a prey to foreign enemies.

When we inquire into the various periods during which the Hebrew people enjoyed the blessings of peace, we find great differences in the several epochs of their history; for often, before there were kings in Israel, we read of 40, and once (but this is beyond all likelihood) of 80 years passed happily without a foreign or civil war. But after the kings had acquired the supreme power, inasmuch as the prize now was not peace and liberty, but glory and conquest, we read that all, with the single exception of Solomon, whose wisdom and tastes had a better field for display in peace than in war, were addicted to war, whereunto was added the uneasy lust of ruling, which made the way to the throne a bloody one to many.

Lastly, under the democracy the laws remained uncorrupted, and were more regularly and willingly observed. For before the epoch of the kings there were few prophets who taught and admonished the people; after the election of kings, however, they appear to have been very numerous; and we read of Obadiah on one occasion rescuing a hundred of them from slaughter and concealing them lest they should perish by the sword. Neither do we see that the people were ever deceived by false prophets until after they had yielded the empire to the kings, with whom these prophets were mostly in alliance. In addition, the people, who are always haughty or abject according to circumstances, readily correct themselves in adversity, return to God, and appeal to the laws, and thus, indeed, mostly find help out of their difficulties and dangers; kings, on the other hand, whose tempers are always alike elate, and who cannot yield without ignominy, cling pertinaciously to all the vice in their system of rule, and rather than bend would perish in the ruins of their country.

From what immediately precedes we see, 1st, how disastrous it is both to religion and the commonwealth to concede to the ministers of religion a right to pass decrees or administer the business of the state; and, on the contrary, that things go on much more smoothly if the religious body are only heard on worldly affairs when their counsel is asked; their proper duty being to teach and to act in conformity with received ideas and accredited custom.

2. How dangerous it is to refer to the divine right things that are purely speculative, and to institute laws to regulate opinions about matters on which men are wont to differ, or may at any time differ; for there assuredly is the government a tyranny where opinions, which are the individual right of every one, and which no one can of his mere will give up, are regarded as crimes. Where such a state of things prevails, indeed, the rage of the multitude is usually found

in place of the law. Pilate, yielding to the dislike of the Pharisees, ordered Christ to be crucified, knowing him all the while to be innocent. Then, too, the Pharisees, that they might wrest their dignities from the more wealthy among the citizens, began an agitation about religious matters, and accused the Sadducees of impiety; and following this example of the Pharisees, the worst of hypocrites possessed by the like wickedness, which they always designate as holy zeal, have still gone on persecuting men of distinguished probity, illustrious for their virtues, and on this very account disliked of the many, proclaiming their opinions detestable and dangerous, and exciting the savage multitude against them.* And this licence, because it wears an appearance of piety, cannot easily be curbed, especially where the ruling powers have been parties to the introduction of a sect of which they themselves were not the originators. For then they are not regarded as the interpreters of the divine law, but as sectarians, or as acknowledging the teachers of the sect who are interpreters of the divine law; consequently, the authority of the magistrate in these circumstances is wont to have little influence with the people, whilst the authority of the teachers is great, so great, indeed, that they have often declared that even kings should bow to them. To escape such evils, nothing better for the commonwealth can be thought of than that piety and religion should be held to consist in good works, that is to say, in the exercise of charity and justice alone, every one being left in all other particulars at entire liberty to follow his own opinions; but on this head I shall have more to say by and by.

3. We have seen how imperative it was, both for the

---

* Socrates done to death by the Sophists, Christ by the Pharisees, twenty thousand good men in the Low Countries by Philip II., *many* thousands in Spain by the Inquisition, some scores in Smithfield by the Papists; Spinoza excommunicated by the Jews of Amsterdam, and his life attempted; the authors of Essays and Reviews anathematized by the bishops and the common herd of intolerant men, who hug their chains for present bread and know better,—so the world goes on—not so cruel as of yore, but the same in spirit.—*Ed*.

commonwealth and religion, that the civil power should be possessed of the authority to decree what was right and lawful, what was wrong and against law. For if this power of determining right and wrong could not be intrusted to even divine prophets without great detriment to the state and religion, much less could it be conceded to those who are unable to predict future events, and who can do no miracles. Of this I shall take occasion to speak particularly in the next chapter.

4. Lastly, we have seen how disastrous it was for the people, unaccustomed to live under kingly rule, and already possessed of established laws for their government, to have the election of the sovereign in their hands. For neither could the people themselves bear such a load of power, nor could the regal authority endure laws and privileges among the people which had been instituted by others of less authority than itself; much less could it be induced heartily to defend these laws and privileges, undoubtedly because at the time of their institution there was no thought of a king, but only of the people, or of a council invested with the supreme power. A king in the position of defender of the ancient rights and privileges of the community would have the appearance of a servant rather than of a master. The new monarch, therefore, would naturally be disposed to give his mind to the institution of new laws, and the introduction of reforms favourable to himself, and to place the people in such a position that they should find it less easy to curtail than to extend the privileges of the Crown. But here I must not omit to say that it is no less dangerous to do away with the kingly office once established, even when he who holds it is acknowledged on all hands to be a tyrant; for the people, accustomed to the royal authority, and only kept in check by it, will despise any less dignified form of government, and make it the subject of their mockery; so that were the king in present possession removed, it will soon become matter of necessity to have another in his place, just as it was formerly with the prophets, and he very certainly will

prove himself a tyrant, less, it may be, of his own will and pleasure than of necessity. For, in case the former king have been put to death, with what eyes should his successor behold his subjects, their hands reddened with the blood of his predecessor, boasting of their deed as something meritorious, and perchance hinting that what had occurred should be an example and a warning to him? If he would be a king indeed, and not have the people for his judges; if he would have his subjects submissive, and not be content himself to reign on the slippery tenure of popular approval; he will revenge the death of the former sovereign, and, by making examples of the leaders of the revolt against him, deter the people from committing a crime of the kind again. But he will not effectually avenge the death of his predecessor by the slaughter of any number of citizens, unless at the same time he defends his cause universally, approves of his deeds, and treads in his steps in everything. Whence it has so commonly happened that peoples have often changed their tyrants, but have never succeeded in getting rid of them altogether; nor has the monarchical yet been permanently changed for any other form of government. The people of England have left a memorable example of this fact, even when they had deposed and with a show of justice put their king to death. The king removed, they could not do less than attempt to change the form of their government; but after much bloodshed, disorder, and disagreement among parties, it came to this, that a new monarch was saluted in a bold soldier by another name—as if the whole question had been one of names!—But this arrangement could not possibly last; and soon after the death of the Protector there seemed but one desire in the general mind, and this was for the restoration of the old royal family. The restoration was accordingly effected under the auspices of another astute soldier, and England, as of yore, was once more nominally ruled by a king.*

* The text in reference to English history here has been condensed and somewhat modified. There was no wanton bloodshed during the great English revo-

Here, however, it may perchance be objected to me, that instances might be quoted from the Roman history in which the people did really get rid of their tyrants. But I am rather of opinion that my view will be found confirmed by any example that can be cited from thence. For, although the Roman people might more easily than common remove a tyrant from among them, and even change the form of their government (the right of choosing a king and appointing his successor lying with the people themselves, and they not having been long accustomed to kingly rule), still, though they put to death three of the six kings they had in the early period of their history, yet in no instance did they accomplish more than that instead of one they obtained several tyrants, who kept them miserably engaged in a series of foreign and domestic wars, until at length the government reverted, with a change of name only, as in England, to a monarchy. With regard to the States of Holland, these, so far as we know, seem never to have had kings for their rulers, but counts, to whom, however, no sort of sovereign right ever belonged. For the high and mighty States of Holland, by an instrument drawn up by them in the time of the Earl of Leicester, plainly declare that they have always kept the supreme authority in their own hands, and reserved to themselves the right and power to direct these counts in the exercise of their authority; that they, with a view to the defence of civil liberty, and to freeing themselves of their officers should they degenerate into tyrants, pronounce all their acts and ordinances null and void unless reviewed and approved by the general council of the States. Whence it follows that the supreme power has always lain with the States-general; and when the last of the counts of Holland did actually attempt to usurp this, the people could not be said

---

lution, no bloodshed whatever in the time of the Commonwealth. Spinoza had seen the Stuarts restored; he did not live long enough to see the very next successor to the throne deposed, driven into exile, and the hated house, because of their misdeeds, their moral turpitude, and tyrannical temper, declared for ever incompetent to sit on the throne of free England!—*Ed.*

to revolt or to rebel against him, when they successfully re-asserted their proper authority, almost lost through his usurpation. These examples I think suffice to prove what we set out by saying, viz. that the form of government which has long obtained in a state ought by all means to be preserved, and that no attempt to change it can be made without extreme danger of total ruin. And this is the conclusion to which I have been desirous to come as the fruit of this portion of my undertaking.

CHAPTER XIX.

ALL AUTHORITY IN SACRED MATTERS RESTS EXCLUSIVELY WITH THE CIVIL POWER; AND RELIGIOUS WORSHIP MUST BE IN HARMONY WITH THE INSTITUTIONS OF THE STATE IF GOD IS TO BE RIGHTLY OBEYED.

WHEN I said above that they who were intrusted with the administration of affairs were the sole arbiters of right, and that all legislation depended on them, I did not mean this to be understood as referring to civil affairs only, but also to things sacred; for I maintain that the government of a country should also be the guardians and interpreters of these. Now, my purpose in this chapter is to enforce this principle; for there are many who deny such a right to civil rulers, and refuse to acknowledge them as interpreters of the divine decretals; whence, further, they assume the liberty of condemning and vilifying, and even of excommunicating their rulers, ex cathedra, as Ambrose did the Emperor Theodosius. But I shall show that such persons seek occasion in this way to divide the state against itself, and even to seize the supreme power for themselves. First, however, I shall demonstrate that a religious system can only acquire the force of law from the decree of those who are at the head of the state, and have the right to command; and that God has no especial empire among men save through those who govern; moreover, that religious worship and pious practices should be arranged harmoniously with the peace and well-being of the commonwealth; consequently, that these are to be determined by the ruling powers alone, who are at the same time to be the judges of their worth and fitness. I speak expressly of pious practices and outward religious observance, not of those sentiments of piety and veneration towards the Supreme Being whereby the mind is inwardly disposed to the worship of God. For inward worship and pious contemplation are the inalienable right of all, the right which cannot be given away nor transferred to another, as has been shown towards the end of Chapter VII. And what I understand by empire or kingdom of God I think is sufficiently explained in Chapter XIV., where I have shown that he fulfils the divine law who studies justice and charity from the commandments of God; whence it follows, that there the kingdom of God truly is where justice and charity have the force of law. And here I say that I acknowledge no distinction or difference, whether God teach and enforce the practice of justice and charity by natural impulse or by revelation; for it matters not how the necessity for their exercise is made known, so as they obtain supremacy, so as they become the chiefest law to man. If, then, I have already shown that justice and charity cannot acquire the force of a law and commandment except by the authority of the government, I conclude from this—inasmuch as the right of command inheres in the supreme authority alone—that religion also only acquires the force of law by the decision of those who have the right of commanding, and that God has no kingdom among men save by those who hold the chief authority. But that the practice of justice and charity does not acquire the force of law save from the right of authority has been already shown in what precedes. In Chapter XVI., for example, it has been demonstrated that in the natural state the empire of appetite was as authoritative as the rule of reason, and that they who lived according to the laws of appetite had as good a right to all they could compass as they who lived in obedience to the laws of reason. From this cause we said that we could not conceive sin as existing in the natural state, nor God, as judge, punishing men for their transgressions, but found that all things went on according to the general laws of nature at large, and that the same thing—to speak with Solomon—was just and unjust, pure and impure, &c., and that there was no place found for justice or charity. That the doctrine of true reason, that is, the divine doctrine, should have the absolute force of law, it were necessary that every one ceded his natural rights, and that each and all transferred these either to all collectively, to a few, or to one; and that then we were first informed of what was justice, what injustice, what was to be done, what left undone, &c. Justice, therefore, and the whole of the doctrines of right reason, and as a consequence of this, neighbourly charity, receive the force of law from the rights of the ruling power alone; in other words, from the decree of him who has, or of them who have, the power to command. And since, as I have already shown, the kingdom of God wholly consists in the supremacy of justice and charity, or of true religion, it follows, as I maintain, that God's kingdom among men exists through those who hold the supreme authority, and is thus, I repeat, ever the same, whether we conceive religion to be derived from our natural faculties or from prophetic revelation. For the proposition is still a general one, inasmuch as religion is always the same, and is equally revealed and given by God, whether it be supposed to have been communicated to man in one way or another. Thus it came to pass, that in order to give even the religion prophetically revealed to the Hebrews the force of law, it was necessary that they should first cede their natural rights, and all determine by common consent only to obey the commands prophetically revealed to them by God; much in the same way as we have seen things done in a democratic state, where all deliberate together, and by common consent agree to live by the rules of right reason alone. The Jews, indeed, besides mutually ceding their rights, transferred them to Jehovah. But this was done mentally rather than in fact; for we have seen that they did verily retain the supreme power among themselves, until it was transferred to Moses, who thenceforward became their absolute king, and God through him disposed of the nation. Moreover, it was from this cause, viz. that a religious system only acquires the force of law by the authority of the ruling power, that Moses could not punish those who broke the Sabbath before the covenant, when every one was still possessed of his natural rights, as he did after the covenant was made, and each man had ceded the rights he naturally possessed, and when observance of the Sabbath had acquired the force of a commandment in virtue of the decree of the ruling power. For the same reason, also, when the Hebrew empire fell, the religion revealed to its people ceased to have the force of law; for it is impossible to doubt that when the Hebrews transferred their rights and allegiance to the king of Babylon, the kingdom of God and the divine law established among them incontinently came to an end. For by this act the compact whereby they bound themselves to obey God in all that he commanded was plainly annulled; nor, indeed, could it now have been enforced, seeing that from this time forward the Hebrew people were no longer their own masters, but servitors to the king of Babylon, whom they were bound to obey in all things. This Jeremiah declares expressly, when he says, "And seek the peace of the city whither I have caused you to be carried away captives; for in the safety thereof shall ye have safety." Now the Jews could have taken no measures for the safety of Babylon as citizens or ministers of the Babylonian empire, for they were slaves; it could only have been by avoiding conspiracy and sedition, by showing themselves obedient to all commands, observant of the rights of the empire and the requirements of the laws, although sufficiently different, perchance, from the laws to which they had been accustomed in their native country. From the whole of these particulars it follows very obviously that religion among the ancient Hebrews acquired the force of law from the fiat of the governing authority alone; and this authority destroyed, religion in itself could no longer be regarded as a system adapted to a single nation, but became a catholic or universal system of reason; I say of reason, for the truly catholic religion was not yet made known to man by revelation.

Let us conclude therefore without reservation that religion, whether revealed by natural inherent capacity or prophetically, receives the force of a mandate only from the decree of those who have the power to command, and that the kingdom of God in the world is in those who hold the supreme authority. This also follows, and is even more appreciable, from what is said in Chapter IV., where we have seen that the decrees of God involve eternal truth and eternal necessity, and that it is impossible to conceive God as a Prince or Legislator, imparting laws to man. Wherefore, the divine precepts, whether made known by natural light or prophetic revelation, do not receive the force of commandments immediately from God, but necessarily from those or by means of those who are in possession of the sovereign authority, and have the power of passing and enforcing their decrees. In the same way, we cannot conceive God otherwise than by their means as reigning over mankind and administering affairs with equity and justice, as is proved by every-day experience; for no traces of divine justice are ever seen save where the just have authority; where it is otherwise (recurring to the words of Solomon) we see the same fate befall the just and the unjust, the pure and the impure, a conclusion which has driven some, who think that God reigns immediately over man and rules the whole universe for his advantage, to doubt of the divine providence.

Since, therefore, experience and reason alike declare that the divine right depends entirely on the decrees of the governing powers, it follows that they also must be the interpreters of this right. In what way they are so we shall now see; for it is time we showed how all outward religious worship, and all pious exercises, should be so regulated as to secure the peace and prosperity of the commonwealth, if God is to be obeyed aright. So much once proven, we shall readily understand in what way the ruling powers are properly the interpreters of the religion and regulators of the pious practices of the country.

It is certain that devotion to our country is the highest virtue that can be shown; for this wanting, nothing good can remain, all runs to confusion, and licence and impiety bear sway, to the terror and damage of all, whence it follows that nothing can be advantageous to any one which is not bad in itself, if it prove injurious to the commonwealth at large; as, on the contrary, no act can be amiss, can be otherwise than absolutely good, if done to the advantage of the commonwealth. For example, it has been held pious to give him who attacks me and would take my cloak, my coat also; but when this decision is brought to the bar of right and reason, and the thing is seen to be injurious to the public at large, as well as to the individual, it becomes an act of piety to bring the robber before the judgment-seat, to the end that he may be punished and the community protected. Manlius Torquatus is renowned because the safety of the republic was of more moment in his eyes than pity and compassion for his son. And if this view be well founded, it follows that the safety of the state is the supreme law, to which all laws, divine and human, must be made to bend. But since it is the office of the government to determine what is for the good of the whole community and necessary to the safety of the state, and to command that to be done which is deemed necessary, it follows that it is also the province of the supreme power alone to determine in what way every one shall comport himself to his neighbour; in other words, in what way every one shall be held bound to obey God. These considerations give us the key to a right understanding of the way and manner in which the ruling power of the state is the interpreter and regulator of its religious system; and also why no one can truly obey God who does not accommodate his religious observances to public utility, and consequently who does not obey the commands of the governing authority. For inasmuch as all without exception by God's commands are ordered to be observant religiously, and to do injury to no one, it follows that it is lawful to do no service to any one who brings damage upon another, much less when he causes detriment to the whole state; no one, therefore, can do service to his neighbours in obedience to God's commands, unless his charitable and pious purpose be found in accordance with the public advantage. But no merely private person can always know what is useful to the commonwealth; this he must learn from the governing authorities and their decrees, the proper business of the ruler being to administer the affairs of the state; consequently, no one can be accounted truly pious, nor obedient to God, unless he obeys the decrees of the government of his country. And all this is confirmed by experience. For any one, whether a native or a stranger, a private person or one in authority, whom the supreme power in the state has adjudged to death, or has declared an enemy, must on no account be sheltered or succoured by a subject. So also, although the Hebrew was ordered to love every one of his neighbours as himself (Levit. xix. 17, 18), he was nevertheless held bound to deliver over to the judge any one who had done aught against the commandments of the law (Levit. v. 1, and Deut. xiii. 8, 9), and even to slay him if he were adjudged worthy of death (Deut. xvii. 7). Again, in order that the Hebrew might preserve his recovered liberty, and possess the land he occupied in safety, it was absolutely necessary that he should accommodate his religious practices to the exigences of the civil power, and keep himself distinct and separate from other nations; therefore was he instructed to love his neighbour, but to hate his enemy (vide Matt. v. 43). After the fall of the Jewish empire, however, and when the people had been led captive to Babylon, Jeremiah taught his countrymen that they should consult the safety of the very state into which they had been taken captive; and after Christ had seen the Jews scattered and in exile over the face of the whole earth, he taught that they should love and do good to all indifferently—friends and foes alike: these things show most obviously that the principles of religion were always accommodated to the exigences and uses of the community. But should it now be asked, By what right and authority did the disciples of Christ, being private men, presume to preach their religion? I reply, It was in virtue of the power which they received from Christ against the impure spirits (Matt. x. 1). For I have already expressly declared that all were to keep faith, even with a tyrant,—all, except him to whom God by a special revelation promised assistance against an oppressor (vide Chap. XVI. towards the end). No one, therefore, can take an example from this, unless he have the power of performing miracles. And this also makes plain the meaning of what Christ said to his disciples when he told them they were not to fear those who had the power of the sword (Matt. xvi. 28); for had this been said to all indiscriminately, the state or commonwealth would have been constituted in vain, and the saying of Solomon (Prov. xxiv. 21), "My son, fear God and honour the king," would have been a mockery, which very certainly it was not intended to be; and so must we necessarily understand the authority which Christ gave his disciples, as having been given to them in especial, and that it was not intended that others should receive any warrant from his words.

I do not pause to discuss the reasons of those who would sever the civil from the religious element in the state, and who maintain that the former rests with the government alone, the latter with the whole body of the Church, for I find these so frivolous as not to deserve a serious refutation. I cannot avoid declaring how miserably, in my opinion, they are deceived who in support of this seditious view (I ask pardon for the hard word) cite the example of the chief priests among the Jews, with whom in ancient times lay the right of administration in sacred things; just as if those pontiffs had not received the right they exercised from Moses, who himself possessed the supreme power, and could not even be deprived of it at his bidding. Moses not only elected Aaron, but his son Eleazar, and his nephew Phineas, and gave them authority to administer the pontificate, which the high priests in succession after them retained in such wise that they appeared like the substitutes of Moses, that is to say, of the supreme civil power, for, as we have seen, Moses elected no successor to himself in the state, but so distributed his various offices that those who came after him seemed his vicars, who administered the government as if the sovereign had been absent, not dead. In the second empire, indeed, the high priests held this right absolutely, when with the pontificate they had usurped the principality also. The pontifical authority, therefore, always depended on the edict of the supreme civil ruler, nor did the high priests ever possess the chief power in the state until after they had usurped the sovereignty. The right of sacred things, indeed, lay with the kings absolutely (as I shall show in what I have still to say at the end of this chapter), with this single exception, that it was not lawful for them to take part in the celebration of the sacred rites within the temple, and this was because all who did not derive their descent from Aaron were held impure, an idea which has no place in the Christian system. We cannot therefore doubt but that the sacred rites of the present day (the administration of which requires peculiar morals, but not family descent, so that no one is now excluded as impure and profane from qualifying himself to take part in them) are entirely in the power of the supreme ruler of the state; and that no one, save by the authority of the sovereign or government, has any right of administration in ecclesiastical affairs, of fixing the foundations and determining the doctrines of the Church, of judging in matters of morality and public piety, of pronouncing excommunications and excluding from or of receiving into the Church, nor, in fine, of providing for the poor and the needy.' And all this is not only demonstrably true, as we have shown, but is indispensably necessary also, as well to religion as to the well-being of the state, for all are aware how much right and authority in sacred things avail with the people, and how much all are dependent on his report who possesses them; it were scarcely too much to say that he bears the most sovereign sway in the minds of men to whom such right and authority are conceded. Any one, therefore, who should attempt to deprive governments of this authority over sacred things, would in effect attempt a division of the state, from which would necessarily arise differences and dissensions as among the Hebrew kings and high priests of old, differences which could never be composed; he, indeed, who should seek to take away this authority from the civil power would rightly be held as aspiring to the sovereign authority for himself. For what were left to the decision of the civil power were the right over religion denied it? Nothing, either in regard to war or peace or any other business, if it were once compelled to bow to the opinion of another who should inform it whether that which it had deemed useful and proper were really just or unjust, right or wrong. No, everything in the well-regulated commonwealth must be done by the decrees of those who are intrusted with the supreme civil power, and with it the right of judging and decreeing what is beneficial or injurious, just or unjust, right or wrong. Examples in illustration of the effects for good or for evil, as one or other of these courses has been followed, abound in history. I shall adduce but one, the papacy, as an epitome of all the rest. Because the absolute right of over-ruling the civil power had been conceded to the Roman pontiff, this priest came by degrees to assert his supremacy over all the kings and principalities of Christendom, until at length the very crown and pinnacle of earthly power and greatness was attained; so firmly was the empire of the Pope established, too, that for ages all that the sovereigns of Europe, and especially the emperors of Germany, attempted against it, proved of non-avail; on the contrary, every fresh endeavour to curb its exorbitant power, in ever so trifling a degree, seemed long but to add immeasurably to its strength. What neither king nor kaiser could accomplish by fire or sword was done by an ecclesiastic, in the middle ages, with the stroke of a pen; a fact from which the immense power of the ecclesiastical order may readily be inferred, and which also shows how necessary it is that civil rulers should keep the sovereign authority in their own hands. And if we but duly reflect on the contents of the preceding chapter, we shall see that this will conduce in no small measure to the increase of piety and true religion. For we have seen above that the prophets themselves, although gifted with divine powers, because they were mere private individuals, often excited and inflamed the people rather than instructed and corrected them, by the freedom of their expostulations and denunciations, when the sovereign, with the right of warning and of punishment in his hand, would have readily bent them to obedience. It is further notorious that the Hebrew kings themselves, solely because they were not firmly established in the right of controlling things sacred, frequently seceded from the national religion, along with almost the whole of the people; and the same thing, from the very same cause, too, has happened on various occasions in Christian countries also.

But here some one perchance will ask, Who is to stand forth to vindicate religion, if they who possess the supreme authority prove themselves careless or irreligious? Shall they in such a case still be held its regulators and interpreters? But I in my turn demand, What if ecclesiastics (who are also men of private station, and whose sole duty it is to mind their own affairs), or they with whom is lodged the right of jurisdiction in sacred things, choose to show themselves impious persons, are *they then to be esteemed the regulators and interpreters of the religious system of the state? This much is certain, indeed, that if they who hold the reins of power may go their own way, without control of any kind, whether they have authority in sacred matters or not, all things, both sacred and profane, never fail to get into disorder, and run on from bad to worse, till they end in ruin; and this by so much the more quickly if there be any meddling by private persons who seek to vindicate the divine right by exciting sedition and rebellion. Wherefore nothing is gained by denying the right over sacred things to the civil power; on the contrary, the evil to the state is but increased; for it inevitably happens that they, like the Hebrew kings of old, who had not the right in question conceded to them absolutely, fall away from their religion, and as a consequence of this the damage to the commonwealth, from uncertain and contingent is made certain and necessary. Whether, therefore, we consider the truth of the thing, or the safety of the state, or, lastly, the increase of piety, we are compelled to admit that even the right divine, or the right over things sacred, depends absolutely on the decision of the supreme civil power in the state, and that this power is also the interpreter, and avenger if need be, of things sacred. From this it follows that they are the true ministers of God's word who teach the people piety on the authority of the ruling powers, seeing that this by other decrees is arranged harmoniously for peace and profit with all the other institutions of the state.

It only now remains for us to point out the cause why in the Christian dispensation there has always been a dispute about the right in question, although among the ancient Hebrews, so far as I know, there never was a difference of opinion on the subject. It does indeed seem monstrous that concerning a thing so manifest, so necessary, there should ever have been any dispute, and that governments should never have exercised their right in this direction without controversy, sometimes, indeed, not without the danger of sedition, and always with great damage to the cause of true religion. And verily, could no definite reason be assigned for this, I could readily persuade myself that all I have set forth in this chapter was speculative only, or of that order of discussion which never comes to use. But when the origin of the Christian religion is inquired into, the reason of the state of things in question becomes abundantly apparent; for the first teachers of the Christian religion were not kings, but private persons, who, against the will of those who governed, and whose subjects they were, were wont to hold secret assemblies for religious worship, to appoint to sacred offices, and to order and conclude in spiritual things among themselves without taking any thought of the government. But by and by, as the Christian religion with the lapse of years began to form an element in the state, the priesthood were applied to by rulers for information on the constitution of their church, and thus came to be considered as the interpreters of the will of God, and finally as his vicars on earth; and in order that Christian kings should not at a future time resume the authority which they then conceded to the Church, the priesthood interdicted matrimony to themselves and their successors in the ministry for ever. In addition to this, the dogmas of the Christian Church grew so prodigiously in number, and were so mixed up with philosophical ideas, that its teachers and interpreters required to be at once consummate philosophers and theologians, and to give their minds to abstruse and profitless speculation, which could only be done by men possessed of abundant leisure, and without family cares or public employments.

But among the ancient Hebrews things were managed very differently; their Church was founded at the same time as their empire, and Moses, the supreme and absolute head of the state, also taught the people religious doctrine, arranged their religious services, and selected the ministers of the temple. And thus, again, it came to pass that the royal authority was the more esteemed of the people, and that the kings of the Jews were mostly held supreme in spiritual as well as in temporal things. For although after Moses' death no one ruled the realm with absolute sway, still the right of commanding, both in sacred and profane matters, remained with the prince or the government. Subsequently, the people were ordered to seek instruction in their religious duties from the judge as well as from the priest (vide Deut. xvii. 9, 11). In conclusion, although the Jewish kings had not that paramount authority possessed by Moses, they still gave almost every order, and made all the appointments required in connection with sacred things. David, for example, gave directions for the whole arrangements of the temple (1 Chron. xxviii.

11, 12, &c.), and chose from among the Levites 24,000 to sing the Psalms,* 6000 to act as judges and officers, 4000 as porters or door-keepers, and finally 4000 as players upon musical instruments (Ib. xxiii. 4, 5). Further, King David divided the Levites into "courses;" to each of which he appointed a leader, that each might be ready to take their turn of duty in the temple and minister in its sacred offices. The priests were also divided into "courses," as the reader will find set forth in the Second Book of Chronicles, from which I shall make but a single quotation in illustration of my position, that the civil power was supreme in all things among the ancient Hebrews. In verses 12 and 13 of the chapter referred to, it is said, "Then Solomon offered burnt offerings unto the Lord, &c., even after a certain rate every day, offering according to the commandment of Moses; and he appointed, according to the order of David his father, the courses of the priests to their service, and the Levites to their charges, &c., for so had David the man of God commanded; and they departed not from *the commandment of the king unto the priests and Levites* concerning any matter, or concerning the treasures." This alone I think is sufficient to prove that the whole of the religious institution and administration of the country depended entirely on the mandate of the king. I have made exception, however, of the appointment of the high priest, and of the right to consult God immediately and to condemn the prophets who exercised their vocation in the life-time of the king, powers which Moses possessed and exercised; I have called attention to this exception for no other reason but because the prophets, in virtue of the authority that belonged to them, could elect a new king, and pardon parricide; but it was not lawful for them to call the king to judgment for any attempt against the laws, or otherwise legally to oppose him.† Wherefore, if there were no

* In the English version the 24,000 "were to set forward the work of the house of the Lord."—*Ed.*

† I particularly request in this place the closest attention to the principles of law laid down in Chapter XVI.

prophet who by a special revelation could safely offer pardon to a parricide, the king had the whole and sole right both in sacred and civil affairs. The ruling powers of the present day, accordingly, who have no prophets, and are not required to receive them (for they are no longer bound by the laws of the Jews), possess this right absolutely, though they are not unmarried; and they must be careful to keep it for ever, unless they would consent to have the dogmas of religion endlessly multiplied, and confounded with the sciences, from which they ought ever to be kept separate.*

* In England the strife between the temporal and spiritual power, with the best will in the world on the part of ambitious prelates and priests to renew it, continues to sleep, kept at peace mainly by the good sense of the community. The clerical element, however, still does battle vigorously as often as the civil power, in its efforts to enlighten the multitude, trenches upon the vantage-ground which the clergy in days of yore acquired for themselves in the control of the popular education. But they are gradually losing their footing here, and none but the very bigots among them would now restrict popular education to the Catechism and the Collects. As to Convocation, so long as the laity see that no two of the members of either house are ever precisely of the same mind, that the upper and the lower chamber always differ from each other, and that even though they were unanimous upon any matter of doctrine or discipline, they are still without power to enforce their decisions,—the laity, we say, continue to regard the transactions of the houses of Convocation with supreme indifference.—*Ed.*

CHAPTER XX.

IN A FREE STATE EVERY ONE IS AT LIBERTY TO THINK AS HE PLEASES, AND TO SAY WHAT HE THINKS.

IF it were as easy to rule the thoughts as to command the tongue, princes would always reign securely, and there would be no such thing as government by force. For every one would then live according to the views of governors, and by their decision alone would conclude as to what was good or bad, true or false, just or unjust. But this is impossible, as has been already shown (Chap. XVII.), inasmuch as no man can yield his mind and understanding absolutely to another; for no one can transfer, nor can he be forced to transfer, to another his natural right or faculty of reasoning freely, and of judging in certain cases. Hence it is that that authority which is exerted over the mind is characterized as tyrannical; and that the ruler oppresses his subjects, and seems to usurp their rights, who attempts to prescribe what shall be received as true or rejected as false, and what ideas shall arouse feelings of devotion towards God in the mind; for these are the natural and inalienable rights of all. I confess, indeed, that the judgment may be preoccupied in so many and such incredible ways, that although it cannot be said to be directly under the authority of another, still it shall depend so entirely on his will as almost to appear to belong to him. But, with all that craft has yet been able to accomplish in this direction, things have never come to such a pass that men have not felt themselves their own masters in respect of judgment and emotion, and that there was not even as great diversity of opinions as of tastes in the world. Moses himself, who secured the confidence of his nation in so remarkable a manner, and by no craft or guile, but by the divine power that was in him, although believed to be more than mortal and to speak and to act under the inspiration of Deity, nevertheless could not always escape the suspicious and sinister interpretations of the multitude. Much less could the rulers who came after Moses avoid suspicion; and if it could in any way or under any circumstances be conceived possible that rulers should escape suspicion, it were certainly in a monarchy; in a democracy it is clearly impossible, the reason for which I presume must be obvious to all.

Although, then, the ruling powers are held to have a right to everything, and to be the interpreters of law and religion, this can never prevent men from having their own views on things in general, and from being influenced by this or that opinion or emotion. It is true, indeed, that governments may rightfully hold all who do not judge or feel with them as enemies; but at present we are not discussing rights, we are speaking of what is useful only; for I allow that princes often rule of right most violently, and send citizens to death for very trifling causes; but all will deny that such things can be done whilst any respect is had to sound reason. Inasmuch, indeed, as such things cannot be done without great peril to the state, we may also deny that rulers have any right to do such deeds, and, consequently, any absolute right whatever; for we have shown that the rights of ruling powers are determined by their capacity to enforce obedience.

If, therefore, no one can give up his title to judge and to think as he lists, but every one by a supreme law of nature is master of his own thoughts, it follows that an attempt can never be made without the most disastrous consequences to the commonwealth, to make all men, though possessed by nature of the most various and even opposite sentiments, to utter no word, save upon the prescription of their governors; for not even the most cautious and cultivated, to say nothing of the many, will at all times be able to hold their tongue. It is, indeed, one of the commonest weaknesses of men that even where silence is most necessary they communicate their views and opinions to others. That regimen were therefore of the most stringent description where all liberty of speech and public discussion are denied; as that, on the contrary, were moderate where such freedom is conceded to all. Nevertheless, as it is impossible to deny that the majesty of authority may be assailed by words as well as deeds, and liberty of speech cannot be altogether denied to subjects, it would be most objectionable were such liberty granted without any restriction. It therefore becomes necessary that we should inquire in how far liberty of speech can and ought to be conceded, consistently with the peace of the commonwealth and the rights of rulers; and I have already said in the beginning of my sixteenth chapter that this inquiry formed a principal feature in my undertaking.

From the foundations of the commonwealth, as already explained, it follows most obviously that its purpose is not dominion, nor the coercion of men by fear, nor that they should act at the arbitrary bidding of others; on the contrary, it is that every one may be free from fear, that he may live securely, in so far as this is possible, that is to say, that he may possess in the best sense his natural right to existence, and to the fruits of his industry. It is not, I say, the end of the state from rational beings to make men brute beasts or automatons; on the contrary, its end is that mind and body may unimpeded perform their functions, that every one may enjoy the free use of his reason, and that hatred, anger, deceit, and strife should cease from among its members. The end and aim of the state, in fact, is LIBERTY. To establish a policied state or commonwealth, however, we have seen that this one condition was indispensable, viz. that the right and authority to pass laws should belong to all its denizens in common, to a limited number of these, or to one of them only. For since the opinions of free men are sufficiently various, and each commonly enough thinks that he alone knows best, as it is impossible that all should think alike on any subject and speak as it were with one mouth, it would be impossible for them to live together in peace, unless each gave up the right of action according to the decision of his individual mind. The right of action on his own judgment then ceases, but the right of action only, not the right of reasoning and judging. The rights of the government having perforce to be respected, however, no one may do aught in the way of action against its decrees; but every one may think and judge, and consequently also declare his views, provided he but express himself simply and conformably to reason, without passion, spite, or insinuation, nor go cunningly about to make his own especial views prevail against the general opinion. If any one, for example, can show that a certain law is repugnant to good sense, and declares that it ought therefore to be abrogated, and at the same time submits his views to the government (whose exclusive privilege it is to make and to abrogate laws), and meantime does nothing in contravention of the law in question, that man, I say, deserves well of the republic, and is a good citizen; but otherwise, if his purpose were to proclaim the magistracy guilty of injustice, and to render the government odious to the people, or were he seditiously to seek the abrogation of a law against the will of the ruling power, such a one is to be accounted a disturber of the public peace and a rebel. We see, then, in what way any one with every regard to the right and authority of the government, in other words, to the peace of the commonwealth, may speak and make known his views; viz. if he leaves the determination touching things to be done in the hands of the ruling powers, and takes no step himself against their decrees, although he may even have to act in opposition to what he believes to be right, and to do what he sees clearly ought not to be done. So much, however, he may do without trenching on propriety; and so much indeed he may occasionally have to submit to if he would prove himself a true subject and peaceable citizen. For we have already shown, as justice depends entirely on the decisions of the higher powers, so no one can be just and pious who does not live in accordance with their commands. That piety, however, is greatest which is exerted in securing the peace and prosperity of the republic, for these could not be regarded were every one to think of living by the rule of his own arbitrary pleasure; and so is it criminal in a subject, on his own mere motion, to do aught against the decree of the supreme power whose subject he is, inasmuch as the ruin of the state must necessarily ensue were every one to allow himself such licence. And what is more, he really does nothing against the dictates of reason who acts in conformity with the decrees of the supreme authority in the state: for reason persuading, he has already ceded to his rulers his right of living agreeably to his own judgment. Now all this can be confirmed by an appeal to experience. In the councils of the greater as well as of the less estates of a realm it seldom happens that any resolution is ever taken by the unanimous consent of the members, yet is everything held to be done by common consent, of those therefore who vote *against* as well as of those who vote *for* the resolution. But I return to my subject.

We have seen from the constitution of the state how every one may, within the limits of reason, use his right of private judgment without detriment to the rights of the ruling powers. On the same grounds, viz. the foundations of the state, we may readily determine what opinions are seditious. They are such as in their mere enunciation go to annul the compact whereby each man cedes his right of acting on his own arbitrary views. For example, should any one maintain that the supreme state power did not exist independently and of its own right, that promises were never to be kept, that it behoved every one to live as he listed without regard to others, and the like, which the afore-mentioned contract directly repudiates, that man is a seditious person, not so much on account of his views and opinions as on account of the actions which such views and opinions involve, viz. because in the fact that he thinks as he does, he either expressly or tacitly breaks faith with the supreme authority. It is for this reason that other mental states which do not involve any breach of the political contract, such as anger, revenge, &c., are not seditious. Such passions, indeed, only come into play in corrupt states, where reason is perverted, and where superstition and ambition have acquired such an ascendency that they have more influence among the people than the government. I would not, however, deny that there are yet other opinions which, whilst they seem merely to regard the true or the false, are nevertheless propounded and spread abroad with an evil intention. But these have already been discussed in Chapter XV., where we have shown that reason nevertheless remains free. And, again, if we consider that faith to the state, like faith to God, can be known from works only—from neighbourly charity, &c.—we shall not have any reason to doubt but that the best republic concedes the same rights to philosophy, as we have shown conceded to the faith of its members. I confess, indeed, that several inconveniences arise from such liberty; but what was ever so wisely ordered that no inconvenience could thence ensue? He who would fix and determine everything by law would inflame rather than correct the vices of the world. What cannot be prevented must be endured, although thereby evil often accrues. For how many are the ills that follow from luxury, envy, avarice, drunkenness, and the like? but these, though vices, are suffered, because they cannot be prevented by legal enactments. But freedom of opinion, which is a positive virtue, and which cannot be controlled, ought much rather to be encouraged. And when we see that no inconvenience can arise from such freedom as will not immediately be met by the authority of the magistrate (as I shall soon show), and that it is essentially necessary to progress in the arts and sciences, which are only successfully cultivated where the mind is free and unfettered, I think enough has been said to show the paramount importance of freedom of thought and freedom of opinion in every well-ordered commonwealth.

But say that this freedom could be so held under, and men so oppressed that they dared not even to whisper anything but what was permitted or prescribed by rulers, still things could never be brought to such a pass but that subjects would have their own thoughts; and then it would necessarily follow that men would daily think otherwise, and speak otherwise than as they said they thought, whereby faith in the commonwealth, which is so indispensable, would be destroyed, and hateful perfidy and sycophancy encouraged; whence cunning and subterfuge, and corruption of all the amiable and social affections. But far from its being possible that men should ever be brought only to speak within certain prescribed limits, it has still happened that the more anxiously freedom of speech has been denied the more resolutely have mankind striven against the restraint,—not flatterers and sycophants indeed, and the other impotent spirits of the world, the chief seasoning in whose lives it is to dwell in the shadow of the great, to possess titles and distinctions, to have money in their purse, and a full belly, but those whom a liberal education and integrity of life have made more free. Now men in general are so constituted that they bear nothing more impatiently than to see opinions which they hold for true regarded as crimes, and all that moves them to piety towards God and charity towards man accounted as wickedness; whence it comes that laws are detested, and whatever can be adventured against authority is held to be not base and reprehensible, but brave and praiseworthy, a state on the back of which soon follow sedition, and riot, and revolution. Human nature being so constituted, then, it follows that laws against opinion bear not upon the worthless but the virtuous, and seem contrived not to restrain the evil-disposed, but rather to irritate the honest and estimable. Such laws therefore cannot be defended or enforced without great peril to the general peace. And then they are absolutely useless; for they who think the opinions sound which are condemned by the law will not be able to obey it; and they, on the contrary, who reject these opinions as false look on the laws which condemn them as privileges, and make so much of them that the government of the country, even though they wished at a later period to rescind them, find themselves unable to do so. To these considerations must be added those which, in Chapter XVIII. § 2, we have derived from the Jewish history. Lastly, schisms in the church, and controversies between its doctors, are mostly referrible to this source, schisms which each party in turn that was uppermost would have had put down by legal enactment; and men have never contended with such acrimony, never yielded to such fell passion, and perpetrated such cold-blooded deeds of cruelty, as when they have succeeded in making governments their partisans in matters of faith and doctrine, and, with the approval of the insensate multitude, have triumphed over their opponents. This is amply shown by reiterated experience, and reason also declares that it must be so. Laws which decree what every one must believe, and forbid utterance against this or that opinion, have too often been enacted to confirm or enlarge the power of those who dared not suffer free inquiry to be made, and have by a perversion of authority turned the superstition of the mob into violence against opponents. But surely it would be more reasonable to take measures to restrain the rage and fury of the multitude, than to make laws which can only be broken by those who love virtue and the arts and sciences, and which bring the commonwealth into such straits as intelligent persons cannot endure. For what greater evil can be conceived to befall a state than that honourable men, men of the most virtuous lives, because they think peculiarly on certain matters of speculation, and know not how to dissemble, should be driven into exile if they would escape worse treatment,—the dungeon, or perchance the stake! What, I say, can be more execrable than that men, for no crime or wickedness, but because they are of liberal mind, should be regarded as criminals, and that the scaffold, the terror of the evil-doer, should be made the stage for the display of fortitude and resignation on the part of suffering virtue, to the infinite scandal of all law and authority! Such men know themselves sincere, have no fear of death like felons, and will suffer any extremity of punishment rather than debase themselves by disguising or gainsaying their opinions; their minds are never racked by remorse for any baseness or wickedness done; on the contrary, they still feel themselves honest men, nor do they think it grief to die for a good and glorious cause. And what is the example given in the death of such men, whose cause the careless and unscrupulous ignore, the despot hates, and the good and great admire? None that the truly noble will not seek to emulate and commend.*

That trust and confidence should prevail then, and not dissimulation and compliance, and that the supreme power may rule in the most beneficial manner for all, nor ever feel compelled to yield to seditious clamour, liberty of opinion must of necessity be conceded, and men so governed that though they notoriously think differently from one another, they may still live together in peace and amity. Nor can it be doubted that such a manner of governing is the best, inasmuch as it is most in accordance with the nature of man. In a democracy (which approaches nearest to the natural state) we have shown that all engage to act under a common arrangement, though not to reason or to judge on any common ground; and it is because all men cannot think alike that they have agreed to abide by the decision of a majority of voices, that what the majority resolves on should have the force of law for all, the minority meanwhile reserving to themselves the right at some future time to propose the repeal of the law. Where men have less liberty conceded them, there the natural state is more departed from, and there consequently must the government be more stringent. Now I could quote many examples to show that no inconvenience is

* There can be little doubt but Spinoza, whilst speaking generally in this fine passage, has the case of the advocate Olden Barneveldt particularly in his eye, Barneveldt having been judicially murdered in 1632, for his patriotic independence, by Maurice, Prince of Orange.—*Ed.*

likely to arise from this liberty which will not be met and provided for by the authority of the government, and that men, though of opposite opinions, may live at peace with one another. I shall select the city of Amsterdam as sufficient for my purpose, where the fruits of this liberty of thought and opinion are seen in its wonderful increase, and testified to by the admiration of every people. In this most flourishing republic and noble city, men of every nation, and creed, and sect live together in the utmost harmony, and, in their transactions with one another, the only questions asked are whether the parties be rich or poor, and whether they are wont to act with good faith or not; there is never a question of religion or creed, for in presence of the judge these have no part in the proceedings, and neither justify nor condemn a man; and here there is no sect, however odious and despised, whose ministers, provided they do injury to none, but give every one his due and live respectably, do not find countenance and protection from the magistrate. In contrast with this, when in former times the religious controversies of the Remonstrants and Counter-remonstrants were taken up by the politicians and nobility of the provinces, the issue after much discord was a schism, and it was then discovered from many instances that laws made in behalf of religion, and with a view to abate controversy, rather aggravated than appeased the strife, and became the cause of licence and misdeeds, rather than of order and good conduct. Moreover, schism does not always arise from the anxious study of truth—the wellspring of humanity and gentleness—but often from the lust of dominion. And from this it is as clear as the sun at noonday that they are rather to be regarded as schismatics who condemn the writings of opponents, and unfairly instigate the unlettered vulgar against their authors, than the writers themselves, who mostly address the learned only, and make no appeal save to reason and calm reflection. They therefore are the true disturbers of the state who in a free commonwealth refuse that liberty of opinion which cannot be repressed.

In the preceding pages it has, I hope, been shown,

1. That it is impossible to take from men the liberty of saying what they think.

2. That this liberty may be conceded to every one, the rights and privileges of the supreme power remaining unaffected, and used by every one, the same supreme power being duly respected, if care be only taken to run into no licence, to force nothing in the shape of law upon the state, and to do nought against acknowledged laws.

3. That every one may enjoy this liberty, the peace of the republic being held sacred, and that no inconvenience can arise from it, which cannot easily be met and obviated.

4. That this same liberty may be enjoyed by every one with all respect to piety and religion.

5. That laws made in regard to speculative matters are useless.

6. That liberty of thought and speech is not only consistent with the peace of the state, with the authority of its government, and the maintenance of its religious institutions, but must even be conceded for the safety and preservation of these. For wherever an attempt is made to take this liberty away, and the opinions of disputants, not their minds, which alone can sin, are summoned to judgment, there examples are sure to be made of the best and noblest ; which are then regarded as martyrdoms, and irritate the nation and move them to pity, if not to revenge, rather than to fear. Peaceful arts and mutual trust thenceforth disappear, flatterers and hypocrites find encouragement, and dogmatism, because concessions have been made to it, and rulers have been arrayed as partizans, by and by ventures to arrogate authority to itself, and does not blush to boast that its professors are the elect of God and the immediate interpreters of his divine decrees, whilst the supreme civil power, as merely human, should be held bound to yield to that which is divine; in other words, to them and their decisions—all which things every one knows are altogether incompatible with the peace and prosperity of a well-ordered state.

Wherefore, in this place and again, as already in Chapter XVIII., we conclude that there is nothing safer for the common weal than that piety and religion should be wholly comprehended in the practice of charity and justice, and that the authority of the ruling power in the state, both as regards sacred and lay affairs, should be restricted to actions ; for the rest, that liberty of thinking as they list, and of saying what they think, should be conceded to all without restriction.

And now I have completed what I had proposed to myself in this Treatise. I have only to add that I have set down nothing which I have not most carefully considered, and submitted to the chief authorities of my native country ; but if aught that I have said contravenes the law, or seems opposed to the common good, I would have it impugned and set right, knowing, as full well I do, that I am a man and liable to err ; but I have taken great pains not to err ; and especially have I been anxious that all I have written should be found in keeping with the laws of my country, with piety, and good manners.

FINIS.

APPENDIX.

The Editor cannot resist the desire he feels to make the reader acquainted with the following appropriate and characteristic letter of Spinoza, in answer to a hostile criticism of this work, which had been sent him by a mutual friend of the critic and himself. The translation is made free, to enhance the pleasure the Editor himself has experienced in turning it into English, and for the sake of the reader; but there is no form of expression he believes which Spinoza's views do not warrant, and which he would not have suffered to pass. The original is the Epist. 49, of the Op. Posth.

Spinoza to I. O.*

"Learned Sir,

"You are doubtless surprised that I have made you wait so long for an acknowledgment of your last letter, but, in truth, it is with difficulty I have brought myself to notice the libellous epistle you enclosed, and, indeed, I only write now to make good my promise to answer it. That I may do as little violence as possible to my proper sentiments, I shall be brief, contenting myself with showing how your correspondent falsifies both my views and my intentions,—whether of set purpose and from malevolence, or through ignorance, I cannot so readily tell. But to the matter.

* Isaac Orobio, M.D., a Jewish physician of Amsterdam.

"Your correspondent in the beginning of his letter says, 'That it is of no consequence to know to what people I belong, or what manner of life I lead.' Had he been duly informed on both of these heads he would not so lightly have taken up the idea that I inculcate atheism. Atheists, for the most part, are worldlings, and seek eagerly after wealth and distinction, but these, all who know me are aware, I have ever held in the very slenderest estimation. He is then pleased to say that 'I must be a man of no mediocre ability,' for the purpose, apparently, of giving point to his next assertion, that 'I have at best skilfully, craftily, and with the worst intentions, advocated the radically bad and pernicious cause of the Deists.' This of itself were enough to show that the writer has not understood my arguments; for who could possibly be of so crafty and hypocritical a temper as to array a host of the most cogent and convincing reasons in favour of a conclusion which he himself believed to be false? Of whom would your correspondent believe that truth and sincerity guided the pen, if he thought that falsehood in disguise could be enforced with the same straightforwardness of purpose as truth itself? But, indeed, I ought not to express surprise here, for even thus was Descartes traduced by Voet; even thus are the best men in the world wont to be met by their opponents.

"The writer next proceeds to say, 'It seems as though, to escape suspicion of superstition, I had thought it requisite to divest myself of all religion.' I do not pretend to divine what he understands by religion and what by superstition here, but I ask, Does he cast off religion who rests all he has to say on the subject, on the ground that God is to be acknowledged as the Supreme Good, that He is with entire singleness of soul to be loved as such; and that in loving God consists our highest bliss, our best privilege, our most perfect freedom? Further, that the reward of virtue is virtue, and the penalty of incapacity and baseness is ignorance and abjectness of spirit? Still further, that every one is bound to love his neighbour as himself, and to obey the laws of the land in which, and the authority under which, he lives? Now all this I have not only insisted on as impressively as I could in words, but I have further adduced the most cogent reasons that presented themselves to me in support of my conclusions.

"But I think I can see whence the hostility of my critic

arises. This person finds nothing in virtuous life and right reason in themselves which satisfy or delight him; it seems as though he would rather live under the empire of his passions, yield to his appetites and lusts, were it not that this one consideration withheld him—the fear of punishment. He must keep himself from doing amiss as a slave; he cannot observe the divine commandments of his own free-will, but crouches before them with a perplexed and unsatisfied soul; he strikes a bargain with the Almighty, and for good conduct looks for much more ample reward, and of a much more sensible kind, than he expects to find in the divine love,—ay, recompense ever the greater as inwardly he feels more averse to good, as reluctantly and perforce he compels himself to effect what good he does. This is the ground of his belief, that all who are not restrained by fear of the kind he feels himself, must live without a curb upon their lusts, and cast out religion from their hearts. But I quit this ungrateful topic, and proceed to the inferences of my censor, and to this one in especial, that 'I with glozing and crafty arguments inculcate Atheism.'

"The grounds of this conclusion appear to be that he thinks I take from God all freedom, that I subject the Supreme to fate. This is utterly false; I do nothing of the sort; on the contrary, I maintain that everything follows by inevitable necessity from the very nature of God. It is universally admitted that God by his nature knows himself, and that this knowledge follows necessarily from the divine nature; but I presume no one thinks that God is therefore controlled by fate. On the contrary, all reasonable men believe that God knows himself freely and necessarily at once; that freedom and necessity, in fact, are terms synonymous when the nature of Deity is in question: God, as author of all, is himself fate, freedom and necessity. In this I can see nothing which every one may not understand, nothing which any one can find fault with; but if my critic nevertheless believes that what I say is said with an evil intention, what, I would ask, must he think of his Descartes, who maintains that nothing happens through our agency which God has not already pre-ordained; yea, that in every moment of our lives we are as it were created anew by God, but that we do not the less act freely according to the power that is given us? a state of things which, as Descartes himself admits, is altogether incomprehensible.

"The necessity of things which I contend for abrogates neither divine nor human laws; the moral precepts, whether they have the shape of commandments from God or not, are still divine and salutary; and the good that flows from virtue and godly love, whether it be derived from God as a ruler and lawgiver, or proceed from the constitution, that is, the necessity, of the Divine Nature, is not on this account the less desirable. On the other hand, the evils that arise from wickedness, are not the less to be dreaded and deplored because they necessarily follow the actions done; and, finally, whether we act with freedom or from necessity we are still accompanied in all we do by hope or fear. My censor, therefore, says falsely that I put the question of morals and religion on such a footing that neither command nor prescription are any longer to be recognized, or, as he has it, 'That there can be no expectation of reward, no fear of punishment, if everything be held subject to fate, or follow of necessity from the nature of God.'

"Here I will not pause to ask whether it be one and the same, or not a very different, thing, to maintain that all happens necessarily from the nature of God, and to hold that the Universe is God? but I beg you to observe how the critic odiously and unjustifiably adds that 'I am minded men should lead virtuous lives, not because of the precepts and commands of God, or moved by the hope of reward or fear of punishment, but,' &c. In the whole of my Tractate I aver that you will find no word to this effect. On the contrary, I declare expressly (vide Chap. IV.) that the sum of the divine law, the law that is written on our hearts and minds by the hand of God (vide Chap. II.), consists in this especially,—that we love God as our supreme good, not through fear of punishment, for love knows nothing of fear and cannot flow from fear, not even from love of aught else that we might wish to enjoy, but wholly and solely from devotion to the Supreme; for were this not the rule, we should then love God less than the thing desired. I have further shown in the same place that this is the very law which God revealed to the prophets; and if I now maintain that this law receives its character of commandment from God, or if I comprehend it in the way I comprehend the other decrees of God as involving an eternal truth, an eternal necessity in itself, it still remains an ordinance of the Almighty, and is doctrine wholesome to mankind. Even so, whether I love God of my own free will or by the necessity of the divine decree,

I still love the Creator and am blessed. I might therefore with reason maintain that this person belongs to that class of men of whom I speak at the end of my preface, and say, that I would much rather they left my book unread, than by perverse interpretations of its views, whilst deriving no benefit from its perusal themselves, they proved hindrances in the way of others who might profit by its contents.

"Although I believe that I have already said enough in the way of explanation of my views, and in answer to my censor, I still think it worth while to make a few further observations. I say, then, that he is mistaken when he imagines that I had in my eye that axiom of theological writers, which draws a distinction between the dogmatic doctrine and the simple narrative discourse of a prophet. If he really understands what I say in my 15th chapter, when quoting the Rabbi Judah Alpakhar, how could he believe that I agreed with the Rabbi, when I was all the while engaged in pointing out the erroneousness of his conclusions? If my critic intended any other axiom than the one I refer to, then I avow that I am not myself acquainted with it, and could not therefore in any way have had it in my eye.

"Further, I cannot see how my censor should say I believed that 'all would agree with me in my views who deny that reason and philosophy are the proper interpreters of Scripture,' seeing that I have pointedly rejected the conclusions as well of those who scout reason, as of Maimonides [who would reconcile Scripture with reason by arbitrarily torturing its text into the shape he desires].

"It were long to recite everything advanced by my critic in which I can see that he does not come to his task of censor with an entirely assured spirit; I therefore proceed at once to the passage where he says, that 'I have no grounds for my opinion that Mahomet was not a true prophet.' This singular conclusion of his he as strangely seeks to make good from the general statements and opinions I propound, in spite of the fact that from all I say of Mahomet I plainly show that I regard him as an impostor, inasmuch as he denies throughout the Koran that liberty which the universal religion, the religion which is revealed by natural as well as by prophetic light, allows—the right to worship God in spirit and in truth, a right which I have maintained must under all circumstances be conceded to mankind. And had I happened not to have done so, I should ask whether I were really bound to show that every one who has spoken oracularly was a false prophet? The prophets of the Old Testament were held on their parts, to prove that they were true prophets [and this, not by signs only, but by the excellence of their doctrine also]. If after all I am met by the reply that Mahomet taught divine precepts and gave sure signs of his mission, then would my critic himself have no grounds for refusing to Mahomet the character of a true prophet.

"As regards the Turks and other nations not included in the pale of Christianity, I am free to confess that I believe if they worship God in love and truth and do justly by their neighbour they have within them that which is equivalent to the Spirit of Christ, and that their salvation is assured, whatever notions they in their ignorance may entertain of Mahomet and his revelations.

"You see, therefore, my dear friend, that my critic fails greatly of the truth; but I do not the less perceive that he does me far less injustice than he does himself, when he ventures to assert that 'with covert wiles and glozing arguments I inculcate Atheism.'

"In conclusion, I venture to hope that in what precedes you will not find anything said too severely, and that is not well merited by my censor. Should you however meet with anything of the sort, I beg you to strike it out, or to soften and amend it as may seem best to you. It is not my wish to vex or irritate him, whoever he may be; neither is it my purpose, in my desire to stand well with you, to make myself a single enemy abroad; indeed, as such adverse criticisms are common enough, I should scarcely have brought myself to reply to this particular one, as I say at the beginning of my letter, had I not pledged you my word that I should. Farewell! I commit this letter to your prudence, and beg you to believe that I am yours, &c.,

"B. DE SPINOZA."

JOHN CHILDS AND SON, PRINTERS.

A CATALOGUE

OF

IMPORTANT WORKS IN ALL DEPARTMENTS OF LITERATURE AND SCIENCE,

PUBLISHED BY

TRÜBNER & CO., 60, PATERNOSTER ROW.

Poetry, Novels, Belles Lettres, Fine Arts, &c.

Barlow. IL GRAN RIFIUTO, WHAT IT WAS, WHO MADE IT, AND HOW FATAL TO DANTE ALLIGHIERI. A dissertation on Verses 58 to 65 of the Third Canto of the Inferno. By H. C. BARLOW, M.D., Author of "Francisca da Rimini, her Lament and Vindication"; "Letteratura Dantesca," etc., etc., etc. 8vo. Pp. 22, sewed, 1s. 1862.

———— IL CONTE UGOLINO E L'ARCIVESCOVO RUGGIERI, a Sketch from the Pisan Chronicles. By H. C. BARLOW, M.D. 8vo. Pp. 24, sewed, 1s. 1862.

———— THE YOUNG KING AND BERTRAND DE BORN. By H. C. BARLOW, M.D. 8vo. Pp. 35, sewed, 1s. 1862.

Barnstorff (D.) A KEY TO SHAKSPEARE'S SONNETS. Translated from the German by T. J. GRAHAM. 8vo.
[*In the Press*

Biglow Papers (THE). By JAMES RUSSELL LOWELL. Newly Edited, with a Preface, by the Author of "Tom Brown's School Days." In 1 vol. crown 8vo. Pp. 196, cloth 2s. 6d.

"Masterpieces of satirical humour, they are entitled, as such, to a permanent place in American, which is English literature."—*Daily News.*

"No one who ever read the '*Biglow Papers*' can doubt that true humour of a very high order, is within the range of American gift."—*Guardian.*

"The book undoubtedly owed its first vogue to party feeling; but it is impossible to ascribe to that cause only, so wide and enduring a popularity as it has now."—*Spectator.*

———— Second Series (Authorised Edition). Part I. containing Birdofredom Sawin, Esq., to Mr. Hosea Biglow.—2. Mason and Slidell: a Yankee Idyll. Crown 8vo., sewed, price 1s. Part II. containing—1. Birdofredum Sawin, Esq., to Mr. Hoseas Biglow. 2. A Message of Jefferson Davis in Secret Session. Cr. 8vo., sewed. Price each part 1s.

Brentano. HONOUR; or, THE STORY OF THE BRAVE CASPAR AND THE FAIR ANNERL. By CLEMENS BRENTANO. With an Introduction, and a Biographical Notice of the Author. By T. W. APPELL. Translated from the German. 12mo. Pp. 74, cloth, 1847. 2s. 6d.

Diary of a Poor Young Gentlewoman. Translated from the German, by M. ANNA CHILDS. Crown 8vo. cloth, 3s. 6d.

Deur and Bertha. A Tale. 18mo. Pp. vi. and 72, 1848. 1s.

Göthe's Correspondence with a Child. 8vo. pp. viii. and 498. 7s. 6d.

Golden A, B, C. Designed by GUSTAV KÖNIG. Engraved by JULIUS THATER. Oblong. 5s.

Gooroo Simple (THE VENERABLE), (*Strange Surprising Adventures of*) *and his Five Disciples, Noodle, Doodle, Wiseacre, Zany and Foozle;* adorned with Fifty Illustrations, drawn on wood, by ALFRED CROWQUILL. A Companion Volume to "Munchausen" and "Owlglass," based upon the famous Tamul tale of the Gooroo Paramartan, and exhibiting, in the form of a skilfully-constructed consecutive narrative, some of the finest specimens of Eastern wit and humour. Elegantly printed on tinted paper, in crown 8vo., richly gilt ornamental cover, gilt edges, price 10s. 6d.

"Without such a specimen as this it would not be possible to have a clear idea of the height to which the Indians carry their humour, and how much they revel in waggery and burlesque. It is a CAPITAL CHRISTMAS BOOK, with engravings worthy of the fun it portrays."—*London Review.*

"It is a collection of *eight extravagantly funny tales*, appropriately illustrated with fifty drawings on wood, by Alfred Crowquill. The volume is handsomely got up, and will be found worthy of close companionship with the '*Adventures of Master Owlglass*,' produced by the same publishers."—*Spectator.*

"Other than quaint, Alfred Crowquill can scarcely be. In some of his heads, too, he seems to have caught with spirit the Hindoo character."—*Athenæum.*

"The humour of these ridiculous adventures is thoroughly genuine, and very often quite irresistible. A more amusing volume, indeed, is rarely to be met with, while the notes in the Appendix display considerable erudition and research. In short, whoso would keep up the good old kindly practice of making Christmas presents to one's friends and relatives, *may go far afield and never fail in with a gift so acceptable* as a copy of the '*Strange Surprising Adventures of the Venerable Gooroo Simple.*'"—*Allen's Indian Mail.*

"A popular satire on the Brahmins current in several parts of India. The excellent introduction to the story or collection of incidents, and the notes and glossary at the close of the volume, will afford a good clue to the various habits and predilections of the Brahmins, which the narrative so keenly satirises. Most telling and characteristic illustrations, from the pencil of Alfred Crowquill, are lavishly sprinkled throughout the volume, and the whole getting up entitles it to rank as *a gift book worthy of special notice.*"—*English Churchman.*

"The public, to their sorrow, have not seen much of Alfred Crowquill lately; but we are glad to find him in the field again, with the story of the 'Goorno Simple.' The book is most excellent fooling, but contains, besides, a mine of recondite Oriental lore, necessitating even the addition of notes and a glossary; and moreover, there is *a vein of quiet philosophy running through it very pleasant to peruse.*"—*Illustrated London News.*

"The story is irresistibly funny, and is aided by fifty illustrations by Alfred Crowquill. The book is got up with that luxury of paper and type which is of itself, and in itself, *a pleasure to look upon.*"—*Globe.*

"The book is amusing, and is, moreover, admirably illustrated by the gentleman known as Alfred Crowquill with no fewer than fifty comic woodcuts. It is no less admirably got up, and beautifully bound, and it will be *most acceptable to a large portion of the public.*"—*Observer.*

Groves. JOHN GROVES. A Tale of the War. By S. E. De M———. 12mo. Pp. 16, sewed, 1846. 6d.

Gunderode. CORRESPONDENCE OF FRAULEIN GUNDERODE and BETTINA VON ARNIM. Cr. 8vo. Pp. 356, cloth. 6s.

Hagen. NORICA; or, Tales from the Olden Time. Translated from the German of August Hagen. Fcp. 8vo., ornamental binding, suitable for presentation. Pp. xiv. and 374. 5s.

"This pleasant volume is got up in that style of imitation of the books of a century ago, which has of late become so much the vogue. The typographical and mechanical departments of the volume speak loudly for the taste and enterprise bestowed upon it. Simple in its style, pithy, reasonably pungent—the book smacks strongly of the picturesque old days of which it treats. A long study of the art-antiquities of Nürnberg, and a profound acquaintance with the records, letters, and memoirs, still preserved, of the times of Albert Durer and his great brother artists, have enabled the author to lay before us a forcibly-drawn and highly-finished picture of art and household life in that wonderfully art-practising and art-reverencing old city of Germany."—*Atlas.*

"A delicious little book. It is full of a quaint garrulity, and characterised by an earnest simplicity of thought and diction, which admirably conveys to the reader the household and artistic German life of the times of Maximilian, Albert Durer, and Hans Sachs, the celebrated cobbler and 'master singer,' as well as most of the artist celebrities of Nürnberg in the 16th century. Art is the chief end and aim of this little history. It is lauded and praised with a sort of unostentatious devotion, which explains the religious passion of the early moulders of the ideal and the beautiful; and, perhaps, through a consequent deeper concentration of thought, the secret of their success."—*Weekly Dispatch.*

"A volume full of interest for the lover of old times; while the form in which it is presented to us may incite many to think of art and look into its many wondrous influences with a curious earnestness unknown to them before. It points a moral also, in the knowledge that a people may be brought to take interest in what is chaste and beautiful as in what is coarse and degrading.—*Manchester Examiner.*

Hearts in Mortmain, and Cornelia. Two Novels. Post 8vo. Pp. 458, cloth, 5s. 1850.

"To come to such writing as 'Hearts in Mortmain, and Cornelia' after the anxieties and roughness of our worldly struggle, is like bathing in fresh waters after the dust and heat of bodily exertion . . . To a peculiar and attractive grace they join considerable dramatic power, and one or two of the characters are conceived and executed with real genius."—*Prospective Review.*

"Both stories contain matter of thought and reflection which would set up a dozen commonplace circulating-library productions."—*Examiner.*

"It is not often now-a-days that two works of such a rare degree of excellence in their class are to be found in one volume; it is rarer still to find two works, each of which contains matter for two volumes, bound up in these times in one cover."—*Observer.*

"The above is an extremely pleasing book. The story is written in the antiquated form of letters, but its simplicity and good taste redeem it from the tediousness and appearance of egotism which generally attend that style of composition."—*Economist.*

"Well written and interesting.—*Daily News.*

"Two very pleasing and elegant novels. Some passages display descriptive powers of a high order.—*Britannia.*

Heine. SELECTIONS FROM THE POETRY OF HENRICH HEINE. Translated by JOHN ACKERLOS. 12mo. Pp. viii. and 66, stiff cover. 1854. 1s.

——— PICTURES OF TRAVEL. Translated from the German of HENRY HEINE. By CHARLES G. LELAND. Crown 8vo., Pp. 472. 1856. 7s. 6d.

Historical Sketches of the Old Painters. By the Author of "Three Experiments of Living," etc. 8vo. sd. 2s.

"That large class of readers who are not accustomed to refer to the original sources of information, will find in it interesting notices of men of whom they may have known little else than the names, and who are daily becoming more the subjects of our curiosity and admiration."—*Christian Examiner.*

Horrocks. ZENO. A Tale of the Italian War, and other Poems. To which are added Translations from Modern German Poetry. By JAMES D. HORROCKS. 12mo. Pp. vii. and 286, cloth. 1854. 5s.

Howitt. THE DÜSSELDORF ARTIST' ALBUM. Twenty-seven superb Lithotint Illustrations, from Drawings by Achenbach, Hubner, Jordan, Lessing, Leutze, Schadow, Tidemand, etc. With Contributions, original and translated, by Mary Howitt, Anne Mary Howitt, Francis Bennoch, etc. Edited by MARY HOWITT. 4to, elegantly bound in cloth, 18s.; or, in fancy leather binding, £1 1s.

Humboldt (ALEX. VON). LETTERS TO VARNHAGEN VON ENSE. Authorised English Translation, with Explanatory Notes, and a full Index of Names. In 1 vol. 8vo., handsomely bound in cloth, price 12s.

"It seldom occurs that the importance and value of a great man's thoughts are so immediately attested as these have been, *by the unequivocal disapprobation of the silly* at their publication."—*Court Circular.*

King. THE PATRIOT. A Poem. By J. W. KING. 12mo. Pp. 56, sewed, 1s. 1853.

Log Cabin (THE); or, THE WORLD BEFORE YOU. Post 8vo. Pp. iv. and 120, cl. 1844. 2s. 6d.

Massey (GERALD.) HAVELOCK'S MARCH; and OTHER POEMS. In one vol. 12mo. cloth, price 5s.

"Among the bands of young poets who in our day have fed on the fiery wine of Festus, or beaten time to the music of 'Pippa Passes,' few have been so healthful and robust in the midst of imitation as Mr. Massey. . . . . 'Robert Blake' is no less good; and, indeed, all the sea pieces have the dash and saltness of the ocean in them. They well deserve to be read, and, if read, are sure to be admired. . . . . Readers who find this vein of reading in their own humour—and there are many such—will get the volume for themselves. Mr. Massey's poetry shows growth. Some of the finest and weakest productions of our generation may be found in this volume."—*Athenæum*, August 17, 1861.

"The exception that we make is in favour of Gerald Massey. He has in him many of the elements of a true poet."—*Patriot*, August 22, 1861.

"Gerald Massey has been heard of ere now as a poet. He has written verses with such touches of nature in them as reach the heart at once. Himself a child of labour, he has felt the labourer's sufferings, and uttered the labourer's plaint; but uttered in such tones as throughout the din of the mills were surely recognised as poetry."—*The Nation*, September 21, 1861.

"Gerald Massey has a large and increasing public of his own. He is one of the most musical, and the most pure in thought, of all the large army of young bards who have so recently stared at little more than the sun and moon. Everybody can read Mr. Massey, and he is worthy of being read by everybody. His words flow with the freedom and impetuosity of a cataract."—*Lloyd's Weekly*, August 25, 1861.

Mayne. THE LOST FRIEND. A Crimean Memory. And other Poems. By COLBOURN MAYNE, Esq. 12mo. Pp. viii. and 134, cloth. 1857. 3s. 6d.

Morley. SUNRISE IN ITALY, etc. REVERIES. By HENRY MORLEY. 4to. Pp. 164, cloth. 1848. 7s. 6d.

Munch. WILLIAM AND RACHAEL RUSSELL; A Tragedy, in Five Acts. By ANDREAS MUNCH. Translated from the Norwegian, and Published under the Special Sanction of the Poet. By JOHN HEYLIGER BURT. 12mo. Pp. 126. London, 1862. 3s. 6d.

Munchausen (BARON). *The Travels and Surprising Adventures of.* With Thirty original Illustrations (Ten full-page coloured plates and twenty woodcuts). By ALFRED CROWQUILL. Crown 8vo. ornamental cover, richly gilt front and back, 7s. 6d.

"The travels of Baron Munchausen are perhaps the most astonishing storehouse of deception and extravagance ever put together. Their fame is undying, and their interest continuous; and no matter where we find the Baron—on the back of an eagle in the Arctic Circle, or distributing fudge to the civilized inhabitants of Africa—he is ever amusing, fresh, and new.

"A most delightful book. . . . . Very few know the name of the author. It was written by a German in England, during the last century, and published in the English language. His name was Rudolph Erich Raspe. We shall not soon look upon his like again."—*Boston Post*.

Owlglass (MASTER TYLL), *The Marvellous Adventures and Rare Conceits of.* Edited, with an Introduction, and a Critical and Bibliographical Appendix, by KENNETH R. H. MACKENZIE, F.S.A., with six coloured full-page Illustrations, and twenty-six Woodcuts, from original designs by ALFRED CROWQUILL. Price 10s. 6d., bound in embossed cloth, richly gilt, with appropriate design; or neatly half-bound morocco, gilt top, uncut, Roxburgh style.

"Tyll's fame has gone abroad into all lands; this, the narrative of his exploits, has been published in innumerable editions, even with all manner of learned glosses, and translated into Latin, English, French, Dutch, Polish. etc. We may say that to few mortals has it been granted to earn such a place in universal history as Tyll: for now, after five centuries, when Wallace's birthplace is unknown, even to the Scots, and the Admirable Crichton still more rapidly is grown a shadow, and Edward Longshanks sleeps unregarded, save by a few antiquarian English, Tyll's native village is pointed out with pride to the traveller, and his tombstone, with a sculptured pun on his name —namely, an Owl and a Glass, still stands, or pretends to stand, at Mollen, near Lübeck, where, since 1350, his once nimble bones have been at rest."—*Thomas Carlyle's Essays*, vol. ii. pp. 287, 288.

"A book for the antiquary, for the satirist, and the historian of satire; for the boy who reads for adventure's sake; for the grown person, loving every fiction that has a character in it. . . . . Mr. Mackenzie's language is quaint, racy, and antique, without a tiresome stiffness. The book, as it stands, is a welcome piece of English reading, with hardly a dry or tasteless morsel in it. We fancy that few Christmas books will be put forth more peculiar and characteristic than this comely English version of the '*Adventures of Tyll Owlglass.*' "—*Athenæum*.

"A volume of rare beauty, finely printed on tinted paper, and profusely adorned with chromo-lithographs and woodcuts in Alfred Crowquill's best manner. Wonderful has been the popularity of Tyll Eulenspiegel, surpassing even that of the '*Pilgrim's Progress*.' "—*Spectator*.

Preciosa; A Tale. Fcp. 8vo. Pp. 326, cloth, 7s. 6d. 1852.

"A bridgeless chasm seems to stand between us and the unexplored world of feeling. We do not hesitate to say that there are passages in it which, for the power of transporting the reader across the intervening depth, and of clothing in an intelligible form the dim creation of passionate imagination, have scarcely a rival in English prose."—*Morning Chronicle*.

"Marked by qualities which we are accustomed to associate with the maturity of a writer's powers."—*Guardian*.

"Exquisitely beautiful writing. . . . . It is full of sighs and lovers' aspirations, with many charming fancies and poetic thoughts. It is Petrarch and Laura over again, and the numerous quotations from the Italian interspersed, together with images suggested by the passionate melodies of the great composers, pretty clearly indicate the burden which runs like a rich refrain throughout. . . . . Of its execution we have the right to speak in terms of unqualified praise."—*Weekly Dispatch*.

Prescott (Miss.) SIR ROHAN'S GHOST; a Romance. Crown 8vo, cloth. 5s.

Proverbs and Sayings. Illustrated by Dusseldorf Artists. Twenty chromo-lithographic Plates, finished in the highest style of art. 4to, bds, gilt, 12s.

Read (THOMAS BUCHANAN). POEMS. Illustrated by KENNY MEADOWS. 12mo. cloth, 6s.

Reade (CHARLES). THE CLOISTER AND THE HEARTH; a Tale of the Middle Ages. In four volumes. Third edition. Vol. I., pp. 360; Vol. II., pp 376; Vol. III., pp. 328; Vol. IV., pp. 435. £1 11s. 6d.

—— Ditto. Fourth Edition. In 3 vols. Cr. 8vo. cl. 15s.

—— CREAM. Contains "Jack of all Trades;" "A Matter-of-Fact Romance," and "The Autobiography of a Thief." 8vo. Pp. 270. 10s. 6d.

—— LOVE ME LITTLE, LOVE ME LONG. In two volumes, post 8vo. Vol. I. p. 390; Vol. II., pp. 35. 8vo, cl. 21s.

—— THE EIGHTH COMMANDMENT. 8vo. Pp. 380. 14s.

—— WHITE LIES; a Story. In three volumes, 8vo. Vol. I., pp. 300; Vol. II., pp. 238; Vol. III., pp.232. £1 1s.

Reynard the Fox; *after the German Version of Göthe.* By THOMAS J. ARNOLD, Esq.

"Fair jester's humour and ready wit
Never offend, though smartly they hit."

With Seventy Illustrations, after the designs of WILHELM VON KAULBACH. Royal 8vo. Printed by CLAY, on toned paper, and elegantly bound in embossed cloth, with appropriate design after KAULBACH; richly tooled front and back. Price 16s. Best full morocco, same pattern, price 24s.; or, neatly half-bound morocco, gilt top, uncut edges, Roxburgh style, price 18s.

"The translation of Mr. Arnold has been held more truly to represent the spirit of Göthe's great poem than any other version of the legend.

"There is no novelty, except to purchasers of Christmas books, in Kaulbach's admirable illustrations of the world-famous '*Reynard the Fox*,' Among all the English translations Mr. T. J. Arnold holds at least his own, and we do not know that this edition, published by Trübner, with the Kaulbach engravings, reduced and faithfully rendered on wood, does not stand in the very first rank of the series we are commenting upon. Mr. Harrison Weir is a good artist, but in true comic power he is far inferior to Kaulbach. We do not see how this volume can, in its way, be excelled."—*Saturday Review.*

"Göthe's '*Reinecke Fuchs*' is a marvel of genius and poetic art. '*Reynard the Fox*' is more blessed than Alexander: his story has been written by one of the greatest of the human race, and another of inimitable genius has added to the poet's narrative the auxiliary light of the painter's skill. Perhaps no artist—not even our own Landseer, nor the French Gavarni—ever excelled Kaulbach in the art of infusing a human expression into the countenances and attributes of brutes; and this marvellous skill he has exerted in the highest degree in the illustrations to the book before us."—*Illustrated News of the World.*

"The illustrations are unrivalled for their humour and mastery of expression and detail."—*Economist.*

"Of all the numerous Christmas works which have been lately published, this is likely to be the most acceptable, not only as regards the binding, the print, and the paper, which are excellent, but also because it is illustrated with Kaulbach's celebrated designs."—*Court Journal.*

Schefer. THE BISHOP'S WIFE. A Tale of the Papacy. Translated from the German of LEOPOLD SCHEFER. By MRS. J. R. STODART. 12mo. cloth, 2s. 6d.

—— THE ARTIST'S MARRIED LIFE: being that of ALBERT DURER. For devout Disciples of the Arts, Prudent Maidens, as well as for the Profit and Instruction of all Christendom, given to the light Translated from the German of LEOPOLD SCHEFER, by MRS. J. R. STODART. Post 8vo. Pp. 98, sewed, 1s. 1853.

Stevens (BROOK B.) SEASONING FOR A SEASONER; or, THE NEW GRADUS AD PARNASSUM; a Satire. 8vo. Pp. 48. 3s.

Swanwick. SELECTIONS FROM THE DRAMAS OF GOETHE AND SCHILLER. Translated with Introductory Remarks. By ANNA SWANWICK. 8vo. Pp. xvi. and 290, cloth. 1846. 6s.

Tegner (F.) THE FRITHJOF SAGA; a Scandinavian Romance. Translated into English, in the original metres, by C. W. HECKETHORN, of Basle. One vol. 18mo. cloth. Price 3s. 6d.

Whipple. LITERATURE AND LIFE. Lectures by E. P. WHIPPLE, Author of "Essays and Reviews." 8vo. Pp. 114, sewed. 1851. 1s.

Wilson. THE VILLAGE PEARL: A Domestic Poem. With Miscellaneous Pieces. By JOHN CRAUFORD WILSON. 12mo. Pp. viii. and 140, cloth. 1852. 3s. 6d.

Winckelmann. THE HISTORY OF ANCIENT ART AMONG THE GREEKS. By JOHN WINCKELMANN. From the German, by G. H. LODGE. Beautifully Illustrated. 8vo. Pp. viii. and 254, cloth, 12s. 1850.

"That Winckelmann was well fitted for the task of writing a History of Ancient Art, no one can deny who is acquainted with his profound learning and genius. . . . He undoubtedly possessed, in the highest degree, the power of appreciating artistic skill wherever it was met with, but never more so than when seen in the garb of antiquity. . . . The work is of 'no common order,' and a careful study of the great principles embodied in it must necessarily tend to form a pure, correct, and elevated taste."—*Eclectic Review.*

"The work is throughout lucid, and free from the pedantry of technicality. Its clearness constitutes its great charm. It does not discuss any one subject at great length, but aims at a general view of Art, with attention to its minute developments. It is, if we may use the phrase, a Grammar of Greek Art, a *sine qua non* to all who would thoroughly investigate its language of form." *Literary World.*

"Winckelmann is a standard writer, to whom most students of art have been more or less indebted. He possessed extensive information, a refined taste, and great zeal. His style is plain, direct, and specific, so that you are never at a loss for his meaning. Some very good outlines, representing fine types of Ancient Greek Art, illustrate the text, and the volume is got up in a style worthy of its subject."—*Spectator.*

"To all lovers of art, this volume will furnish the most necessary and safe guide in studying the pure principles of nature and beauty in creative art. . . . We cannot wish better to English art than for a wide circulation of this invaluable work."—*Standard of Freedom.*

"The mixture of the philosopher and artist in Winckelmann's mind gave it at once an elegance, penetration, and knowledge, which fitted him to a marvel for the task he undertook. . . Such a work ought to be in the library of every artist and man of taste, and even the most general reader will find in it much to instruct, and much to interest him."—*Atlas.*

Wise, Captain Brand, of the "Centipede;" a Pirate of Eminence in the West Indies: His Loves and Exploits, together with some Account of the Singular Manner in which he departed this Life. By Lieut. H. A. Wise, U.S.N. 12mo. Pp. 304. 6s.

Geography, Travels, etc.

Barker. A Short Historical Account of the Crimea, from the Earliest Ages to the Russian Occupation: and a Description of the Geographical Features of the Country, and of the Manners, Customs, etc., of its Inhabitants, with Appendix. Compiled from the best authorities, by W. Burckhardt Barker, Esq., M.R.A.S., Author of "Lares and Penates," the "Turkish Reading Book," "Turkish Grammar;" and many years resident in Turkey, in an official capacity. Map. Fcp. 8vo. 3s. 6d.

Benisch. Travels of Rabbi Petachia of Ratisbon: who, in the latter end of the twelfth century, visited Poland, Russia, Little Tartary, the Crimea, Armenia, Assyria, Syria, the Holy Land, and Greece. Translated from the Hebrew, and published, together with the original on opposite pages. By Dr. A. Benisch; with Explanatory Notes, by the Translator and William F. Ainsworth, Esq., F.S.A., F.G.S., F.R.G.S. 12mo. pp. viii. and 106. 5s.

Bollaert (William). Antiquarian, Ethnological, and other Researches, in New Granada, Equador, Peru, and Chili; with Observations on the Pre-Incarial, Incarial, and other Monuments of Peruvian Nations. With numerous Plates. 8vo. 15s.

Falkener (Edward). A Description of some Important Theatres and other Remains in Crete, from a MS. History of Candia, by Onorio Belli, in 1586. Being a Supplement to the "Museum of Classical Antiquities." Illustrations and nine Plates. Pp. 32, royal 8vo. cloth. 5s. 6d.

Golovin (Ivan). The Caucasus. In one vol. 8vo. cloth. 5s.

——— The Nations of Russia and Turkey, and their Destiny. Pp. 370, 8vo. cloth. 9s.

Kohl. Travels in Canada, and through the States of New York and Pennsylvania. By I. J. Kohl. Translated by Mrs. Percy Sinnett. Revised by the Author. Two vols., post 8vo. Pp. xiv. and 794, cloth, 21s. 1861.

Krapf. Travels, Researches, and Missionary Labours, during an Eighteen Years' Residence on the Eastern Coast of Africa. By the Rev. Dr. J. Lewis Krapf, late Missionary in the service of the Church Missionary Society in Eastern and Equatorial Africa; to which is prefixed a concise Account of Geographical Discovery in Eastern Africa, up to the present time, by J. E. Ravenstein, F.R.G.S. In demy 8vo., with a Portrait, two Maps, and twelve Plates, price 21s., cloth.

"Dr. Krapf and his colleagues have largely contributed to the most important geographical discovery of modern time—namely, that the centre of Africa is not occupied, as was formerly thought, by a chain of mountains, but by a series of great inland lakes, some of which are hundreds of miles in length. Hardly any one discovery has thrown so much light on the formation of the earth's surface as this."—*Saturday Review.*

"Dr. Krapf's work is superior in interest to the well-known narrative of Moffatt; in some parts, it is equal in novelty to the most attractive chapters of Barth and Livingstone. Dr. Krapf travels well, and writes as a traveller should write, and seldom claims any indulgence from the reader."—*Athenæum.*

"Scarcely any pages in Livingstone exceed in interest some of Dr. Krapf's adventures. The whole volume, so full of interest, will well repay the most careful perusal."—*Literary Gazette.*

Lange. The Upper Rhine: Illustrating its finest Cities, Castles, Ruins, and Landscapes. From Drawings by Messrs. Rohbock, Louis and Julius Lange. Engraved by the most distinguished Artists. With a History and Topographical Text. Edited by Dr. Gaspey. 8vo. Pp. 494. 134 Plates. London, 1859. £2 2s.

Paton. RESEARCHES ON THE DANUBE AND THE ADRIATIC; or, Contributions to the Modern History of Hungary and Transylvania, Dalmatia and Croatia, Servia and Bulgaria. By A. A. PATON, F.R.G.S. In 2 vols. 12mo Pp. 850, cloth, price 12s.

"We never came across a work which more conscientiously and accurately does exactly what it professes to do."—*Spectator.*

"The interest of these volumes lies partly in the narrative of travel they contain, and partly in the stores of information on all kinds of subjects with which they abound."—*Saturday Review.*

"The work is written in a pleasant and readable style, and will be a necessary companion for travellers through the countries of which it treats."—*Literary Gazette.*

Ravenstein. THE RUSSIANS ON THE AMUR; its Discovery, Conquest, and Colonization, with a Description of the Country, its Inhabitants, Productions, and Commercial Capabilities, and Personal Accounts of Russian Travellers. By E. G. RAVENSTEIN, F.R.G.S., Correspondent F.G.S. Frankfurt, with an Appendix on the Navigation of the Gulf of the Amur. By CAPTAIN PRUTZ. In one volume, 8vo., 500 pp. of Letter Press, 4 tinted Lithographs, and 3 Maps, handsomely bound. Price 15s., in cloth.

"This is a work of real and permanent value. Mr. Ravenstein has set himself a weighty task, and has performed it well. It is, we think, impossible to name any subject bearing upon the Amur, which is not considered in this volume."—*Economist.*

"Mr. Ravenstein's work is worthy of high commendation. It throws much additional and interesting light on a country but comparatively little known."—*Morning Advertiser.*

"It is a perfect handbook of the Amur, and will be consulted by the historian, the politician, the geographer, the naturalist, the ethnologist, the merchant and the general reader, with equal interest and profit."—*Colburn's New Monthly Magazine.*

"The most complete and comprehensive work on the Amur that we have seen."—*New Quarterly Review.*

"The expectations excited by the announcement of this pregnant volume are amply fulfilled by its execution. ... The book bears evidence in every page of the toil and conscientiousness of the author. It is packed full with valuable information. There is not a word thrown away; and the care with which the facts are marshalled, attests the great pains and consideration that have been bestowed upon the plan of the work."—*Home News.*

"It is a thoroughly conscientious work, and furnishes very full information on all points of interest. The illustrations are extremely good; the maps are excellent."—*The Press.*

"Mr. Ravenstein has produced a work of solid information—a capital book of reference—on a subject concerning which Englishmen will, before long, desire all the trustworthy information they can get."—*Globe.*

"Mr. Ravenstein's book contains the fullest and latest accounts of Russia's annexations in oriental quarters, and is, therefore, a highly valuable and useful addition to English knowledge thereof."—*Dublin Nation.*

"In conclusion, we must compliment Mr. Ravenstein on the skill which he has shown as a compiler. He himself has never visited the Amur; and has composed his work entirely from the accounts of previous travellers. But he has done it so well, that few readers except those whose business it is to be suspicious, would have found it out, if it had not been acknowledged in the preface."—*Literary Budget.*

"The book has, of course, no pretensions to the freshness of a narrative of personal exploration and adventure, but it is by no means unpleasant reading, even from this point of view, while for those who are possessed of a geographical taste, which is in some degree a thing apart, it will have a high degree of interest."—*Spectator.*

"This book is a good honest book—a book that was needed, and that may be referred to as a reliable source of information."—*Athenæum.*

"The work before us is full of important and accurate information."—*London Review.*

"His book is by far the most comprehensive review of all that has been observed and ascertained of a little-known portion of Asia."—*Guardian.*

"There is a breadth and massiveness about the work which mark it off very distinctly from the light books of travel or history which are written to amuse a railroad traveller, or a subscriber to Mudie's."—*China Telegraph.*

"The volume deserves a careful perusal, and it will be found exceedingly instructive."—*Observer.*

"The aim of Mr. Ravenstein has been to make his book one of authority, and in this he has certainly been most successful."—*Bell's Messenger.*

"We are fortunate, too, in our opportunity, for it would be hard to find a more careful or trustworthy guide than Mr. Ravenstein, who has not only availed himself of all accessible publications on the subject, but has also enjoyed the immense advantage of holding personal communication with Russian officers who had served on the Amur."—*Allen's Indian Mail.*

"The book to which we are indebted for our information is a perfect magazine of knowledge, and must become the standard work on the Amur. It does not affect liveliness or brilliancy, but is constantly perspicuous, interesting, and complete. We have never opened a more satisfactory and well-arranged collection of all that is known on any given subject, than Ravenstein's Russians on the Amur."—*Liverpool Daily Post.*

"A well-written work."—*Morning Post.*

"The account by Mr. Ravenstein of their long-continued efforts and recent success, is one of the most complete books we have ever met with—it is an exhaustive monograph of the political history and natural resources of a country of which but little was before known in Europe, and that little had to be extracted from obscure sources. This labour has been most conscientiously performed by the author. The various journeys of Russian explorers, the early predatory incursions, the narratives of missionaries, and the accounts of the Chinese themselves, are brought together with great skill and success."—*Westminster Review.*

Sartorius (C.). MEXICO. Landscapes and Popular Sketches. Edited by Dr. GASPEY, with Engravings by distinguished Artists, from original Sketches. By MORITZ RUGENDAS. 4to. cloth gilt. 18s.

Schlagintweit. RESULTS OF A SCIENTIFIC MISSION TO INDIA and UPPER ASIA. By HERMANN, ADOLPHUS, and ROBERT DE SCHLAGINTWEIT. Undertaken between 1854 and 1858, by order of the Honourable East India Company. In nine vols. 4to, with an Atlas in folio. (*Dedicated, by permission, to Her Majesty*). Vol. I. and folio atlas, Vol. II. and atlas, each £4 4s.

Seyd (ERNEST). CALIFORNIA AND ITS RESOURCES. A Work for the Merchant, the Capitalist, and the Emigrant. 8vo cloth, plates, 8s. 6d.

Ware. SKETCHES OF EUROPEAN CAPITALS. By WILLIAM WARE, Author of "Zenobia; or, Letters from Palmyra," "Aurelian," &c. 8vo. Pp. 124, 1s. 1851.

Memoirs, Politics, History, etc.

Address of the Assembled States of Schleswig to His Majesty the King of Denmark. 8vo. Pp. 32, 1s. 1861.

Administration (the) of the Confederate States. Correspondence between Hon. J. A. CAMPBELL and Hon. W. H. SEWARD, all of which was laid before the Provisional Congress, on Saturday, by PRESIDENT DAVIS. 8vo. Pp. 8, sewed, 1s. 1861.

Americans (the) Defended. By an AMERICAN. Being a Letter to one of his Countrymen in Europe, in answer to inquiries concerning the late imputations of dishonour upon the United States. 8vo. Pp. 38, sewed, 1s. 1844.

Austria, and her Position with regard to Hungary and Europe. An Address to the English Press. By a HUNGARIAN. 8vo. Pp. 32, sewed, 1s. 1861.

Bell. THE ENGLISH IN INDIA. Letters from Nagpore, written in 1857-8. By CAPTAIN EVANS BELL. Post 8vo. Pp. 2, cloth. 4s. 1859.

Benjamin. SPEECH OF HON. J. P. BENJAMIN, of Louisiana, on the Right of Secession, delivered in the Senate of the United States, Dec. 31st, 1860. Royal 8vo. Pp. 16, sewed, 1s.

Bicknell. IN THE TRACK OF THE GARIBALDIANS THROUGH ITALY AND SICILY. By ALGERNON SIDNEY BICKNELL. Cr. 8vo. Pp. xx. and 344, cloth, 10s. 6d. 1861.

Blind. AN OUTLINE OF THE STATE OF THINGS IN SCHLESWIG-HOLSTEIN. By KARL BLIND. 8vo. Pp. 16, sewed. 1862. 6d.

Bunsen. MEMOIR ON THE CONSTITUTIONAL RIGHTS OF THE DUCHIES OF SCHLESWIG AND HOLSTEIN, presented to Viscount Palmerston, by CHEVALIER BUNSEN, on the 8th of April, 1848. With a Postscript of the 15th of April. Published with M. de Gruner's Essay, on the Danish Question, and all the official Documents, by Otto Von Wenkstern. Illustrated by a Map of the Two Duchies. 8vo. Pp. 166, sewed. 1848. 2s. 6d.

Chapman. REMARKS ON THE LEGAL BASIS REQUIRED BY IRRIGATION IN INDIA. By JOHN CHAPMAN. 8vo. Pp. 20. 1s. 1854.

—————— INDIAN POLITICAL REFORM. Being Brief Hints, together with a Plan for the Improvement of the Constituency of the East India Company, and the Promotion of Public Works. By JOHN CHAPMAN. Pp. 36, cloth, 1s. 1853.

—————— BARODA AND BOMBAY; their Political Morality. A Narrative drawn from the Papers laid before Parliament in relation to the Removal of Lieut.-Col. Outram, C.B., from the Office of Resident at the Court of the Gaekwar. With Explanatory Notes, and Remarks on the Letter of L. R Reid. Esq., to the Editor of the *Daily News*. By J. CHAPMAN. 8vo. Pp. iv. and 174. sewed, 3s. 1853.

—————— THE COTTON AND COMMERCE OF INDIA, considered in relation to the Interests of Great Britain: with Remarks on Railway Communication in Bombay Presidency. By JOHN CHAPMAN, Founder of the Great India Peninsula Railway Company. 8vo. Pp. xvii. and 412, cloth. 1s. 1851.

Civilization in Hungary: SEVEN ANSWERS TO THE SEVEN LETTERS addressed by M. BARTH DE SZEMERE, late Minister of the Interior in Hungary. to Richard Cobden, Esq., M.P. for Rochdale. By a HUNGARIAN. 12mo., Pp. xii. and 232. 6s.

Clayton and Bulwer Convention, OF THE 19TH APRIL, 1850, BETWEEN THE BRITISH AND AMERICAN GOVERNMENTS, CONCERNING CENTRAL AMERICA. 8vo. Pp. 64, 1s. 1856.

Coleccion de Documentos ineditos relativos al Descubrimiento y á la Historia de las Floridas. Los ha dado á luz el Senor Don BUCKINGHAM SMITH, segun los manuscritos de Madrid y Sevilla. Tomo primero, folio, pp. 216, con retrato del Rey D. Fernando V. 28s.

Constitution of the United States, with an Index to each article and section. By A CITIZEN OF WASHINGTON. 8vo. Pp. 64, sewed, 1s. 1860.

Deliberation or Decision? being a Translation from the Danish, of the Reply given by Herr Raasloff to the accusations preferred against him on the part of the Danish Cabinet; together with an Introductory Article from the Copenhagen "Dagbladet," and Explanatory Notes. 8vo. Pp. 40. sewed, 1s. 1861.

Dewey. AMERICAN MORALS AND MANNERS. By ORVILLE DEWEY, D.D. 8vo. Pp. 32, sewed, 1s. 1844.

Dirckinck-Holmfeld. ATTIC TRACTS ON DANISH AND GERMAN MATTERS. By BARON C. DIRCKINCK-HOLMFELD. 8vo. Pp. 116, sewed, 1s. 1861.

Emerson. THE YOUNG AMERICAN. A Lecture. By RALPH WALDO EMERSON. 8vo. Pp. 24, 1s. 1844.

—— REPRESENTATIVE MEN. Seven Lectures. By R. W. EMERSON. Post 8vo. Pp. 215, cloth. 5s. 1850.

Emperor of Austria versus Louis Kossuth. A few words of Common Sense. By AN HUNGARIAN. 8vo. Pp. 28, 1s. 1861.

Everett. THE QUESTIONS OF THE DAY. An Address. By EDWARD EVERETT. Royal 8vo. Pp. 46, 1s. 6d. 1861.

—— SELF GOVERNMENT IN THE UNITED STATES. By the Hon. EDWARD EVERETT. 8vo. Pp. 44, sewed, 1s. 1860.

Filippo Malincontri; or, STUDENT LIFE IN VENETIA. An Autobiography. Edited by GIROLAMO VOLPE. Translated from the unpublished Italian MS. by C. B. CAYLEY, B.A. Two vols., post 8vo. Pp. xx. and 646, 18s. 1861.

Furdoonjee. THE CIVIL ADMINISTRATION OF THE BOMBAY PRESIDENCY. By NOWROZJEE FURDOONJEE, fourth Translator and Interpreter to Her Majesty's Supreme Court, and Member of the Bombay Association. Published in England at the request of the Bombay Association. 8vo. Pp. viii. and 8s, sewed, 2s. 1853.

Germany and Italy. Answer to Mazzini's "Italy and Germany." By RODBERTUS, DE BERO, and L. BUCHER. 8vo. Pp. 20, sewed, 1s. 1861.

Herbert. THE SANITARY CONDITION OF THE ARMY. By the Right Honorable SIDNEY HERBERT, M.P. 8vo Pp. 48. sewed. London. 1859. 1s. 6d,

Herzen. LE MONDE RUSSE ET LA REVOLUTION. Mémoires de A. HERZEN. Traduit par H. DELAVEAU. Trois volumes in 8vo., broché. 5s. each.

Herzen. DU DEVELOPPEMENT des Idées Révolutionnaires en Russie, par ISCANDER. 2s. 6d.

—— LA FRANCE OU L'ANGLETERRE? Variations Russes sur le thême de l'attentat du 14 Janvier 1858, par ISCANDER. 1s.

—— FRANCE OR ENGLAND? 6d.

—— MEMOIRES DE L'IMPERATRICE CATHERINE II. Ecrits par elle-même. et précédés d'une préface, par A. HERZEN. Seconde Edition. Revue et augmentée, de huit Lettres de Pierre III., et d'une Lettre de Catherine II. au Comte Poniatowsky. 8vo. Pp. xvi. and 370. 10s. 6d.

—— MEMOIRS OF THE EMPRESS CATHERINE II., written by Herself. With a Preface by A. HERZEN. Translated from the French. 12mo. cloth. 7s. 6d.

Higginson. WOMAN AND HER WISHES. An Essay. By THOMAS WENTWORTH HIGGINSON. Post 8vo., sewed, 1s. 1854.

Hole. LECTURES ON SOCIAL SCIENCE AND THE ORGANIZATION OF LABOUR. By JAMES HOLE. 8vo. Pp. xi. and 182, sewed. 2s. 6d. 1851.

Humboldt. LETTERS OF WILLIAM VON HUMBOLDT TO A FEMALE FRIEND. A complete Edition. Translated from the Second German Edition by CATHERINE M. A. COUPER, with a Biographical Notice of the Writer. Two vols. Crown 8vo. Pp. xxviii.and 592, cloth. 10s. 1849.

"We cordially recommend these volumes to the attention of our readers . . . . . The work is in every way worthy of the character and experience of its distinguished author."—*Daily News.*

"These admirable letters were, we believe, first introduced to notice in England by the 'Athenæum;' and perhaps no greater boon was ever conferred upon the English reader than in the publication of the two volumes which contain this excellent translation of William Humboldt's portion of a lengthened correspondence with his female friend."—*Westminster and Foreign Quarterly Review.*

"The beautiful series of W. von Humboldt's letters, now for the first time translated and published complete, possess not only high intrinsic interest, but an interest arising from the very striking circumstances in which they originated . . . . . We wish we had space to verify our remarks. But we should not know where to begin, or where to end; we have therefore no alternative but to recommend the entire book to a careful perusal, and to promise a continuance of occasional extracts into our columns from the beauties of thought and feeling with which it abounds."—*Manchester Examiner and Times.*

"It is the only complete collection of these remarkable letters, which has yet been published in English, and the translation is singularly perfect; we have seldom read such a rendering of German thoughts into the English tongue."—*Critic.*

Humboldt. THE SPHERE AND DUTIES OF GOVERNMENT. Translated from the German of BARON WILHELM VON HUMBOLDT, by JOSEPH COULTHARD, Jun. Post 8vo. 5s.

"We have warmly to thank Mr. Coulthard for adding to English literature, in so faithful a form, so valuable a means of extending the range and elevating the character of our political investigation."—*Westminster Review.*

Hutton. MODERN WARFARE: its positive Theory and True Policy. With an application to the Russian War. By HENRY DIX HUTTON. 8vo. Pp. 74, sewed. 1s. 1855.

Jay. THE AMERICAN REBELLION: its History, its Aims, and the Reasons why it must be suppressed. An Address. By JOHN JAY. Post 8vo. Pp. 50, sewed, 1s. 1861.

——— THE GREAT CONSPIRACY. An Address. By JOHN JAY. 8vo. Pp. 50, 1s. 1861.

Jones, Peter. AN AUTOBIOGRAPHY. Stage the First. 12mo. Pp. 220, cloth, 3s. 1848.

Kossuth. Speeches of Louis Kossuth in America. Edited, with his sanction, by F. W. NEWMAN. Pp. 388, post 8vo, boards. 5s.

——— Sheffield and Nottingham Evening Speeches. Edited by himself. 2d.

——— Glasgow Speeches. Edited by himself. 2d.

Langford. ENGLISH DEMOCRACY; its History and Principles. By JOHN ALFRED LANGFORD. Fcp. 8vo., stiff cover. Pp. 88. 1s. 6d. 1854.

Letter to Lord Palmerston, concerning the Question of Schleswig-Holstein. 8vo. sewed. Pp. 32. 1850. 1s.

Martineau. LETTERS FROM IRELAND. By HARRIET MARTINEAU. Reprinted from the *Daily News.* Post 8vo. Pp. viii. and 220, cloth. 6s. 6d. 1852.

"Every one of these letters contains passages worthy of attention. . . . The republication of Miss Martineau's Letters, as a very late description of Ireland, will be universally acceptable."—*Economist.*

". . . We entertain no doubt, then, that our readers will rejoice with us in having these contributions brought together and presented again to their notice in a compact and inviting form."—*Inquirer.*

——— A HISTORY OF THE AMERICAN COMPROMISES. Reprinted with additions from the *Daily News.* By HARRIET MARTINEAU. 8vo. Pp. 35, sewed, 1s. 1856.

Memoires de la Cour d'Espagne SOUS LE RÈGNE DE CHARLES II., 1678-1682. Par le Marquis DE VILLARS. 8vo, pp. xxxix. and 380. Londres, 1861 £1 10s.

Michel. LES ECOSSAIS EN FRANCE ET LES FRANÇAIS EN ECOSSE. Par FRANCISQUE MICHEL. Two vols. of more than 1,200 pages, with numerous Woodcuts. Handsomely bound in appropriate style, £1 12s. Also a splendid Edition in 4to., with red borders, and four Plates, in addition to the Woodcut Illustrations. This Edition is printed in 100 copies only, and will contain a list of Subscribers. Bound in half Morocco. Price £3 3s.

Mission (the) of South Carolina to Virginia. From *De Bow's Review,* December, 1860. 8vo. Pp. 34, sewed, 1s. 1861.

Morell. RUSSIA AND ENGLAND; THEIR STRENGTH AND THEIR WEAKNESS. By JOHN REYNELL MORELL, Author of " Russia as it is," &c. Fcap. 8vo., 1s.

Morentin (MANUEL MARTINEZ DE). RULES AND PEOPLE; or, Thoughts upon Government and Constitutional Freedom. An Essay. 12mo. Pp. 50. 2s.

Motley. CAUSES OF THE CIVIL WAR IN AMERICA. By JOHN LOTHROP MOTLEY, LL.D. Reprinted from the *Times.* 8vo. Pp. 30, sewed, 1s. 1861.

Neale (Rev. ERSKINE, Rector of Kirton). MY COMRADE AND MY COLOURS; or, Men who know not when they are Beaten. 12mo, sewed. 1s.

Newman. LECTURES ON POLITICAL ECONOMY. By FRANCIS WILLIAM NEWMAN. Post 8vo., cloth, 5s.

"The most able and instructive book, which exhibits, we think, no less moral than economical wisdom." *Prospective Review.*

——— THE CRIMES OF THE HOUSE OF HAPSBURG AGAINST ITS OWN LIEGE SUBJECTS. By F. W. NEWMAN. 8vo. Pp. 60, sewed, 1s. 1853.

Ogareff. ESSAI SUR LA SITUATION RUSSE. Lettres à un Anglais. Par N. OGAREFF. 12mo. Pp. 150, stitched, 3s.

Our North-West Frontier. With Map. 8vo. Pp. 20. 1s. 1856.

Partnership, with Limited Liability. Reprinted with additions, from *The Westminster Review.* New Series, No. viii., October, 1853. Post 8vo., sewed, 1s. 1854.

Petruccelli. PRELIMINAIRES DE LA QUESTION ROMAINE de M. ED. ABOUT. 8vo. Pp. xv. and 364. 7s. 6d.

Policy of the Danish Government, and the "Misunderstandings." A Key to the Budget Dispute. 8vo. Pp. 74, sewed, 1s. 1861.

Pope's Rights and Wrongs. An Historical Sketch. 12mo. Pp. xiv. and 97. 2s. 6d.

Richter. THE LIFE OF JEAN PAUL FR. RICHTER. Compiled from various sources. Together with his Autobiography, translated from the German. 2 vols. Pp. xvii. and 465, paper in cover, 7s. 1845.

Schimmelfennig. THE WAR BETWEEN TURKEY AND RUSSIA. A Military Sketch. By A. SCHIMMELFENNIG. 8vo., 2s.

Schoelcher. DANGERS TO ENGLAND OF THE ALLIANCE WITH THE MEN OF THE COUP-D'ETAT. By VICTOR SCHOELCHER, Representative of the People. Pp. 190, 12mo., sewed, 2s.

Serf (the) and the Cossack; or, Internal State of Russia. Second Edition, revised and enlarged. 12mo., sewed, 6d.

Smith. LOCAL SELF-GOVERNMENT AND CENTRALIZATION. The Characteristics of each; and its Practical Tendencies as affecting Social, Moral, and Political Welfare and Progress. Including Comprehensive Outlines of the English Constitution. With copious Index. By J. TOULMIN SMITH, Esq., Barrister-at-Law. Post 8vo. Pp. viii. and 409, cloth, 5s. 1851.

"This is a valuable, because a thoughtful treatise upon one of the general subjects of theoretical and practical polities. No one in all probability will give an absolute *assent* to all its conclusions, but the reader of Mr. Smith's volume will in any case be induced to give more weight to the important principle insisted on."—*Tait's Magazine*.

"Embracing, with a vast range of constitutional learning, used in a singularly attractive form, an elaborate review of all the leading questions of our day."—*Eclectic Review*.

"This is a book, therefore, of immediate interest, and one well worthy of the most studious consideration of every reformer; but it is also the only complete and correct exposition we have of our political system; and we mistake much if it does not take its place in literature as our standard text-book of the constitution."

"The special chapters on local self-government and centralization will be found chapters of the soundest practical philosophy; every page bearing the marks of profound and practical thought."

"The chapters on the crown, and on common law, and statute law, display a thorough knowledge of constitutional law and history, and a vast body of learning is brought forward for popular information without the least parade or pedantry."

"Mr. Toulmin Smith has made a most valuable contribution to English literature; for he has given the people a true account of their once glorious constitution; more than that, he has given them a book replete with the soundest and most practical views of political philosophy."—*Weekly News*.

"There is much research, sound principle, and good logic in this book; and we can recommend it to the perusal of all who wish to attain a competent knowledge of the broad and lasting basis of English constitutional law and practice."—*Morning Advertiser*.

Smith. SOCIAL ASPECTS. By JOHN STORES SMITH, Author of "Mirabeau," a Life History. Post 8vo. Pp. iv. and 258, cloth, 2s. 6d. 1850.

"This work is the production of a thoughtful mind, and of an ardent and earnest spirit, and is well deserving of a perusal *in extenso* by all those who reflect on so solemn and important a theme as the future destiny of their native country."—*Morning Chronicle*.

"A work of whose merits we can hardly speak too highly."—*Literary Gazette*.

"This book has awakened in us many painful thoughts and intense feelings. It is fearfully true—passionate in its upbraidings, unsparing in its exposures—yet full of wisdom, and pervaded by an earnest, loving spirit. The author sees things as they are—too sad and too real for silence—and courageously tells of them with stern and honest truth. . . . We receive with pleasure a work so free from polite lispings, pretty theorizings, and canting progressionisms; speaking, as it does, earnest truth, fearlessly, but in love."—*Nonconformist*

Spellen (J. N.) THE INNER LIFE OF THE HOUSE OF COMMONS. 12mo. sd, 6d.

Spencer. A THEORY OF POPULATION, deduced from the general law of Animal Fertility. By HERBERT SPENCER, Author of "Social Statics." Republished from the *Westminster Review*, for April, 1852. 8vo., paper cover, price 1s.

—— STATE EDUCATION SELF DEFEATING. A Chapter from Social Statics. By HERBERT SPENCER. Fifth Thousand. 12mo. Pp. 24, 1s. 1851.

Story. LIFE AND LETTERS OF JOSEPH STORY, Associate Justice of the Supreme Court of the United States, and Dane Professor of Law at Harvard University. Edited by his Son WILLIAM W. STORY. Two vols. Royal 8vo. Pp. xx.—1,250, cloth, 20s. 1851.

"Greater than any Law Writer of which England can boast since the days of Blackstone."—*Lord Campbell, in the House of Lords, April 7, 1843*.

"We look in vain over the legal literature of England for names to put in comparison with those of Livingstone, Kent, and Story. . . . After reading his (Judge Story's) Life and Miscellaneous Writings, there can be no difficulty in accounting for his personal influence and popularity."—*Edinburgh Review*.

"The biography before us, written by his son, is admirably digested, and written in a style which sustains the attention to the last, and occasionally rises to true and striking eloquence."—*Eclectic Review*.

—— THE AMERICAN QUESTION. By WILLIAM W. STORY. 8vo. Pp. 68, sewed, 1s. 1862.

Taney. THE OPINION OF THE HON. ROGER BROOKE TANEY, Chief Justice of the Supreme Court of the United States in the Habeas Corpus Case of John Morryman, of Baltimore County, Md. 8vo. Pp. 24, sewed, 1s. 1861.

The Rights of Neutrals and Belligerents, from a Modern Point of View. By a CIVILIAN. 8vo., sewed, 1s.

The Rights of Schleswig-Holstein and the Policy of England. Published by order of the Executive Committee of the German National Verein. 8vo. Pp. 54, stitched, 1s. 1862.

Thomson. THE AUTOBIOGRAPHY OF AN ARTIZAN. By CHRISTOPHER THOMSON. Post 8vo. Pp. xii. and 408, cloth. 6s. 1847.

Three Experiments of Living. Within the Means. Up to the Means. Beyond the Means. Fcp. 8vo., ornamental cover and gilt edges. Pp. 86, 1s. 1848.

Education.

Classical Instruction: ITS USE AND ABUSE: reprinted from the *Westminster Review* for October, 1853. Post 8vo. Pp. 72, 1s. 1854.

Jenkins (JABEZ.) VEST POCKET LEXICON; an English Dictionary, of all except Familiar Words, including the principal Scientific and Technical Terms, and Foreign Moneys, Weights, and Measures. Omitting what everybody knows, and containing what everybody wants to know, and cannot readily find. 32mo. pp. 563. 2s. 6d.

Pick (Dr. EDWARD.) ON MEMORY, and the Rational Means of Improving it. 12mo. Pp. 128. 2s. 6d.

Watts and Doddridge. HYMNS FOR CHILDREN. Revised and altered, so as to render them of general use. By Dr. WATTS. To which are added Hymns and other Religious Poetry for Children. By Dr. DODDRIDGE. Ninth Edition. 12mo. Pp. 48, stiff covers. 6d. 1857.

ATLASES.

Menke (Dr. T.) ORBIS ANTIQUI DESCRIPTIO, for the use of Schools; containing 16 Maps engraved on Steel and coloured, with descriptive Letter-press. Half-bound morocco, price 5s.

Spruner's (Dr. KARL VON) HISTORICO-GEOGRAPHICAL HAND-ATLAS; containing 26 coloured Maps, engraved on copper plates: 22 Maps devoted to the General History of Europe, and 4 Maps specially illustrative of the History of the British Isles. Cloth lettered, 15s.; or half-bound morocco, £1 1s.

The deserved and widely spread reputation which the Historical Atlas of Dr. Spruner has attained in Germany, has led to the publication of this English Edition, with the Author's co-operation and the authority of the German Publisher, Mr. Justus Perthes. Inasmuch as an inferior, unauthorised, and carelessly prepared Atlas has recently appeared, in which Dr. Spruner's Maps have been reproduced without reference to the copyright of the Author, or to the demand which the public make for accuracy and fulness, it is necessary to be particular in specifying the "Author's Edition."

A detailed Prospectus, with a specimen Map, will be forwarded on application, on receipt of one postage stamp.

HEBREW.

Gesenius' HEBREW GRAMMAR. Translated from the Seventeenth Edition, by Dr. T. J. CONANT. With a Chrestomathy by the Translator. 8vo, cloth. 10s. 6d.

—————— HEBREW AND ENGLISH LEXICON OF THE OLD TESTAMENT, including the Biblical Chaldee, from the Latin. By EDWARD ROBINSON. Fifth Edition. 8vo, cloth. £1 5s.

SYRIAC.

Uhlemann's SYRIAC GRAMMAR. Translated from the German by ENOCH HUTCHINSON. 8vo, cloth. 18s.

LATIN.

Ahn's (Dr. F.) New, Practical, and Easy Method of Learning the Latin Language. [*In the Press*

Harkness (ALBERT, Ph. D.) LATIN OLLENDORFF. Being a Progressive Exhibition of the Principles of the Latin Grammar. 12mo, cloth. 5s.

GREEK.

Ahn's (Dr. F.) New, Practical, and Easy Method of Learning the Greek Language. [*In the Press*

Kendrick (ASAHEL C.) GREEK OLLENDORFF. A Progressive Exhibition of the Principles of the Greek Grammar. 8vo, half calf. 6s.

Kühner (Dr. RAPH). GRAMMAR OF THE GREEK LANGUAGE for the use of High Schools and Colleges. Translated from the German by B. B. EDWARDS and S. H. TAYLOR. Fourth Edition. 8vo, cloth. 10s. 6d.

Kühner (Dr. Raph). An Elementary Grammar of the Greek Language. Translated by Samuel H. Taylor. One vol. Thirteenth edition. 8vo, cloth. 9s.

MODERN GREEK.

Felton (Dr. C. C.) Selections from Modern Greek Writers, in Prose and Poetry. With Notes. 8vo, cloth. 6s.

Sophocles (E. A.) Romaic or Modern Greek Grammar. 8vo, half-bound. 7s. 6d.

ITALIAN.

Ahn's (Dr. F.) New, Practical, and Easy Method of Learning the Italian Language. First and Second Course. One vol. 12mo. 3s. 6d.

———— Key to ditto. 12mo. 1s.

Millhouse (John). New English and Italian Pronouncing and Explanatory Dictionary. Vol. I. English-Italian. Vol. II. Italian-English. Two vols. square 8vo, cloth, orange edges. 14s.

———— Dialoghi Inglesi ed Italiani. 18mo, cloth. 2s.

Camerini (E.) L'Eco Italiano; a Practical Guide to Italian Conversation. With a Vocabulary. 12mo, cl, 4s. 6d.

GERMAN.

Ahn's (Dr. F.) New, Practical and Easy Method of Learning the German Language. First and Second Course. Bound in one vol., 12mo, cloth. 3s.

———— Practical Grammar of the German Language (intended as a sequel to the foregoing Work), with a Grammatical Index and a Glossary of all the German Words occurring in the Work. 12mo, cloth. 4s. 6d.

———— Key to ditto. 12mo, cloth. 1s. 6d.

———— Manual of German and English Conversations, or Vade Mecum for English Travellers. 12mo, cloth. 2s. 6d.

———— Poetry of Germany. A Selection from the most celebrated Poets. 12mo, sewed. 3s.

Trübner's Series of German Plays, for Students of the German Language. With Grammatical and Explanatory Notes. By F. Weinmann, German Master to the Royal Institution School, Liverpool, and G. Zimmermann, Teacher of Modern Languages. No. I. Der Vetter, Comedy in three Acts, by Roderick Benedix. [In the Press.

Oehlschlager's German-English and English-German Pocket Dictionary. With a Pronunciation of the German Part in English Characters. 24mo, roan. 4s.

Wolfram (Ludwig.) The German Echo. A Faithful Mirror of German Every-day Conversation. With a Vocabulary by Henry Skelton. 12mo, cloth. 3s.

FRENCH.

Ahn's (Dr. F.) New, Practical, and Easy Method of Learning the French Language. In Two Courses, 12mo, sold separately, at 1s. 6d. each.

The Two Courses, in 1 vol. 12mo, cloth, price 3s.

———— Manual of French and English Conversation. 12mo. cloth. 2s. 6d.

Le Brun's (L.) Materials for Translating from English into French; being a Short Essay on Translation, followed by a Graduated Selection in Prose and Verse, from the best English Authors. 12mo, cloth, price 4s.

Fruston (F. de La.) Echo Français. A Practical Guide to French Conversation. With Vocabulary. 12mo, cloth. 3s.

Nugent's Improved French and English and English and French Pocket Dictionary. 24mo, cloth. 3s. 6d.

Van Laun. Leçons Graduées de Traduction et de Lecture; or, Graduated Lessons in Translation and Reading, with Biographical Sketches, Annotations on History, Geography, Synonym and Style, and a Dictionary of Word and Idioms. By Henry Van Laun. 12mo. Pp. vi. and 476. 5s. 1862.

RUSSIAN.

Cornet (Julius). A Manual of Russian and English Conversation. 12mo. 3s. 6d.

Reiff (Ch. Ph.) Little Manual of the Russian Language. 12mo, sewed. 2s. 6d.

DUTCH.

Ahn. A Concise Grammar of the Dutch Language; with a Selection from the best Authors, in Prose and Poetry. By Dr. F. Ahn. Translated from the Tenth Original German Edition, and remodelled for the use of English Students. By Henry Van Laun. 12mo. Pp. 170, cloth, 3s. 6d.

PORTUGUESE.

A Practical Grammar of Portuguese and English, exhibiting in a Series of Exercises, in Double Translation, the Idiomatic Structure of both Languages, as now written and spoken. Adapted to Ollendorff's System by the Rev. Alexander J. D. D'Orsey, of Corpus Christi College, Cambridge, and Professor of the English Language in that University. In one vol. 12mo, cloth, boards. 7s.

Colloquial Portuguese, or THE WORDS AND PHRASES OF EVERY-DAY LIFE. Compiled from Dictation and Conversation, for the use of English Tourists and Visitors in Portugal, The Brazils, Madeira, and the Azores. With a Brief Collection of Epistolary Phrases. Second edition, considerably enlarged and improved. In one vol. 12mo, cloth, boards. 3s. 6d.

SPANISH.

Ahn (Dr. F.) A NEW PRACTICAL AND EASY METHOD OF LEARNING THE SPANISH LANGUAGE. Post 8vo [*In the Press*

———— KEY to ditto. Post 8vo. sewed. [*In the Press*

Cadena (MARIANO VELASQUEZ DE LA). AN EASY INTRODUCTION TO SPANISH CONVERSATION: containing all that is necessary to make a rapid progress in it; particularly designed for those who have little time to study, or are their own instructors. 18mo. Pp. 160, cloth. 2s.

———— A NEW SPANISH READER; consisting of Passages from the most approved Authors in Prose and Verse. With a copious Vocabulary. (Sequel to the Spanish Grammar upon the Ollendorff Method. 8vo. Pp. 352, cloth. 6s. 6d.

———— A DICTIONARY OF THE SPANISH AND ENGLISH LANGUAGES. For the use of young Learners and Travellers. In Two Parts. I. Spanish-English; II. English-Spanish. Crown 8vo. Pp. 860, roan. 10s. 6d.

Cadena (RAMON PALENZUELA y JUAN DE LA C). METODO PARA APRENDER A LEER, ESCRIBIR Y HABLAR EL INGLES, segun el sistema de Ollendorff. Con un tratado de Pronunciacion al principio, y un Apéndice importante al fin, que sirve de complemento á la obra. Un tomo en 8vo. de 500 páginas. 12s.

Cadena. Clave al mismo. En 8vo. 6s.

Hartzenbusch (J. E.) and **Lemming** (H.) ECO DE MADRID: a Practical Guide to Spanish Conversation. Post 8vo. Pp. 240, cloth. 5s.

Morentin (M. DE). A SKETCH ON THE COMPARATIVE BEAUTIES OF THE FRENCH AND SPANISH LANGUAGES. Part I., 8vo, pp. 38, sewed, 1s. 6d. Part II., 8vo, pp. 60, sewed, 2s

Velasquez and Simonne. A NEW METHOD TO READ, WRITE, AND SPEAK THE SPANISH LANGUAGE. Adapted to Ollendorff's System. Post 8vo. Pp. 558, cloth. 6s.

———— KEY to ditto. Post 8vo. Pp. 174, cloth. 4s.

Ahn's (Dr. F.) GERMAN COMMERCIAL LETTER-WRITER, with Explanatory Introductions in English, and an Index of Words in French and English. 12mo, cloth, price 4s. 6d.

———— FRENCH COMMERCIAL LETTER-WRITER, on the same Plan. 12mo, cloth, price 4s. 6d.
———— SPANISH do. [*In the Press*
———— ITALIAN do. [*In the Press*

Levy (MATTHIAS). THE HISTORY OF SHORTHAND WRITING; to which is appended the System used by the Author. cr. 8vo, cloth. 5s.

Taylor's System of Shorthand WRITING. Edited by MATHIAS LEVY. Crown 8vo. Pp. 16, and three plates, stiff cover, 1s. 6d. 1862.

Theology.

American Bible Union. REVISED VERSION OF THE HOLY SCRIPTURES. viz.:

BOOK OF JOB. The common English Version, the Hebrew Text, and the Revised Version. With an Introduction and Notes. By T. J. CONANT. 4to. Pp. xxx., and 166. 7s. 6d.

GOSPEL BY MATTHEW. The Common English Version and the Received Greek Text; with a Revised Version, and Critical and Philological Notes. By T. J. CONANT, D.D. Pp. XL. and 172. With an APPENDIX on the Meaning and Use of Baptizein. Pp. 106. 4to. 8s.

GOSPEL ACCORDING TO MARK. Translated from the Greek, on the Basis of the Common English Version, with Notes. 4to. Pp. vi. and 134. 5s.

GOSPEL BY JOHN. Ditto. 4to. Pp. xv. and 172. 5s.

ACTS OF THE APOSTLES. Ditto. 4to. Pp. iv. and 224. 6s.

EPISTLE TO THE EPHESIANS. Ditto. 4to. Pp. vi, and 40. 3s. 6d.

EPISTLES OF PAUL TO THE THESSALONIANS. Ditto. 4to. Pp. viii. and 74. 4s. 6d.

EPISTLES OF PAUL TO TIMOTHY AND TITUS. Ditto. 4to. Pp. vi. and 78. 2s. 6d.

EPISTLE OF PAUL TO PHILEMON. Ditto. 4to. sewed. Pp. 404 1s. 6d. 12mo. cloth, 2s.

EPISTLE TO THE HEBREWS. Pp. iv. and 90. 4to. 4s.

SECOND EPISTLE OF PETER, EPISTLES OF JOHN AND JUDE AND THE REVELATION. Ditto. 4to. Pp. 254. 5s.

Beeston. THE TEMPORALITIES OF THE ESTABLISHED CHURCH as they are and as they might be; collected from authentic Public Records. By WILLIAM BEESTON. 8vo. pp. 36, sewed. 1850. 1s.

Bible. THE HOLY BIBLE. First division the Pentateuch, or Five Books of Moses, according to the authorized version, with Notes, Critical, Practical, and Devotional. Edited by the Rev. THOMAS WILSON, M.A., of Corpus Christi College, Cambridge. 4to. Part I. pp. vi. and 84; part II. pp. 85 to 176; part III. pp. 177 to 275, sewed. 1853–4. each pt.5s., the work compl.20s.

Campbell. NEW RELIGIOUS THOUGHTS. By DOUGLAS CAMPBELL. Post 8vo. Pp. xii. and 425, cloth. 1860. 6s. 6d.

Conant (T. J., D.D.) THE MEANING AND USE OF BAPTIZEIN PHILOLOGICALLY AND HISTORICALLY INVESTIGATED. 8vo. Pp. 164. 2s. 6d.

Confessions (The) of a Catholic Priest. Post 8vo. Pp. v. and 320, 1858. 7s. 6s.

Crosskey. A DEFENCE OF RELIGION. By HENRY W. CROSSKEY. Pp. 48. 12mo., sewed, 1s. 1854.

Foxton. THE PRIESTHOOD AND THE PEOPLE. By FREDERICK J. FOXTON, A.B., Author of "Popular Christianity," etc. 8vo. sewed, price 1s. 6d.

Froude. THE BOOK OF JOB. By J. A. FROUDE, M.A., late fellow of Exeter College, Oxford. Reprinted from "The Westminster Review." New Series, No. VII., October, 1853. 8d.

Fulton. THE FACTS AND FALLACIES OF THE SABBATH QUESTION CONSIDERED SCRIPTURALLY. By HENRY FULTON. 12mo. Pp. 108, cloth, limp. 1858. 1s. 6d.

Gervinus. THE MISSION OF THE GERMAN CATHOLICS. By G. G. GERVINUS, Professor of History in the University of Heidelberg. Translated from the German. Post 8vo., sewed, 1s. 1846.

Giles. HEBREW RECORDS. An Historical Enquiry concerning the Age, Authorship, and Authenticity of the Old Testament. By the Rev. DR. GILES, late Fellow of Corpus Christi College, Oxford. Second Edition. 8vo. Pp. 356, cloth. 1853. 10s. 6d.

Hennell. THE EARLY CHRISTIAN ANTICIPATION OF AN APPROACHING END OF THE WORLD, and its bearing upon the Character of Christianity as a Divine Revelation. Including an investigation into the primitive meaning of the Antichrist and Man of Sin; and an examination of the argument of the Fifteenth Chapter of Gibbon. By SARA S. HENNELL. 12mo. Pp. 136., cloth, 2s. 6d.

Hennell. AN ESSAY ON THE SCEPTICAL TENDENCY OF BUTLER'S "ANALOGY." By SARA S. HENNELL. 12mo. Pp. 66. in paper cover, 1s.

———— THOUGHTS IN AID OF FAITH, Gathered chiefly from recent works in Theology and Philosophy. By SARA S. HENNELL. Post 8vo. Pp. 427, cloth. 10s. 6d.

Hitchcock (EDWARD, D.D., LL.D.). RELIGIOUS LECTURES ON PECULIAR PHENOMENA OF THE FOUR SEASONS. Delivered to the Students in Amhurst College, in 1845-47-48-49. Pp. 72, 12mo., sewed, 1s.

Hunt. THE RELIGION OF THE HEART. A Manual of Faith and Duty. By LEIGH HUNT. Fcap. 8vo. 6s.

Professor Newman has kindly permitted Mr. Chapman to print the following letter addressed to him—

"Mr. Leigh Hunt's little book has been very acceptable to me. I think there is in it all that tenderness of wisdom which is the peculiar possession and honour of advanced years. I presume he regards his book as only a *contribution* to the Church of the Future, and the Liturgical part of it as a mere sample. I feel with him that we cannot afford to abandon the old principle of a 'public recognition of common religious sentiments;' and I rejoice that one like him has taken the lead in pointing out the direction in which we must look.

(Signed) F. W. NEWMAN."

"To the class of thinkers who are feelers also, to those whose soul is larger than mere logic can compass, and who habitually endeavour, on the wings of Imagination, to soar into regions which transcend reason, this beautiful book is addressed. . . . It cannot be read even as a book (and not accepting it as a ritual) without humanizing and enlarging the reader's mind."—*Leader.*

"The 'Religion of the Heart' is a manual of aspiration, faith, and duty, conceived in the spirit of natural piety. . . . It is the object of the book to supply one of those needs of the popular mind which the speculative rationalism is apt to neglect, to aid in the culture of sound habits and of reasonable religious affections. If the time has not yet arrived for the matured ritual of natural religion, the present endeavour will at least be regarded as a suggestion and help in that direction."—*Westminster Review.*

"This volume deserves to be read by many to whom, on other grounds, it may perhaps prove little acceptable, for the grave and thoughtful matter it contains, appealing to the heart of every truthful person. . . . Kindly emotions and a pure morality, a true sense of the beneficence of God and of the beauty of creation, a heightened sensibility that shuns all contact with theology, and shrinks only with too much dread from the hard dogmas of the pulpit,—make up the substance of this book, of which the style throughout is exquisitely gentle and refined. . . . Mr. Hunt never, on any occasion, discredits, by his manner of stating his beliefs, the comprehensive charity which sustains them. The most rigidly orthodox may read his book, and, passing over diversities of opinion, expressed always in a tone of gentle kindliness, may let his heart open to receive all that part (the main part) of Mr. Hunt's religion, which is, in truth, the purest Christianity."—*Examiner.*

Mann. A FEW THOUGHTS FOR A YOUNG MAN. A Lecture delivered before the Boston Mercantile Library Association, on its 29th Anniversary. By HORACE MANN, First Secretary of the Massachusetts Board of Education. Second Edition. Pp. 56, 16mo., sewed, 6d.

Newman. A HISTORY OF THE HEBREW MONARCHY from the Administration of Samuel to the Babylonish Captivity. By FRANCIS WILLIAM NEWMAN, formerly Fellow of Balliol College, Oxford, and Author of "The Soul; its Sorrows and Aspirations," etc. Second Edition. 8s. 6d.

Parker. TEN SERMONS ON RELIGION. By THEODORE PARKER. Post 8vo. cloth. 8s.

CONTENTS:
I. Of Piety, and the relation thereof to Manly Life.
II. Of Truth and the Intellect.
III. Of Justice and the Conscience.
IV. Of Love and the Affections.
V. Of Conscious Religion and the Soul.
VI. Of Conscious religion as a Source of Strength.
VII. Of Conscious Religion as a Source of Joy.
VIII. Of the Culture of the Religious Powers.
IX. Of Conventional and Natural Sacraments.
X. Of Communion with God.

"We feel that in borrowing largely from his (Parker's) pages to enrich our columns, we are earning the reader's gratitude."—*Leader.*

———— THEISM, ATHEISM, AND THE POPULAR THEOLOGY. Sermons by THEODORE PARKER, author of "A Discourse of Matters pertaining to Religion," etc. A portrait of the author engraved on steel is prefixed. Price 9s.

The aim of this work is defined by its author at the beginning of the first Discourse as follows:—"I propose to speak of Atheism, of the Popular Theology, and of pure Theism. Of each first, as a Theory of the Universe, and then as a Principle of Practical Life; first as Speculative Philosophy, then as Practical Ethics."

"To real thinkers and to the ministers of the Christian gospel, we emphatically say—Read them. (Parker's books) and reflect on them . . . there are glorious bursts of eloquence, flashings of true genius."—*Nonconformist.*

"Compared with the sermons which issue from the majority of pulpits, this volume is a treasure of wisdom and beauty."—*Leader.*

"The method of these discourses is practical, addressing their argument to common sense. Atheism and the popular theology are exhibited in their repulsive relations to common life, while from the better conception of divine things, of which the writer is the chief apostle, there is shown to arise, in natural development, the tranquil security of religious trust, guidance, and comfort in all social duty, and the clear hope of the world to come."—*Westminster Review.*

Parker. BREAD CAST UPON THE WATERS. BY SOWERS OF THOUGHT FOR THE FUTURE. With four Sermons by THEODORE PARKER. 12mo. Pp. 104, sewed, 1s. 1860.

———— THEODORE PARKER'S EXPERIENCE AS A MINISTER, with some account of his Early Life and Education for the Ministry. Third thousand, 12mo. Pp. 80, sewed, 1s. 1860.

———— THE PUBLIC FUNCTION OF WOMAN. A Sermon preached at the Music Hall, March 27, 1853. By THEODORE PARKER. Post 8vo., sewed, 1s. 1855.

Priaulx. QUESTIONES MOSAICÆ, or the First Part of the Book of Genesis, compared with the remains of Ancient Religions. By OSMOND DE BEAUVOIR PRIAULX. Second edition, corrected and enlarged. 8vo. Pp. vii. and 548, cloth. 1854. 12s.

Ripley (HENRY J., Professor of Sacred Rhetoric and Pastoral Duties in Newton Theological Institute). SACRED RHETORIC; or, Composition and Delivery of Sermons. To which are added, HINTS ON EXTEMPORANEOUS PREACHING. By HENRY WARE, Jun., D.D. Pp. 234. 12mo., cloth, 2s. 6d.

Simonides (CONSTANTINE, Ph. D.) FAC-SIMILES OF CERTAIN PORTIONS OF THE GOSPEL OF ST. MATTHEW, AND OF THE EPISTLES OF ST. JAMES AND ST. JUDE, Written on Papyrus in the First Century, and preserved in the Egyptian Museum of Joseph Mayer, Esq., Liverpool; with a Portrait of St. Matthew, from a fresco Painting at Mount Athos. Edited and Illustrated, with Notes and Historical and Literary Prolegomena, containing confirmatory Fac-similes of the same portions of Holy Scripture, from Papyri and Parchment MSS. in the Monasteries of Mount Athos, of St. Catherine on Mount Sinai, of St. Sabba, in Palestine, and other sources. Folio. £1 11s. 6d.

Tayler. A RETROSPECT OF THE RELIGIOUS LIFE OF ENGLAND; or, the Church, Puritanism, and Free Inquiry. By J. J. TAYLER, B.A. New Revised Edition. Large post 8vo. 7s. 6d.

"This work is written in a chastely beautiful style, manifests extensive reading and careful research, is full of thought, and decidedly original in its character It is marked also by the modesty which usually characterises true merit."—*Inquirer.*

"Mr. Tayler is actuated by no sectarian bias, and we heartily thank him for this addition to our religious literature."—*Westminster Review.*

"It is not often our good fortune to meet with a book so well conceived, so well written and so instructive as this. The various phases of the national mind, described with the clearness and force of Mr. Tayler, furnish inexhaustible material for reflection. Mr. Taylor regards all parties in turn from an equitable point of view, is tolerant towards intolerance, and admires zeal and excuses fanaticism wherever he sees honesty. Nay, he openly asserts that the religion of mere reason is not the religion to produce a practical effect on a people; and therefore regards his own class only as one element in a *better principle church*. The clear and comprehensive grasp with which he marshals his facts, is even less admirable than the impartiality, nay, more than that, the general kindliness with which he reflects upon them."—*Examiner*.

Thom. ST. PAUL'S EPISTLES TO THE CORINTHIANS; An Attempt to convey their Spirit and Significance. By the Rev. JOHN HAMILTON THOM. Post 8vo., cloth. 7s.

"A volume of singularly free, suggestive, and beautiful commentary."—*Inquirer*.

Twenty-five Years' Conflict in the Church, and its Remedy, 12mo. Pp. viii. and 70, sewed. 1855. 1s. 6d.

Philosophy.

An Exposition of Spiritualism; comprising two Series of Letters, and a Review of the "Spiritual Magazine," No. 20. As published in the "Star and Dial" With Introduction, Notes, and Appendix. By SCEPTIC. 8vo. Pp. 330, cloth, 6s.

Atkinson and Martineau. LETTERS ON THE LAWS OF MAN'S NATURE AND DEVELOPMENT. By HENRY GEORGE ATKINSON, F.G.S., and HARRIET MARTINEAU. Post 8vo. Pp. xii. and 390, cloth. 1851. 5s.

"Of the many remarkable facts related in this book we can say little now. What rather strikes us is the elevating influence of an acknowledgment of *mystery* in any form at all. In spite of all that we have said, there is a tone in Mr. Atkinson's thoughts far above those of most of us who live in slavery to daily experience. The world is awful to him—truth is sacred. However wildly he has wandered in search of it, truth is all for which he cares to live. If he is dogmatic, he is not vain; if he is drying up the fountain of life, yet to him life is holy. He does not care for fame, for wealth, for rank, for reputation, for anything except to find truth and to live beautifully by it; and all this because he feels the unknown and terrible forces which are busy at the warp and woof of the marvellous existence."—*Fraser's Magazine*.

"A book, from the reasonings and conclusions of which, we are bound to express our entire dissent, but to which it is impossible to deny the rare merit of strictest honesty of purpose, as an investigation into a subject of the highest importance, upon which the wisest of us is almost entirely ignorant, begun with a sincere desire to penetrate the mystery and ascertain the truth, pursued with a brave resolve to shrink from no results to which that inquiry might lead, and to state them, whatever reception they might have from the world."—*Critic*.

"A curious and valuable contribution to psychological science, and we regard it with interest, as containing the best and fullest development of the new theories of mesmerism, clairvoyance, and the kindred hypotheses. The book is replete with profound reflections thrown out incidentally, is distinguished by a peculiar elegance of style, and, in the hands of a calm and philosophical theologian may serve as a useful *précis* of the most formidable difficulties he has to contend against in the present day."—*Weekly News*.

"The letters are remarkable for the analytical powers which characterise them, and will be eagerly read by all those who appreciate the value of the assertion, that 'the proper study of mankind is man.' The range of reading which they embody is no less extensive than the sincerity as well as depth of thought and earnestness in the search after truth, which are their principal features. Without affectation or pedantry, faults arrived at by so easy a transition, they are marked by simplicity of diction, by an ease and grace of language and expression that give to a subject, for the most part intricate and perplexing, an inexpressible charm."—*Weekly Dispatch*.

Awas I Hind; or, a Voice from the Ganges. Being a Solution of the true Source of Christianity. By an INDIAN OFFICER. Post 8vo. Pp. xix. and 222, cloth, 5s. 1861.

Baconi, Francisci, VERULAMIENSIS SERMONES FIDELES, sive interiora rerum, ad Latinam orationem emendatiorem revocavit philologus Latinus. 12mo. pp. xxvi. and 272. 1861. 3s.

Channing. SELF-CULTURE. By WILLIAM E. CHANNING. Post 8vo. Pp. 56, cloth, 1s. 1844.

Comte. THE CATECHISM OF POSITIVE RELIGION. Translated from the French of Auguste Comte. By RICHARD CONGREVE. 12mo. Pp. vi. and 428, cloth, 6s. 6d. 1858.

—— THE POSITIVE PHILOSOPHY OF AUGUSTE COMTE. Translated and Condensed by HARRIET MARTINEAU. 2 vols. Large post 8vo, cloth 16s.

"A work of profound science, marked with great acuteness of reasoning, and conspicuous for the highest attributes of intellectual power."—*Edinburgh Review*.

"The 'Cours de Philosophie Positive' is at once a compendious cyclopædia of science and an exhibition of scientific method. It defines rigorously the characteristics of the several orders of phenomena with which the particular sciences are concerned, arranges them in an ascending scale of complexity and speciality, beginning with mathematics and ending with social physics or sociology, and assigns to each science its proper method in accordance with the nature of the phenomena to be investigated. . . . Because it is not merely a cyclopædia of scientific facts, but an exhibition of the methods of human knowledge and of the relations between its different branches, M. Comte calls his work philosophy; and because it limits itself to what can be proved, he terms it positive philosophy."—*Spectator*.

"The world at large has reason to be grateful to all concerned in this publication of the *opus magnum* of our century. . . . Miss Martineau has confined herself rigorously to the task of translating freely and condensing the work, adding nothing of illustration or criticism, so that the reader has Comte's views presented as

Comte promulgated them ... In the whole range of philosophy we know of no such successful abridgment."—*Leader.*

"A wonderful monument of ratiocinative skill."—*Scotsman.*

"Miss Martineau's book, as we expected it would be, is an eloquent exposition of M. Comte's doctrines."—*Economist.*

Cousin (VICTOR). ELEMENTS OF PSYCHOLOGY: included in a Critical Examination of Locke's Essay on the Human Understanding, and in additional pieces. Translated from the French, with an Introduction and Notes, by CALEB S. HENRY, D.D. Fourth improved edition, revised according to the Author's last corrections. Crown 8vo. Pp. 568. 1861. cloth, 7s.

——— THE PHILOSOPHY OF KANT. Lectures by VICTOR COUSIN. Translated from the French To which is added, a Biographical and Critical Sketch of Kant's Life and Writings. By A. G. HENDERSON. Large post 8vo, cloth. 9s.

Duncanson. THE PROVIDENCE OF GOD MANIFESTED IN NATURAL LAW. By JOHN DUNCANSON, M.D. Post 8vo. Pp. v. and 354. cloth. 1861. 7s.

Emerson. ESSAYS BY RALPH WALDO EMERSON. First Series, embodying the Corrections and Editions of the last American edition; with an Introductory Preface by THOMAS CARLYLE, reprinted, by permission, from the first English Edition. Post 8vo. 2s.

——— ESSAYS BY RALPH WALDO EMERSON. Second Series, with Preface by THOMAS CARLYLE. Post 8vo. cloth. 3s. 6d.

Feuerbach. THE ESSENCE OF CHRISTIANITY. By LUDWIG FEUERBACH. Translated from the Second German Edition, by MARIAN EVANS, Translator of Strauss's "Life of Jesus." Large post 8vo. 10s. 6d.

Fichte. THE POPULAR WORKS OF J. G. FICHTE. Two vols. Post 8vo., cloth, £1.

——— ON THE NATURE OF THE SCHOLAR, AND ITS MANIFESTATIONS. By JOHANN GOTTLIEB FICHTE. Translated from the German by WILLIAM SMITH. Second Edition. Post 8vo. Pp. vii. and 131, cloth, 3s. 1848.

"With great satisfaction we welcome this first English translation of an author who occupies the most exalted position as a profound and original thinker; as an irresistible orator in the cause of what he believed to be the truth; as a thoroughly honest and heroic man. . . . The appearance of any of his works in our language is, we believe, a perfect novelty. . . . These orations are admirably fitted for their purpose: so grand is the position taken by the lecturer, and so irresistible their eloquence."—*Examiner.*

"This work must inevitably arrest the attention of the scientific physician, by the grand spirituality of its doctrines, and the pure morality it teaches. . . . Shall we be presumptuous if we recommend these views to our professional brethren? or if we say to the enlightened, the thoughtful, the serious, This—if you be true scholars—is your Vocation? We know not a higher morality than this, or more noble principles than these: they are full of truth."—*British and Foreign Medico-Chirurgical Review.*

Fichte. THE CHARACTERISTICS OF THE PRESENT AGE. By JOHANN GOTTLIEB FICHTE. Translated from the German by WILLIAM SMITH. Post 8vo. Pp. xi. and 271, cloth, 6s. 1847.

"A noble and most notable acquisition to the literature of England."—*Douglas Jerrold's Weekly Paper.*

"We accept these lectures as a true and most admirable delineation of the present age: and on this ground alone we should bestow on them our heartiest recommendation: but it is because they teach us how we may rise above the age, that we bestow on them our most emphatic praise.

"He makes us think, and perhaps more sublimely than we have ever formerly thought, but it is only in order that we may the more nobly act.

"As a majestic and most stirring utterance from the lips of one of the greatest German prophets, we trust that the book will find a response in many an English soul, and potently help to regenerate English society."—*The Critic.*

——— THE VOCATION OF A SCHOLAR. By JOHANN GOTTLIEB FICHTE. Translated from the German by WILLIAM SMITH. Post 8vo. Pp. 78, sewed, 1s. 6d., cloth, 2s. 1847.

"'The Vocation of a Scholar . . . . is distinguished by the same high moral tone, and manly, vigorous expression' which characterize all Fichte's works in the German, and is nothing lost in Mr. Smith's clear, unembarrassed, and thoroughly English translation."—*Douglas Jerrold's Newspaper.*

"We are glad to see this excellent translation of one of the best of Fichte's works presented to the public in a very neat form. . . . No class needs an earnest and sincere spirit more than the literary class: and therefore the 'Vocation of the Scholar,' the 'Guide of the Human Race,' written in Fichte's most earnest, most commanding temper, will be welcomed in its English dress by public writers, and be beneficial to the cause of truth."—*Economist.*

——— THE VOCATION OF MAN. By JOHANN GOTTLIEB FICHTE. Translated from the German by WILLIAM SMITH. Post 8vo. Pp. xii. and 198, cloth, 4s. 1848.

"In the progress of my present work, I have taken a deeper glance into religion than ever I did before. In me the emotions of the heart proceed only from perfect intellectual clearness; it cannot be but the clearness I have now attained on this subject shall also take possession of my heart."—*Fichte's Correspondence.*

"'The Vocation of Man' is, as Fichte truly says, intelligible to all readers who are really able to understand a book at all: and as the history of the mind in its various phases of doubt, knowledge, and faith. it is of interest to all. A book of this stamp is sure to teach you much, because it excites thought. If it rouses you to combat his conclusions, it has done a good work: for in that very effort you are stirred to a consideration of points which have hitherto escaped your indolent acquiescence."—*Foreign Quarterly.*

"This is Fichte's most popular work, and is every way remarkable."—*Atlas.*

"It appears to us the boldest and most emphatic attempt that has yet been made to explain to man his restless and unconquerable desire to win the True and the Eternal."—*Sentinel.*

Fichte. THE WAY TOWARDS A BLESSED LIFE; or, the Doctrine of Religion. By JOHANN GOTTLIEB FICHTE. Translated by WILLIAM SMITH. Post 8vo. Pp. viii. and 221, cloth, 5s. 1849.

—— MEMOIR OF JOHANN GOTTLIEB FICHTE. By WILLIAM SMITH. Second Edition. Post 8vo. Pp. 168, cloth, 4s. 1848.

".... A Life of Fichte, full of nobleness and instruction, of grand purpose, tender feeling, and brave effort! ..... the compilation of which is executed with great judgment and fidelity."—*Prospective Review.*

"We state Fichte's character as it is known and admitted by men of all parties among the Germans, when we say that so robust an intellect, a soul so calm, so lofty, massive, and immoveable, has not mingled in philosophical discussion since the time of Luther .... Fichte's opinions may be true or false; but his character as a thinker can be slightly valued only by such as know it ill; and as a man, approved by action and suffering, in his life and in his death, he ranks with a class of men who were common only in better ages than ours."—*State of German Literature, by Thomas Carlyle.*

Foxton. POPULAR CHRISTIANITY; its Transition State, and Probable Development. By FREDERICK J. FOXTON, A.B., formerly of Pembroke College, Oxford, and Perpetual Curate of Stoke Prior and Docklow, Herefordshire. Post 8vo. Pp ix. and 226, cloth. 1849. 5s.

"Few writers are bolder, but his manner is singularly considerate towards the very opinions that he combats—his language singularly calm and measured. He is evidently a man who has his purpose sincerely at heart, and indulges in no writing for effect. But what most distinguishes him from many with whom he may be compared is, the positiveness of his doctrine. A prototype for his volume may be found in that of the American, Theodore Parker—the 'Discourse of Religion.' There is a great coincidene e in the train of ideas. Parker is more copious and eloquent, but Foxton is far more explicit, definite, and comprehensible in his meaning."—*Spectator.*

"He has a penetration into the spiritual desires and wants of the age possible only to one who partakes of them, and he has uttered the most prophetic fact of our religious condition, with a force of conviction, which itself gives confidence, that the fact is as he sees it. His book appears to us to contain many just and profound views of the religious character of the present age, and its indications of progress. He often touches a deep and fruitful truth with a power and fulness that leave nothing to be desired."—*Prospective Review, Nov.,* 1849.

"It contains many passages that show a warm appreciation of the moral beauty of Christianity, written with considerable power."—*Inquirer.*

".... with earnestness and eloquence."—*Critic.*

"We must refer our readers to the work itself, which is most ably written, and evinces a spirit at once earnest, enlightened, and liberal; in a small compass he presents a most lucid exposition of views, many of them original, and supported by arguments which cannot fail to create a deep sensation in the religious world."—*Observer.*

Hall. THE LAW OF IMPERSONATION AS APPLIED TO ABSTRACT IDEAS AND RELIGIOUS DOGMAS. By S. W. HALL. Second Edition, enlarged. Crown 8vo. Pp. 120. Bound in cloth, 4s. 6d.

Hickok. A SYSTEM OF MORAL SCIENCE. By LAWRENS P. HICKOK, D.D., Author of "Rational Psychology." Royal 8vo. Pp. viii. and 432, cloth. 1853. 12s.

Langford. RELIGION AND EDUCATION IN RELATION TO THE PEOPLE. By JOHN ALFRED LANGFORD. 12mo. Pp. iv, 133, cloth, 1852. 2s.

—— RELIGIOUS SCEPTICISM AND INFIDELITY; their History, Cause, Cure, and Mission. By JOHN ALFRED LANGFORD. Post 8vo. Pp. iv. and 246, cloth. 1850. 2s. 6d.

Maccall (WILLIAM). NATIONAL MISSIONS. A Series of Lectures. 8vo. Pp. viii. and 382. 10s. 6d.

—— SACRAMENTAL SERVICES. Pp. 20, 12mo., sewed, 6d.

—— THE AGENTS OF CIVILIZATION. A Series of Lectures. Pp. 126, 12mo., cloth, 1s. 6d.

—— THE DOCTRINE OF INDIVIDUALITY. A Discourse delivered at Crediton, on the 28th of May, 1843. Pp. 22, 12mo., sewed, 6d.

—— THE EDUCATION OF TASTE. A Series of Lectures. Pp. 104, 12mo., sewed, 1s.

—— THE ELEMENTS OF INDIVIDUALISM. A Series of Lectures. Pp. 358, 8vo., cloth, 7s. 6d.

—— THE INDIVIDUALITY OF THE INDIVIDUAL. A Lecture delivered at Exeter on the 29th March, 1844, before the Literary Society. Pp. 40, 12mo., sewed, 6d.

—— THE LESSONS OF THE PESTILENCE. A Discourse delivered at Royston, on the 23rd September, 1849. Pp. 22, 12mo. ,sewed, 6d.

—— THE UNCHRISTIAN NATURE OF COMMERCIAL RESTRICTIONS. A Discourse delivered at Bolton, on Sunday, the 27th September, 1840. Pp. 14, 12mo., sewed, 3d.

Mackay. INTELLECTUAL RELIGION; being the Introductory Chapter to "The Progress of the Intellect, as Exemplified in the Religious Development of the Greeks and Hebrews." By R. W. MACKAY, M.A. 8vo. paper cover, 1s. 6d.

Mackay THE PROGRESS OF THE INTELLECT, as Exemplified in the Religious Development of the Greeks and Hebrews. By R. W. MACKAY, M.A. 2 vols. 8vo., cloth, 24s.

"The work before us exhibits an industry of research which reminds us of Cudworth, and for which, in recent literature, we must seek a parallel in Germany, rather than in England, while its philosophy and aims are at once lofty and practical. Scattered through its more abstruse disquisitions, are found passages of preeminent beauty—gems into which are absorbed the finest rays of intelligence and feeling. We believe Mr. Mackay's work is unique in its kind. . . . The analysis and history of the theory of mediation, from its earliest mythical embodiments, are admirable, both from their panoramic breadth and their richness in illustrative details. We can only recommended the reader to resort himself to this treasury of mingled thought and learning."—*Westminster Review, Jan. 1, 1851.*

————— THE RISE AND PROGRESS OF CHRISTIANITY. By R. W. MACKAY, M.A. Author of "The Progress of the Intellect as exemplified in the Religious Development of the Greeks and Hebrews." Large post 8vo., cloth. 10s. 6d.

CONTENTS:
Part I. Idea of Early Christianity.
„ II. The Pauline Controversy and its Issues
„ III. Idea of Catholicity.
„ IV. Origin of the Church, and its Conflict with Heathenism.
„ V. Origin and Progress of Dogma.
„ VI. Rise of the Papacy.
„ VII. Theology of the Church.
„ VIII. Decline of the Papacy.

"A work of this nature was much wanted and will be highly useful. Mr. Mackay has executed his task with great skill; he is profoundly acquainted with the whole German literature of his subject, and he has successfully fused into one continuous and consistent view the latest results obtained and chief topics treated by the freest and ablest of the critics of Germany."—*Westminster Review.*

"Our readers may rest assured that this book is on every account worthy of special and attentive perusal. . . . Mr. Mackay writes moderately as well as fearlessly, with the spirit of a philosopher and the candour of an honest man."—*Leader.*

Mann (HORACE). A FEW THOUGHTS FOR A YOUNG MAN. A Lecture delivered before the Boston Mercantile Library Association, on its 29th Anniversary. Second Edition. 12mo. Pp. 56. 6d.

Newman. CATHOLIC UNION: Essays towards a Church of the future, as the organization of Philanthropy. By F. W. NEWMAN. Post 8vo., cloth, 3s. 6d.

————— PHASES OF FAITH; or Passages from the History of My Creed. By FRANCIS WILLIAM NEWMAN. Sewed, 2s., post 8vo., cloth, 3s. 6d.

"Besides a style of remarkable fascination, from its perfect simplicity and the absence of all thought of writing, the literary character of this book arises from its display of the writer's mind, and the narrative of his struggles. In addition to the religious and metaphysical interest, it contains some more tangible biographical matter, in incidental pictures of the writer's career, and glimpses of the alienations and social persecutions he underwent in consequence of his opinions."—*Spectator.*

"The book altogether is a most remarkable book, and is destined, we think, to acquire all the notoriety which was attained a few years since by the 'Vestiges of Creation,' and to produce a more lasting effect."—*Weekly News.*

"No work in our experience has yet been published, so capable of grasping the mind of the reader, and carrying him through the tortuous labyrinth of religious controversy; no work so energetically clearing the subject of all its ambiguities and sophistications; no work so capable of making a path for the new reformation to tread securely on. In this history of the conflicts of a deeply religious mind, courageously seeking the truth, and conquering for itself, bit by bit, the right to pronounce dogmatically on that which it had heretofore accepted traditionally, we see reflected, as in a mirror, the history of the last few centuries. Modern spiritualism has reason to be deeply grateful to Mr. Newman: his learning, his piety, his courage, his candour, and his thorough mastery of his subject, render his alliance doubly precious to the cause."—*The Leader.*

"Mr. Newman is a master of style, and his book, written in plain and nervous English, treats of too important a subject to fail in commanding the attention of all thinking men, and particularly of all the ministers of religion."—*Economist*

"As a narrative of the various doubts and misgivings that beset a religious mind, when compelled by conviction to deviate from the orthodox views, and as a history of the conclusions arrived at by an intelligent and educated mind, with the reasons and steps by which such conclusions were gained, this work is most interesting and of great importance."—*Morning Advertiser.*

Newman. THE SOUL: HER SORROWS AND HER ASPIRATIONS. An Essay towards the Natural History of the Soul, as the Basis of Theology. By FRANCIS WILLIAM NEWMAN, formerly Fellow of Balliol College, Oxford. Sewed, 2s., post 8vo., cloth, 3s. 6d.

"The spirit throughout has our warmest sympathy. It contains more of the genuine life of Christianity than half the books that are coldly elaborated in its defence. The charm of the volume is the tone of faithfulness and sincerity which it breathes—the evidences which it affords in every page, of being drawn direct from the fountains of conviction."—*Prospective Review.*

"On the great ability of the author we need not comment. The force with which he puts his arguments, whether for good or for evil, is obvious on every page."—*Literary Gazette.*

"We have seldom met with so much pregnant and suggestive matter in a small compass, as in this remarkable volume. It is distinguished by a force of thought and freshness of feeling, rare in the treatment of religious subjects."—*Inquirer.*

Novalis. CHRISTIANITY OF EUROPE. By NOVALIS (FREDERICK VON HARDENBERG). Translated from the German by the Rev. JOHN DALTON. Post 8vo. Pp. 34, cloth, 1844. 1s.

Owen (ROBERT DALE). FOOTFALLS ON THE BOUNDARY OF ANOTHER WORLD. An enlarged English Copyright Edition. Ten editions of this work have been sold within a very short time in America. In the present edition, the author has introduced a considerable quantity of new matter. In 1 vol., post 8vo., neatly bound in cloth, 7s. 6d.

"It is as calm and logical a work as exists in the English language."—*Weldon's Register.*

"Mr. Owen is a thorough conscientious man, an acute reasoner, and a cultivated and accomplished writer.—*Atlas.*

"But his book is not merely curious and amusing, its utility may be recognised, even by those who dissent most strongly from the author's conclusions."—*Spectator.*

Quinet. ULTRAMONTISM; or, THE ROMAN CHURCH AND MODERN SOCIETY. By E. QUINET, of the College of France. Translated from the French (Third Edition), with the Author's approbation, by C. COCKS, B.L. Post 8vo., Pp. ix. and 184, cloth, 5s. 1845.

Religious Thoughts (The) and Memoranda of a Believer in Nature. Post 8vo. Pp. viii. and 225, cloth. 1855. 2s. 6d.

Science of Happiness. Developed in a Series of Essays on Self Love. By a Friend to Humanity. 8vo. Pp. xii. and 141, 3s. 6d.

Strauss. THE OPINIONS OF PROFESSOR DAVID F. STRAUSS, AS EMBODIED IN HIS LETTER TO THE BURGOMASTER HINZEL, PROFESSOR ORELLI, AND PROFESSOR HIZIG AT ZURICH. With an Address to the People of Zurich. By PROFESSOR ORELLI. Translated from the Second Edition of the original. 8vo. Pp. 81, sewed, 1s. 1844.

Ullmann. THE WORSHIP OF GENIUS, AND THE DISTINCTIVE CHARACTER OR ESSENCE OF CHRISTIANITY. By PROFESSOR C. ULLMANN. Translated by LUCY SANDFORD. Post 8vo. Pp. 110, cloth. 3s. 6d.

What is Truth? Post 8vo. Pp. 124, cloth. 1854. 3s.

Wilson. CATHOLICITY SPIRITUAL AND INTELLECTUAL. An attempt at vindicating the Harmony of Faith and Knowledge. A series of Discourses. By THOMAS WILSON, M.A., late Minister of St. Peter's Mancroft, Norwich; Author of "Travels in Egypt," etc. 8vo. Pp. 232, cloth. 1850. 5s.

Philology.

ENGLISH.

Asher (DAVID, PH. D.). ON THE STUDY OF MODERN LANGUAGES in general, and of the English Language in particular. An Essay. 12mo., cloth, pp. viii. and 80. 2s.

"I have read Dr. Asher's Essay on the Study of the Modern Languages with profit and pleasure, and think it might be usefully reprinted here. It would open to many English students of their own language some interesting points from which to regard it, and suggest to them works bearing upon it, which otherwise th y might not have heard of. Any weakness which it has in respect of the absolute or relative value of English authors does not materially affect its value.—RICHARD C. TRENCH, *Westminster,* June 25, 1859.

Bartlett (JOHN RUSSELL). DICTIONARY OF AMERICANISMS: A Glossary of Words and Phrases colloquially used in the United States. Second Edition, considerably enlarged and improved. 1 vol. 8vo. Pp. xxxii. and 524, cloth, 16s.

Bowditch (N. I.). SUFFOLK SURNAMES. Third Edition. 8vo. Pp. xxvi. and 758, cloth, 15s.

Chapman. THE NATURE AND USE OF LANGUAGE, POPULARLY CONSIDERED. A Lecture. By EDWIN CHAPMAN. 8vo. 1826. Pp. 82, 1s.

Canones Lexicographici: or Rules to be observed in editing the New English Dictionary of the Philological Society, prepared by a Committee of the Society. 8vo. Pp. 12, sewed, 6d.

Coleridge (HERBERT, Esq., of Lincoln's Inn, Barrister-at-Law). A GLOSSARIAL INDEX to the printed English Literature of the Thirteenth Century. 1 vol. 8vo., cloth. Pp. 104, 5s.

An Etymological Analysis of all English Words, being a list of all the Prefixes, Roots, and Suffixes in English, with all the words containing each Prefix, Root, and Suffix under it. Made by Dr. C. LOTTNER, of the University of Berlin, and edited by F. J. FURNIVALL, Esq., M.A., Trin. Hall, Cambridge, Editor of the Philological Society's Proposed New English Dictionary. 8vo.

A Concise Early English Dictionary for the period 1250—1520, the Beginning of Early English to the Date of the First English New Testament. Edited by F. J. FURNIVALL, Esq., M.A. Trin. Hall, Cambridge. 8vo.

A Concise Middle-English Dictionary for the period 1526—1674, the date of the First English New Testament to Milton's death. Edited by F. J. FURNIVALL, Esq., M.A. 8vo.

Philological Society. PROPOSALS FOR THE PUBLICATION OF A NEW ENGLISH DICTIONARY. 8vo. Pp. 32, sewed, 6d.

The Philological Society's New English Dictionary. Basis of Comparison. Third Period. Eighteenth and Nineteenth Centuries. Part I., A to D. 8vo. Pp. 24, sewed, 6d.

Wedgwood (HENSLEIGH, M.A. late Fellow of Christ's College, Cambridge). A DICTIONARY OF ENGLISH ETYMOLOGY. 3 vols. Vol. 1, embracing letters A to D. 8vo. Pp. xxiv. and 508, cloth, 14s.

"Dictionaries are a class of books not usually esteemed light reading; but no intelligent man were to be pitied who should find himself shut up on a rainy day, in a lonely house, in the dreariest part of Salisbury Plain, with no other means of recreation than that which Mr. Wedgwood's Dictionary of English Etymology could afford him. He would read it through, from cover to cover, at a sitting, and only regret that he had not the second volume to begin upon forthwith. It is a very able book, of great research, full of delightful surprises, a repertory of the fairy tales of linguistic science."—*Spectator*.

SPANISH.

Morentin (MANUEL M. DE). ESTUDIOS FILOLOGICOS ó sea Exámen razonado de las dificultades Principales en la Lengua Española. Un tomo en 8vo. mayor, de 576 páginas. 12s.

——— A SKETCH OF THE COMPARATIVE BEAUTIES of the French and Spanish Languages. Part I. 8vo. Pp. 38, sewed, 1s. 6d. Part II. 8vo. Pp. 60, sewed, 2s.

MODERN GREEK.

Sophocles (E. A.). A GLOSSARY of later and Byzantine Greek. 4to. Pp. iv. and 624, cloth, £2 8s.

AFRICAN.

Osburn (WILLIAM, R.S.L.). THE MONUMENTAL HISTORY OF EGYPT, as recorded on the Ruins of her Temples, Palaces, and Tombs. Illustrated with Maps, &c. &c. 2 vols. 8vo. Pp. xii and 461; vii. and 643, £2 2s.

Vol. I.—From the Colonization of the Valley to the Visit of the Patriarch Abram.
Vol. II.—From the Visit of Abram to the Exodus.

Grout (REV. LEWIS, Missionary of the American Board; and Corresponding Member of the American Oriental Society). THE ISIZULU, A Grammar of the Zulu Language; accompanied with a Historical Introduction, also with an Appendix. 8vo. Pp. lii. and 432, cloth, 21s.

JAPANESE.

Alcock (RUTHERFORD, Resident British Minister at Jeddo). A PRACTICAL GRAMMAR of the Japanese Language. 4to. Pp. 61, cloth, 18s.

Hoffmann (J., Japanese Interpreter to the Government of the Dutch East Indies). SHOPPING DIALOGUES in Japanese, Dutch, and English. Oblong 8vo., sewed, 3s.

CHINESE.

Hernisz (STANISLAS, M.D., Attaché to the U. S. Legation at Paris; late Attaché to the U. S. Legation in China; Member of the American Oriental Society, etc., etc.). A GUIDE TO CONVERSATION in the English and Chinese Languages, for the use of Americans and Chinese, in California and elsewhere. Square 8vo. Pp. 274, sewed. 18s.

The Chinese characters contained in this work are from the collections of Chinese groups, engraved on steel, and cast into movable types, by Mr. Marcellin Legrand, Engraver of the Imperial Printing Office at Paris; they are used by most of the Missions to China.

Legge. THE CHINESE CLASSICS. With a Translation, Critical and Exegetical, Notes, Prolegomena, and Copious Indexes. By JAMES LEGGE, D.D., of the London Missionary Society. In seven vols. Vol. I., containing Confucian Analects, the Great Learning, and the Doctrine of the Mean. 8vo. Pp 526, cloth, price £2 2s. Vol. II., containing the Works of Mencius. 8vo. Pp. 634, cloth, price £2 2s.

Medhurst. CHINESE DIALOGUES, QUESTIONS, and FAMILIAR SENTENCES, literally rendered into English, with a view to promote commercial intercourse, and assist beginners in the language. By the late W. H. MEDHURST, D.D. A new and enlarged edition. Part I. Pp. 66. 8vo. price 5s.

SANSKRIT.

Goldstücker (THEODOR, Ph. D., Professor of the Sanskrit Language and Literature in University College, London). A DICTIONARY, SANSKRIT AND ENGLISH, extended and improved from the second edition of the Dictionary of Professor H. H. WILSON, with his sanction and concurrence; together with a Supplement, Grammatical Appendices, and an Index, serving as a Sanskrit-English Vocabulary. Parts I. to IV. 4to. Pp. 1—320. 1856—1860. Each Part 6s.

——— PANINI: His Place in Sanskrit Literature. An Investigation of some Literary and Chronological Questions which may be settled by a study of his Work. A separate impression of the Preface to the Facsimile of M.S. No. 17 in the Library of Her Majesty's Home Government for India, which contains a portion of the MANAVA-KALPA-SUTRA, with the Commentary of KUMARILA-SWAMIN. Imperial 8vo. Pp. 268, cloth, 12s.

Manava-Kalpa-Sutra; being a portion of this ancient work on Vaidik Rites, together with the Commentary of KUMARILA-SWAMIN. A Facsimile of the MS. No. 17 in the Library of Her Majesty's Home Government for India. With a Preface by THEODORE GOLDSTÜCKER. Oblong folio. pp. 268 of letterpress, and 121 leaves of facsimiles. Cloth, £4 4s.

Rig-Veda Sanhita. A Collection of Ancient Hindu Hymns, constituting the Fifth to Eighth Ashtakas, or Books of the Rig-Veda, the oldest authority for the Religious and Social Institutions of the Hindus. Translated from the original Sanskrit by the late HORACE HAYMAN WILSON, M.A., F.R.S., etc. Edited by JAMES R. BALLANTYNE, LL.D., late Principal of the Government Sanskrit College of Benares. Vols. IV., V., and VI. 8vo., cloth.
[*In the Press.*

Select Specimens of the Theatre of the Hindus, translated from the Original Sanskrit. By HORACE HAYMAN WILSON, M.A., F.R.S. Second Edition. 2 vols. 8vo., cloth. Pp. lxx. and 384, 415. 15s.

CONTENTS.

Vol. I. Preface—Treatise on the Dramatic System of the Hindus—Dramas translated from the Original Sanskrit—The Mrichchakati, or the Toy Cart—Vikrama and Urvasi, or the Hero and the Nymph—Uttara Ramá Cheritra, or continuation of the History of Ramá.

Vol. II. Dramas translated from the Original Sanskrit—Malati and Madhava, or the Stolen Marriage—Mudrá Rakshasa, or the Signet of the Minister—Retnávala, or the Necklace—Appendix, containing short accounts of different Dramas.

Wilson. WORKS BY THE LATE HORACE H. WILSON, M.A., F.R.S., Member of the Royal Asiatic Societies of Calcutta and Paris, and of the Oriental Society of Germany, etc., and Boden Professor of Sanskrit in the University of Oxford. Vol. I. Also under this title, ESSAYS AND LECTURES, CHIEFLY ON THE RELIGION OF THE HINDUS. By the late H. H. WILSON, M.A., F.R.S., etc. etc. Collected and Edited by DR. REINHOLD ROST. In two vols. Vol. I., containing "A Sketch of the Religious Sects of the Hindus." 8vo. Pp. 612, cloth, price 10s. 6d.

The Series will consist of twelve volumes. A detailed Prospectus may be had on application.

Wise (T. A., M.D., Bengal Medical Service). COMMENTARY ON THE HINDU SYSTEM OF MEDICINE. 8vo. pp. xx. and 432, cloth, 7s. 6d.

Young (ROBERT, F.E.S.L.). GUJARATI EXERCISES; or a New Mode of Learning to Read, Write or Speak the Gujarati Language, on the Ollendorffian System. 8vo. pp. 500, sewed, 12s.

RUSSIAN.

Kelsyeff (BASIL). A NEW RUSSIAN GRAMMAR, based upon the phonetic laws of the Russian Language. 8vo.
[*In the Press*

ZEND.

Haug. OUTLINE OF A GRAMMAR OF THE ZEND LANGUAGE. By MARTIN HAUG, Dr. Phil. 8vo. Pp. 82, sewed. 14s. 1861.

——— ESSAYS ON THE SACRED LANGUAGES, WRITINGS, AND RELIGION OF THE PARSEES. By MARTIN HAUG, Dr. Phil., Superintendent of Sanskrit Studies in the Poona College. 8vo. Pp. 278, cloth, 21s. 1862.

AMERICAN.

Colleccao de Vocabulos e Frases usados na Provincia de S. Pedro do Rio Grande do Sul no Brazil. 16mo. pp. 32, sewed, 2s. 6d.

Evangeliarium, Epistolarium et Lectionarium Aztecum, sive Mexicanum, ex Antiquo Codice Mexicano, nuper reperto, depromptum cum praefatione interpretatione adnotationibus Glossario edidit BERNARDINUS BIONDELLI. Folio. Pp. 1. and 574. 1858. (Only 400 copies printed, on stout writing-paper. Bound half Morocco, gilt top, uncut edges). £6 6s.

The very interesting Codex of which the above is a careful reprint, was discovered in Mexico by Boltrami, in the year 1826. It is composed in the purest and most elegant Nahuatl, that was ever written, by Bernardino Sahagun, a Spanish Franciscan, assisted by two princes of the royal house of Anahuac, one the son of Montezuma, the other the son of the Prince of Tozcuco—and purports to be a "postilla" (post illa scilicet textus verba) on the Gospels and Epistles. Sahagun arrived at Mexico in the year 1529, and lived and laboured with great success in that country for fully sixty years. Mr. Biondelli has accompanied Sahagun's text by a Latin version, has added a copious Vocabulary Nahuatl and Latin, and, by his introductory observations, has thrown considerable light not alone upon the Nahuatl language, its affinity to other families of languages, its grammatical peculiarities, but also upon the traditions, institutions, and monuments of the Aztecs—thus forming a complete treasury of everything appertaining to the ancient Aztecs.

POLYNESIAN.

Grey. MAORI MEMENTOS; being a Series of Addresses, presented by the Native People to His Excellency SIR GEORGE GREY, K.C.B., F.R.S., With Introduction, Remarks, and Explanatory Notes. To which is added a small Collection of LAMENTS, etc. By CHARLES OLIVER B. DAVIES. 8vo. Pp. 227, 12s.

Williams. First Lessons in the Maori Language, with a short Vocabulary. By W. L. WILLIAMS, B.A. Square 8vo. Pp. 80., cloth. London, 1862. 3s. 6d.

POLYGLOTS.

Triglot. A COMPLETE DICTIONARY, ENGLISH, GERMAN, AND FRENCH, on an entirely new plan, for the use of the Three Nations. In Three Divisions. One vol. small 4to, cloth, red edges. 10s. 6d.

Tetraglot. NEW UNIVERSAL DICTIONARY OF THE ENGLISH, FRENCH, ITALIAN, AND GERMAN LANGUAGES, arranged after a new system. Small 8vo, cloth. 7s. 6d.

Grammatography. A MANUAL OF REFERENCE TO THE ALPHABETS OF ANCIENT AND MODERN LANGUAGES. Based on the German Compilation of F. BALLHORN. In one vol. Royal 8vo. Pp. 80, cloth, price 7s. 6d.

The "Grammatography" is offered to the public as a compendious introduction to the reading of the most important Ancient and Modern Languages. Simple in its design, it will be consulted with advantage by the Philological Student, the Amateur Linguist, the Bookseller, the Corrector of the Press, and the diligent Compositor.

ALPHABETICAL INDEX.

Afghan (or Pushto).
Amharic.
Anglo-Saxon.
Arabic.
Arabic Ligatures.
Aramaic.
Archaic Characters.
Armenian.
Assyrian Cuneiform.
Bengali.
Bohmian (Czechian).
Bugis.
Burmese.
Canarese (or Carnataca).
Chinese.
Coptic.
Croato-Glagolitic.
Cufic.
Cyrillic (or Old Slavonic).
Czechian (or Bohemian).
Danish.
Demotic.
Estrangelo.
Ethiopic.
Etruscan.
Georgian.
German.
Glagolitic.
Gothic.
Greek.
Greek Ligatures.
Greek (Archaic).
Gujerati (or Guzerattee).
Hieratic.
Hieroglyphics.
Hebrew.
Hebrew (Archaic).
Hebrew (Rabbinical).
Hebrew (Judæo-German)
Hebrew (current hand).
Hungarian.
Illyrian.
Irish.
Italian (Old).
Japanese.
Javanese.
Lettish.
Mantshu.
Median Cuneiform.
Modern Greek (or Romaic).
Mongolian.
Numidian.
Old Slavonic (or Cyrillic).
Palmyrenian.
Persian.
Persian Cuneiform.
Phœnician.
Polish.
Pushto (or Afghan).
Romaic (or Modern Greek).
Russian
Runes.
Samaritan.
Sanscrit.
Servian.
Slavonic (Old).
Sorbian (or Wendish).
Swedish.
Syriac.
Tamil.
Telugu.
Tibetan.
Turkish.
Wallachian.
Wendish (or Sorbian).
Zend.

A Latin, English, Italian, and Polyglot Anthology, with a variety of Translations and Illustrations. To be published once a year; designed to contribute to the cause of classical learning, as well as to forward the cultivation of the English language and literature in Italy, and that of the Italian in Great Britain, America, and Australia. Edited by JOHN SPAGGIARI. Oct. 1861. No. 1, oblong 4to. 2s. 6d.

A Handbook of African, Australian, and Polynesian Philology, as represented in the Library of His Excellency SIR GEORGE GREY, K.C.B., Her Majesty's High Commissioner of the Cape Colony. Classed, Annotated, and edited by SIR GEORGE GREY, and DR. H. J. BLEEK.

Vol. I. Part 1. South Africa, 8vo pp. 186. 7s. 6d
Vol. I. Part 2. Africa (North of the Tropic of Capricorn), 8vo. pp. 70. 2s.
Vol. I. Part 3. Madagascar, 8vo. pp. 24. 1s.
Vol. II. Part 1. Australia, 8vo. pp. iv., 44. 1s. 6d.
Vol. II. Part 2. Papuan Languages of the Loyalty Islands and New Hebrides, comprising those of the Islands of Nengone, Lifu, Aneiteum, Tana, and others, 8vo. pp. 12. 6d.
Vol. II. Part 3. Fiji Islands and Rotuma (with Supplement to Part 2, Papuan Languages, and Part 1, Australia), 8vo. pp. 31. 1s.
Vol. II. Part 4. New Zealand, the Chatham Islands, and Auckland Islands, 8vo. pp. 76. 3s. 6d.
Vol. II. Part 5 (continuation). Polynesia and Borneo, 8vo. pp. 77 to 154. 3s. 6d.

The above is, without exception, the most important addition yet made to African Philology. The amount of materials brought together by Sir George, with a view to elucidate the subject, is stupendous; and the labour bestowed on them, and the results arrived at, incontestably establish the claim of the author to be called the father of African and Polynesian Philology.

OPINIONS OF THE PRESS.

"We congratulate the Governor of the Cape on the production of a most important aid to the study of the twin sciences of philology and ethnology, and look forward to the completion of the catalogue itself as a great and permanent step towards the civilization of the barbarous races whose formation, habits, language, religion, and food, are all, more or less, most carefully noted in its pages."—*Leader*.

"It is for these substantial reasons, that we deemed it worth a brief notice to call attention to these excellently-arranged catalogues (with important notes), describing the various works in the library of Sir George Grey, and by which this great philanthropist will greatly aid in civilizing the numerous peoples within the limit of the colony of the Cape of Good Hope."—*Brighton Gazette*.

Natural History, Ethnology, etc.

Agassiz (LOUIS). AN ESSAY ON CLASSIFICATION. 8vo, cloth. 12s.

Blyth and Speke. REPORT ON A ZOOLOGICAL COLLECTION FROM THE SOMALI COUNTRY. By EDWARD BLYTH, Curator of the Royal Asiatic Society's Museum, Calcutta. Reprinted from the Twenty-fourth volume of the Journal of the Royal Asiatic Society of Bengal; with Additions and Corrections by the Collector, Capt. J. H. SPEKE, F.R.G.S., &c., 8vo. Pp.16. One Coloured Plate. 2s. 6d.

Dana (JAMES D., A.M., Member of the Soc. Cies. Nat. Cur. of Moscow, the Soc. Philomatique of Paris, etc.) A SYSTEM OF MINERALOGY: comprising the most recent Discoveries; including full Descriptions of Species and their Localities, Chemical Analyses and Formulas, Tables for the Determination of Minerals, with a Treatise on Mathematical Crystallography and the Drawing of Figures of Crystals. Fourth Edition, re-written, re-arranged, and enlarged. Two vols. in one. Illustrated by 600 woodcuts. 8vo. Pp. 860, cloth. £1 4s.

—————— Supplements to ditto, 1 to 8. 1s. each.

—————— MANUAL OF MINERALOGY; including Observations on Mines, Rocks, Reduction of Ores, and the Applications of the Science to the Arts; designed for the use of Schools and Colleges. New edition, revised and enlarged. With 260 Illustrations, 12mo. Pp. xii and 456. 1860. 7s. 6d.

Nott and Gliddon. TYPES OF MANKIND; or Ethnological Researches based upon the Ancient Monuments, Paintings, Sculptures, and Crania of Races, and upon their Natural, Geographical, Philological, and Biblical History, by J. C. NOTT, M.D., Mobile, Alabama; and GEO. R. GLIDDON, formerly U.S. Consul at Cairo. Plates. Royal 8vo. Pp. 738. Philadelphia, 1854, cloth. £1 5s.

Nott and Gliddon. The same, in 4to. £1 16s.

—————— INDIGENOUS RACES OF THE EARTH; or, New Chapters of Ethnological Inquiry: including Monographs on Special Departments of Philology, Iconography, Cranioscopy, Palæontology, Pathology, Archæology, Comparative Geography, and Natural History, contributed by Alfred Maury, Francis Pulszky, and J. Aitken Meigs, M.D.; presenting Fresh Investigations, Documents, and Materials, by J. C. NOTT, M.D., and GEO. R. GLIDDON. Plates and Maps. 4to. Pp. 656. London and Philadelphia, 1857, sewed. £1 16s.

Nott and Gliddon. The same, royal 8vo. £1 5s.

Pickering THE GEOGRAPHICAL DISTRIBUTION OF ANIMALS AND PLANTS. By CHARLES PICKERING, M.D. 4to. Pp. 214, cloth, 1854. £1 11s. 6d.

Sclater. CATALOGUE OF A COLLECTION OF AMERICAN BIRDS belonging to Philip Lutley Sclater, M.A., Ph.D., F.R.S., &c. The figures will be taken from Typical Specimens in the Collection. 8vo. With Twenty Coloured Plates. £1 10. [*In Preparation.*

The Ibis. A MAGAZINE OF GENERAL ORNITHOLOGY. Edited by PHILIP LUTLEY SCLATER, M.A. Vol. I. 1859. 8vo, cloth. Coloured Plates. £1 12s.

—————— Vol. II., 1860. £1 12s.

—————— Vol. III., 1861. £1 6s.

The Oyster: Where, How, and When to Find, Breed, Cook, and Eat it. 12mo. Pp. viii. and 96. 1s.

Medicine, etc.

Althaus (J., M.D.). A TREATISE ON MEDICAL ELECTRICITY, THEORETICAL AND PRACTICAL. 8vo, cloth. 7s. 6d.

—————— THE SPAS OF EUROPE. By JULIUS ALTHAUS, M.D. 8vo., cloth. [*In the Press.*

—————— CASES TREATED BY FARADISATION. By JULIUS ALTHAUS, M.D. 12mo. Pp. 16, sewed, 1s.

Catlin (GEORGE). THE BREATH OF LIFE. (Manugraph.) 8vo, with Illustrations. 2s. 6d.

Chapman. CHLOROFORM AND OTHER ANÆSTHETICS; their History and Use during Childbed. By JOHN CHAPMAN, M.D. 8vo., sewed, 1s.

—————— CHRISTIAN REVIVALS; their History and Natural History. By JOHN CHAPMAN, M.D. 8vo., sewed, 1s.

Dunglison (ROBLEY). A DICTIONARY OF MEDICAL SCIENCE; containing a Concise Explanation of the Various Subjects and Terms of Anatomy, Physiology, Pathology, Hygiene, Therapeutics, Pharmacology, Pharmacy, Surgery, Obstetrics, Medical Jurisprudence, Dentistry, &c.; Notices of Climate, and of Mineral Waters; Formulæ for Officinal, Empirical, and Dietetic Preparations, &c.; with French and other Synonymes. By ROBLEY DUNGLISON, M.D., LL.D. Revised and very greatly enlarged. 8vo. pp. 292. 18s.

Of print, this new edition — the third — has been undertaken by the present proprietors of the copyright, with the view not only of meeting the numerous demands from the class to which it was primarily addressed by its learned author, but also for extending its circulation to the general reader, to whom it had, heretofore, been all but inaccessible, owing to the peculiar mode of its publication, and to whom it is believed it will be very acceptable, on account of the great and growing interest of its subject-matter, and the elegant and successful treatment thereof. The volume is a verbatim reprint from the second edition; but its value has been enhanced by the addition of a paper on "Child-Pilgrimages," never before translated; and the present edition is therefore the *first* and *only* one in the English language which contains *all* the contributions of Dr. Hecker to the history of medicine.

Hecker (J. F. C., M.D.) THE EPIDEMICS OF THE MIDDLE AGES. Translated by G. B. BABINGTON, M.D., F.R.S. Third Edition, completed by the Author's Treatise on CHILD-PILGRIMAGES. 8vo, cloth, pp. 384, price 9s.

CONTENTS:—The Black Death—The Dancing Mania—The Sweating Sickness—Child Pilgrimages.

This volume is one of the series published by the Sydenham Society, and, as such, originally issued to its members only. The work having gone out

Parrish (EDWARD). AN INTRODUCTION TO PRACTICAL PHARMACY; designed as a Text-Book for the Student, and as a Guide for the Physician and Pharmaceutist. With many Formulas and Prescriptions. Second edition, greatly Enlarged and Improved. With Two Hundred and Forty-six Illustrations. 8vo. pp. xxi. and 720. 1261. 15s.

Sick Chamber (THE). 18mo. Pp. 60, cloth, 1s. 1846.

Practical Science.

Austin. CEMENTS AND THEIR COMPOUNDS; or, A Practical Treatise of Calcareous and Hydraulic Cements, their Preparation, Application, and Use. Compiled from the highest authorities, and from the Author's own experience during a long period of professional practice. To which is added Information on Limes and Cements. By JAMES GARDNER AUSTIN. 12mo. [*In the Press.*

Calvert. ON IMPROVEMENTS AND PROGRESS IN DYEING AND CALICO PRINTING SINCE 1851. Illustrated with Numerous Specimens of Printed and Dyed Fabrics. By Dr. F. CRACE CALVERT, F.R.S., F.C.S. A Lecture delivered before the Society of Arts. Revised and Enlarged by the Author. 12mo., pp. 28, sewed, 1s.

O'Neill. CHEMISTRY OF CALICO PRINTING, DYEING, AND BLEACHING, including Silken, Woollen, and Mixed Goods, Practical and Theoretical. With copious references to original sources of information, and abridged specifications of the Patents connected with these subjects, for the years 1858 and 1859. By CHARLES O'NEIL. 8vo. Pp. XII., 408. 18s.

Paterson. TREATISE ON MILITARY DRAWING. With a Course of Progressive Plates. By CAPTAIN W. PATERSON, Professor of Military Drawing, at the Royal Military College, Sandhurst. 4to., boards.

Bibliography.

Allibone (AUSTIN S.) A CRITICAL DICTIONARY OF ENGLISH LITERATURE, AND BRITISH AND AMERICAN AUTHORS, from the Earliest Accounts to the Middle of the Nineteenth Century. (Vol. I. is now published.) Two vols' imp. 8vo, cloth. To Subscribers, £1 16s. : to Non-subscribers, £2 8s.

Berjeau (F. PH.) CANTICUM CANTICORUM. Reprinted in Facsimile from the Scriverius Copy in the British Museum; with an Historical and Bibliographical Introduction. In folio, 64 pp. Only 150 copies printed, on stout tinted paper; bound in the antique style. £2 2s.

Caxton. THE GAME OF CHESS. A reproduction of WILLIAM CAXTON'S GAME OF CHESS, the first work printed in England. Small folio, bound in vellum, in the style of the period. Price £1 1s.

Frequently as we read of the works of Caxton, and the early English Printers, and of their black letter books, very few persons have ever had the opportunity of seeing any of these productions, and forming a proper estimate of the ingenuity and skill of those who first practised the " Noble Art of Printing."

This reproduction of the first work printed by Caxton at Westminster, containing 23 woodcuts, is intended, in some measure, to supply this deficiency, and bring the present age into somewhat greater intimacy with the *Father of English Printers*.

The type has been carefully imitated, and the cuts traced from the copy in the British Museum. The paper has also been made expressly, as near as possible like the original.

Delepierre. ANALYSE DES TRAVAUX DE LA SOCIÉTÉ DES PHILOBIBLON DE LONDRES. Par OCTAVE DELEPIERRE. Small 4to., laid paper, bound in the Roxburgh style. [*In the Press.*
(Only 250 copies will be printed).

——— HISTOIRE LITTERAIRE DES FOUS. 12mo, cloth. 5s.

Edwards (EDWARD). MEMOIRS OF LIBRARIES, together with a PRACTICAL HANDBOOK OF LIBRARY ECONOMY. Two vols. royal 8vo. Numerous Illustrations. Cloth. £2 8s.

——— DITTO, large paper, imperial 8vo. £4 4s.

Gutenberg (JOHN). FIRST MASTER PRINTER, His Acts, and most remarkable Discourses, and his Death. From the German. By C. W. 8vo, pp. 141. 10s. 6d.

Le Bibliomane. No. I., 8vo, pp. 20; No. II., pp. 20. 2s. each.

Nouvelles Plaisantes Recherches D'UN HOMME GRAVE SUR QUELQUES FARCEURS. 8vo. Pp. 53. 10s. 6d.

Uricoechea (EZEQUIEL, Dr., de Bogota, Nueva Granada). MAPOTECA COLOMBIANA: CATALOGO DE TODOS LOS MAPAS, PLANOS, VISTAS, ETC., RELATIVOS A LA AMERICA-ESPANOLA, BRASIL, E ISLAS ADYACENTES. Arreglada cronologicamente i precedida de una introduccion sobre la historia cartografica de America. One vol. 8vo, of 232 pages. 6s.

Van de Weyer. LES OPUSCULES DE M. SYLVAIN VAN DE WEYER de 1823 à 1861. Première Serie. Small 4to., printed with old face type, on laid paper, expressly made for the purpose. Suitably bound in the Roxburgh style.
[*In the Press.*
(The Edition will consist of 300 copies only).

Ludewig (HERMANN E.) THE LITERATURE OF AMERICAN ABORIGINAL LANGUAGES. With Additions and Corrections by Professor WM. W. TURNER. Edited by NICOLAS TRÜBNER. 8vo, fly and general Title, 2 leaves; Dr. Ludewig's Preface, pp. v.—viii; Editor's Preface, pp. iv—xii; Biographical Memoir of Dr. Ludewig, pp. xiii, xiv; and Introductory Bibliographical Notices, pp. xiv—xxiv, followed by List of Contents. Then follow Dr. Ludewig's Bibliotheca Glottica, alphabetically arranged, with Additions by the Editor, pp. 1—209; Professor Turner's Additions, with those of the Editor to the same, also alphabetically arranged, pp. 210—246; Index, pp. 247—256; and list of Errata, pp. 257, 258. One vol. handsomely bound in cloth, price 10s. 6d.

This work is intended to supply a great want, now that the study of Ethnology has proved that exotic languages are not mere curiosities, but essential and interesting parts of the natural history of man, forming one of the most curious links in the great chain of national affinities, defining as they do the reciprocity existing between man and the soil he lives upon. No one can venture to write the history of America without a knowledge of her aboriginal languages; and unimportant as such researches may seem to men engaged in the mere bustling occupations of life, they will at least acknowledge that these records of the past, like the stern-lights of a departing ship, are the last glimmers of savage life, as it becomes absorbed or recedes before the tide of civilization. Dr. Ludewig and Prof. Turner have made most diligent use of the public and private collections in America, access to all of which was most liberally granted to them. This has placed at their disposal the labours of the American Missionaries, so little known on this side of the Atlantic that they may be looked upon almost in the light of untrodden ground. But English and Continental libraries have also been ransacked; and Dr. Ludewig kept up a constant and active correspondence with scholars of " the Fatherland," as well as with men of similar tastes and pursuits in France, Spain, and Holland, determined to leave no stone unturned to render his labours as complete as possible. The volume, perfect in itself, is the first of an enlarged edition of Vater's *Linguarum totius orbis Index.*" The work has been noticed by the press of both Continents, and we may be permitted to refer particularly to the following

OPINIONS OF THE PRESS.

" This work, mainly the production of the late Herr Ludewig, a German, naturalized in America, is devoted to an account of the literature of the aboriginal languages of that country. It gives an alphabetical list of the various tribes of whose languages any record remains, and refers to the works, papers, or manuscripts, in which such information may be found. The work has evidently been a labour of love; and as no pains seem to have been spared by the editors, Prof. Turner and Mr. Trübner, in rendering the work as accurate and complete as possible, those who are most interested in its contents will be best able to judge of the labour and assiduity bestowed upon it by author, editors, and publisher."—*Athenæum*, 5th April, 1858.

" This is the first instalment of a work which will be of the greatest value to philologists; and is a compendium of the aboriginal languages of the American continents, and a digest of all the known literature bearing upon those languages. Mr. Trübner's hand has been engaged *passim*, and in his preface he lays claim to about one-sixth of the whole; and we have no doubt that the encouragement with which this portion of the work will be received by scholars, will be such as to inspire Mr. Trübner with sufficient confidence to persevere in his arduous and most honourable task."—*The Critic*, 15th Dec., 1857.

"Few would believe that a good octavo volume would be necessary to exhaust the subject; yet so it is, and this handsome, useful, and curious volume, carefully compiled by Mr. Ludewig, assisted by Professor Turner, and edited by the careful hand of Mr. Trübner, the well-known publisher, will be sure to find a place in many libraries."—*Bent's Advertiser*, 6th Nov., 1857.

"The lovers of American linguistics will find in the work of Mr. Trübner scarcely any point omitted calculated to aid the comparative philologer in tracing the various languages of the great Western Continent."—*Galway Mercury*, 30th Jan., 1858.

"Only those deeply versed in philological studies can appreciate this book at its full value. It shows that there are upwards of seven hundred and fifty aboriginal American languages."—*Gentleman's Magazine*, Feb. 1858.

"The work contains an account of no fewer than seven hundred different aboriginal dialects of America, with an introductory chapter of bibliographical information; and under each dialect is an account of any grammars or other works illustrative of it."—*The Bookseller*, Jan. 1858.

"We have here the list of monuments still existing, of an almost innumerable series of languages and dialects of the American Continent. The greater part of Indian grammars and vocabularies exist only in MS., and were compiled chiefly by Missionaries of the Christian Church; and to Dr. Ludewig and Mr Trübner, we are, therefore, the more indebted for the great care with which they have pointed out where such are to be found, as well as for enumerating those which have been printed, either in a separate shape, in collections, or in voyages and travels, and elsewhere."—*Leader*, 11th Sept. 1858.

"I have not time, nor is it my purpose, to go into a review of this admirable work, or to attempt to indicate the extent and value of its contents. It is, perhaps, enough to say, that apart from a concise but clear enumeration and notice of the various general philological works which treat with greater or less fulness of American languages, or which incidentally touch upon their bibliography, it contains not less than 256 closely-printed octavo pages of bibliographical notices of grammars, vocabularies, etc., of the aboriginal languages of America. It is a peculiar and valuable feature of the work that not only the titles of printed or published grammars or vocabularies are given, but also that unpublished or MS. works of these kinds are noticed, in all cases where they are known to exist, but which have disappeared among the *debris* of the suppressed convents and religious establishments of Spanish America."—*E. G. Squier, in a paper read before the American Ethnological Society*, 13th Jan., 1858.

"In consequence of the death of the author before he had finished the revisal of the work, it has been carefully examined by competent scholars, who have also made many valuable additions."—*American Publishers' Circular*, 30th Jan., 1858.

"It contains 256 closely-printed pages of titles of printed books and manuscripts, and notices of American aboriginal languages, and embraces references to nearly all that has been written or published respecting them, whether in special works or incidentally in books of travel, periodicals, or proceedings of learned societies."—*New York Herald*, 26th Jan., 1858.

"The manner in which this contribution to the bibliography of American languages has been executed, both by the author, Mr. Ludewig, and the able writers who have edited the work since his death, is spoken of in the highest terms by gentlemen most conversant with the subject."—*American Historical Magazine*, Vol. II., No. 5, May, 1858.

"Je terminerai en annonçant le premier volume d'une publication appelée à rendre de grands services à la philologie comparée et à la linguistique générale. Je veux parler de la Bibliotheca Glottica, ouvrage devant renfermer la liste de tous les dictionnaires et de toutes les grammaires des langues connues, tant imprimés que manuscrits. L'éditeur de cette précis une bibliographie est M. Nicolas Trübner, dont le nom est honorablement connu dans le monde oriental. Le premier volume est consacré aux idiomes Américaines; le second doit traiter des langues de l'Inde. Le travail est fait avec le soin le plus consciencieux, et fera honneur à M. Nicolas Trübner, surtout s'il poursuit son œuvre avec la même ardeur qu'il amise à le commencer."—*L. Leon de Rosny, Revue de l'Orient, Février*, 1858.

"Mr. Trübner's most important work on the bibliography of the aboriginal languages of America is deserving of all praise, as eminently useful to those who study that branch of literature. The value, too, of the book, and of the pains which its compilation must have cost, will not be lessened by the consideration that it is first in this field of linguistic literature."—*Petermann's Geographische Mittheilungen*, p. 79, Feb., 1858.

"Undoubtedly this volume of Trübner's Bibliotheca Glottica ranks amongst the most valuable additions which of late years have enriched our bibliographical literature. To us Germans it is most gratifying, that the initiative has been taken by a German bookseller himself, one of the most intelligent and active of our countrymen abroad, to produce a work which has higher aims than mere pecuniary profit, and that he too, has laboured at its production with his own hands; because daily it is becoming a circumstance of rarer occurrence that, as in this case, it is a bookseller's primary object to serve the cause of literature rather than to enrich himself."—*P. Tromel, Borsenblatt*, 4th Jan., 1858.

"In the compilation of the work the editors have availed themselves not only of the labours of Vater, Barton, Duponceau, Gallatin, De Souza, and others, but also of the MS. sources left by the missionaries, and of many books of which even the library of the British Museum is deficient, and furnish the fullest account of the literature of no less than 525 languages. The value of the work, so necessary to the study of ethnology, is greatly enhanced by the addition of a good Index."—*Berliner National-Zeitung*, 22nd Nov., 1857.

"The name of the author, to all those who are acquainted with his former works, and who know the thoroughness and profound character of his investigations, is a sufficient guarantee that this work will be one of standard authority, and one that will fully answer the demands of the present time."—*Petzholdt's Anzeiger*, Jan., 1858.

"The chief merit of the editor and publisher is to have terminated the work carefully and lucidly in contents and form, and thus to have established a new and largely augmented edition of '*Vater's Linguarum totius orbis Index*,' after Professor Jülg's revision of 1847. In order to continue and complete this work the editor requires the assistance of all those who are acquainted with this new branch of science, and he sincerely hope it may be accorded to him."—*Magazin fur die Literatur des Auslandes*, No. 58, 1858.

"As the general title of the book indicates, it will be extended to the languages of the other continents, in case it meet with a favourable reception, which we most cordially wish it."—*A. F. Pott, Preussische Jahrbucher*, Vol. II., part I.

"Cette compilation savante est sans contredit, le travail bibliographique le plus important que notre époque ait vu surgir sur les nations indigènes de l'Amérique."—*Nouvelles Annales des Voyages*, Avril, 1859.

"La Bibliotheca Glottica, dont M. Nicolas Trübner, a commencé la publication, est un des livres les plus utiles qui aient jamais été rédigés pour faciliter l'étude de la philologie comparée. Le premier tome de cette grand bibliographie linguistique comprend la liste textuelle de toutes les grammaires, de tous les dictionnaires et des vocabulaires même les moins étendus qui ont été imprimés dans les différents dialectes des deux Amériques; en outre, il fait connaître les ouvrages manuscrits de la même nature renfermés dans les principales bibliothèques publiques et particulières. Ce travail a dû nécessiter de longues et patientes recherches; aussi mérite-t-il d'attirer tout particulièrement l'attention des philologues. Puissent les autres volumes de cette bibliothèque être rédigés avec le même soin et se trouver bientôt entre les mains de tous les savants auxquels ils peuvent rendre des services inappréciables."—*Revue Americaine et Orientale*, No. 1., Oct. 1858.

"To every fresh addition to the bibliography of language, of which we have a most admirable specimen in this work, the thoughtful linguist will ever, as the great problem of the unity of human speech approaches towards its full solution, turn with increasing satisfaction and hope.

"But Mr. Nicolas Trübner, however, has perhaps, on the whole, done the highest service of all to the philologer, by the publication of "The Literature of American Aboriginal Languages." He has, with the aid of Professor Turner, greatly enlarged, and at the same time most skilfully edited, the valuable materials acquired by his deceased friend H. Ludewig. We do not, indeed, at this moment, know any similar work deserving of full comparison with it. In its ample enumeration of important works of reference, and careful record of the most recent facts in the literature of its subject, it, as might have been expected, greatly surpasses Jülg's ' Vater,' valuable and trustworthy though that learned German's work undoubtedly is."—*North British Review*, No. 59, February, 1859.

The Editor has also received most kind and encouraging letters respecting the work, from Sir George Grey, the Chevalier Bunsen, Dr. Th. Goldstücker, Mr. Watts (of the Museum), Professor A. Fr. Pott (of Halle), Dr. Julius Petzholt (of Dresden), Hofrath Dr. Grasse (of Dresden), M. F. F. de la Figanière (of Lisbon), E. Edwards (of Manchester), Dr. Max Müller (of Oxford), Dr. Buschmann (of Berlin), Dr. Jülg (of Cracow), and other linguistic scholars.

Trübner (NICOLAS). TRÜBNER'S BIBLIOGRAPHICAL GUIDE TO AMERICAN LITERATURE; a Classed List of Books published in the United States of America, from 1817 to 1857. With Bibliographical Introduction, Notes, and Alphabetical Index. Compiled and Edited by NICOLAS TRÜBNER. In One vol. 8vo, of 750 pages, half-bound, price 18s.

This work, it is believed, is the first attempt to marshal the Literature of the United States of America during the last forty years, according to the generally received bibliographical canons. The Librarian will welcome it, no doubt, as a companion volume to Brunet, Lowndes, and Ebert; whilst, to the bookseller, it will be a faithful guide to the American branch of English Literature—a branch which, on account of its rapid increase and rising importance, begins to force itself daily more and more upon his attention. Nor will the work be of less interest to the man of letters inasmuch as it comprises complete Tables of Contents to all the more prominent Collections of the Americana, to the Journals, Memoirs, Proceedings, and Transactions of their learned Societies—and thus furnishes an intelligible key to a department of American scientific activity hitherto but imperfectly known and understood in Europe.

OPINIONS OF THE PRESS.

"It has been reserved for a foreigner to have compiled, for the benefit of European readers, a really trustworthy guide to Anglo-American literature. This honourable distinction has been fairly won by Mr. Nicholas Trübner, the intelligent and well-known publisher in Paternoster-row. That gentleman has succeeded in making a very valuable additon to bibliographical knowledge, in a quarter where it was much wanted."—*Universal Review*, Jan., 1859.

"'Trubner's Bibliographical Guide to American Literature' deserves praise for the great care with which it is prepared, and the wonderful amount of information contained in its pages. It is compiled and edited by Mr. Nicholas Trübner, the publisher, of Paternoster Row. It comprises a classified list of books published in the United States during the last forty years, with Bibliographical Introduction, Notes, and Alphabetical Index. The introduction is very elaborate and full of facts, and must be the work of a gentleman who has spared no pains in making himself master of all that is important in connection with American literature. It certainly supplies much information not generally known in Europe."—*Morning Star*, January 31st, 1859.

"Mr. Trübner deserves much credit for being the first to arrange bibliography according to the received rules of the art. He began the labour in 1855, and the first volume was published in that year; constituting, in fact, the earliest attempt, on this side of the Atlantic, to catalogue American books. The present volume, of course, is enlarged, and is more perfect in every respect. The method of classification is exceedingly clear and useful.

"In short, it presents the actual state of literature, as well as the course of its development, from the beginning. Into the subject-matter of this section we shall have to look hereafter; we are now simply explaining the composition of Mr. Trübner's most valuable and useful book." -*Spectator*, February 5, 1859.

"Mr. Trübner's book is by far the most complete American bibliography that has yet appeared, and displays an amount of patience and research that does him infinite credit. We have tested the accuracy of the work upon several points demanding much care and inquiry, and the result has always been satisfactory. Our American brethren cannot fail to feel complimented by the production of this volume, which in quantity almost equals our own London catalogue."—*The Bookseller*, February 24, 1859.

"To say of this volume that it entirely fulfils the promise of its title-page, is possibly the highest and most truthful commendation that can be awarded to it. Mr. Trübner deserves, however, something beyond general praise for the patient and intelligent labour with which he has elaborated the earlier forms of the work into that which it now bears. What was once but a scanty volume, has now become magnified, under his care, to one of considerable size; and what was once little better than a dry catalogue, may now take rank as a bibliographical work of first-rate importance. His position as an American literary agent has, doubtless, been very favourable to Mr. Trübner, by throwing matter in his way; and he confesses, in his preface, that it is to this source that he is mainly indebted for the materials which have enabled him to construct the work before us. Mr. Trübner's object in compiling this book is, he states, two-fold: 'On the one hand, to suggest the necessity of a more perfect work of its kind by an American, surrounded, as he necessarily would be, with the needful appliances; and, on the other, to supply to Europeans a guide to Anglo-American literature —a branch which, by its rapid rise and increasing importance, begins to force itself more and more on our attention.' It is very modest in Mr. Trübner thus to treat his work as a mere suggestion for others. It is much more than this; it is an example which those who attempt to do anything more complete cannot do better than to follow a model, which they will do well to copy, if they would combine fulness of material with that admirable order and arrangement which so facilitates reference, and without which a work of this sort is all but useless.

"All honour, then, to the literature of Young America—for young she still is, and let her thank her stars for it—and all honour, also, to Mr. Trübner, for taking so much pains to make us acquainted with it."—*The Critic*, March 19, 1859.

"This is not only a very useful, because well executed, bibliographical work—it is also a work of much interest to all who are connected with literature. The bulk of it consists of a classified list, with date of publication, size, and price, of all the works, original or translated, which have appeared in the United States during the last forty years; and an alphabetical index facilitates reference to any particular work or author. On the merits of this portion of the work we cannot, of course, be expected to form a judgment. It would require something of the special erudition of Mr. Trübner himself, to say how far he has succeeded or fallen short of his undertaking —how few, or how many, have been his omissions. There is one indication, however, of his careful minuteness, which suggests the amount of labour that must have been bestowed on the work—namely, the full enumeration of all the contents of the various Transactions and Scientific Journals. Thus, the 'Transactions of the American Philosophical Society,' from the year 1769 to 1857—no index to which has yet appeared in America—are in this work made easy of reference, every paper of every volume being mentioned seriatim. The naturalist, who wishes to know what papers have appeared in the Boston Journal of Natural History during the last twenty years, that is, from its commencement, has only to glance over the five closely-printed pages of this guide to satisfy himself at once."— *The Saturday Review*, April 2, 1859.

"We have never seen a work on the national literature of a people more carefully compiled than the present, and the bibliographical prolegomena deserves attentive perusal by all who would study either the political or the literary history of the greatest republic of the West."— *The Leader*, March 26, 1859.

"The subject of my letter to-day may seem to be of a purely literary character, but I feel justified to claim a more general interest for it. That subject is connected with the good reputation of the United States abroad. It is likewise connected with the general topic of my two former letters. I have spoken of the friends and the antagonists of the United States among European nations, and among the different classes of European society. I have stated that the antagonists are chiefly to be found among the aristocracy, not only of birth, but 'of mind'—as it has been called—likewise; not only among the privileged classes, and those connected with the Government interests, but among those who live in the sphere of literature and art, and look down with contempt upon a society in which utilitarian motives are believed to be paramount. And I have asserted that, these differences in the opinions of certain classes left aside, the Germans, as a whole, take a more lively and a deeper interest in American affairs than any other nation. Now, I am going to speak of a book just ready to leave the press of a London publisher, which, while it is a remarkable instance of the truth of my assertion in reference to the Germans, must be considered as serving the interests of the United States, by promoting the good reputation of American life in an uncommon degree.

"The London book trade has a firm, Trübner & Co., of whose business transactions American literature, as well as literature on America, form a principal branch. It is the firm who have lately published the bibliography of American languages. Mr. Nicolas Trübner is a German, who has never inhabited the United States, and yet he risks his time, labour, and money, in literary publications, for which even vain endeavours would have been made to find an American publisher.

"The new publication of Mr. Trübner, to which I have referred, is a large 8vo. volume of 860 pages, under the title of 'Bibliographical Guide to American Literature. A classified List of Books published in the United States of America, from 1817 to 1857. With Bibliographical Introduction, Notes, and Alphabetical Index. Compiled and edited by Nicolas Trübner.

"This last remark has but too much truth in it. The United States, in the opinion of the great mass of even the well-educated people of Europe, is a country inhabited by a nation lost in the pursuit of material interest, a country in which the technically applicable branches of some sciences may be cultivated to a certain degree, but a country essentially without literature and art, a country not without newspapers —so much the worse for it—but almost without books. Now, here, Mr. Trübner, a German, comes out with a list of American books, filling a thick volume, though containing American publications only, upward from the year 1817, from which time he dates the period of a more decided literary independence of the United States.

"Since no native-born, and even no adopted, American, has taken the trouble of compiling, arranging, digesting, editing, and publishing such a work, who else but a German could undertake it? who else among the European nations would have thought American literature worth the labour, the time, and the money? and, let me add, that a smaller work of a similar character, 'The Literature of American Local History,' by the late Dr. Hermann Ludewig, was the work of a German, likewise. May be that the majority of the American public will ascribe but an inferior degree of interest to works of this kind. The majority of the public of other nations will do the same, as it cannot be everybody's business to understand the usefulness of bibliography, and of books containing nothing but the enumeration and description of books. One thing, however, must be apparent: the deep interest taken by some foreigners in some of the more ideal spheres of American life; and if it is true, that the clear historical insight into its own development, ideal as well as material, is one of the most valuable acquisitions of a nation, future American generations will acknowledge the good services of those foreigners, who, by their literary application, contributed to avert the national calamity of the origin of the literary independence of America becoming veiled in darkness."— *New York Daily Tribune*, December, 1858.

"It is remarkable and noteworthy that the most valuable manual of American literature should appear in London, and be published by an English house. Trübner's Bibliographical Guide to American Literature is a work of extraordinary skill and perseverance, giving an index to all the publications of the American press for the last forty years."— *Harper's Weekly*, March 26th, 1859.

"Mr. Trübner deserves all praise for having produced a work every way satisfactory. No one who takes an interest in the subject of which it treats can dispense with it; and we have no doubt that booksellers in this country will learn to consider it necessary to them as a shop manual, and only second in importance, for the purposes of their trade, to the London Catalogue itself. That a foreigner, and a London bookseller, should have accomplished what Americans themselves have failed to do, is most creditable to the compiler. The volume contains 149 pages of introductory matter, containing by far the best record of American literary history yet published; and 521 pages of classed lists of books, to which an alphabetical index of 33 pages is added. This alphabetical index alone may claim to be one of the most valuable aids for enabling the student of literary history to form a just and perfect estimate of the great and rising importance of Anglo-American literature, the youngest and most untrammelled of all which illustrate the gradual development of the human mind."—*The Press, Philadelphia*, Oct. 11, 1858.

"We do not so much express the wish by this notice, that Mr. Trübner may not find a public ungrateful for his labour, as congratulate, especially American Bibliophiles, upon the advantage within their reach, by the acquisition and use of what Mr. Trübner has so opportunely supplied."—*Washington National Intelligencer*, March 22nd, 1859.

"This volume contains a well-classified list of books published in the United States of America during the last forty years, preceded by a tolerably full survey of American literary enterprise during the first half of the nineteenth century. The value of such a guide, in itself tolerably evident, becomes more so upon glancing over the five hundred and forty pages of close print which display the literary activity pervading the country of Prescott and Motley, of Irving and Hawthorne, of Poe and Longfellow, of Story and Wheaton, of Moses Stuart and Channing. This volume will be useful to the scholar, but to the librarian it is indispensable."—*Daily News*, March 21, 1859.

"There are hundreds of men of moderate scholarship who would gladly stand on some higher and more assured point. They feel that they have acquired much information, but they also feel the need of that subtle discipline, literary education, without which all mere learning is the *rudis indigesta moles*, as much of a stumbling-block as an aid. To those in such a condition, works on bibliography are invaluable. For direction in classifying all reading, whether English or American, Allibone's Dictionary is admirable; but, for particular information as to the American side of the house, the recently published Bibliographical Guide to American Literature, by Nicolas Trübner, of London, may be conscientiously commended. A careful perusal of this truly remarkable work cannot fail to give any intelligent person a clear and complete idea of the whole state of American bookmaking, not only in its literary aspect, but in its historical, and, added to this, in its most mechanical details."—*Philadelphia Evening Bulletin* March 5th, 1859.

"But the best work on American bibliography yet published has come to us from London, where it has been compiled by the well-known bibliophile, Trübner. The work is remarkable for condensation and accuracy, though we have noted a few errors and omissions, upon which we should like to comment, had we now space to do so."—*New York Times*, March 26th, 1859.

"Some of our readers, whose attention has been particularly called to scientific and literary matters, may remember meeting, some years since, in this country, a most intelligent foreigner, who visited the United States for the purpose of extending his business connections, and making a personal investigation into the condition of literature in the New World. Mr. Nicholas Trübner—the gentleman to whom we have made reference—although by birth a German, and by education and profession a London bookseller, could hardly be called a 'stranger in America,' for he had sent before him a most valuable 'letter of introduction,' in the shape of a carefully compiled register of American books and authors, entitled 'Bibliographical Guide to American Literature,' &c., pp. xxxii., 108. This manual was the germ of the important publication, the title of which the reader will find at the commencement of this article. Now, in consequence of Mr. Trübner's admirable classification and minute index, the inquirer after knowledge has nothing to do but copy from the Bibliographical Guide the titles of the American books which he wishes to consult, despatch them to his library by a messenger, and in a few minutes he has before him the coveted volumes, through whose means he hopes to enlarge his acquisitions. Undoubtedly it would be a cause of well-founded reproach, of deep mortification to every intelligent American, if the arduous labours of the learned editor and compiler of this volume (whom we almost hesitate to call a foreigner), should fail to be appreciated in a country to which he has, by the preparation of this valuable work, proved himself so eminent a benefactor"—*Pennsylvania Enquirer*, March 26th, 1859.

The editor of this volume has acquired a knowledge of the productions of the American press which is rarely exhibited on the other side of the Atlantic, and which must command the admiration of the best informed students of the subject in this country. His former work on American bibliography, though making no pretensions to completeness, was a valuable index to various branches of learning that had been successfully cultivated by our scholars; but, neither in comprehensiveness of plan nor thoroughness of execution, can it be compared to the elaborate and minute record of American literature contained in this volume. The duty of the editor required extensive research, vigilant discrimination, and untiring diligence; and in the performance of his task we are no less struck with the accuracy of detail than with the extent of his information. The period to which the volume is devoted, comprises only the last forty years; but within that time the literature of this country has received its most efficient impulses, and been widely unfolded in the various departments of intellectual activity. If we were permitted to speak in behalf of American scholars, we should not fail to congratulate Mr. Trübner on the eminent success with which he has accomplished his plan, and the ample and impartial justice with which he has registered the productions of our native authorship. After a careful examination of his volume, we are bound to express our high appreciation of the intelligence, fairness, and industry which are conspicuous in its pages; for exactness and precision it is no less remarkable, than for extent of research; few, if any, important publications are omitted on its catalogue, and although, as is inevitable in a work of this nature, an erroneous letter has sometimes crept into a name, or an erroneous figure into a date, no one can consult it habitually without learning to rely on its trustworthiness, as well as its completeness."—*Harper's Magazine*, April, 1859.

"Nor is the book a dry catalogue only of the names and contents of the publications of America. Prefixed to it are valuable bibliographical prolegomena, instructive to the antiquary, as well as useful to the philologist. In this portion of the work, Mr. Trübner had the assistance of the late Dr. Ludewig, whose early death was a great loss to philological science. Mr. Moran—the assistant-secretary to the American Legation, has added to the volume a historical summary of the literature of America; and Mr

Edward Edwards is responsible for an interesting account of the public libraries of the United States. To Mr. Trübner's own careful superintendence and hard work, however, the student must ever remain indebted for one of the most useful and well-arranged books on bibliographical lore ever published. In addition to this, it is right to congratulate Mr. Trübner on the fact, that his present work confirms the opinion passed on his 'Bibliotheca Glottica,' that among the booksellers themselves honourable literary eminence may exist, without clashing with business arrangements. The booksellers of old were authors, and Mr. Trübner emulates their example."—*Morning Chronicle*, March 22, 1859.

"Mr. Trübner, who is not only a bibliopole but a bibliophile, has, in this work, materially increased the claim which he had already upon the respect of all book-lovers everywhere, but especially in the United States, to whose literature he has now made so important and useful a contribution. So much larger than a former book, under a similar title, which he published in 1855, and so much more ample in every respect, the present constitutes a new implement for our libraries, as well as the most valuable existing aid for those students who, without libraries, have an interest in knowing their contents."—*Baltimore American*, 2nd April, 1859.

"Lastly, published only the other day, is Trübner's Bibliographical Guide to American Literature, which gives a classed list of books published in the United States during the last forty years, with bibliographical introduction, notes, and alphabetical index. This octavo volume has been compiled and edited by Mr. Nicholas Trübner, the well-known head of one of the great foreign publishing and importing houses of London, who is also editor of Ludewig and Turner's Literature of American Aboriginal Languages. Besides containing a classed list of books, with an alphabetical index, Mr. Trübner's book has an introduction, in which, at considerable fulness, he treats of the history of American literature, including newspapers, periodicals, and public libraries. It is fair to state that Mr. Trübner's Bibliographical Guide was published subsequent to Allibone's Dictionary, but printed off about the same time."—*Philadelphia Press*, April 4th, 1859.

"This is a valuable work for book buyers. For its compilation we are indebted to a foreign bibliomaniac, but one who has made himself familiar with American literature, and has possessed himself of the most ample sources of information. The volume contains :—I. Bibliographical Prolegomena ; II. Contributions towards a history of American literature ; III. Notices of Public Libraries of the United States These three heads form the introduction, and occupy one hundred and fifty pages. IV. Classed list of books ; V. Alphabetical list of authors. This plan is somewhat after that adopted in Watts's celebrated 'Bibliotheca Britannica,' a work of immense value, whose compilation occupied some forty years. The classified portion of the present work enables the reader to find readily the names of all books on any one subject. The alphabetical index of authors enables the reader to ascertain instantly the names of all authors and of all their works, including the numerous periodical publications of the last forty years. Mr. Trübner deserves the thanks of the literary world for his plan, and its able execution."—*New York Courier and Enquirer*, April 11th, 1859.

"L'auteur, dans une préface de dix pages, expose les idées qui lui ont fait entreprendre son livre, et le plan qu'il a cru devoir adopter. Dans une savante introduction, il fait une revue critique des différents ouvrages relatifs à l'Amérique ; il signale ceux qui ont le plus contribué à l'établissement d'une littérature spéciale Américaine, et il en fait l'histoire, cette partie de son travail est destinée à lui faire honneur, elle est méthodiquement divisée en période coloniale et en période Américaine et renferme, sur les progrès del' imprimerie en Amérique, sur le salaire des auteurs, sur le commerce de la librairie, les publications périodiques, des renseignements très intéressants, que l'on est heureux de trouver réunis pour la première fois Cette introduction, qui n'a pas moins de 150 pages, se termine par une table statistique de toutes les bibliothèques publiques des différents Etats de l'Union.

"Le catalogue méthodique et raisonné des ouvrages n'occupe pas moins de 521 pages, il forme 32 sections consacrées chacune à l'une des branches des sciences humaines: celle qui donne la liste des ouvrages qui intéressent la géographie et les voyages (section xvi.) comprend près de 600 articles, et parmi eux on trouve l'indication de plusieurs ouvrages dont nous ne soupçonnions même pas l'existence en Europe. Un index général alphabétique par noms d'auteurs qui termine ce livre, permet d'abréger des recherches souvent bien pénibles. Le guide bibliographique de M. Trübner est un monument élevé à l'activité scientifique et littéraire Américaine et comme tel, il est digne de prendre place à côte des ouvrages du même genre publiés en Europe par les Brunet, les Lowndes, et les Ebert. (V. A. Malte-Brun)."—*Nouvelles Annales des Voyages*, April, 1859.

Addenda.

Cobbe. AN ESSAY ON INTUITIVE MORALS. Being an attempt to popularize Ethical Science. By FRANCIS TOWER COBBE. Part I. THEORY OF MORALS. Second Edition. Crown 8vo, Pp 296. cloth.
Part II. PRACTICE OF MORALS. Book I. RELIGIOUS DUTY. Second Edition. Crown 8vo., cloth, *in the Press*.

Sclater. CATALOGUE OF A COLLECTION OF AMERICAN BIRDS belonging to Mr. PHILIP LINSLEY SCLATER, M.A., Th. Doc., F.R.S. Fellow of Corpus Christi College, Oxford ; Secretary to the Zoological Society of London ; Editor of " The Ibis." 8vo. Pp. 354, and 20 coloured Plates of Birds, cloth, 30s.

Rowan. MEDITATIONS ON DEATH AND ETERNITY. Translated from the German (by command) by FREDERICA ROWAN. Published by Her Majesty's Gracious permission. In one volume, crown 8vo., cloth.

Compte Rendu du Congrès International de bienfaisance de Londres. Troisième Session. 2 volumes, 8vo. (one French, one English) *In the Press.*

Paton. A HISTORY OF THE EGYPTIAN REVOLUTION, from the Period of the Mamelukes to the Death of Mohammed Ali; from Arab and European Memoirs, Oral Tradition, and Local Research. By A. A. PATON, F.R.G.S., Author of "Researches on the Danube and the Adriatic." Two volumes, 8vo, cloth.

Ticknor. A HISTORY OF SPANISH LITERATURE. Entirely rewritten. By GEORGE TICKNOR. Three volumes, Crown 8vo., cloth.

Parker. THE COLLECTED WORKS OF THEODORE PARKER; containing his Theological, Polemical, and Critical Writings, Sermons, Speeches, and Addresses, and Literary Miscellanies. In Twelve Volumes, Crown 8vo., cloth.

Renan. AN ESSAY ON THE AGE AND ANTIQUITY OF THE BOOK OF NABATHÆAN AGRICULTURE. To which is added an Inaugural Lecture on the position of the Shemitic Nations in the History of Civilization. By M. ERNEST RENAN, Membre de l'Institut. In one Volume. Crown 8vo., cloth.

Bleek. A COMPARATIVE GRAMMAR OF SOUTH AFRICAN LANGUAGES. By Dr. W. H. I. BLEEK. In one Volume, Crown 8vo., cloth.

Wilson. ESSAYS AND LECTURES CHIEFLY ON THE RELIGION OF THE HINDUS. By H. H. WILSON, M.A., F.R.S., late Boden Professor of Sanskrit in the University of Oxford. Collected and Edited by Dr. REINHOLD ROST. Vol. II.

Wedgwood. A DICTIONARY OF ENGLISH ETYMOLOGY. By HENSLEIGH WEDGWOOD, M.A., late Fellow of Christ College, Cambridge. (Volume II.—E. to P.) 8vo.

WERTHEIMER AND CO., PRINTERS, CIRCUS PLACE, FINSBURY CIRCUS.

www.ingramcontent.com/pod-product-compliance
Lightning Source LLC
Chambersburg PA
CBHW020105020526
44112CB00033B/925